Acclaim for *Spymaster*

'An exemplary biography . . . it is full of perceptive intimacies
and plenty of tradecraft, subterfuge, deception and revelation.
I cannot think of a better biography of a spy chief'
RICHARD DAVENPORT-HINES, *Spectator*

'Gripping and candid'
The Times

'A welcome biography of a man able to combine warm family
and personal relationships with hard-headed intellectual
analysis, taking the cold decisions needed to succeed in the
most unaccountable and secret of government agencies'
RICHARD NORTON-TAYLOR, *Guardian*

'A fascinating insight into the complex world of a master spy'
CHARLES CUMMING, author of *A Divided Spy*

'A lively, readable and delightful portrait of one of the most
charming men to emerge from the shadows'
Sunday Telegraph

'A frank and clear-eyed, if affectionate, biography of a great public servant, cruelly traduced'
MATTHEW PARRIS, *Spectator,* Books of the Year 2016

'A revealing study of this most unlikely of spy chiefs, the clever farmer's son from Derbyshire who reached the top of the most class-bound of professions. Pearce paints a rounded portrait of an enigmatic personality, but one whose skilful reading of human nature and empathy with colleagues made him a popular "Chief" of the Secret Intelligence Service in the dangerous days of the Cold War'
ROGER HERMISTON, author of *The Greatest Traitor*

'Fuller and more rounded than previous accounts . . . Pearce amplifies and clarifies our image of a man who contributed significantly to the national zeal and, arguably, world peace'
ALAN JUDD, *Literary Review*

'Riveting'
Daily Express

For J.T.P. and Grandma Sadie

Contents

Introduction: Uncle M   1

1   The Worst Thirty-Six Hours   7
2   A Derbyshire Lad   24
3   The Manchester Years   40
4   A Good War   59
5   From Cairo With Love   86
6   Into His Majesty's Secret Service   104
7   Go East Young Man   130
8   To London – and the World   163
9   The Horrors   183
10   Return to the East   195
11   The Tenant of Waterside Drive   210
12   Khrushchev – Kennedy – Oldfield   229
13   Mesmerized by Moles   254
14   Close to the Summit   273
15   Frustration   289
16   A Waiting Game   301
17   M = C Part One   316

18	M = C Part Two	346
19	A Lonely Man in Stormont	375
20	Anatomy of a Smear	402
Acknowledgements		435
Picture Acknowledgements		439
Sources		441
Bibliography		459
Index		465

Introduction: Uncle M

APART FROM AN enduring love of the James Bond films –
especially the early ones – until I started researching
this book I didn't have a particular interest in spies or
espionage. What I did have was an uncle who was, for a time,
probably the most famous spymaster in the world. Had he
been a famous footballer, or an actor, or a pop star, I would
have known all about him and what he did. When your
uncle is a spymaster, all you really know is his name and his
job title – everything else is just speculation. Was he really
James Bond's boss, the grumpy 'M'? Or was he George
Smiley from the John le Carré novels, films and television
series? Or was he nothing of the kind?

Sir Maurice Oldfield was the oldest brother of my
grandma, Sadie Pearce. Even though he had ten brothers
and sisters, it was always Sadie to whom he was the closest,
to whom he spoke the most, in whom he confided the most.
Their brother Joe said to me when I was asking him about
Maurice, 'Martin, you probably know more about his work
than I do. You have to remember he went away to Manchester

and then to the war when I was still very young, and when he came back we talked about village life and farming. He really spoke mostly to your grandma.'

I remember Uncle Maurice very well. As children he always had time for us, his great-nephews and -nieces, and would tell us about his travels and the people he met. He never forgot a birthday, and given that the number of his blood relations was probably doubled by the multiple god-children he had, such attentiveness was quite an achievement. I remember telling him that I would like to write stories, and being delighted when for my eighth Christmas a typewriter arrived, with a tag saying 'Send me a copy of your first book, Merry Christmas, M'. Sadly that was not to happen: I couldn't figure out how to change the ribbon.

What was mysterious about Uncle Maurice was that, given he was a spymaster, he really never seemed very mysterious at all. He was funny, friendly and kind, and the only thing that seemed different about him from the rest of the family was that he 'spoke posh', as we Derbyshire folk would say. But then, people have told me that he would occasionally, when dealing with the posh, speak Derbyshire in order to disarm them.

I remember Grandma being called to London and hang-ing up her apron or kicking off her farming boots to go and accompany him to dinner with politicians; I can recall the drama of his appointment to Northern Ireland, the great sadness and worry of his last few months in 1981 when Grandma was away from home to care for him, and the hurt that was caused by rumour six years after he died. Since his passing there has barely been a year when he has not been in the papers for some reason or another; sometimes being spoken of favourably in Parliament or the media during discussion of an intelligence disaster of the day, sometimes in a list of people involved in a sex scandal. And, of course, every time a new Bond film comes out.

The biography of Maurice that came out thirty years ago was for me something of a disappointment. This wasn't because of factual mistakes, or personal details I knew to be wrong, but because it didn't describe the person I knew. It nearly got him, but not quite. Family members and friends have always told little stories about Maurice, and as his surviving siblings and colleagues are ageing dramatically and their recollections destined to be lost, I felt it was time to try to build as complete a picture of him as I could. I set about talking to as many of Maurice's old colleagues, friends and family members as would speak with me, and have studied hundreds of papers, books and archives.

Maurice's papers from his London flat were taken by MI6 within hours of his death in 1981, and from looking into what might have become of them I suspect anything too sensitive would have been returned when he retired as Chief of MI6 in 1978. This view is supported by an intriguing incident I discovered early in my research, and which is explored later in the book. It's also worthy of note that when Maurice died his lawyers told the family that his remaining, vetted, papers and his vast library of books would be given to Manchester University – but when I approached the archivist about this I was told nothing had ever been handed over. There were, though, personal things he kept out of official hands by making sure the family had them before he died – and so I have his many address books, several notebooks, his passports and various day diaries he kept out of

MI6's way in Derbyshire. I hope all of this has helped to provide as complete a picture of Maurice and his life as it's possible to achieve without access to MI6's own files.

When you speak to anyone who actually works in espionage, as I have recently had cause to do, you soon realize that the world of secret intelligence has little in common with Ian Fleming's superhero. It's far more complex and nuanced, rooted in politics, personalities, international relations and, in Britain, historically at least, an underlying culture of class issues. Bond is the eternally cool icon, all action yet casually dusting down his dinner jacket after his latest scrap and then smoothly getting the girl, but the reality is very different.

Unlike its American counterpart the Central Intelligence Agency, the British Secret Intelligence Service has retained its secrecy. Whereas the CIA has been scrutinized by politicians, the British equivalent has always been able to operate in the knowledge that its files will never be released. While it is answerable to the Foreign Secretary, and ultimately the Prime Minister, what goes on behind its closed doors remains shrouded in mystery. The organization is even known by two different acronyms, SIS and MI6, depending on to whom you are talking.

What the Service does have in common with the world of James Bond is that its main purpose is to protect British interests around the world. Whereas MI5 operates in British territory, MI6 operates globally. It seeks to discover the motivations of foreign governments, politically and economically, and assess how those motivations might affect Britain. Sometimes it has taken steps to intervene overseas in support of British interests, via subversive techniques or

– Maurice's favourite – by getting 'agents of influence' into foreign governments. These are contacts, maybe ministers or officials, who supply information to MI6 – or obtain selected information from MI6 – sometimes even without the agent's knowledge.

MI6 has stations the world over, usually operating out of, or in conjunction with, British embassies, under the protection of diplomatic immunity. The officers directly working for MI6 will usually be described as being 'attached to the Foreign Office', or as 'Counsellors'. Beneath those officers are agents and sub-agents, not employees, whose motivations for helping MI6 can be many and varied. Some are double or even triple agents, working for multiple countries for ideological reasons; some are simply paid to do a job; some are being blackmailed; some just want to help; some are a combination of these. The relationships are often complex, and always secret. The atmosphere in which these people work is frequently dark and uncertain, and sometimes dangerous: there are plenty of countries that don't want British Intelligence knowing what they are up to and will take extreme steps to stop that happening.

The Chief of MI6 – known by the initial 'C' since the first incumbent, Sir Mansfield Smith Cumming, who signed himself thus on documents – has to decide how to balance the risks taken by his officers and agents in the field against the potential rewards of what they might find out. Imagine, for example, how different the world might have been post-2002 had MI6 been able to learn that Saddam Hussein possessed none of those feared weapons of mass destruction. The risks in getting someone into a position to obtain such information would have been huge; the rewards, had that been achieved, could have been far greater. A war could have been prevented. The Chief also has to convey the intelligence that is gathered from MI6's worldwide network – when he or she is satisfied with it once it has been analysed, cross-checked and weighted for accuracy – to the government so they can use that information to influence their policies.

Most books on the subject of espionage are, I have found, like the subject itself, riddled with codenames, acronyms and arcane language. Sometimes these are unavoidable, sometimes I have wondered if the authors used them to demonstrate their knowledge. I have consciously decided to use such terms only when absolutely necessary. The purists will not need them; the people who are interested only in Maurice's story do not need them. Those who find them interesting will, I hope, refer to more academic books on the subject.

My aim in this book is to explore how Maurice Oldfield came to rise to the very top of MI6 from the most humble of backgrounds, and how his story fitted in with some of the most important events of the twentieth century. Whatever he did, wherever he went, Maurice's life always brought him back to his Derbyshire roots and his family, and it is from that context that I set out to learn how he managed to achieve all he did.

1

The Worst Thirty-Six Hours

I T WAS A RATHER strange, almost sedate end to the SIS career of its most decorated Chief. It had been a turbulent thirty-three years since the close of the Second World War, during which fear, treachery and mistrust had gripped Britain's – indeed the world's – intelligence services. Traitors had been exposed and their crimes buried or covered up to prevent embarrassment to the services and their political masters, with only the occasional incident reaching the public domain. The activities of the likes of Burgess, Maclean and Philby – characters so infamous that their surnames alone build a picture of Cold War intrigue – fascinated and dismayed the public in equal measure. The Cuban Missile Crisis, the Vietnam War, the Troubles in Northern Ireland: these events, apparently unrelated, overshadowed the permissive optimism of the 1960s and the economic turmoil of the 1970s by creating an era of military uncertainty in the post-war world.

One man had been at the centre of British Intelligence in guiding the nation's reactions through all these events

– counselling President John F. Kennedy through the intelligence reports over Cuba, convincing Harold Wilson to keep Britain out of Vietnam, and sowing the earliest seeds of the peace process in Northern Ireland. But by the spring of 1978, having been at the top of his profession for the best part of two decades, Sir Maurice Oldfield had completed his farewell tour of the world's intelligence agencies and was set to return to the genteel life in academia from which Hitler's war had wrenched him almost forty years before. Oldfield retired having been decorated by the international counterparts of his own SIS: on that farewell trip he gathered the CIA Seal Medal (presented by future President George H. W. Bush), the Peace of Jerusalem Medal, Ceremonial Daggers from the Kings of Morocco and Jordan, and the Medal of the Royal Canadian Mounted Police.

Despite Oldfield having been the first Chief of SIS to be publicly named and photographed in the press – he was outed in 1968 as an SIS officer by the aforementioned Kim Philby in his mischievous KGB-monitored memoir *My Silent War* – the public was not aware of his phenomenal contribution to world affairs. In a time when the Secret Service was officially still exactly that, its existence not even admitted to by the government, press reports largely confined themselves to speculation over whether Oldfield was the model for James Bond's boss, M, or John le Carré's enigmatic George Smiley. Or both. Or neither. When Oldfield was reported as having dined with Alec Guinness when the latter was preparing to bring Smiley to the small screen, press speculation grew. The actual work done by Oldfield and his organization was barely known, let alone reported or commented upon, beyond the occasional lapse when a traitor was revealed or a badly chosen associate was named in relation to some other matter.

The convention of failing to admit to, or 'avow', the existence of SIS was by the 1970s becoming increasingly anachronistic, and successive government ministers were determined to – in their view – rectify the situation. The Cabinet Secretary, Sir John Hunt, had successfully lobbied James Callaghan, when he became Prime Minister in 1976, to get rid of the anomaly. And David Owen, the last Foreign Secretary under whom Oldfield served, was initially as keen as Callaghan to avow the SIS. For the first time in the organization's history the Chief of MI6 was authorized by the Prime Minister to brief the Leader of the Opposition on intelligence matters; and so it was that Oldfield began to make the case to Margaret Thatcher, along with Callaghan and Owen, for maintaining the secrecy of the Secret Service despite the obvious democratic deficit in doing so. Owen recalls that Oldfield told him, 'I am very aware, Foreign Secretary, that by its very nature the SIS is effectively taking liberties with people's liberty, but the best way of minimizing this is to keep our work out of the glare of publicity. And we must be trusted to recruit only agents of the highest integrity. Avowing the Service would allow the minutiae of our work to be put under scrutiny and this could put officers' lives at risk.' Given the then relatively recent history of treachery and betrayal among SIS agents, it is a testament to the esteem in which Oldfield was held that he was able to persuade Callaghan, Owen and Thatcher of the importance of maintaining the status quo when the politically easy answer would have been to support avowal. And persuade them he did: the avowal of the Service was not sanctioned until 1994, some thirteen years after Oldfield's death.

Owen was also persuaded to Oldfield's view that for the SIS to be successful it needed to be kept largely free from political control, though of course remaining a servant of the government of the day – a very difficult line to draw, and one which only someone with a particular and complex blend of characteristics, such as Oldfield, could effectively deliver.

There can be little doubt that the avowal of SIS inevitably led to its creeping politicization, to the point where by 2002, just prior to the Iraq War, government spin doctors were able to influence and amend intelligence reports to fit their masters' aims. By then SIS was being asked to, or expected to, provide intelligence that selectively supported the politicians' preferred world view rather than intelligence that could itself effectively influence government reaction to world events.

It was during a brief period of relative calm in international affairs, in the spring of 1978, that Sir Maurice Oldfield handed the reins of the Secret Intelligence Service to his successor, Sir Arthur Franks – known as Dickie – and moved into retirement. When appointing a deputy the year before, Oldfield had hoped to pave the way into the role for his preferred candidate, Brian Stewart, with a view to Stewart succeeding him as Chief in due course. Stewart, father of the Conservative MP Rory Stewart, was without doubt an able officer, but he was not especially popular with certain colleagues, and thought to be somewhat cold – a marked contrast to the ebullient Oldfield. This was an example of the criticism most commonly levelled at Oldfield by his normally supportive colleagues: he could be a poor judge of character and would tend to favour those to whom he took a shine. In an unprecedented move, senior colleagues in the Service united to convince Oldfield to abandon Stewart's elevation.

In 1978 the Cold War was still decidedly frosty, but against the background of the previous four decades it was a sensible time for the sixty-two-year-old Chief to stand aside. Oldfield's assiduous cultivation of relations with the Shah of Iran – the two men's personal friendship had allowed Oldfield to encourage the Shah to rein in his autocratic tendencies and allow a Western-style economy to develop in Iran – along with his links with Jordan, Israel and the Saudis had helped maintain a period of comparative peace in the Middle East. The Americans had pulled out of Vietnam, and there had been a lull in Irish terrorist activity, at least partly aided by Oldfield's work in the Province.

Having spent a few months in 1978 visiting old colleagues and friends around the globe, Oldfield had had ample time to plan his retirement. His restless, enquiring mind would need plenty to keep it occupied, and, having been offered a Fellowship at All Souls College, Oxford, his initial thought was to write a biography of the first Chief of SIS, Sir Mansfield Cumming. Cumming, who had established the Service in 1909, was what might now be described as a 'colourful' character. His known adventures hinted at a fascinating story to be told, but once Oldfield began his research he was frustrated by the lack of documentary evidence about his illustrious predecessor. When he looked at what was available, the archivist was only able to show him a typed manuscript covering the period from 1909 to early 1914.

This would appear to be because of the rather haphazard way the papers were organized at the time. It wasn't until twenty years later that former MI6 officer Alan Petty, writing as Alan Judd, revisited the by now reorganized papers and discovered hand-written volumes the archivist in Oldfield's day was unaware of, running from 1914 up to Cumming's death in 1923. Judd was at last able to write the book Oldfield had planned.

By mid September 1979 Oldfield had more or less established himself in some sort of routine for the first time in forty years. His weeks were spent in London or Oxford, his weekends with the family in Over Haddon, Derbyshire, helping on the farm. On Monday, 24 September, having decided to wait until Tuesday to take his train back to the city, he spent the day at Bakewell Market with his brother Joe, brother-in-law Warren Pearce and his nephew, Warren's son John. The family weren't planning to buy or sell any livestock that day; it was a simple trip to market to see how cattle prices were moving, and to have a few drinks with other farming friends in the town's pubs. Ever the chameleon, Oldfield liked to blend with the locals, and the slightly tattered tweed jacket and woven tie made him indistinguishable from his brothers to the naked eye, though the plumpish face and smooth, clean hands would have betrayed to the keener observer the fact that this wasn't a man who had spent many hours of his life toiling on a windswept hill farm.

As Joe cleared the back of the Land Rover to make room for the Pearces for the trip to Bakewell, Maurice chatted with their elderly mother in front of the open fire that blazed in the cast-iron range. An Indian September it may well have been – the farmhouse door was open to allow the morning sun to illuminate the kitchen – but if the family wanted hot water then the range had to be kept alight.

Renee Oldfield answered a phone call, and summoned Maurice as the caller had requested.

The caller, it transpired, was the Prime Minister's Private Secretary, Sir Clive Whitmore, and the purpose of the call was to ask Oldfield to go directly to 10 Downing Street where the new PM, Margaret Thatcher, needed to meet with him. She had offered to send a car to collect him, but Oldfield told Whitmore that he was already committed to going 'out with the lads' that day and would travel to London under his own steam the following morning.

As planned, he and his family went to the market, then on to the Wheatsheaf in the middle of Bakewell. The pub was, as ever on market day, bustling, noisy with chatter and getting louder the more the beer flowed. His family recall that, unusually for him, Maurice was quiet and preoccupied and did not join in with the traditionally earthy banter.

After returning to Over Haddon, Joe Oldfield and John Pearce dealt with the milking on their respective farms while Maurice and Warren Pearce walked down to the village pub, where Maurice nursed half a pint of bitter for nearly an hour, still quiet and detached. He then returned home and packed a bag for his trip to Downing Street before retiring to bed. It was only as John drove him the thirteen miles to Chesterfield Station the following morning that his uncle at last began to speak about the previous day's phone call.

Oldfield had been trying to work out what it was that had sparked Thatcher's mysterious invitation. His initial thought was that it might be something to do with the situation in

Rhodesia. At the time the protracted Lancaster House negotiations that eventually led to independence for the country were being held in London under the stewardship of Foreign Secretary Lord Carrington, and it would have been no surprise had Oldfield, with his depth of knowledge on the matter, been consulted.

His other theory – equally plausible – was that the call was related to the Sir Anthony Blunt affair. Blunt, a distinguished art historian who had been Surveyor of the Queen's Pictures, had been unmasked as a Soviet spy in 1964 but, in return for a confession and the naming of several other traitors, had been granted anonymity for fifteen years. He had even been able to carry on in his royal post despite Her Majesty having been informed of his treachery. His time was now up, and speculation had been stoked in *Private Eye* magazine; it would not be long before Margaret Thatcher formally went public on the matter. Back in 1964 Blunt had been interrogated in Oldfield's bugged London flat, and there is no doubt that as a high-ranking SIS officer at the time, Oldfield was knowledgeable about the entire business.

In the event Oldfield was proved entirely wrong in his musings. That Tuesday he was ushered into the Prime Minister's study where Thatcher offered him his final assignment.

A month earlier, on 27 August, the Queen's cousin Lord Mountbatten had been assassinated when his boat was blown up as he fished off the coast near his home at Mullaghmore in County Sligo. On the same day, eighteen British soldiers had been killed at Warrenpoint in County Down. Mountbatten had been advised not to visit his Irish retreat by the Garda, and by Maurice Oldfield personally, due to intelligence that suggested the IRA was planning to target the royal family.

These were the latest – and also the most dramatically publicized – in a series of atrocities that had been inflicted on Britain as 'the Troubles', by which name the situation in Northern Ireland was somewhat understatedly known, rumbled on. The lull in 1978 had proved a false dawn. Margaret Thatcher had been personally affected in March 1979 when her friend Airey Neave was murdered: a magnetic bomb placed under his car exploded as he left the House of Commons car park. The Irish National Liberation Army (INLA) claimed responsibility for the assassination, though conspiracy theorists placed the blame on the SIS itself. Neave was Shadow Northern Ireland Secretary at the time and was likely to be appointed Secretary of State if the Conservatives came to power in May. His hard-line stance against terrorists on all sides led a member of the political wing of the INLA to tell Neave's biographer, the journalist Paul Routledge, that Neave 'would have been very successful at that job. He would have brought the armed struggle to its knees.' Neave had also been Thatcher's campaign manager when she became leader of the Tories in 1975; his escape from the prisoner-of-war camp at Colditz Castle in 1942 was typical of the kind of dashing derring-do she admired in a man. He was one of her few close allies in the party, and his loss was a devastating blow, not least because within two days of his death she was faced with fighting a general election campaign when James Callaghan's Labour government dramatically lost a confidence motion by a single vote.

Terrorist atrocities dominated the newspapers and television news programmes throughout the summer of

1979, and the fear of terror really did grip the British public. Press speculation mounted that a further attack on the mainland was inevitable, and to the new Conservative government it became clear that *something must be done*. Thatcher asked her Northern Ireland Secretary, Humphrey Atkins, the Defence Secretary, Francis Pym, and their civil servants to come up with proposals.

A study of the situation in the Province reached the inescapable conclusion that the multiple agencies charged with dealing with the Troubles – the British Army, the Royal Ulster Constabulary, MI5 and SIS (responsible for intelligence gathering in the Irish Republic) – were, far from cooperating in the common good, in many cases actively antagonistic to one another, to the point where conspiracy theories such as the one about Neave's assassination were able to gain credence.

The solution to this, it was decided, was to create a new post, Security Coordinator for Northern Ireland, with an overarching brief to tighten up security, ensure that the work of the agencies did not overlap, and basically bang a few heads together. The new Coordinator would chair meetings between the heads of these agencies, and set the context in which they would work to counter terrorism. It was felt by both secretaries of state that the impression given to the public should be that of stability: business as usual, but with a focus on making normal policing more effective. The desired effect would be the appearance of a calm, measured response, with a reassuring and non-confrontational presence that wouldn't inflame a situation where tensions were running dangerously high.

At the Northern Ireland Office, the proposal was for the

Secretary of State to have greater involvement in security, with the Coordinator being a 'strong official beavering away on operational matters'. The recommendation was for the post to hold no extra powers, and for there to be – perhaps surprisingly given the atrocities that had prompted the creation of the post – no change in policy. Their favoured candidate was Sir Alan Donald, who was at the time the British Ambassador to Zaire, Congo, Burundi and Rwanda, based in Kinshasa.

The Ministry of Defence proposed that the Coordinator should be directly accountable to the Northern Ireland Secretary, be the Deputy Chairman of Security Policy Meetings, and have 'some powers over security and related matters'. Their suggested candidates were, again, firmly from the diplomatic camp. Lord Moran, most notable for being the son of Winston Churchill's doctor, was the ambassador to Portugal, while Sir Oliver Wright was ensconced in Bonn as ambassador to West Germany. Sir Antony Duff, later to become head of MI5, was Deputy Governor of Southern Rhodesia, and Sir John Killick was Britain's Permanent Representative to NATO.

A meeting between Francis Pym and Humphrey Atkins with the aim of thrashing out the issue was 'inconclusive', to the point where Pym described the atmosphere to his officials as having been 'neurotic'. Other names began to be bandied about, including that of Sir Donald Maitland, upon whom Pym and Atkins felt they could agree – but as Ted Heath's retired press secretary he was unlikely to find much favour with Margaret Thatcher. Besides, the Foreign Office was said to be 'busily collecting reasons why Maitland was not suitable'. William Pile, the former Director of Prisons and a colleague of the late Lord Mountbatten, was another, and a man the Northern Ireland Office felt they could work with – but he was also a candidate officials felt would be vetoed by the Prime Minister.

By 19 September a job description for the Security Coordinator, running to seven pages, had been agreed upon. This was a typically convoluted document, making it perfectly clear that the occupant of the new role would not be taking away any power or prestige from the Secretary of State and also, very sensibly, that the role would not be held by someone with a high public profile. A distinguished public servant who could inspire confidence among civil servants and reassure the public without exciting the press would be the perfect fit. The criteria were boiled down to the following:

i.   A strong personality, able to cooperate by persuasion and in a style appropriate to dealing with both police officers and soldiers;
ii. having planning and operational experience and ingenuity;
iii. but NOT a 'commander';
iv. and not a public figure.

The officials who concocted the brief quite clearly did not have in mind the most high-profile spymaster in the history of the Secret Intelligence Service, the man who had spent the previous six years being associated in the public eye, erroneously or not, with the boss of the most high-profile action hero in the history of cinema. Typically, the Prime Minister was less than impressed that these officials should think so pressing a role ought to be filled by a career diplomat. She was convinced the job needed to be taken by someone with a background in intelligence. After a day of briefings and meetings and agonizing a compromise candidate was agreed upon, and the post was offered to Sir John Killick. He was a low-profile and highly regarded if abrasive career diplomat, which suited the Civil Service. He had also been the British Ambassador in Moscow at a time when ninety Russian agents masquerading as embassy staff were expelled from London and another fifteen told they were not to return. Thus Killick had become embroiled in the minutiae of Cold War espionage, and was widely held to have acquitted himself well in extreme circumstances. He seemed the perfect fit for this most sensitive of posts.

Sir John Killick met with the Prime Minister in Downing Street on 20 September, and she put to him 'cogently in all respects' the details of what she was asking him to do. Despite initial enthusiasm, and pride at being asked, after a night of reflection Killick wrote to Mrs Thatcher to turn down the job. Its potential security implications had not been lost on Sir John – or, more tellingly, Lady Killick. In his note to the Prime Minister, Sir John wrote: 'The prospect that the assignment may only last six months is not much consolation to her given the risk that I might not survive it!' He was also doubtful about his capability to do the job, conscious in particular of his lack of knowledge of and experience in the peculiar circumstances of Northern Ireland. In a frank appraisal, Sir John went on: 'Although I have never been conspicuously reluctant in the past to "have a go", I have to form a view, not only of my own limitations, but also of the "do-ability" of what I'm asked to "have a go" at. So all in all, and without neglecting what I do not regard as old fashioned to refer to as "the call of duty", I reach the conclusion that, if the task is "do-able" at all, it is not "do-able" by me. And it must be a matter of supreme importance to the Prime Minister to have someone with demonstrable confidence.'

With Killick out of the equation, more names were needed. The mandarins in the Northern Ireland Office and the Ministry of Defence came up with Sir Arthur Hockaday, another career diplomat, but this time with experience in Northern Ireland. The Prime Minister herself had expanded her consultation to include her trusted and vastly experienced colleagues William Whitelaw, the Home Secretary, and Lord Carrington, the Foreign Secretary. When they met in Downing Street on the morning of Saturday, 22 September, this triumvirate came up with an as yet unconsidered name.

While Margaret Thatcher was being briefed on intelligence matters as Leader of the Opposition by the then head of the Secret Intelligence Service, she and Maurice Oldfield had developed a mutual respect; and it is no coincidence that Airey Neave is known to have been an avowed Oldfield fan. Thatcher, Carrington and Whitelaw agreed that Sir Maurice Oldfield would be the most suitable candidate, notwithstanding the stated job description, and that Hockaday should be the back-stop in the event that Oldfield declined.

On the Monday morning at 9.30 Atkins and Pym visited Number 10 and agreed to the Prime Minister's proposal. By eleven, Thatcher had instructed Sir Clive Whitmore to make the phone call to Derbyshire, and so it was that Oldfield was summoned at the Prime Minister's personal request to be invited to take on the most challenging – and ultimately thankless – assignment of his life.

Their meeting took place the following evening. Thatcher went through the brief with Oldfield in the privacy of the Prime Minister's study. Oldfield was not slow to grasp the importance of the job he was being offered, or the terrifying risks taking it on would bring to him and his family. His mind flashed back to the times when his life had been threatened in the past – events we will explore in later chapters – especially the menacing notes he and his sister had found hidden in prayer books as they took communion in St Matthew's Church, Westminster, in 1977. Had Maurice also taken the chance in retirement to indulge his long-hidden homosexuality, safe in the knowledge that with his public life over, and freed from responsibility, he could finally relax and enjoy a full private life? Did he suspect he might already have potentially compromised his position by doing this?

Whatever was going through his mind, the fact remains that Oldfield asked the Prime Minister for three days to consider the offer, and she granted that request.

Oldfield spent the morning of 26 September under the stewardship of the Cabinet Secretary, Sir John Hunt, meeting with the civil servants who would be dealing with his new post (should he accept it), Whitmore on behalf of the Prime Minister, and the heads of both MI5 and MI6 – respectively Sir Howard Smith and Sir Dickie Franks – to go through the details of the job. From there, as ever accompanied by his bodyguard Ken Dyer, he took the train to Oxford to talk things through with his old friend Betty Kemp. In the evening he dined with his former protégé Anthony Cavendish and the Conservative MP and erstwhile Foreign Minister Julian Amery.

Unlike Killick, whose musings of only a few days before had led to a decision that was influenced by his wife, Oldfield had no wife or partner with whom to share his agonizing. He was all too aware that his bachelor status left him both uniquely placed to take on the role and entirely alone in his decision-making. He worried that in taking on the job he would potentially be placing his mother and wider family in greater danger than they had ever faced before, but he also knew that his sense of duty would not allow him to let his country down. And that his family would understand that.

At noon on Thursday, 27 September, Sir Maurice Oldfield telephoned the Prime Minister's office to say he was ready to take on the role of Security Coordinator in Northern Ireland. In a minute to her officials, Margaret Thatcher stressed that henceforth the safety of Oldfield and his family must be paramount.

With the security arrangements in place, Oldfield travelled back to Derbyshire on the morning of 1 October, surrounded by bodyguards including the ubiquitous Ken Dyer, and spent the day explaining to his family what was happening.

In Downing Street, Mrs Thatcher approved the press release to accompany the appointment, which was due to be announced on Wednesday the 3rd. But by Tuesday morning news of Oldfield's appointment had already started to leak, and Humphrey Atkins was forced to bring forward his announcement. The statement was dry and deliberately low-key:

Sir Maurice Oldfield will assist the Secretary of State in improving the coordination and effectiveness of the fight against terrorism in Northern Ireland. He will be based in

Northern Ireland and will be supported by a joint staff drawn from the Royal Ulster Constabulary, the Army and the Civil Service, which will be operational twenty-four hours a day.

The following morning, on the doormats of Britain, the newspaper headlines screamed 'M Returns to Fight the IRA'.

2

A Derbyshire Lad

HEADS OF THE Secret Intelligence Service tend to be drawn from an almost identikit background. True, the early Chiefs – starting with William Melville who founded the Secret Service Bureau, and Mansfield Cumming, the first head of MI6 when the Bureau was split into sections according to their area of responsibility – were colourful characters with interesting roots, but those two were both middle class with planned careers in law enforcement or the military. Melville, the Irish-born son of a baker-cum-publican, joined the Metropolitan Police at the age of twenty-two and progressed through the Criminal Investigations Department to Special Irish Branch, eventually becoming head of Special Branch and on into the evolving Secret Service. Cumming hailed from a business background and trained at the Royal Naval College at Dartmouth, leading to a twenty-nine-year career in the Navy.

Since Cumming vacated the office in 1923 there have been fifteen Chiefs of the SIS. Fourteen came from what would be deemed Establishment backgrounds, whether old money, private education, or careers in diplomacy – and in most cases all three, with Oxbridge thrown in. The fifteenth was from possibly the most contrasting heritage one could imagine and yet ended up the most decorated holder of the post.

Maurice Oldfield arrived in his grandparents' kitchen in their farmhouse in the Derbyshire Peak District on 16 November 1915. Meadow Place Farm shelters in a hollow behind a bleak hillside in the parish of Youlgreave, about midway between that village and Over Haddon, the village where Oldfield grew up and which he called home for the whole of his life. The villages are separated by Lathkill Dale, now a tourist trap and celebrated as one of the most beautiful spots in the national park. Historically, though, it had been best known for its lead mining, and the haunting remains of that industry make for a striking contrast with the rural tranquillity that now prevails. The steep banks of Lathkill Dale made life and work challenging for the people who farmed it, and in the early twentieth century these included the Oldfields and the Dickens.

The world into which Maurice Oldfield was born could not be fairly described as one of dark, satanic, grinding poverty in the way we think of it from accounts of life in industrial urban areas. His was poverty all right, but the air was clean, the fields and dales a playground, and people simply mucked in. In Over Haddon there was no real industry beyond farming, and with the poor soil and lack of mechanization, even those in work faced relative poverty so low were the wages. The workhouse in Bakewell was, as a result, a busy place. But this part of the Peak District is also one of the most stunning, wild and enticing places in England, and its influence ran deep for the Oldfield family.

Joseph Oldfield, Maurice's father, was born in 1885 and had found himself almost abandoned in Over Haddon as a baby. He was the eldest of the six children born to Fred Oldfield, a farm worker in the village whose family had featured in the parish records for over two centuries, and his wife Margaret Lupton, daughter of the local fish-keeper. Joseph was only a few months old when his parents took up the tenancy of Woodthorpe Hall Farm, a handsome property in the north-east Derbyshire coalfields some twenty miles from Over Haddon. Fred himself had sprung from difficult beginnings, the illegitimate product of a brief liaison between farmer's daughter Sarah Oldfield and a farmer's lad from a neighbouring village by the name of Robert Broome (it's somehow difficult to picture a spymaster called Maurice Broome), so when Fred and Margaret Oldfield were offered the chance to take on what was, by their standards, a prestigious tenancy, it must have been difficult to resist.

Unwilling, and possibly unable, to start their new life and new business with the inconvenience of a baby, Fred and Margaret left little Joseph in the care of his elderly maiden great-aunts, spinsters Annie and Mary Wildgoose – joint landladies of the Lathkill View Hotel in Over Haddon – the intention being that he would eventually join his parents at Woodthorpe.

The Lathkill View Hotel was in those days a typical public house of the time, though with extraordinary views over the wooded valley of Lathkill Dale to the villages, hills and dales beyond. Now, having been named in 2012 among Britain's

50 Best Country Pubs by the *Independent*, the place – extended in build, and abbreviated in name to the Lathkill Hotel – attracts tourists from all over the world. But in the early 1900s it was a much smaller, parochial hostelry, mostly serving the local farm workers. The pub sits on a loop in the road at the eastern end of Over Haddon, with only Hall Hill Cottage and the Wesleyan Reform Chapel occupying the same small island. To the rear is a high limestone wall; to the front the wall disguises a fifteen-foot drop to the fields below. The natural security provided by the Lathkill's location was not lost on Maurice Oldfield. It was very easy to block off the road, and in the 1970s he took advantage of this, using the pub to host sensitive meetings far from the public gaze.

The Wildgoose sisters served beer in jugs from their kitchen, and this basically topped up what little they earned from the hens, pigs and few dairy cattle they had on their smallholding. This gave Joseph a wide range of chores, responsibilities and experiences – and an appetite for hard work. It also imbued him with the desire to keep *his* family together when the time came. Having often to be 'front of house' at the pub as he grew up, Joseph – or Joe, as he preferred – was always immaculately turned out. He sported highly polished boots, collar, tie and waistcoat, and topped it all off with a tweed cap. He took on a coal round with his pony and trap, and was known as a dapper little chap, barely five feet small, and something of a one for the ladies.

Joe Oldfield never did join his parents at Woodthorpe. Things didn't work out for them and by 1905 they were back in the Peak District, renting a far more humble farm in the village of Little Longstone. Fred played the role of gentleman farmer, leaving his other sons, Joe's younger brothers Herbert and Walter, to do the work while Fred held court in the Packhorse Inn nearby. For the remaining twenty-five years of his life Fred pottered between pub and farmhouse, existing on Bass Best Bitter and pickled eggs, and proudly never missing a session in the Packhorse.

Ada Annie Dicken, younger daughter of Ellis Dicken and Elizabeth Featherstone, was a girl of eighteen living at Meadow Place Farm, part of an extended family that included her brothers Tom, Reginald and William, her sister Elizabeth, and Elizabeth's husband Edwin Cawley, when she ran into Joe Oldfield at Bakewell Market in 1911. The Dicken family had come from nearby Flagg in the mid nineteenth century, when a farmer named Reginald Dicken (known as Original Dicken) had two sons and encouraged them to take on farm tenancies. The elder, Ellis, went to Meadow Place, the younger, Robert, to a farm in South Normanton in east Derbyshire. (Going down four generations, the South Normanton side of the family tree leads to Nellie Dicken, who married an American GI and moved to the USA. Nellie's granddaughter is the actress and former Bond girl Halle Berry.)

Annie (as she was called, unless her father was angry with her, when she became Ada) and Joe married after a short courtship, and rented Hall Hill Cottage, the tiny dwelling next to the Lathkill. By the start of the First World War Joe had taken on the licence of the place from his aunts.

Maurice Oldfield's later personal and professional life always retained its links with his Derbyshire childhood, which was the firm root in his life however seemingly far removed from that background he grew. As a schoolboy he began a collection of books about Derbyshire, from guides and histories to fiction that featured Derbyshire settings. This included such diverse writers as George Eliot, Jane Austen, the poet Thomas Moult, and a former Lady Manners Grammar School alumna, Alison Uttley. He maintained connections with family and wider Derbyshire people around the world, and would use them as eyes and ears to suit his needs. When travelling in Canada in 1977 as head of MI6, Oldfield looked up some Lupton relatives – whose parents had migrated to Canada in the 1870s with a rail ticket that gave them each a quarter section of land, which saw them accidentally become owners of much of what would become downtown Calgary – and was tickled to find that they still took the *Derbyshire Times* half a century on. The old family names served him well over the years, and his preferred aliases for checking into hotels were the splendidly named characters Featherstone Lupton and Dicken Cawley. Wherever he went, whatever he did, all roads led back to Derbyshire. The depth of affection and sense of history Maurice felt for his family and its geographical roots were to colour his attitude to life in a way that extended to his career. He understood that what motivated him motivated people at the most basic level the world over – and this in turn helped him grasp that, when stripped to its bones, intelligence is about people.

Maurice's arrival gave his father the opportunity to shower the boy with the attention he'd been denied by his own parents, and he was joined by sisters Margaret, Sadie and Renee over the next six years. Joe Junior, Brian, Derrick, John and Freda followed in turn, which made Hall Hill Cottage – a tiny two-up two-down – a rather cosy place to be. Maurice quickly showed himself to be bright, thriving at Over Haddon School where he worked solidly to try and earn a County Minor Scholarship to Lady Manners School, a couple of miles down the hill in the centre of Bakewell.

The scholarship didn't come to Maurice, despite the fact that his aptitude for study and capacity for work were already well known. The sheer size of the Oldfield family, and the limited income that could be generated even by Joe and Annie's best endeavours, meant there was no prospect of his parents funding Maurice's education beyond Over Haddon School. All through the summer Maurice worked on the farm, taking responsibility for the hens, while his parents reassured him that they would always have a job for him there.

In the end, just as summer was drawing to a close and he was resigning himself to life as a farmer, a stroke of luck took both Maurice and a schoolmaster who was to become one of his closest friends to Lady Manners School on the same day in September 1926. Joe and Annie Oldfield feigned to be disappointed to be losing their son from the farm but were, in truth, both relieved and delighted for the boy.

The curate of St Anne's Church in Over Haddon was one L. G. Evans, known as 'Tubby'. The Reverend Evans doubled up as a teacher of history, divinity and games at Lady Manners. The Oldfield family were regular communicants at St Anne's, and Tubby Evans was well aware of young Maurice's burgeoning talents. When Evans was offered, and accepted, a post as Minor Canon of Llandaff Cathedral back in his native Wales, two vacancies were created at Lady Manners School. Evans's young son gave up his free place as a pupil, and the clergyman recommended to the school that the place should be offered to Maurice Oldfield. A former teacher from Winchester College, Reginald Harvey, took up Evans senior's teaching post. The new pupil and his master were to become firm, lifelong friends, each having a lasting influence on the other, and the school. Tubby Evans's legacy also went beyond enabling the introduction of these two great figures to Lady Manners: he introduced rugby union to the school and helped found the Old Mannerians Rugby Club that still thrives today.

Maurice's scholarship at the school was topped up by the enterprises of Joe and Annie, and he was eventually joined at Lady Manners by his two eldest sisters – a commitment that really did stretch the family's precarious finances. These had taken a hit at the end of the war when Annie, who had hated the long hours running the pub, insisted that Joe give up the licence to focus on the farm.

Much of Over Haddon belonged to the Melbourne Estate and had passed by marriage through the ownerships of two Prime Ministers, Lord Melbourne and Lord Palmerston, before in 1909 – again by marriage – becoming the possession of Captain Walter Kerr, heir to the Marquess of Lothian. The land and properties were by 1920 being managed on behalf of the Melbourne Estate by the Kerrs' land agent Thomas Pearce, and as parcels of farm land became available for lease Joe Oldfield would take them on as he tried to develop the business and support his ever-growing family.

Maurice also played his part in helping to fund his way through school and with varying degrees of success mucked in to help on the farm. His brothers remember that despite his keenness to help Maurice wasn't the most practical of people in his endeavours. He was renowned as a spectacularly bad horseman with an unfortunately regular habit of falling off. His efforts at tractor driving (once the family at last acquired one of these newfangled beasts to replace the four-legged variety) still draw shaking heads and wry smiles from the surviving Oldfields as they recall having to rebuild limestone walls, and run in blind panic in front of the rampaging vehicle to warn pedestrians when Maurice was behind the wheel.

In 1973, when he was first asked to list his recreations in *Who's Who* and after very little deliberation went for 'farming', Maurice was on the end of a substantial amount of ribbing from his family – to the point where Maurice claimed it was a misprint; he'd actually put 'farting', but the editor had, well, edited it. He did, though, develop his talent for music, and taught himself how to play the organ, inspired by Joe, who liked to entertain the family on his harmonium. This gave Maurice the opportunity to do what he could to bring money to the table, and he was paid to play the organ at various churches around the Peak District, sometimes cramming in three services a day – quite a feat when you consider the distances between churches, the bleak hills involved, and the fact that Maurice, never naturally built for cycling, was travelling between them on a rickety old bike.

Lady Manners School was, in the days of that generation of Oldfield pupils, a small establishment in the centre of Bakewell, adjacent to the Town Hall and Bath Gardens, with barely two hundred scholars. Maurice would walk down after morning milking, and after school sneak away to the big house where his cousin, Clara Cawley, was in service. Clara was renowned for making the thinnest cucumber sandwiches in Bakewell, but Maurice tended to prefer her cakes. He'd have one of those if he could get away with it, a gossip and a mug of tea, and then trek the two miles back up the hill in time for his evening chores.

The emphasis at Lady Manners was firmly on the academic, and in that atmosphere Maurice thrived. He entered what was called 'Shell' form, a class of thirty-one pupils under the tutelage of Mrs Olive Faber, who was to be his form teacher for three years until she moved to North Yorkshire. Mrs Faber spotted Maurice's potential from very early in their association, and it was she who encouraged him to aim for university when his instinct was to return to the farm. His school reports show a pupil that was at the top or thereabouts across the range of subjects. The most appropriate statement, one that could be applied to any of his subjects, whether at school or later at university, was provided by his English teacher in 1928: 'Maurice shows a remarkably quick understanding of the most complex texts, and absorbs information readily. He has a concise way of answering questions. His economy with words is a great strength.' By slight contrast, in the more practical subjects Maurice was, unsurprisingly to his family, not at his best. Under 'Drawing' in his 1927 report, Mrs Faber wrote: 'A keen worker usually, but he is getting rather messy with his paints. This is apt to spoil it.' His 'Manual Work' teacher added: 'Good, though he is slow.'

He was a popular schoolmate too, with a solid bank of friends and interests that set him apart from the conventional bookworm. Maurice's sporting prowess was at a similar level to that of his tractor driving, yet he would occasionally turn out for the school rugby XV or shamble around in the cross-country races. In matters such as these he was utterly unselfconscious. He knew his limitations, was comfortable with his limitations, and indeed could laugh at them, and would join in to give enthusiastic support where it was needed. Maurice was remembered as very much a team player, certainly not its star, content to let the more talented and more vocal members of the squad take the glory while he, a barely adequate prop forward, kept his head down and worked.

The headmaster at Lady Manners School in Maurice's early days was a remarkable character and a major influence on changing the way his pupils approached their lives. It must be borne in mind that the Derbyshire countryside of the 1920s was about as far removed from a bustling metropolis as it's possible to imagine. The radio revolution was barely out of short trousers, and in the same way as there are now inner-city children who have to be bussed out to the sticks so that they might see a cow, there were people in rural Derbyshire who had never seen a bus, let alone been on one. Many had never left their native village.

So when Ian Pendlebury Macdonald swept into town in 1924 to take up the post of headmaster in his new silver Alvis two-seater sports car, with a colourful past in his wake, the impression he made on the wide-eyed children of the Bakewell area was both immediate and long-lasting. Immaculately qualified for the job, having graduated in history from Oxford University and been a master at both Oundle School and Wellington College, of more interest to his pupils was the fact that he had been a motor-racing champion. Macdonald was an early version of John Surtees with accomplishments on both two and four wheels, winning Gold Medals in the English and Scottish Six-day

Autocycle Trials, and Silver in the Junior Car Club High Speed Trials. He had also seen active service with the 28th Punjab Regiment in the bloody battles on the Tigris Front during the First World War, and reached the rank of Lieutenant. Reginald Harvey recalled that Macdonald 'had an aura of authority. Whether striding down South Church Street, refereeing rugger matches, taking Prayers, or making his Annual Report at Speech Day, he was always and obviously the headmaster. The use of the collection of canes in his study was minimal.'

Macdonald saw it as his role to 'open windows' for the normally insular pupils in his provincial domain, and a lasting legacy of his time at Lady Manners School was that he instilled the public school ethos of keeping his charges busy with a range of activities, requiring and inspiring loyalty, manners, behaviour, and a high standard of dress. For the first time the school undertook trips – nowadays commonplace, in the 1920s extremely rare – starting with visits to relatively local industrial sites: the coalmines of east Derbyshire, the DP Battery factory in Bakewell, the brake linings manufacturer Ferodo in Chapel-en-le-Frith; by 1930 pupils were being sent on trips to Paris and Bruges and visited the battlefields and war graves of northern France and Belgium. Maurice Oldfield was sponsored to go on both those trips.

Macdonald's time at the school was relatively brief – he left in 1930 to become director of the British Institute in Naples – but his successor, Leslie Wilks, was another highly decorated veteran of the First World War and a graduate of Cambridge University who ensured that the Macdonald ethos prevailed.

He may have had the benefit of Ian Macdonald's teaching for only four years, but its impact on the teenage Maurice Oldfield was to endure. Maurice's sister Sadie, who joined her brother at Lady Manners School in Macdonald's final year, remembered that Maurice would often come home relating tales of wartime derring-do that had been shared by the headmaster. 'Mr Macdonald really inspired Maurice to read,' Sadie recalled. 'Before that he was mainly interested in Derbyshire books and Bible stories, but he became fascinated by travel writing, history and atlases once he got to Lady Manners.'

In a household such as the Oldfields', it was essential that everyone took Maurice's approach to getting stuck in. And they did. The family finances did not extend to putting all of the younger offspring through Lady Manners, so the next raft of boys went straight from Over Haddon School to working on the farm. Such a household was not conducive to study, and unquestionably not at the level Maurice intended, so he would wait until his younger siblings were asleep before starting work by oil lamp or candlelight – there was no mains electricity in Over Haddon and there is still no gas. His parents realized that Maurice wasn't destined to go into farming so did all they could to support him – though he was still expected to combine study with looking after the smaller children while the others were at work. It wasn't unheard of for the family to come home to find that Maurice had set himself up with a desk in the garden and hung Freda on the washing line to stop her toddling off while he worked.

The Oldfield family was a large and resourceful unit, and this extended to managing family holidays. There was no prospect of such an enormous group, with all the inherent responsibilities of the farm, holidaying en masse, so a different approach was needed. What they did have was an extensive collection of relatives, mostly with farms, in the surrounding area. And in Over Haddon, the village yeast man, Albie Cooke, had a round that covered most of the Peak District, including the outlying farms. So Maurice and his siblings would be dispatched, usually in pairs so the farm was never shorthanded, on Albie's horse and cart, and dropped at some or other relative's farm for a break. They would then be collected and brought back the next time the yeast round went that way. One of the children's favourite trips was to see their Grandpa Fred at Little Longstone; Joseph Oldfield may never have been close to his father, but old Fred doted on his grandchildren.

In Over Haddon, a place many of its 150 or so residents had never left (barring the very few who were sent off to fight in the Great War), these gallivanting Oldfields were considered quite exotic. For the Oldfield children, just the fact of spending time away from their parents, even if only a few miles away and with relatives, gave them an independence of spirit and an appetite for travel that set them apart from many of their village mates. This travel may by today's standards seem scant and parochial, but the holidays at Black Harry Farm, high on Longstone Edge and backing on to the gaping Backdale Quarry, or at Hazlewood Farm near the Chevin Golf Course at Duffield remained etched in the memories of all the young Oldfields. The use of wider family connections to suit the needs of the moment was certainly a tactic Maurice was to employ in later life.

The farming way of life in a remote Derbyshire village in

the early twentieth century was hard, relentless and unforgiving but it became firmly engrained in Maurice's psyche. The sloping churchyard, clinging to the side of Lathkill Dale and containing Oldfield ancestors dating back as far as 1879 – before the church was even built – helped to give Maurice a sense of history and place he was never to lose. He was also fascinated by the large, somewhat incongruous memorial at the bottom of the churchyard, inscribed to Charles John Abraham, first Bishop of Wellington in New Zealand, who had died on a visit to Bakewell in 1903 and was buried in Over Haddon. In this one small field, in Maurice's racing mind, were the roots that bound him inextricably to his home village, and a symbol of the wider world he was yet to know. As a profile of Oldfield in the *New Statesman* in 1978 was to point out, 'When the clubland heroes looked into [Oldfield's] background, they didn't just find grassroots in Bakewell, they found gravestones.'

Maurice's achievements at Lady Manners School were as consistent as they were impressive. All through his school career he was well rewarded at the annual Speech Day, amassing prizes for English, history or languages, or form prizes for all-round achievement. And these prizes were always books – the start of what would eventually become an extensive library. By the time of his final year he had been appointed Head Boy and become a regular member of the rugby 1st XV, and his Higher School Certificate results were so outstanding – including the first, and last, distinction in divinity in the history of Lady Manners – that the whole school was given a day off in his honour. That, more than any other achievement, cemented his place in the memories of his contemporaries as their time at grammar school ended.

History had become established as Maurice's subject of choice very early in his time at school, and his exam results saw him offered a place at Manchester University. He was the recipient of a Jones Open History Scholarship worth £40 per year, another £40 per year in the shape of the William Hulme Bursary to Manchester University, and a Hulme Hall Scholarship worth a further £20 per year. On 16 September 1934, Maurice took the train from Bakewell Station to Manchester to take up his place.

3

The Manchester Years

To go from a situation where study was virtually a luxury – snatched hours of reading by candlelight after days of farming, childcare and walking to and from school – to the academic surroundings of Manchester University was the biggest and most defining change of Maurice Oldfield's early life.

The first, most prosaic change he had to deal with was that of what to wear, how to *be*: how to invent himself as a character. For the preceding eight years, as he had grown up and gone through school, he had switched between farming clothes and the obligatory uniform of Lady Manners. It had rather suited him not to have to think beyond that because, as some in his family used to say, 'Our Maurice doesn't really *suit* clothes.' He was used to his slightly ungainly manner and his portly appearance and had grown accustomed to rising above it by appearing unselfconscious, and by deploying his wit, warmth and intelligence. He really hadn't known any different.

But then he had never been put in the position of having

to choose his own style, or having the freedom to live his life exactly as he pleased. His family were not in any way oppressive, but his situation was. Through his young life Maurice had lots of friendships, but no intimate relationships. In 1920s rural Derbyshire a permissive society must have seemed a lot further away than the forty-odd years it would turn out to be. This wasn't a time or a place for homophobia – in fact the word itself had yet to be invented. Homosexuality was rarely spoken of in public, and certainly not in small, agricultural communities. You'd have been more likely to hear tales of bestiality than of buggery. Even in 1987, twenty years after homosexual activity between people over the age of twenty-one was legalized in the United Kingdom by Roy Jenkins's Sexual Offences Act, when reports of Oldfield's homosexuality started to feature in the press, his closest family and friends were utterly dismayed at the very suggestion.

For someone so defensive of, and devoted to, his family, and who had great emotional as well as intellectual intelligence, the desire to keep his sexual preference a secret must have been every bit as powerful as it was to be essential later in his professional life. So before he was eighteen there was never the merest hint of homosexuality about Oldfield. As the studious one of the family who was either buried in a book or working on the farm, the lack of a girlfriend never became an issue. There was plenty of time for all that. From the very moment he became aware of his sexuality it must have been absolutely second nature to repress it. And if his university contemporaries were aware of Maurice's proclivities, then in the main they were entirely discreet about it.

The sole contemporary ever to address the matter publicly, Ronald Reed, did so only retrospectively. Reed, who became Professor of Chemistry at Glasgow University, made no claim to be a particular friend – or enemy – of Oldfield's, just someone who was there at the same time and who had a measure of close-quarters knowledge. Reed arrived in Manchester in 1938 with Oldfield already graduated and Senior Man at Hulme Hall while taking his Masters, and paints quite a vivid picture of Oldfield as he appeared to a freshman with no preconceptions: 'Maurice was short and fat, pale and pasty, with full lips and a mop of unruly dark auburn hair. He wore an ill-fitting dark pinstriped suit, whose collar seemed to be there for the sole purpose of catching dandruff. Visually, he put me very much in mind of the actor Charles Laughton.'

Reed shared a room with one of Oldfield's acolytes, James Crompton – with whom, Reed suspected, Oldfield had a relationship. 'Jimmy avidly attended all seminars in the History Department and the private goings-on in Maurice's room in Hall – ostensibly as a history student interested in matters medieval. Many in Hall suspected that there were other reasons for these meetings in Maurice's room; "gay" people are more obvious than they think. I have no definite proof that homosexual practices were followed on these occasions – but at least all the signs were there.'

It wasn't until after the Senior Man's death that Reed felt he needed to address the matter of Oldfield's sexuality, and even then, aside from a detailed and quite scientific look at homosexuality more generally, it only forms a relatively small part of his appraisal. Other university colleagues, including lifelong friends such as David Wiseman, remained entirely silent on the matter. This could be in no small part down to the arrival at Manchester in 1937 of Betty Kemp.

Tall, striking, witty, and boasting a curly red head of hair, Betty was a year younger than Maurice, but came to Manchester three years after he did. A relatively local girl hailing from Bowdon, on the outskirts of Manchester but then emphatically in prosperous Cheshire, Betty had passed her Higher School Certificate aged just sixteen – two years younger than Maurice when he achieved the same. But rather than head straight to university, Betty had gone from Altrincham High School for Girls to work in the Manchester office of the Inland Revenue. Four years of that was enough for Betty's restless mind and she enrolled at the university where she became, alongside Oldfield, one of the foremost historians in the faculty.

Maurice and Betty very quickly struck up a friendship, one which was to endure until Maurice died. For him, as well as the simple fact of having a close female confidante beyond his sisters, his relationship with Betty presented an opportunity. In the spring of 1938 the couple took a week-end break to visit the Oldfield family in Over Haddon, and Betty was introduced as Maurice's girlfriend. They spent evenings in the Lathkill meeting the villagers and old friends such as Reg Harvey, and camped out in a tent in Warren Pearce's field to the rear of Hall Hill Cottage. Whatever passed between them physically under the canvas can only ever be a matter of conjecture, but at a stroke Maurice's heterosexuality was confirmed to those who mattered most to him.

Aside from the breakthroughs in Maurice's personal life, at Manchester he was fortunate to come under the auspices of three of the most significant teachers he could have hoped for, at a time when the History School at the university had a soaring reputation. In Lewis Namier, Ernest Jacob and A. J. P. Taylor, Oldfield found himself being tutored by some of the most distinguished academics of their age. Until that period, history had been very much a dry study of facts; the trio at Manchester, from the paternalistic 'Uncle Lewis' (as his pupils knew him) to the progressive Taylor, with Jacob the link in approach, offered a more comprehensive, engaging and challenging tuition package.

In straightforward academic terms, the biggest influences on Oldfield were Jacob and Taylor. Alan Taylor, only nine years older than Oldfield, brought a youthful energy and vigour to his work that stimulated his students in a way seldom seen in so traditional a field. By the time he took up his target post as Fellow of History at Magdalen College, Oxford, in 1938 (which he retained until 1976), Taylor's lectures had become so popular that doors had to open at 8.30 a.m. to cope with the demand. A noted socialist, Taylor's new take on history, with its political undertones, brought a new depth and dimension to the subject. His popularity was such that he became a regular contributor to radio discussions, and ultimately one of the first television historians.

Oldfield, though inspired by Taylor's studious rigour and willingness to challenge accepted norms, and the way he applied history to the issues of the day, never took to the lecturer's brand of politics. The university at the time was quite polarized politically: a substantial number of students were supporters of Oswald Mosley's right-wing Blackshirts and they were balanced by an equally vocal group of communists – and all points in between were represented too. In the student debates, whether formal or among fellow residents in house, Oldfield notably kept his own political views very much to himself, and interjected only to make a nuanced, non-confrontational comment – or a disarming, defusing aside.

Only once in written recollections did a contemporary mention Oldfield having been drawn politically. A freshman, John Robinson, had come to Manchester from Redcar on the north-east coast where he had worked as a seaman and travelled extensively to the ports of Eastern Europe. This was in the run-up to war, when all talk was of the threat posed by Nazi Germany, and a group of students in the Junior Common Room at Hulme Hall, where Oldfield was Senior Man, were discussing the growing crisis. Oldfield listened intently before saying, 'Of course the longer-term threat we will have to face will come from Russia, not Germany.' Robinson leapt to his feet and towered over the Senior Man, fixing him with an unsmiling gaze. 'And when have *you* ever been to Russia?' he asked. From then on Robinson barely concealed his dislike of Oldfield, while Oldfield, suitably chastened, kept his counsel.

Generally, though, in Hall Oldfield was a popular character. He had a gently mischievous sense of humour and was thought a kind and considerate character who wore his obvious intelligence quite lightly. He could join in any conversation without dominating it and offer uncontroversial comment without seeming tedious. In his understated way he built great affection and respect, without those involved even particularly noticing it at the time. That really is quite a skill, and not one that can be readily taught or learned.

Jimmy Crompton, by contrast, was considered by their contemporaries to be kind of 'Oldfield lite'. He tried to emulate Maurice in manner and appearance, but was just that bit more gauche, that bit more slovenly, and that bit less amusing. Reed described it as though 'Crompton had tried to do a Mike Yarwood version of Maurice. You knew what he was about, but it was never quite right.' He was, though, a clever and successful man, and was recruited to the Intelligence Corps not long after Oldfield, and probably by him. By all accounts age improved Crompton, and he was to remain close to Kemp and Taylor (though not Oldfield) until he died in 1975. Maybe their university relationship was something Maurice felt he had to park in the post-war world. Certainly Jimmy doesn't feature in Maurice's later address and contact books.

A. J. P. Taylor would remain a good friend of Oldfield's throughout his life, though their paths diverged and their respective celebrity grew in very different ways. Taylor, the populist historian, lived a colourful life. For a while he and his first wife, Margaret, shared a house with the journalist and television reporter Malcolm Muggeridge and his wife Kitty, where it was alleged that Taylor and Mrs Muggeridge embarked on an affair. Margaret Taylor, for her part, became besotted with the poet Dylan Thomas, who moved first into the summerhouse in the Taylors' garden in Oxford, then into successive houses bought for him by Margaret, culminating in the Boat House in Laugharne where Thomas saw out the last four years of his brief, turbulent life. Heartbroken and financially threatened by Margaret's obsession with Dylan Thomas, Taylor went on to have two further wives, Eve and Eva. Oldfield was close to all of them.

Oldfield's other major academic influence, Ernest Jacob, who with his love of medieval history and status as a long-standing member of the Church Assembly had interests that dovetailed neatly with Oldfield's, reinforced his pupil's commitment to the Church. In later life Jacob was accused of plagiarizing the work his students were doing, but he was also renowned as being a link between the old and the new; the traditionalists who studied the structures of medieval history and the new wave, stimulated to no small effect by Jacob, who introduced socio-political aspects into their work. Oldfield found the study of medieval history and the world of intelligence to have striking parallels and Jacob's influence can be seen in that.

Perhaps the most important contribution Jacob made from Oldfield's point of view, though, was in ensuring that Lewis Bernstein Namier – the third and professionally most pivotal of his Manchester tutors – came to the university in 1931. Namier had been born in eastern Poland, as Ludwik Niemirowski, in 1888. After studies at a university in the Ukraine, and then at Lausanne and the London School of Economics, he formally emigrated to the United Kingdom in 1907, and went on to study at Balliol College, Oxford.

Namier became a British citizen in 1913 and his service in the First World War saw him set about being a British soldier with the zeal of a convert. Poor eyesight and serious injury meant his career as a serviceman was short-lived, but in the departments dealing with propaganda and information he found his ideal wartime role, and from 1918 to 1920 he served at the Foreign Office in the Political Intelligence Department, as part of which job he was a member of the British delegation at the Versailles Peace Conference in 1919.

Just as Taylor was a left-winger, so Namier was of the right, and together they brought balance to Oldfield's political education. More importantly, when, in 1938, the first overtly aggressive stirrings of Hitler's prelude to war began, Namier had already long identified Oldfield as being someone his friends in the Foreign Office could usefully deploy in intelligence when the time was right.

With Namier's encouragement, Oldfield had taken his schoolboy travels to a higher and more focused level. He spent the summer of 1935 at the German Academy of Politics in Berlin, and was dismayed to find that many of the esteemed, predominantly Jewish tutors he had been expecting to find there had already fled to escape Hitler's growing repression. He began to learn German, and got to know much of the character of the German people. In a letter to his sister Sadie, he spoke of the sense of oppression in the country, and how desolate he found the Academy: 'there are many people here that cannot bear Herr Hitler. But equally they seem to feel there is little they can <u>do</u> about him. There's a word they use, "sinnlosigkeit". Look it up, sister dear.' She did. It meant 'futility'.

Maurice's student activities were taking him far beyond Over Haddon, and even Manchester. He was involved in pan-university international relations groups, and by 1936 had been made president of the British Universities League of Nations Society, aided by the fact that he quite readily picked up foreign languages and was already on his way to fluency in French and German. This took him to conferences at universities around Britain and Europe; he did some interpreting work, and twice went to International Summer Schools in Zurich. He retained the group photograph of the delegates at a conference near Stockholm, and hand-drew a map of all their faces, matched to their names. Even then Oldfield was assiduous when it came to details, and seemed to have had one eye on the names and faces he might deal with in the future.

It's one of the myths about Maurice Oldfield that it was the onset of war alone that propelled him into the murky world of intelligence. In truth it was Manchester, and his association with the Polish immigrant Namier, that pointed his life in that direction. Even had war not ensued it seems very likely that he would have been steered into a diplomatic role, albeit possibly not so quickly. The real jump from his humble roots to the career he was to inhabit came in those few short university years. And yet these two parts of his life were regularly to coincide, and Over Haddon kept him grounded. His academic achievements made it highly likely that Maurice could have carved out a permanent and distinguished career as a tutor, but family pressures meant that he needed to earn money more quickly than that.

Maurice Oldfield graduated with a First Class Honours degree in Medieval History on 6 July 1937, the only one in his year to do so. After the summer he was granted a graduate research scholarship in history, and a travelling scholarship by the University of Geneva, both tenable at Manchester, which enabled him to complete his Masters degree. His exceptional academic results led to Maurice being awarded a Fellowship worth £100 a year to be a history tutor at Hulme Hall from the autumn of 1938 – about double the average wage of a farm worker at that time and justification in itself for leaving the farm to continue his studies – and this was topped up with £20 to support him in doing extra research in London. As a single man this would have been more than reasonable – but Maurice was entirely committed to supporting his family.

By 1937 Joseph and Annie Oldfield's breeding programme had expanded to ten children. Yet the family was still squeezed into the tiny Hall Hill Cottage, and the land holding was barely large enough to provide the field space for the quantity of livestock necessary to feed them all, no matter how industrious Joseph and his two young farm-working sons, Joe and Brian, were. So when the opportunity offered to Maurice by Namier's friends in the Foreign Office came about, to earn a little extra by committing himself to joining their service, the sense of duty that drove him on was as much from family necessity as patriotic loyalty. The sums involved are not recorded, and were probably not huge in many people's eyes, but to the Oldfield family they made all the difference.

For some reason, given his motoring record – one can only assume he'd been 'advised' that it might be sensible in the light of plans his new employers had for him – Maurice decided to take a driving test. Until 1935 the test had been optional, and how he kicked himself for not simply applying for a licence when he still could. By 1938, in order to get one he had to take the test. A friend in Over Haddon, Vic Smith – another farmer's son – gave Maurice a few lessons in his dad's Austin 7 calf-carrying van, which terrified both of them, and soon enough he was presenting himself at the Manchester test centre in a car he'd borrowed from Jimmy Crompton. The test was a disaster. A near miss with a bus was followed by a steady roll backwards down a slope as he attempted his hill start. The shaken examiner, once he'd regained his composure, politely suggested that Maurice needed a little more practice.

So it was back to Over Haddon and a conference over a pint with Vic Smith. Vic was frank with his friend. 'Look, Maurice, the fact is you're just not very good at driving. Do you really need to put yourself through this?' Maurice insisted that he did, and that there was only one thing for it. On 27 May 1938, the day before Hitler announced his intention to destroy Czechoslovakia by military force, Maurice Oldfield arrived at the test centre in Buxton to have another go – or at least that was the name on the birth certificate that was handed over to the examiner by way of evidence of identity. By five o'clock in the evening 'Maurice Oldfield' was being inscribed on a new driving licence, and Vic Smith, back from Buxton, was being presented with a pound note by a grateful friend.

It had become common, if largely unspoken, knowledge in his Masters year at Manchester that Maurice had some-how become attached to the Foreign Office. His friends recalled that his whole approach and conduct changed. In his earlier years at Manchester Maurice had been fully engaged in all the livelier aspects of student life. He might never have got into the extremes of student initiations as we may now know them, but he was not shy about getting involved with bawdy behaviour. His organ playing, while still most regularly used in the church as it had been in his Over Haddon days, was a regular accompaniment to what are probably best described as rugby songs. He adopted the fast-paced playing style that had become the fashion of the day, and his party-piece was a full-bodied version of 'The Bastard King of England'.

But now, in Hall, Maurice became more reserved and circumspect. While his colleagues were spending their free time nervously debating the gathering clouds of war and what it might mean for them, the Senior Man would sit, watch, mull over things. While there was quietly frenetic energy as the uncertainty of their future dominated the students' thoughts, Maurice, according to Ronald Reed, 'seemed to exude a strange medieval calm. There was an unusual serenity about him.' At the time his fellow students put this down to being nothing more than his way of dealing with the unfolding events; in retrospect they felt he was more likely preparing for his next career move and already had a reasonable idea of what lay ahead of him. He seemed to his colleagues suddenly to have money. He was never particularly flash or ostentatious, but he and Jimmy Crompton bought new suits and developed a taste for fine wines.

More troubling still, needing an exercise regime Maurice took up tennis. Sport had not featured greatly in his plans since his Lady Manners days, and then only because it was compulsory. In a repeat of his brief rugby career, Maurice threw himself into tennis despite having no discernible aptitude for it. He was quite light on his feet – he'd always been a reasonably competent dancer – but his running style was ungainly and his tennis clothing typically ill-fitting. The sweat he built up, however, convinced him that it must be doing him some good, and that he was sure to be losing weight, not that he ever troubled a set of scales with the matter. That would have been extreme.

It was a proud day for Maurice when on Lady Day 1939 he was able to help his father pay the £125 2s 4d that enabled him to become the tenant of Mr Blore Heathcote, and take on Mona View Farm in Over Haddon. Mona View Farm boasted a large farmhouse – large enough for each of the children to have a bed – several extra fields, an orchard, and a 'dairy in good condition including a sterilizing plant for milk and a 175-gallon cooler unit'. It was what Joseph needed to secure his family's future. In time Maurice was able to help the family buy the freehold of the farm, which continued to grow. His assistance, put alongside his siblings' hard work, saw the farm expand over the next twenty years from a couple of bare paddocks to a three-hundred-acre holding with houses for all his brothers. It is difficult to see how that might have been possible had Maurice devoted his life to medieval history.

Rather than a break from university spent helping the family as they got stuck in at the new farm, the summer of 1939 was, for Maurice, one of more travel. As Europe teetered ever more precariously on the brink of war he visited Paris, Zurich and Brussels, attending more international events and, in the parlance we'd use today, 'networking'. At an international students rally in Boulogne-sur-Mer in northern France he encountered vociferous anti-war campaigners, and was dismayed by what he saw as their naivety. Oldfield felt that while calling for peace was laudable, it was naive in the extreme for the campaigners to advertise the fact that they wouldn't fight whatever the provocation. It was at the Boulogne rally that Oldfield heard a student leader named James Klugmann address the crowd. The Over Haddon man's assessment was that Klugmann was 'very brilliant, but a communist first and foremost, with home and country very much second and third. Not like some of our friends, whose communism is in third place.' It was not to be the last time the two men's paths crossed – and Oldfield's judgement was, in his case, found to be fair.

Closer to home was an international convention in Oxford. As was Maurice's wont, he later numbered all the faces on a photograph – including himself at number 11, typically tucked away in the centre right of the picture and clutching a pipe that draws the eye away from his face – and drew a plan with a key. On the rear of the photograph are the names and numbers of just five of the delegates. At first glance there is no obvious link between them, and the names meant little to me, but a little research showed them to be:

John Strachey (number 2). At the time a noted Marxist theorist who was later to become Secretary of State for War in Clement Attlee's government.

Bernard Floud (number 26). A known communist sympathizer, later to become Labour MP for Acton, and who would be accused by the espionage journalist Chapman Pincher of having worked for the KGB.

Roy Timberlake (number 32). A former civil servant at the Ministry of Information who became a pioneer of trade deals with Mao Zedong's Chinese regime.

Denis 'Jakes' Ewer (number 38). A zoologist and physi-ologist whose reason for inclusion is unclear – until you learn that he was a Cambridge contemporary of Kim Philby, and that his father 'Trilby' Ewer was a committed communist who had been kept under surveillance by MI5 since the Russian Revolution.

Ralph Nunn May (number 47). Another with no obvious reason for special treatment – until you learn that his brother Alan had been spotted at communist meetings in 1938 and was later revealed to be the Soviet agent ALEX who had been supplying details of Canada's nuclear programme to the KGB.

Whatever the exact reasons for Maurice's notes, made in the late 1940s, there seems no doubt that he was doing his homework on the people he was meeting, and actively putting names to faces. He could never be sure when this information might be useful to him.

On 3 September 1939, the inevitable happened, and Britain and France declared war on Germany. Oldfield wasted no time in volunteering for military service. He returned to his work in Manchester and waited for the call to come. To his colleagues at the university he made it clear that they had to do their duty. 'We academics have no right whatsoever to expect to be able to do what millions of others cannot possibly do – to sit back in our ivory towers' was how he put it.

In the end, ironically given his preparation in international affairs, it was to be other Oldfield family members who first rallied to the war effort. Early in 1940, twenty-year-old Sadie – who had trained as a draughtswoman at the DP Battery factory in Bakewell after leaving Lady Manners School – was told to take her skills to Rolls-Royce in Derby, where she worked on the design of Merlin engines for Spitfire fighter planes. The trip to Derby was a tortuous one; the thirty-mile train trip from Bakewell took what felt like an age, and as the station only had a southbound platform, travellers coming back from the county town had to trail all the way to the High Peak village of Chinley some eighteen miles north of Bakewell and wait for a train coming back from Manchester to be able to alight.

One night Sadie arrived back from her usual day in Derby, long train journey and two-mile trek up the hill to Over Haddon looking battered and unkempt, her skirt and stockings in tatters. She looked for all the world as though she'd been attacked and had to restrain her brothers from going off in search of the culprit. After a bath and a cup of tea, the truth emerged. It transpired that Sadie had got stuck in the lavatory at Chinley and, worried about missing her connection, had scaled the wooden door – which was topped with metal spikes – in what she recalled as a 'most unladylike fashion'. From then on she took digs in Derby during the week.

Younger sister Renee, who was nineteen, learned to drive heavy goods vehicles with considerably more success than her elder brother had managed in a car. She was dispatched to Catterick Barracks in North Yorkshire, and convoyed supplies around the camp in her lorry. Joseph and the boys were, as farmers, in a reserved occupation. With Joe and Warren Pearce and villagers Jim Taylor, Jim Mellor, Joe Sherrat and Jack Thurlby they joined the Bakewell Home Guard. Warren took the Hodges role as he, along with Bill Bibbee, was a Special Constable.

The Over Haddon contingent had a hut high on the hill above the village, looking over Bakewell and the Wye Valley towards Sheffield to the north, and the village and Lathkill Dale towards Derby to the south. One wag, having studied a map in the hut, and finding no hills higher between the two, claimed to be able to see France on a clear day. Also in the hut was a hand-cranked field telephone, which was to be used to call in any suspicious sightings from the summit. On the face of it Over Haddon was fairly well insulated from the war and was a popular place to dispatch evacuees from the cities, but when the air raids lit up the sky over Sheffield and the anti-aircraft guns fired in defence, the terrible distant noise felt all too close. Allied planes would often be seen over the village as they circled, heading in apparently the wrong direction but in fact just reaching the right height to mount their raids over Europe.

The most exciting night for the village's crack defence unit came early in 1941 when a fighter plane crashed in Lathkill Dale. The pilot managed to evacuate and parachuted into Over Haddon to be met by the Home Guard, who had hurried to the scene with torches and weapons. Unharmed and incomprehensible as he struggled with the English language, the man was marched at rifle and bayonet point to Constable Bibbee's house, where he was held securely until German-speaking back-up arrived. The villagers locked their doors and took to their cellars lest more of the murderous Hun had Over Haddon in their sights. Some hours later, in daylight, back-up did indeed arrive, and the hostage proved to be Scottish – a friendly airman who'd become lost on the way back from a raid.

Maurice's time came in June 1941, when his call-up papers arrived at Hulme Hall. He was to join the South Staffordshire Regiment based at Whittington Barracks in Lichfield. He travelled back to Over Haddon, accompanied by two lady friends from Manchester: Betty Kemp, of course, and another close friend, Elsa Dean. A leaving party was held at the Lathkill. A long night of festivities ensued, culminating in the locals – family and friends – dancing while Maurice accompanied them on the violin. The following evening there was another leaving party, for Manchester friends, at the Royal George Hotel in Knutsford, south of the city.

Betty was at the station to wave Maurice off. She, Manchester and Over Haddon were soon to feel a long way away.

4

A Good War

FOR ALL THE fuss and farewells that accompanied Maurice's departure to fight for his country in June 1941, the first step of the journey was a mere sixty-mile trip from Knutsford to Lichfield Trent Valley Station, and onward to his digs in the Wrottesley Block at the South Staffordshire Regiment's base, Whittington Barracks at Lichfield. And for all his preparations – travelling around Europe, learning the politics and the languages, his attachment to the Foreign Office – the next ten weeks were spent doing the basic training that every other Army recruit had to go through.

The few weeks after that saw Maurice go almost full circle: he was transferred to the Field Security Police, a junior part of the Intelligence Corps, and sent for training barely eight miles from home. John Smedley's imposing Hydro, its hulking gritstone presence looming over the town of Matlock since 1853, had, until the outbreak of the war, been one of the country's most prestigious spas, with luminaries as diverse as Robert Louis Stevenson and Ivor Novello travelling there to take the waters. The building is still imposing and now in use as the headquarters of Derbyshire County Council. But from 1939 it was called into service as the Midlands base and training school of the Intelligence Corps. So it was in the familiar surroundings of the Derbyshire Dales that Oldfield was taught the techniques of the field agent: surveillance and security, decoding and interrogation.

The Intelligence Corps was one area where Britain had been underprepared going into the Second World War. The Corps had been largely disbanded after 1918, and in the run-up to the second conflict the Army was less ready to reinstate it than it had been for the first. It was essentially the work of one man, Major Gerald Templer, which stirred the wartime Corps back into action. He quickly organized the training of enough personnel to enable the British Expeditionary Force to deploy thirty-one Field Security Units into France, and the Intelligence Corps was formally reinstated by King George VI on 15 July 1940. Templer oversaw a steady build-up in numbers, eventually reaching a total strength of 8,970 bodies, comprising 3,040 officers and 5,930 other ranks.

The skills of the Intelligence Corps were put to use in every military facet of the war effort. Their most famous contributions were in the decoding work at Bletchley Park, where Intelligence Corps operatives made up around 40 per cent of the Army staff working there, and in the Special Operations Executive (SOE). 'Set Europe ablaze' was Winston Churchill's instruction to the SOE, whose role was to get in behind enemy lines, infiltrate and sabotage. Intelligence Corps staff brought subtlety to the SOE, a notable achievement being that of Captain Harry Ree, who single-handedly disabled a Peugeot factory in the Alsace that was making tank parts for the Nazis. Attempts by the RAF to destroy the plant from above had failed, but Ree succeeded by using his best Manchester French to persuade the factory owner to sabotage his own plant. Other important work done by the Intelligence Corps, but less heralded, included being part of the formation of the Special Air Service (SAS), and photographic interpretation. It was work by the Corps' photographic people on the ground that enabled the RAF to target various German weapons stores and troop locations, and that later assisted the Dambusters in their raid on the Möhne dams.

Lance Corporal Maurice Oldfield's role in the organization started at the lowest possible level but in a fascinating location for someone of his enquiring mind. In early September 1941 he was sent to the Suez Canal Zone in the north-east of Egypt, where he joined Field Security Section 273, based in the Ismailia district. The basic role of the section was to protect Army bases in the area, which extended beyond just keeping a beady eye out for things going on in and around the campuses to using what were termed 'Black' and 'White' lists of information provided by MI6, SOE and – with Egypt being technically considered a home station – MI5. The Black List contained names and details of known enemy agents such as members of the Gestapo or the SS, collaborators and sympathizers, while the White List was populated by people known to be sympathetic to the cause, whether members of the local resistance or just friendly locals with information. The Field Security Section had the power of arrest, and the aim was to interrogate anyone apprehended from the Black List and translate any documents or messages they discovered. White List clients were questioned and sometimes given information to feed back into their communities. Information acquired from either source was then assessed for accuracy and passed on to the relevant section of the military that could use it best.

Oldfield started out keeping an eye on the military stores but was quickly deployed to Passport Control at the crucial Suez Canal crossing point of Kantara (El-Qantara el-Sharqiyya in Arabic). This key strategic location was a melting pot of national and religious cultures and rivalries at the best of times; in the war it was a key access route to the North African campaign. The name El-Qantara means 'the bridge', but the bridge in question was considered a hindrance to shipping in the First World War and had been removed, so at the time Oldfield took charge of Passport Control at the crossing the job of the bridge was being done by a ferry, which took trains from the Palestine railway to the east and linked them to the Egyptian State Railway to the west. In a precursor to his future life, the role of Passport Control officer had traditionally been a cover for MI6 agents going back to the days of Mansfield Cumming, not least because it gave them the opportunity to check people's papers to whatever degree they saw fit.

It was Maurice's calm, efficient and effective work at the Kantara crossing that brought him to the attention of the first great influence of his Army career. Major 'Monty' Trethowan, a solicitor from Salisbury in Wiltshire in civilian life, was a Defence Security Officer in the Intelligence Corps, and was overseeing the Suez Canal Area on behalf of Security Intelligence Middle East, known as SIME. There had been a quick and notable increase in arrests on Oldfield's watch, and the beneficiaries of the intelligence that was flowing from Kantara – the more senior Army officers operating in the area – conveyed their appreciative comments to Major Trethowan. At that time, Trethowan had been asked by his superior in SIME to identify an appropriate non-commissioned officer who could speak French to become the liaison officer between the British and the French at the Free French internment camp at Mieh Mieh in southern Lebanon.

Despite Maurice only having been in his post for a few weeks, Monty Trethowan had no hesitation in recommending him for the job, and in late September Maurice found himself promoted to Sergeant and heading to Mieh Mieh, just south of Beirut. If the situation in Ismailia had been complex, the position in Mieh Mieh was more so. In the aftermath of the First World War and the partition of the Ottoman Empire, the League of Nations gave the control of Syria – including the Lebanon – to France under the so-called French Mandate. This arrangement worked tolerably well, until 1940 and the advent of the Vichy French government which allowed the Germans to infiltrate the area, and which necessitated intervention from the Allies.

It was in the aftermath of this intervention, the Syria–Lebanon campaign, which had lasted from 8 June to 14 July 1941 and resulted in the Vichy French being driven out of the region by the British-led Allies and the Free French being given control, that Oldfield arrived at Mieh Mieh. He initially lived in at the camp – a former school that had been converted for the purpose, surrounded by a barbed-wire fence and searchlights – and developed a good relationship with his counterparts among the French. And it was in this setting that he learned a lasting lesson about dealing with people being held under arrest.

Under the French Mandate, French law prevailed, and under French law people arrested for spying could be (and were) convicted and shot without further ado. Oldfield's senior officer, Major Irvine Gray, came to an arrangement with the French camp commander that anyone arrested by the British could be detained for a fortnight before the French intervened. The senior Free French officer in the area, Capitaine Paul Repiton-Préneuf, who was later to be awarded the OBE for his efforts, initially approved the arrangement on an informal basis – then, when it proved successful, made it permanent. The effect of this was that the British could work on a spy they'd apprehended and try to get him to work against his own side. The intelligence derived from using this approach often proved more reliable than that obtained at the point of a gun. It was, for Maurice, the first example he saw in action of what was to become his maxim: 'Defectors are like grapes; the first pressings are always the best.' He found, through experience, that once someone had yielded his initial information, especially under duress, subsequent pressure tended to produce increasingly unreliable results as the informer tried to dredge up – or make up – information of the kind he thought his interrogator would want to hear. The idea of obtaining information under torture was completely anathema to Oldfield, not just because of his Christian beliefs, but simply because he considered the practice pointless and counterproductive.

When asked to summarize Maurice, Major Gray recalled that he was a most unlikely-looking soldier, but that 'he soon proved very efficient, and as an acting Sergeant displayed an astonishing grasp of Lebanese politics'. It wasn't long before

Gray was recommending to their chief, the enigmatic, Ukrainian-born Lieutenant Colonel Douglas Roberts, that Oldfield ought to be given a commission; but for now, at least, Roberts resisted, and Oldfield ploughed on with his work. The decisions about which people were to be released and which interned were usually entrusted to the British, and Maurice gained a reputation for generally reaching the right conclusion – and even forged friendships with some of the interned.

Monty Trethowan joined Maurice once more in Mieh Mieh in June 1942, as assistant to Douglas Roberts, and both men came to admire the quality of Oldfield's work. His quick and accurate assessment of reports, his formidable memory and his easy way of dealing with people at every level made an indelible impression.

SIME's *raison d'être* was the collection and analysis of security information throughout the Middle East, and passing it to the military leaders who needed it. One of SIME's key relationships was with Advanced Headquarters 'A' Force, led by the legendary Brigadier Dudley Clarke. 'A' Force was set up by Clarke in 1941, on the instructions of the British Commander in Chief, General Sir Archibald Wavell, to orchestrate deceptions to confound and confuse the enemy, often by spreading and fomenting misinformation. Soldiers were dressed in fake SAS uniforms and sent out to wander around Cairo, Port Said and Alexandria sparking rumours that the Allies had greater military might than was in fact the case. Rumours of a non-existent British Twelfth Army in Egypt were propagated. Even when an imaginary force like this turned out not to be where German Intelligence had told their military it should be, this was put down not to deception but to Allied plans having changed.

Dudley Clarke was a colourful character and had gained a measure of fame in October 1941 when he was arrested in Madrid by Spanish Intelligence en route to Cairo – dressed as a woman. In his debrief to his superiors after being released, Clarke claimed he was delivering the clothes to a female friend in the Spanish capital and was merely having a joke. They accepted his explanation, with the footnote that it seemed highly coincidental that the woman's clothes, including lingerie and shoes, should have fitted Brigadier Clarke quite so well.

The work Maurice was doing undercover involved going to the bars and nightclubs of Beirut, generally taking on the persona of a more senior officer to lend credibility and kudos, engaging with people who had been identified as potential enemies – sometimes Syrian nationalists, sometimes members of one of the German intelligence services: either Heinrich Himmler's sinister Sicherheitsdienst, or SD ('Security' in English), the intelligence agency of the SS, or the Abwehr ('Defence' in English) – and attempting to 'turn' them to work for the British. It was a potentially perilous task, but Maurice's sangfroid and natural affability, along with his increasingly honed talent for assessing a person, tended to militate against the risks.

The Versailles Treaty after the First World War explicitly forbade Germany from operating any form of intelligence service, but from 1920 on the German defence ministry had started to develop a group of agents with the aim, on the face of things, of defending the country from foreign spies. The Abwehr grew slowly in its early years, but once Captain Konrad Patzig took over in 1932 its presence expanded and

Abwehr officers began to be stationed in the German embassies of friendly and neutral countries. The SD, by contrast, was a 1932 invention of the Nazi Party, and a sister agency of the Gestapo. Perhaps unsurprisingly, it was the Abwehr that was to become the prime, and most fruitful, target of SIME.

In 1935 Patzig was replaced as Chief of the Abwehr by Admiral Wilhelm Canaris, an appointment that was to be of great significance for the war generally and for the efforts of British Intelligence specifically. A fluent English speaker, Canaris started in his post as a strong German nationalist, though never a Nazi, and initially he approved of the renewed strength Adolf Hitler brought to the country, particularly in the face of the rising threat of Soviet communism. He was, however, very much anti-war, and in touch with MI6 – though the British were understandably suspicious of the motives of this powerful military man. In 1938 Canaris was sent to Spain by the Führer to try to persuade General Franco to join forces with Germany in their plans for world domination. In fact Canaris told Franco that he was convinced Germany could not win a war, and encouraged the Spanish dictator to maintain his country's neutrality and, importantly, to deny the Germans access via Spain to Gibraltar.

Canaris's network of intelligence had given him significant doubts about Hitler, and in particular his plans for the Jews, and through his contacts with MI6 he had tried to press the British to declare war when Germany attempted to absorb Czechoslovakia – which would have given him the opportunity to mount an operation to overthrow the Nazi regime. Neville Chamberlain's appeasement policy scuppered that plan, as Hitler was able to play the world statesman and secure growing support at home. Admiral Canaris was left to think again. He appointed a key anti-Nazi ally, Colonel Hans Oster, as his deputy, and they worked covertly and cautiously to make the Abwehr, which should have been one of Hitler's key weapons, more or less neutral, if not effectively part of the resistance.

This made the work of the likes of Maurice Oldfield, charged with turning enemy spies, easier than it should have been. From his time in Berlin before the war, Oldfield knew that there was a significant proportion of the German population for whom Hitler was already far from being the inspirational hero of the nation – a position that was to be further weakened from the Führer's point of view by the defeat at El Alamein in November 1942. A significant proportion of the Abwehr staff was of that mindset, so when they were approached by a personable German-speaking English officer who understood their motivations and who could convince them that their future would be better served in a Hitler-free state after a war they were sure to lose, many of them – though by no means all – came round to his way of thinking. Some of the suspected enemies apprehended by Oldfield and crew were turned and sent back to work as double agents, spreading both information and misinformation about the likelihood of Germany ultimately being defeated; some were interned. Maurice's reputation as a friendly and engaging companion extended to the interns, and some were to remain friends for life.

Oldfield was involved in a small way in the 'A' Force deceptions in the run-up to the battles of El Alamein, assisting in the running of four important double agents acquired from the Abwehr. Three of these were obtained when a boat heading from Athens to Syria was intercepted by the Royal Navy off the Syrian coast. On board were an attractive Greek woman named Anna Agiraki, mistress of the Italian Military Information Chief in Athens (who had apparently sent her to spy in Beirut for the Abwehr as she'd been attracting unwanted attention from the Gestapo in Athens), a former Gestapo thug named Bonzos, and a Greek radio operator called George Liossis. All agreed to be double agents.

Agiraki was jailed in Palestine, but to her Abwehr handlers she was very much at large, and given the codename GALA. Bonzos was also sent to jail, but alter ego RIO carried on his work. Liossis was placed in a secure villa midway between Damascus and Beirut with twenty-four-hour security provided by a group of African guards who spoke no language recognizable by the Europeans. He became QUICKSILVER. The final member was Demetrios, one of a trio of Greek Abwehr agents known as the PESSIMISTS, who had been apprehended near Tripoli. Two of the PESSIMISTS, X and Z, were jailed; Demetrios, with the codename PESSIMIST Y to the Allies or MIMI to the Germans, was placed in the same villa as QUICKSILVER.

The SIME team gave full vent to their imaginations as they invented adventures for GALA, who had been sent by the Abwehr to become a high-class hooker. GALA sent intelligence, all entirely fabricated, that 'she' had been acquiring from the indiscreet Allied officers with whom 'she' was having relations in the hotels of Beirut. RIO had, as far as the Abwehr was concerned, carried out his mission to become a part of the Greek Navy and reported back from the Mediterranean ports to QUICKSILVER with details of the Allies' impressive amphibious operations and their new anti-submarine weapons. QUICKSILVER, who was supposedly radioing from Beirut, then relayed this intelligence back to Athens. PESSIMIST Y, who was supposedly in Damascus, sent information on Allied military deployments to his handlers in Sofia. The location of QUICKSILVER and PESSIMIST's villa (soon known as Q and P Hall) between the two cities meant signals sent to the Abwehr could easily be identified as coming from either place.

One of Oldfield's jobs was to keep QUICKSILVER and PESSIMIST occupied during the long days and hours they spent ensconced in the close confines of Q and P Hall, and having obtained permission from above, he arranged for two local prostitutes to call and offer their services. The whole thing went belly up, Oldfield told a friend later, when the girls insisted that the agents use condoms for the liaison, a suggestion that was considered grossly offensive by the Greeks.

The success of Clarke's 'A' Force – supported by SIME – was the catalyst for the more celebrated deceptions that were to be so important later on in winning the war, and his Operation Bertram in the Second Battle of El Alamein was central to Bernard Montgomery's Desert Rats' victory over the Desert Fox, Erwin Rommel, in the autumn of 1942. Clarke's plan involved such deceptions as covering piles of rubbish in cargo nets so the enemy would mistake them for ammunition stores, building dummy tanks using scaffolding poles draped in calico, and sending false radio transmissions to give the Germans the impression that the Allied forces were much further to the south. Real tanks were disguised as lorries and field guns were hidden under boxes.

The victory at El Alamein was a critical turning point in

the war, one that Winston Churchill was to describe as 'The end of the beginning'. He was later able to reflect that 'Before Alamein we never had a victory. After Alamein we never had a defeat.' The role of British Intelligence in the success is seldom celebrated, falling in the shadow of Montgomery's self-publicity, but it was a major part of the groundwork that made that victory possible.

The effectiveness of the ingenious deceptions in the Middle East and North Africa enabled future plans of the kind to be easily sold to Churchill, who embraced them with such delight that his military leaders had to restrict their reports to the Prime Minister in case he got carried away in his enthusiasm and inadvertently let slip details of operations that only worked in conditions of absolute secrecy. There was also genuine concern over how such reports might be received by the Home Secretary in the Coalition government, Labour's cautious Herbert Morrison. It was decided that operations of deception would be put into monthly reports to Churchill, in as low-key a manner as possible. As the then Director General of MI5, Sir David Petrie, put it, 'It is a disadvantage of security work, by and large, that the results are apt to be mainly negative; that is to say, the better it is done the less there is to show for it. Also, by its very nature, its secrets can be confined only to the few.' Petrie felt it important, though, that the 'good work of the service' should be brought to the attention of the Prime Minister and 'certain other high quarters', so the monthly reports were kept free from details of counter-subversion operations that might not be approved of in these 'certain other high quarters'. These reports were contracted into a précis by an official, one Anthony Blunt – later, of course, to be exposed as a KGB agent. The Security Service didn't know it at the time, but it is likely that Stalin was more fully briefed on the Allies' deception operations than Churchill himself.

Oldfield would always be notable for the extent of his travelling for the Secret Intelligence Service; this part of the war was the only time during which he worked as what fans of fictional espionage would recognize as a secret agent – running missions away from base, often working undercover. Monty Trethowan recorded how Oldfield applied what he called 'Over Haddon common sense' to every challenge: any difficulty confronted, however complex on the face of it, had to be dealt with as it would have been on the farm. As always, his close-knit family helped keep Maurice grounded. In the heat of wartime espionage and deception in November 1942, news reached him that his sister Margaret had given birth to his first nephew, Richard, in blitz-battered Sheffield. It was a reminder of what his efforts were all for.

Maurice's down-to-earth approach, when he'd seen how some agents would spend hours and hours indulging themselves in 'personal' activities then produce overblown intelligence reports to justify the time spent generating the information, demonstrated to him the importance of the job of the analyst. One of the skills he learned, which was probably to serve him more productively than any other – and it was something that couldn't really be taught – was that of analysis. Getting a feel for reports and their sources – what was likely to be reliable, what was not – and having the confidence to 'sell' that intelligence to the decision-makers was ultimately one of the biggest strengths Oldfield possessed professionally. It may not sound very cutting edge or glamorous, but it saved many, many lives.

This was also the only time in his life when Maurice needed to use the driving licence he'd acquired via Vic Smith's efforts back in Manchester. He hated it, but did it out of duty as part of the team – and was known as a 'very serious driver', one who was very much two hands on the wheel and focused on the road, his usual chat commuted to a vow of silence. Unusually for the time, he wouldn't have even a drop to drink if it was his turn to drive. The horrors of his past attempts at piloting a vehicle no doubt added an extra level to his concentration.

In the war-torn Middle East, Army personnel hankered for what aspects of normal life they could grab, and Oldfield was involved in organizing 'Smoking Concerts', a popular entertainment where men would gather to sing lewd songs, talk politics, drink and, well, smoke. Some of the internees were encouraged to attend as part of their indoctrination. Maurice accompanied the singing on a piano, and alongside the old standards such as 'The Bastard King of England', he and Major Gray adapted a well-known song to suit the group:

> Oh dear, what can the matter be?
> This was an office renowned for spy-catchery,
> Now it's a matrimonial agency –
> Who'll be the third one this year?
>
> We once had a Colonel who loved to disparage
> The ancient and grim institution of marriage,
> But he flew home from leave and got caught in the
>   barrage –
> He'll do no more flying, we fear.

Now there's old Maurice O who looks rather monastic
(They say his conscience is made of elastic),
To get him a wife we must do something drastic –
There are lots of nice girls in Mieh Mieh.

The Colonel referred to in the song was Douglas Roberts. On 13 April 1943, Maurice Oldfield became a commissioned officer and joined Monty Trethowan on Roberts's staff at SIME headquarters in Beirut, in what was then a new office building, not far from the landmark St Georges Hotel, close to the Mediterranean. The building was in joint use between the Field Security Section and MI6, so Maurice was now engaged in what was effectively a combined operation of MI5 and MI6. The Beirut station was one of only two in the Middle East that had access to the Enigma decoding machine, and was thus able to decipher German messages and communicate wirelessly back to London – or to the Generals on the battlefields. As the historian Andrew Roberts put it, in relation to El Alamein, 'Montgomery, when he put a picture of Rommel up in his caravan, wanted it to appear as if he was reading his mind. In fact he was reading his mail.'

As Oldfield's reputation continued to grow, the two men formed an unlikely double act. Douglas Roberts, a military man through and through, and blessed with a military bearing, was steeped in the British military Establishment: born in 1898, the son of the British Consul in Odessa, he was a Russian speaker who had served in the Royal Artillery in the First World War and, as aide-de-camp to General Pyotr Wrangel (known as the Black Baron), in the White Russian Army fighting the Bolsheviks in the Russian Civil War. Oldfield, the farmer's son and academic, short, squat and owlish, was the thoughtful analyst to Roberts's confident 'front-of-house' figurehead. It was a pairing that was to endure for the remainder of the war and beyond, described by the eminent historian Sir Alistair Horne – who served under them later, in Cairo – as being 'a kind of Hindenburg-Ludendorff relationship, though in this case the Hindenburg input was often hard to discern'.

In February 1944, the Allies' fruitful relationship with the Abwehr began to unravel. Erich Vermehren – belatedly recruited as an Abwehr agent and sent to Istanbul – and his wife Elisabeth, a well-connected German couple who were strongly anti-Nazi, defected to the British. The Vermehrens had been involved in the Solf Circle, a group of German intellectuals who were committed to resisting the Nazi regime, and who had held a tea party in Berlin the previous September to discuss their plans. One guest at the party, Dr Paul Reckzeh, turned out to be a Gestapo spy, and one by one the Solf Circle began to be rounded up and executed for plotting against Hitler. The Vermehrens headed back to Istanbul separately, fearing for their lives. A petrified Elisabeth was arrested by the Gestapo in Sofia when her train stopped in the Bulgarian capital; Erich, somehow, got back unscathed, probably on the back of his Abwehr papers. The German Ambassador in Sofia, an Abwehr sympathizer, used his connections in the Service to spirit Elisabeth from custody and on to a diplomatic courier plane to join her husband in Istanbul.

In Istanbul, Erich Vermehren got in touch with an MI6 contact he knew, Nicholas Elliott, and arranged a swift defection. The Vermehrens were first taken to Cairo, where they were debriefed by Oldfield and company, and then back to London, where Elliott arranged for them to have a safe billet in a basement flat belonging to a willing colleague's mother. To the British, these German defectors, with up-to-date Abwehr intelligence on Canaris's plans, ought to have been a carefully managed, discreet asset, like so many of the other defectors and double agents that had come onside during the conflict. They could have merely 'disappeared' in Istanbul and the German authorities would have been none the wiser.

It was at this point that things took a strange, unexpected turn. Someone in MI6 let it be known that the Vermehrens had defected, and that they had knowledge of Abwehr operations. Hitler, who had suspected for a while that the Abwehr had been infiltrated, also mistakenly believed the Vermehrens had supplied the British with their secret codes. He summoned Admiral Canaris, fired him on the spot, and abolished the Abwehr on 18 February. It was that quick. The functions of the Abwehr were transferred to the Reich Main Security Office, and the Allies and the anti-Nazi resistance were left without access to German intelligence. The best chance of Hitler being overthrown from within, and the war ending early, was lost.

Canaris was given the meaningless title of Chief of the Office of Commercial and Economic Warfare, and the conspiracy against Hitler continued. The German war effort was falling apart, and with a variety of motivations – chiefly a desire to get a German government in power that was acceptable to the Allies so that the war could be stopped before Stalin's Red Army took over their country – a group of senior politicians and officers led by Claus von Stauffenberg, Henning von Tresckow and Canaris's old colleague from the Abwehr Hans Oster formulated Operation Valkyrie, part of a plot to rid the country of the Nazi leadership. By late June the conspirators had recruited the old Desert Fox himself. Erwin Rommel, considered even by his opponents to be an honourable man and a fine General, would have preferred Hitler to be brought before a war crimes court to answer for his crimes, but he went along with the plans, and his agreement gave great credibility to the operation. The German military commander in France, General Carl-Heinrich von Stulpnagel, was recruited too, and he was in Paris, poised to make peace with the Allies as soon as Hitler was gone.

Von Stauffenberg was appointed Chief of Staff at the Army Reserve Headquarters in Berlin on 1 July, and this gave him access to Hitler's military conferences. The plan was for von Stauffenberg to attend a meeting with Hitler while carrying two time bombs in his briefcase, pop to the loo leaving the briefcase behind, and then make his way to safety. The first opportunity was lost when the conspirators decided the plan would only work if they got rid of Himmler and Goering at the same time. The second was foiled when Hitler popped to the loo before von Stauffenberg, who had to grab his briefcase and reset the timers.

Word reached the plotters that the Gestapo had got wind of an assassination plan, so it was decided to act quickly, and get Hitler at a military conference in his Wolfsschanze (Wolf's Lair) near Ketrzyn in Poland on 20 July, whether the other two targets were present or not. Von Stauffenberg, struggling to prime the bombs quickly outside the room as he'd lost one hand and two fingers from the other in battle, managed to get only one bomb ready before being called into the meeting. He had to go for it, and calmly put his explosive briefcase under the table near where Hitler stood.

As planned, von Stauffenberg was summoned from the room to take a phone call. Someone by the table accidentally nudged the briefcase behind one of its sturdy legs, and when the bomb went off Hitler was left with nothing worse than singed trousers, a perforated eardrum and a bad temper. Four others in the room were killed. Hitler's response was predictably ferocious: the conspirators were shot the next day, and the Gestapo arrested anyone who could have been plausibly associated with the plot, their friends and relatives – an astonishing seven thousand people. Over two thirds of them – 4,980 people, including Canaris – were executed. Rommel, such a popular figure in the country that Hitler couldn't risk making a martyr of him, was allowed to take a cyanide capsule.

Despite Hitler's continued aggression, his war was disintegrating. As the 20 July Plot was failing, the Allies were liberating Caen in Normandy, the last remaining Nazi stronghold there after the D-Day landings a month earlier. The Soviets were driving the Germans into retreat from the east, the Allies from north, west and south. So for Maurice Oldfield and the SIME group, their job was becoming increasingly concerned with planning for the aftermath of war.

By Christmas 1944, Oldfield was living in a small flat on the outskirts of Cairo, not far from the Maadi Interrogation Camp in which he was due to start work the coming January. Douglas Roberts was promoted to Brigadier and made head of SIME; Oldfield was promoted to Lieutenant Colonel in succession to Monty Trethowan and made head of the 'A'

Section of SIME, responsible for political and administrative affairs. It was a complex, challenging brief against a changing backdrop, and he'd only recently turned twenty-nine. Nominally the Germans were still the enemy, and that was the official focus of the work. But the threat posed by the Soviet Bloc in the aftermath of war was now of more concern.

On 6 January 1945, the Russian issue planted itself with a thud on Oldfield's desk in the shape of a note to say that Dr Alexander Radó was on his way to Maadi. Radó was a Jewish cartographer of Hungarian Catholic ancestry who had joined the Hungarian Communist Party in 1918 as a nineteen-year-old, and moved to study in Austria and Germany in the 1920s. The rise of the Nazi Party in the 1930s saw Radó and his wife move to France, and ultimately to Switzerland. He was recruited to the Soviet Military Intelligence Agency (GRU) in 1935, with a brief to report on the growth of fascism. From his base in Geneva he travelled to Italy to analyse the fascist support for Franco's Spain, and around Germany where he saw first-hand the Hitler-mania that was sweeping the country.

Using the cover of his cartographic agency in Geneva, Geopress, during the early war years Radó, codenamed DORA, became linked through his network to several other spy networks that fed information about German movements to Moscow. The complexity of these networks leaves the details open to speculation to this day, but the key elements here are the links to Leopold Trepper, another GRU agent and a component of two spy rings, Die Rote Kapelle ('The Red Orchestra') and Lucy, operated by Rudolf Roessler from his little publishing house, and called Lucy simply because it was based in Lucerne.

To add a further layer of complexity, Radó's radio operator was a Liverpool-born Yorkshireman with a Scottish father by the name of Alexander Foote. Foote was, even by the standards of his profession, an enigmatic figure. A committed anti-fascist, he fought for the republican side in the Spanish Civil War, then decided that the most effective way he could fight the fascists would be to volunteer for the Red Orchestra. From there he started working for Radó, and so voluminous was the information he was feeding via the Lucy ring to Moscow, it was feared he was working for MI6.

Radó's efforts provided the Soviets with reams and reams of intelligence, some of which they used. But in December 1941 the Red Orchestra was uncovered and shut down by German security forces, and Leopold Trepper went on the run before finally being arrested a year later and agreeing to act as a double agent. Radó must have known that his network might have been compromised, but he and Foote continued to feed information to Moscow nonetheless, until late 1943 when the Germans persuaded the Swiss authorities to track and close down their transmitters. Radó went into hiding, and Foote was arrested – though later released when it emerged that he had not done anything that could be considered anti-Swiss. The men met again in Paris. Foote made his own way there, Radó after being spirited out of Switzerland by train with the help of the Maquis (part of the French Resistance) in September 1944.

Radó and Foote contacted a Soviet agent in Paris, Lieutenant Colonel Novicov, and the two were recalled to Moscow and put on the first flight available, which was not until 6 January 1945. Due to the ongoing warfare in central Europe, the flight could not take the direct route so it went via a stopover in Cairo. Foote, a more confident character than his travelling companion, carried on to Moscow to fight his corner; Radó slipped away from his hotel and made for the British Embassy where he sought political asylum, and whence he was sent to Maadi Camp for interrogation.

A fellow internee at Maadi, the German Johannes Eppler, who was at the time sweating on a death sentence, recalled that Maurice Oldfield was sympathetic to Radó, and welcomed the opportunity his potential defection presented to the British. After all, here, in front of Oldfield, was a key member of a spy network who potentially had detailed information about both the Germans on whom he'd been spying and his own Soviet masters. Under the terms of Oldfield's brief, though, he could not unilaterally award asylum without first seeking authority from MI6 (in the guise of the Foreign Office) in London. The Russians put in an extradition request to the Egyptian government, but at that point Britain could still have granted asylum and the threat of extradition would have gone away. So the message went out from Maadi to seek guidance from MI6. The reply was quick and unsigned: 'release the subject to the Egyptian police for onward transit to Moscow'.

If this puzzled Oldfield, it terrified Radó, who had already told Foote he feared a fate worse than death in the Soviet capital. As soon as he was back in his cell he tried to slit his throat. When his guards did their checks they found his bed dripping with blood and Radó lying semi-conscious, a blanket around his head; he was revived but resisted, according to the records, shouting 'Let me die! Let me die!' A report went back to MI6 explaining the situation and that the asylum request appeared genuine. The same unsigned response was the result: release to the Egyptian police for onward transit to Moscow. The following morning Radó tried to steal his guard's pistol, again with every intention of killing himself. Under interrogation by Captains Bidmead and Dunkerley 'on behalf of the Lieutenant Colonel [Oldfield]' as to why he was trying to commit suicide, Radó said, 'I came to you for protection and you arrested me.'

The unsigned instructions from the Foreign Office kept coming, insisting – incredibly – that Radó was of no interest to Britain and should be sent to Moscow, even after he had been sent to Zeitoun Camp, the Egyptian Police internment centre, and even though he was a Hungarian national not a Russian. As late as June messages were still coming stating 'Please telegraph present position RADO case. Is he still in hands of Egyptian police?' Someone was anxious to get Radó to Moscow.

As soon as Radó was back in Moscow, and had been sentenced, without trial, to ten years' hard labour in Siberia, the official tune from MI6 changed and cables started to arrive in Cairo saying that he was very much of interest to them and that efforts should be made to get him back. This persisted over the next year. Fast-forwarding for a moment to 17 August 1946, Maurice Oldfield sent what appears to be a rather sarcastic reply: 'The question no longer arises as by a remarkable coincidence, OSS [the Office of Strategic Services, the wartime precursor to the American CIA] have just received a series of documents from Washington relating to Alexander RADO, Leopold TREPPER, Vladimir CERVINKA [a small cog in Rote Kapelle] and the Rote Kapelle case . . .'

In other words, MI6 had blown its chance.

The Vermehren and Radó cases nagged away at the back of Oldfield's mind as he saw out the last months of the war. They begged more questions than they answered. In the former case, Oldfield had been convinced that Canaris could have brought about an early end to the war – only for this to be blown apart by the Vermehrens' defection being so noisily leaked. Was this British incompetence? Or was someone in the Foreign Office secretly wanting to see Hitler cling to power? And in the matter of Radó, why had someone so obviously of use to Britain, and so frightened that he was almost sure to talk, been hurried out of Egypt to a dubious fate in Moscow? And why did the official line change as soon as he was out of harm's way? Again, was this mere official incompetence or something darker?

The answers, and the sinister link between them, were not to become clear for some years, as we shall see.

In late April 1945, Oldfield was granted a week's leave and travelled back to Over Haddon – for the first time in three and a half years – for his sister Sadie's wedding to Warren Pearce. All through the war, whenever he could, Maurice had sent money back to help his family improve the farm and buy more cows; now at last he had the chance to see how things had gone. His younger brothers Joe, Brian and Derrick were all working on the farm with their father, while Annie was dealing with the younger members of the brood, John, Freda and the youngest, Catherine, who had been less than a year old when Maurice went off to war. Another brother, Geoffrey, had been stillborn.

The wedding day itself, on the morning of 28 April – the day Mussolini was killed, and the day before the German surrender in Italy – was the first time the whole family had been together. Renee was back from her Army service, and Margaret and her family came over from Sheffield. Betty Kemp came as Maurice's partner for the day, except this time she and he stayed at the Lathkill rather than in a tent behind it. The wedding service took place at All Saints' Church in Bakewell, where Maurice met for the first time the young curate responsible for Over Haddon, Kenneth Skelton, who was to become a good friend. The service was followed by a reception at the Lathkill, and then drinks back at Mona View. The wedding guests all had name cards in their places, and one, perhaps mischievously – or maybe out of pride – was inscribed 'Lieutenant Colonel Maurice Oldfield'. The man himself took out his pen and quietly put a line through the title. Betty would later tell Sadie that Maurice had said to her, 'Lieutenant Colonels are for wars. Today I'm Maurice Oldfield from Over Haddon. Sadie's brother.'

Back at Mona View, Maurice had put on a barrel of beer for the guests, and the party went on into the night. When it was time to leave, his brother Joe had availed himself of sufficient ale to have lost his sense of direction, and it took several attempts for him – on foot – to get through the wide-open eight-foot gateway, as he kept hitting first the left and then the right gatepost. Maurice was heard to mutter 'it's a little like my driving'. Joe eventually got through by taking a long run up and putting his head down – and earned himself a round of applause to accompany the helpless laughter.

This brief snippet of his old life gave Oldfield pause for thought as he pondered heading back to Cairo for the last few weeks of the war – for what his family thought would be the last time before he resumed his work as a lecturer in

Manchester. The easy familiarity with which he'd fitted back in, away from the heat, the intrigue and the tension of the war-torn Middle East, would have made it a simple and quite logical step to go back to all that. His family were settled and doing well, Betty was an independent woman forging her own path as a history tutor at St Hugh's College, Oxford, and the comfortable, peaceful History Faculty would have had him back like a shot.

But his family *were* settled and doing well, Betty *was* an independent woman forging her own path, and the History Faculty *was* comfortable and peaceful. All had carried on without him. He'd also come to appreciate the value of the work he'd been doing. Some, mostly more long-term Army colleagues of the old school, viewed intelligence gathering as rather shabby and ungentlemanly, and regarded the whole business as somewhat lacking in taste. What Oldfield had learned, though, and passed on to his juniors, was that used properly, intelligence could be a lifesaver. Time spent turning an enemy could be far more constructive than merely blustering into a gung-ho military operation and needlessly risking lives. Plus, the fact was, he'd come to enjoy intelligence work. He loved the game.

5

From Cairo With Love

THE END OF the Second World War didn't mean the end of SIME's work in the Middle East. Far from it. The nature of the work changed from 1945 going into 1946, but the political balance was still tense and highly charged and marked by a growing perception that the enemy in the background was communism in general, and Stalin's Soviet Russia in particular, rather than the cowed, battered Axis powers. Ostensibly an ally for the war period, political differences held in cautious abeyance for the duration, Stalin's regime with its expansionist nature was now the focus of Western attention. The Middle East, a geographical road, rail, canal and sea junction between Europe, Asia and Africa, was further complicated by the thousands of Jews heading for their spiritual home of Jerusalem after years of murder and persecution by Hitler's Nazis and being repressed by Stalin, despite 'Uncle Joe's' publicly pro-Jewish stance.

Palestine remained under the British Mandate from after the First World War, so it fell to Britain, and Clement Attlee's new Labour government, to take the lead in trying to reach a balanced settlement for the future in the wake of the Second World War – against the backdrop of increased anti-British terrorism from three Zionist paramilitary outfits, aimed at driving the British out of Palestine and establishing a Jewish state. The terror groups Lehi (founded by Avraham Stern and consequently known to the British as the Stern Gang) and Irgun (known to the British as IZL) were the prime agitators; Haganah, a more moderate Zionist group, and one that had been helpful to the Allies in the war, would form an occasional loose alliance with the other two. A key scalp for the terrorists had come in 1944 with the assassination of Walter Guinness, Lord Moyne, who was Winston Churchill's Minister of State in Palestine. This had infuriated Churchill and strengthened Britain's resolve to bring matters to a conclusion – before Churchill himself was driven from office, his wartime work done.

Despite the fact that a Hebrew unit of the British Army in the war, known as the Jewish Brigade, had played an important role in the conflict, the terms of the British Mandate in Palestine allowed for only a minimal amount of Jewish immigration to the area. When the Jewish Brigade was disbanded, they used parts of their uniforms, papers, anything really, to smuggle Jews across the borders. British government policy was to police the borders aggressively, especially after the Moyne assassination, and this served to heighten the aggression of the Stern Gang in particular – one of the first groups in the world actually to describe itself as 'terrorist'.

Labour's new Foreign Secretary, the blunt-speaking Ernest Bevin, came into office in 1945 steeped in years of trades union negotiations, and confident that he could bring those skills to bear in delivering a peaceful settlement to the Middle East – so much so that he staked his reputation on it. He was initially thought to be a supporter of the creation of an independent Jewish state, and Labour policy had been to relax the limits on Jewish immigration. Within a few days of having Bevin in post, though, the Arabists in the Foreign Office had, at least in part justified by the presence of the Jewish terrorist threat, persuaded him to change his mind.

As Christopher Andrew explains in his history of MI5, *The Defence of the Realm*, in the aftermath of the Second World War the focus of the Security Service under its new chief, the successor to Sir David Petrie, Percy Sillitoe, was on dealing with the Zionist terrorists. Despite the looming Soviet problem, the threat from the Stern Gang in particular was felt to be more imminent given that they had started to talk of propagating attacks on British mainland targets. When Bevin not only dismissed a request from American President Harry S. Truman to take a hundred thousand Jewish refugees into Palestine with immediate effect, but rather limited the level of immigration to 1,500 per month, and then appeared to suggest flippantly at the Labour Party conference that the reason for Truman's intervention was that he didn't want all the Jews turning up in New York, he was accused of anti-Semitism and became a target of the Stern Gang.

The job of implementing this rather confused policy of policing the borders on the ground in the Middle East and trying to quell the Zionist terrorists fell to Security Intelligence Middle East, which changed (in theory) from a military to a policing organization, reflecting the move (technically at least) from wartime to peacetime.

Brigadier Douglas Roberts remained in charge of SIME, reporting to MI5 in London, with Lieutenant Colonel Maurice Oldfield as his deputy, and now in charge of what was known as 'B' Division. Oldfield's division was mainly concerned with fighting the terrorists while the politicians sought a diplomatic solution, and his principal opponents were, of course, the Stern Gang and Irgun. One thing Oldfield understood was that the Zionist terrorists could not be treated in isolation. The tentacles of the Soviet Bloc twisted and crept and oozed into every receptive organization, and these Middle Eastern terrorists, with their strongholds in the strategic territory around Suez, the oilfields and the eastern Mediterranean, were obvious targets for penetration.

Avraham Stern had tried to ally his gang with the Germans in the war – bizarrely, given their violent anti-Semitism – and then with the Soviets afterwards, believing either or both would be more sympathetic to the Jewish cause than the British given the latter's (recently reaffirmed) policy of restricting Jewish migration to Palestine. In view of Stalin's expansionist plans, it was importantto find ways of limiting the terrorists' communications with Moscow, and one of the first things Oldfield had to do was oversee the 'tidying up' of the spy networks that had served so well in the war.

One that needed attention, and which illustrates the complexities involved, was in relation to the agent known as KISS. A German engineer of Persian ancestry, KISS was rare if not unique in being run jointly by the British (as lead partner) and the Russians, in the full knowledge of both and using the same ciphers. In early 1945 Moscow had been in touch to say they wanted to terminate the KISS arrangement, but KISS, with his Persian connections, was still useful to British Intelligence in the Middle East, even if the quality of the intelligence he was providing was diminishing. This left SIME, who were handling him, in a quandary over how to proceed.

Three options were considered, all of which had to take into account the delicate intricacy of the situation. The first option was simply to close down the KISS network, do away with it altogether – but this was rejected in case it looked like an act of weakness, or that the British had some reason to prevent Russia from continuing to read the transmissions. Secondly, the cipher could be changed. This too was rejected, on the grounds that it could be considered hostile to a supposed ally. The third, and favoured, option was to 'express disappointment' that Russia had withdrawn from the network, carry on with KISS – in the knowledge that the Russians would continue to listen in anyway – and then feed them information separately that might encourage them to ask for the arrangement to be reinstated. In any event, KISS was thought to have got well past 'first pressings', in Maurice's parlance, so the potentially diminishing returns from his information was a price worth paying for a tidy way out.

It was this kind of wheels-within-wheels intriguing, reading of personalities and motivations and foreseeing reactions that fascinated Oldfield, and he had got very good at it. He realized that rather than just bludgeoning away at the terror groups – which, like other terror groups, contained people who would later become internationally known politicians, such as Yitzhak Shamir and Menachem Begin – the best way to get the Jewish leaders on side would be to talk to the moderates and try to reach a peaceable way forward from within. One of Oldfield's key talents, thanks in no short measure to his innate warmth and humour, was the ability to form useful long-term friendships around the world. In an early example of this he met, and became firm, lifelong friends with, one of the most influential Jewish politicians of the twentieth century.

Born in Hungary in 1911 as Kollek Tivador, Teddy Kollek grew up in Vienna, part of a left-leaning Zionist family. He and his family left Europe for Israel – already under the British Mandate – in 1935 as the first stirrings of ugly Nazism were beginning to be felt. In the early 1940s Kollek joined the Jewish Agency, the largely peaceful organization that was to lay the foundation stones for the state of Israel, and he spent the early war years lobbying for Jewish interests, particularly in London. In 1942 he became the Jewish Agency's deputy chief of intelligence, and by the end of the conflict he was the organization's liaison officer with MI5 and SIME. Pivotal to this role was Kollek's personal relationship with Maurice Oldfield.

The two men were introduced in the spring of 1945 by Douglas Roberts, who was due to sail back to London on leave. The line in the Army mess song was not just a convenient rhyme: Roberts had previously been a keen amateur pilot, but had been involved in a narrow squeak in an air crash which left him with an understandable phobia and lung damage that rendered flying impossible; he even had it written into his work contract that he did not, could not and would not fly. Thus, Roberts was handing the reins, and this important contact, to Maurice for several months. The temporary Chief of SIME was a more cerebral and pragmatic character than his boss, and determined to take the opportunity to improve relations with the Jewish nationalists.

Teddy Kollek, though supportive of bringing Jewish refugees into Palestine against the strictest letter of the regulations, was opposed to the deadly methods employed by the terrorists in pushing for the establishment of a Jewish state. Doubtless at no small risk to himself, Kollek passed information regarding the activities of the Stern Gang and Irgun to SIME, while Oldfield, taking some personal and professional risks himself, demonstrated his support for Kollek by letting him know of places where immigrants would be likely to find their path to Palestine from the USSR the most straightforward.

This arrangement bore fruit in August 1945 when Kollek gave details to SIME of an Irgun training camp near Binyamina, and suggested it would be a good idea to raid the place. The raid was successful, and twenty-seven Irgun plotters were arrested. Given the overarching brief from the Foreign Office, which was, if not actively anti-Jewish, certainly balanced in favour of the Arabs, Oldfield's understanding of, and cultivation of, his Jewish contacts could have caused him major problems; but he thrived in the pressured environment. Sir Alistair Horne, who as a twenty-one-year-old was sent to work under Oldfield in SIME, recalls that his boss was 'certainly in the minority in terms of his attitude to Palestine. His views were not shared by the pro-Arab Foreign Secretary Ernest Bevin, or the vast majority of British soldiery in the Middle East.' It was an early demonstration of how Maurice, while ostensibly on his way to becoming part of 'the Establishment', remained an independently minded outsider. His rural background and provincial university education had left him without the preconceptions of the Arab world that tended to prevail, and being thrust into war had been a great leveller in terms of the old British class system that was so engrained in the Establishment.

Horne was initially surprised – though it made sense as he grew to know Oldfield better – to find, for example, that Maurice's office in Cairo had three doors. One of these opened into the main office occupied by SIME, one to the waiting room for his counterpart in Arab Intelligence, and the third to Teddy Kollek's waiting room. His great skill was in ensuring the three elements never met – and maintaining beneficial relationships with all.

In September 1945, just a week before Brigadier Roberts was due to return to Cairo from leave, he was enjoying an evening in his London club White's with an old friend, Sir Stewart Menzies, the head of MI6, when he was offered an interesting mission. In Istanbul, an officer of the NKVD (Stalin's murderous law enforcement agency) had arrived at the British Consulate claiming that he wanted to defect to the West. In return for £27,000, Vice Consul Konstantin Volkov claimed he would give MI6 the details of three British traitors: one 'fulfilling the duties of head of department' in an intelligence agency in London, one working in the Foreign Office, and another in the British Embassy in Washington DC, along with all the documents they had supplied to Moscow. The matter needed to be handled with the utmost care as Volkov was potentially in grave danger if his status became known before he left Istanbul. It was also vital to establish his bona fides before agreeing to part with what would be about £750,000 at today's prices.

While chatting to Roberts, Menzies realized that his old pal was just the man for the job. He was an experienced intelligence officer and, even more vitally, the only Russian speaker working at that level in British Intelligence. He was also heading back to the Middle East and so could collect Volkov from Istanbul en route and take him on to Cairo for interrogation. The stumbling block, the non-negotiable obstacle, was Roberts's fear of flying; but it was agreed nonetheless that this would be the best way to spirit Volkov out of Istanbul. To one nervous, panicky man running a section in an intelligence agency in London who was busily trying to come up with a plan and maintain his poker face, this was just about the most miraculous news he could have hoped for.

Three weeks later, Roberts arrived at the British Consulate in Istanbul to find no sign of Volkov. A man from MI6 had been out too, and it was, Roberts was told, all a bit mysterious. The British Vice Consul, Chantry Hamilton Page, had been in regular touch with Volkov since their first contact, though the two had been obliged to speak via an interpreter as Volkov spoke no English. Page had been instructed to stay at arm's length until MI6 were in place, and when the representative arrived – some days before Roberts – he instructed Page to telephone Volkov at the Russian Consulate. Someone came to the phone purporting to be Volkov but speaking perfect English. This puzzled Page, who had spoken to Volkov numerous times and knew exactly what he sounded like, but his MI6 colleague told him to remain calm and to try phoning again the following day. He did, and was told 'Volkov's gone to Moscow'. Enraged, Page went straight round in person and was dismayed to find not a trace of the man. Volkov? They'd never heard of him.

The whole matter was put down to being a diplomatic cock-up, scepticism about Volkov's bona fides being cited unofficially, and Roberts proceeded to Cairo – where he told the curious story of Volkov to his deputy, Maurice Oldfield. Maurice deposited the information in one of the vaults in his formidable memory and locked the door.

As well as making enduring friendships with Alistair Horne and Teddy Kollek, it was in 1946 in Cairo that Oldfield met a colleague who was to become one of his closest and most trusted confidants. Anthony Cavendish (known as Tony Castle until 1954, when he changed his name by deed poll, presumably to sound more aristocratic) was struck by the lack of formality he encountered when he was sent to be interviewed for entry into SIME in Cairo. 'I saw a plump and owl-faced lieutenant colonel with untidy hair, wearing spectacles and dressed in a rumpled khaki drill bush shirt and shorts, with one sock dangerously lower than the other.' It was not the stiff military officer he'd expected to find glowering at him. That role, he realized, was carried out by Brigadier Roberts, described by Cavendish as a 'magnificent soldier', nearer by far the imposing physical presence the young recruit had been preparing to face.

Horne's first impressions of Maurice were remarkably similar, and both Horne and Cavendish had been introduced to him by another Lieutenant Colonel working in intelligence, the dapper, openly and flamboyantly homosexual Claude Dewhurst. Oldfield 'reminded me a little of Charles Laughton playing Captain Bligh . . . a pasty face which had not drunk deeply of the Egyptian sun, with thick Billy Bunter tortoiseshell glasses. Behind them the eyes were penetrating but warm and friendly. His uniform was nondescript, calling out for the dhobi and looking more suitable to an Intelligence Corps sergeant – which, indeed, Maurice had been not so many years previously. His cloth badges of rank seemed deliberately faded and obscure, if not purloined. Everything about the man (in contrast to the ever immaculately elegant Claude) was low-key, designed – except that it was not designed – for anonymity.'

Both Cavendish and Horne were to work under Oldfield in the Middle East only for what amounted to a few months, but for both – and others in their orbit – the influence he had on them was massively disproportionate to the time spent in his employ. Horne had joined the Intelligence Corps in early 1945 as a nineteen-year-old and had been sent to the Middle East, where he started out in Cairo doing low-key and, in his view, fairly tedious topographical work, not the 'real' intelligence stuff he had in mind. He showed enough initiative and promise in his reporting for Claude Dewhurst to arrange a more interesting transfer, to the Balkans, where he was employed in observing and reporting on the movement of Soviet troops. Success there saw him back in Cairo within a few months, and put to work under Oldfield.

Alistair Horne was the beneficiary of the fact that SIME was short-staffed as a lot of their people had been demobbed, and he found himself, aged twenty-one, effectively doing the job of a Major but without a formal promotion as, according to Oldfield, 'the command is tough on the intelligence establishment. They call us "the funnies".' Horne's job was to 'get among the communists'. Oldfield put faith in his young protégé on the basis of Dewhurst's recommendation, and put him in charge of a new section entitled 'Russian Inspired Activities: Satellite Powers'. His first weeks with

Oldfield were, for Horne, like being in a series of 'sparkling tutorials'. Horne said of the time: 'I studied his style. He did not believe in the narrow, need-to-know principle, where officers worked in small cells and were not encouraged (or even permitted) to see what was going on elsewhere. For Maurice the history don (who, as a good historian, always had one eye on the portents of the future), those he trusted had to see the whole picture.'

As if they were in a tutor and student relationship, on his first weekend in Cairo Horne was sent home with two documents to read, for discussion on Monday morning. One was the dark espionage novel *Darkness at Noon* by Arthur Koestler (which, years later, President Bill Clinton was to say felt like his life during the Monica Lewinsky scandal), and the other was the official report by the Royal Canadian Mounted Police into the defection of Soviet spy Igor Gouzenko the previous September. Gouzenko had presented the Canadians with 109 documents that illustrated all too graphically Stalin's attempted espionage against the West, from trying to steal nuclear secrets to planting sleeper agents in Western organizations. The Canadian historian Jack Granatstein was to describe the Gouzenko affair as being, as far as public opinion was concerned, the effective start of the Cold War. Given that within a few months reports on the episode were guiding British intelligence officers in the Middle East, that view appears reasonable.

Horne was instructed by Oldfield to read and digest the documents 'to give you an idea of what we are up against'. It illustrated to him for the first time 'Maurice's passionate abhorrence of Soviet Intelligence and the inhumanity it represented'. For a young man who in his formative years had admired the bravery of the Red Army during the war against Hitler, the revelation of the true nature of the Soviet threat was quite an eye-opener. The practicalities of his job were taken up to a large degree with filing, analysing reports and identifying their reliability, but also with some more engaging field work, such as tracking the remnants of, and successors to, the Red Orchestra. Were Alexander Radó and Leopold Trepper *really* in Russian prisons, for example, or were they in fact running agents into the Middle East? (They were in prison.)

Cavendish's role was in counter-terrorism against the Stern Gang and Irgun, aiming to identify and scupper potential 'spectaculars'. The reality of the job was brought sharply home to him shortly after he started work when, on 22 July 1946, the King David Hotel in Jerusalem was blown up by the terrorists, and ninety-one people were killed. Despite (and possibly, occasionally, because of) the obvious dangers and risks, life in Cairo was for Cavendish – a handsome young man barely out of his teens – in his view 'paradise'. He was able to rent a flat (Oldfield made it clear that as part of his posting Cavendish had to live in the community, not at a military base), buy an old Triumph 350 motorbike, and he had an interesting job with allowances and £100 per month – 'to me a fortune at the time'.

Both men were delighted to be issued with a SIME Green Card, which entitled the pictured bearer to be 'in any place, at any time, in any dress'; moreover, 'all persons subject to Military Law are enjoined to give him every assistance in their power and all others are requested to give him all facilities in carrying out his duty'. Cavendish described his Green Card as 'invaluable'; Horne expressed a little disappointment that his didn't give him automatic access to the belly-dancers at Madame Bardia's Opera House, but commented that 'in those happy days the Green Card did carry considerable weight in Europe'.

The work done by people such as Cavendish and Horne shows the diversity of the tasks under Oldfield's control in terms of dealing with the present and the future of the Middle East – attempting to contain the terrorists, and countering the creeping Russian menace. But, as Oldfield was apt to recall, in other ways they were still fighting the war, including dealing with the hunting down of Nazis and with Nazi prisoners of war. One mission that didn't go as well as hoped was when a group of escaped Nazi POWs was tracked down to an area of Cairo where they had assimilated themselves into the community and were trying to stir up nationalist, anti-British tendencies in the Egyptian Army. A fluent Swiss-German speaker, Tony Cavendish infiltrated the group and in pretending to lead an anti-British uprising lured them to an ambush where a coterie of young, armed, plain-clothed Field Security Police rounded up the Nazis in trucks and set off back to the POW camp in the desert. The Nazis, though, were too cunning for the naive British guards and overpowered them before stripping them all down to their underwear – including Cavendish – and making off with their weapons and clothes. Cavendish and his embarrassed chums were left to trudge back to base for what might have been deemed a dressing down had they been dressed.

Oldfield's roles continued to revolve around doing the government's bidding in trying to improve the security situation against the terrorists, in an atmosphere where the politics were moving towards Britain withdrawing from the Mandate for Palestine, and on a personal level, because he knew that ultimately there would be a need to do so, building relations with the Jewish Agency in the shape of Teddy Kollek.

The Palestinian Police, at that time under British control, lacked knowledge and experience in the techniques of interrogation, and on the recommendation of Douglas Roberts, Maurice Oldfield and Claude Dewhurst it was agreed that they would use the Combined Services Detailed Interrogation Centre at Suez to improve their questioning of apprehended terrorists. The centre had been hugely successful in the war years, a key player there being Harold Shergold, known affectionately by his colleagues as Shergy and later to become a legendary and revered figure in MI6 renowned for his interrogation techniques. The ideas that had served so well there were brought to bear now. Along with Shergy, two policemen who were to feature later in Maurice's life became involved in trying to improve the policing in the dying years of the British Mandate. One, Dick Catling (later Sir Richard), would go on to be Chief of Police in Kenya, while a young detective named Ken Newman would thirty years later become Chief Constable of the RUC in Northern Ireland, and earn praise from Anthony Cavendish as being 'the finest policeman this country has yet produced'.

Maurice's efforts with Teddy Kollek had proved directly useful in the Irgun training camp raid, and more generally in terms of a building of trust between their respective organizations; but theirs was quite a specific, personal relationship, and people higher up in MI5 found the Jewish Agency an occasionally frustrating ally. The Deputy Director

General of MI5, Guy Liddell, noted in his diary in November 1946 that he had reported to Clement Attlee on the matter – though not that his report was somewhat disingenuous:

> I told Attlee that the measure of this cooperation was limited; it had never led to the actual pinpointing of terrorists – it had generally taken the form of notifying us that something was likely to happen somewhere within the next 24 or 48 hours, or that the terrorist was believed to be in Jerusalem. In fact, the Agency told the authorities just as much as they thought was good for them and had always endeavoured to keep the strings in their own hands and to imply that they were the people who were governing Palestine and not the British government. The P.M. remarked that they were singularly tortuous people to deal with.

With advice like that going Attlee's way, it's small wonder that his government found its position increasingly challenging. Had Liddell added a 'but' to qualify his remarks and gone on to describe some of the positive work that was being done, things might have been different. It must be remembered that the Jewish Agency, an organization committed to creating an independent Jewish state, could scarcely become an open and unequivocal supporter of the British position, though it was perfectly tenable – and potentially a building block to better things – for individuals such as Kollek who were opposed to terrorism to help the security situation.

By the end of 1946 the British presence in the Middle East had gone from being dangerously overstretched to numbering in excess of a hundred thousand soldiers. Well overdue for demobilization, Maurice and Brigadier Roberts left the Army. To Alistair Horne, and other acolytes from the time such as Anthony Cavendish, Michael Wrigley and even the pre-war Shakespearean actor and baronet Sir Gyles Isham, their time working with Oldfield was considered a golden period. It's a measure of their feelings for the man that all would go on not only to work under him in some capacity, but to have him in their lives as a friend, best man or godfather to their children.

Douglas Roberts was replaced as Chief of SIME by what Horne described as 'a fairly unimpressive figure called Alec Kellar'. A career civil servant with a lisp, protruding teeth and a little grey moustache who reminded those under him of a drowned water rat, Kellar's favoured phrase was 'Men, we mustn't over-exercise ourselves.' The entire operation was moved from Cairo to a grey, sandy compound in the Suez Zone, and with the government's priority in the light of the ongoing terrorism being to extract themselves from Palestine, the focus of SIME moved from what Roberts and Oldfield had identified as the biggest issue – the Soviet threat – to being almost entirely focused on the Palestinian problem. Horne and Wrigley were promoted to Captain, but in their view 'gone were the glory days of MO's regime'. The British Mandate was to continue, without a peaceful settlement or any definitive agreement, until 14 May 1948, when David Ben-Gurion declared the establishment of the State of Israel.

In January 1947 Maurice Oldfield was given a Commendation by the Commander of British Land Forces Middle East, General Sir Miles Dempsey, 'as a token of my appreciation for the outstanding service you have rendered', and was awarded the MBE by King George VI. Despite this personal recognition, years later, reflecting on the perception of British military intelligence and its contribution to the war effort, Oldfield felt that the official history, *British Intelligence in the Second World War*, written by a group of academics, had failed to take into account the work of agents in the field. 'What is remarkable is that there are so few names [in the history]. You get the impression that the intelligence war was won by committees in Whitehall rather than by people. How can anyone write a book about Intelligence in the Middle East without mentioning people like Brigadier Roberts? I am thinking of writing a review of the book, and my opening line will be "This is a book by a committee, about committees, for committees."'

Maurice returned to Over Haddon to what passed for a hero's welcome in the Derbyshire countryside of the 1940s – a few pints at the Lathkill and his first demonstration of some new milking machinery he'd helped to purchase. In February came what he described as 'the proudest moment of his life' when his parents accompanied him to London on the train for the MBE ceremony at Buckingham Palace. It was the first time Joe and Annie Oldfield had visited the capital, and they absorbed every second.

6

Into His Majesty's Secret Service

WITH HIS ARMY service over, at the beginning of 1947 there was never any real prospect of the thirty-one-year-old Maurice Oldfield MBE going back to his academic life at Manchester University. He made the right noises and visited the old place, but much had changed. Betty Kemp was now in her tutorial post at St Hugh's College, Oxford, where she was to remain for the rest of her career, A. J. P. Taylor was at Magdalen College, Oxford, and Ernest Jacob had become a professor at All Souls in Oxford. Of Oldfield's former colleagues only Lewis Namier remained – and it was he who had encouraged Maurice down the Foreign Office route in the first place. All was well (one of Maurice's favourite phrases) on the farm at Over Haddon, and besides, he loved intelligence work. So when his wartime boss, Brigadier Douglas Roberts, was asked to join MI6 and head up the R5 Section, dealing with counterespionage, communism and running the Soviet Desk, and agreed to do so on condition his old colleague could join him as deputy, Oldfield had little hesitation in grasping the opportunity.

From 1947 he was officially a diplomat attached to the Foreign and Commonwealth Office, and that's exactly what he told anyone who asked until he retired from the Service thirty-one years later. In reality he was working on the seventh floor of a rambling, outwardly nondescript, inwardly overcrowded and under-maintained office block known as Broadway Buildings, not far from St James's Park tube station, with a plaque on the wall indicating that it was the registered office of the Minimax Fire Extinguisher Company. At the time, despite being an organization that officially didn't exist, MI6 was colloquially known as 'Broadway' after its headquarters. For the three years of this, his first stint in London, Maurice was, on the face of it, more or less your average commuter. For all legal purposes he was resident at Over Haddon, and during the week he would lodge with friends – for most of that period Bryan (later Sir Bryan, economic adviser to Chancellor of the Exchequer Denis Healey) and Renee Hopkin and their children at their home in north London. Most Friday evenings Maurice would catch the train from St Pancras back to Derbyshire, and leave for London again on Sunday afternoon. He'd go to Broadway straight from the train to trawl through papers and ensure he was fully briefed and ahead of the game for Monday morning, then get back to the Hopkins' for dinner with the family.

On his Derbyshire weekends Maurice would follow a fairly regular routine. He'd head from the train to the Wheatsheaf pub in Bakewell where he'd catch up with friends including the Hudson family who ran the place, and wait to be picked up by one of his brothers. Saturdays would be spent helping on the farm in the morning, and on winter afternoons he'd go and watch his brother John play rugby for the Old Mannerians. Sundays were taken up with a wander down the dale to play the organ at St Anne's Church in Over Haddon, a gently boozy early lunchtime at the Lathkill, a family meal, then back to the station. It was a placid, pleasant way of life, and a sharp contrast to the complexity of the voluminous work that filled his time at Broadway.

In adjusting to life after war, MI6 had undergone a reorganization under the auspices of a new committee, the snappily titled 'Chief of the Secret Service Committee on Secret Intelligence Service Organization', comprising, as chairman, the Chief himself, Sir Stewart Menzies, a deputy chairman in Maurice Jeffes who had been head of Passport Control since before the war, and three high-flying senior officers: Colonel Charles Howard 'Dick' Ellis, Colonel John 'Bill' Cordeaux, and the then head of counterintelligence and the Soviet Desk, Harold 'Kim' Philby. The committee needed to absorb the remnants of the Special Operations Executive and to decide whether to structure MI6 vertically, with sections organized from top to bottom on a country-by-country basis and reporting back to Broadway, or horizontally, with regionally based intelligence being shared across the organization. Those favouring a horizontal reorganization, led by Kim Philby, were more trenchant in their arguments, and won the day. As Philby put it, 'something that cropped up in Canada could be connected to something in Switzerland, and a horizontal reorganization would flag this up'. It seemed eminently sensible.

Kim Philby was a man whose legacy was to loom over MI6 for the next thirty years – the entire length of Maurice

Oldfield's time in the Service. Born Harold Adrian Russell Philby in India in 1912, this was a man who was absolutely the perfect fit for a Secret Service agent of the mid twentieth century. His father, St John Philby, was, like Joseph Oldfield, born in April 1885 – but there ended the similarities between the two families. St John himself was an exotic character: a Westminster School- and Cambridge-educated intelligence officer, an Orientalist who converted to Islam, and the first socialist to join the Indian Civil Service. He married Kim's mother, Dora, in 1910, with his cousin Bernard Montgomery (the victor of Alamein) as best man, and became head of British Intelligence in Palestine under the British Mandate in 1922, working alongside T. E. Lawrence (of Arabia) and Allen Dulles (later head of the CIA).

With a background like that, the similarly educated, immaculately connected Kim Philby – so nicknamed after St John said of him as a child that he behaved like 'a proper little Kim', the eponymous character in the Rudyard Kipling story – found his passage into MI6 an easy one. It was an organization steeped in the upper classes. Eton and Harrow, Oxford and Cambridge, Sandhurst and Dartmouth – these were the breeding grounds of the Secret Intelligence Service, not Lady Manners and Manchester. Trust funds and tiaras, not tractors and trailers.

For people with the right background and connections, gaining entry to MI6 was similar to acquiring membership at London's more exclusive clubs – relatively easy. Kim Philby graduated from Cambridge with a 2:1 in Economics in 1933, and through a Cambridge acquaintance, the Marxist Professor Maurice Dobb, he was introduced to the World Federation for the Relief of Victims of German Fascism.

Politically motivated like many students throughout history, Philby went to Vienna to help refugees fleeing from the beginnings of Nazi Germany, and he soon fell for a pretty young Austrian girl of communist Jewish Hungarian background named Litzi Friedmann.

To the charming twenty-one-year-old Philby, his public school manners and elegant dress sense hiding a nervous stutter, the twenty-three-year-old and already divorced Litzi (Friedmann was her married name), with her thick, short-cropped hair, sleeveless dresses and bare legs, was an intoxicating, intelligent and rebellious figure (she had served time in prison for being a Communist Party member). Utterly smitten, the suave Englishman wielded his charm and his engaging stutter and the two were soon an item. If Philby was to be believed, which he often wasn't, the couple first made love in a snow-filled alleyway on a harsh Vienna winter's night; according to Philby, it was 'surprisingly quite warm when you got used to it'. His friends claimed that was Kim's first sexual encounter. If so, he spent the rest of his life making up for lost time.

In early 1934 the fascist government in Austria began rounding up known communists again. Worried for his daughter's safety, especially given her history, Litzi's father pushed for his daughter and Kim to marry, so that as the wife of a British citizen she might escape. The wedding was held on 24 February in Vienna, where a notable guest – in retrospect – was a friend of Litzi's family named Teddy Kollek. Two months later the new Mr and Mrs Philby fled to England. Once in London, Litzi introduced her husband to a friend, the Austrian-born photographer and communist sympathizer Edith Tudor Hart, and she in turn introduced the couple to a graduate of the University of Vienna, a short, squat, mysterious man of dubious ancestry called Arnold Deutsch. Deutsch impressed Philby with his warmth, his communist idealism and his talk of loving Paris and Rome, and this new friend had an idea to run by Kim.

In mid 1930s Europe the big, glowering fear was of Hitler's Nazis, with their persecution of the Jews and their terrifying fascist rhetoric. A super salesman like Arnold Deutsch was able to paint an attractive picture of the life that could be had if only the world would embrace Soviet communism. The British Establishment, clinging to the remnants of their empire and a bewilderingly complacent idea of its standing in the world, was typified by Winston Churchill's (then still in his wilderness years) description of Stanley Baldwin's government policy on rearmament as being 'decided only to be undecided, resolved only to be irresolute, adamant for drift, solid for fluidity, all-powerful to be impotent'. The only world power offering a credible alternative to Nazism was, in Deutsch's view, Stalin's Russia. If only he could recruit some intelligent, willing young British talent, the sort that was likely to find itself working steadily up to the higher echelons of government, and who would be willing to spy for the Soviets and find out exactly what were the motivations and capabilities of the British government and its Western allies – then, well, anything was possible. Philby, encouraged by his vivacious young wife, was sold on the idea.

Deutsch asked his new recruit to recommend people with communist sympathies from his time at Cambridge who might be interested in helping with the plan. After all, plenty of impressionable, privileged students were known to have flirted with communism only to have it written off, usually correctly, as a university fad. Philby asked for a little time to think, then presented Deutsch with a list of seven names to try. With his colleague and eventual successor as handler, Theodore Maly, Deutsch got to work. At least four of them were found to be suitable and, with Philby making five, were codenamed STANLEY, HOMER, HICKS, LISZT and JOHNSON. This group went on to be possibly the most notorious KGB spy ring in history.

At Deutsch's suggestion, Philby took a course in Russian, though he never became fluent, and driven on by Litzi started working as a journalist, contributing articles to magazines such as the *World Review of Reviews* and the *Anglo-Russian Trade Gazette*. He was encouraged to start distancing himself from his communist past, to dismiss it as a folly of youth, and publicly to express right-wing views – again, a common trait of the born-again in these circumstances. And at some point he split from Litzi. Whether this was at the behest of his Soviet masters as part of the cleansing process or whether the passion had simply burned itself out can only ever be a matter of speculation. What is known is that the two of them remained friends and didn't divorce for another ten years.

In 1937–8, a time when Maurice Oldfield was still safely ensconced at Manchester University studying for his Masters, Philby's right-wing credentials got a boost when he travelled to Seville to report on the Spanish Civil War for *The Times*, and began supplying information to British Intelligence (as well as, of course, to his Russian friends) while becoming close to the anti-communist Francisco Franco's nationalists. Indeed, he was able to speak with Franco personally and pass on to MI6 the assurance that Spain would never permit the Nazis to access Gibraltar via the mainland. By March 1938 Franco had awarded Philby the Red Cross of Military Merit and any suggestion of communist leanings could henceforth be dismissed with a waft of this symbol of right-wing approval.

From his Spanish success Philby went back to work for *The Times* in London, and started reporting from France as the Second World War began. It was now time for him to wheedle his way into MI6 and start actively working against his own country from within. The process was, surely, more simple than he could ever have expected. Firstly a journalistic colleague introduced him to the head of MI6's Section D – the section responsible for spreading propaganda, and thus ideal for a gifted journalist – the formidable Miss Marjorie Maxse. Miss Maxse, who was also, conveniently for Philby's need for right-wing connections, an officer of the Conservative Party, actively encouraged him to join the intelligence effort rather than the Army. An MI5 appraisal found him to be clean, and then the Deputy Chief of MI6, Valentine Vivian, reported that he knew Philby's family – he'd been acquainted with St John Philby – and that they were good eggs. That was it. He was in.

On a personal level, Philby met the perfect woman for his new persona. Aileen Furse was a store detective in the Marble Arch branch of Marks & Spencer, well connected in a 'country' kind of way, with little interest in politics or reading but intelligent and practical – and fiercely patriotic and loyal. Kim and Aileen moved in together in 1940, and though he was still officially married to Litzi, the couple had produced three children and had another on the way when they eventually married in September 1946. As someone probably ought to have said, treachery begins at home, and initially at least Aileen had no idea of what her husband really did when he went out to work.

Perhaps even more so than Maurice Oldfield's, Philby's progress through the Service was meteoric. His work was considered to be of the highest quality, he built friendships and loyalty, and by September 1941 he was working for Section V, a precursor to R5, and involved in counter-intelligence. This work gave him carte blanche to build legitimate contacts with the Soviets: as allies in the fight against Hitler it wasn't just acceptable for Philby to be passing details his section discovered about Nazi movements and plans to Russian Intelligence, it was a requirement. From then on any queries about Philby's true affiliation could be easily dismissed as just part of his job. The award from Franco was now mere garnish. For Philby, this MI6-given cover was about as perfect as he could have wished for. It was this period of Philby's career that Oldfield would later describe as being the traitor's most important.

By 1943 Philby was so highly rated that he was being used to train both MI6 and OSS (the precursor to CIA) officers who were based in London in the arts of counterintelligence. An American agent of the time recalled that Philby 'gave a one- to one-and-a-half-hour talk on turning agents – double agents. I do remember being very impressed. He really knew what he was doing.' One of the British agents working under Philby was the author Graham Greene, who said of his boss: 'No one could have been a better chief than Kim Philby. He worked harder than anyone and never gave the impression of labour. He was always relaxed, completely unflappable.'

It was in this context that Philby met a scrawny, cerebral young OSS man whose career would be inextricably interlinked with his for the next twenty years. James Jesus Angleton was a twenty-five-year-old American with a background almost as exotic as that of Philby. Angleton's parents met in Mexico when his father, also James, was serving in the cavalry under General Pershing, then they moved to Milan when James senior bought the Italian franchise of the National Cash Register Corporation. The young Angleton was thus an American growing up in Italy, and was then sent to Malvern College to get an English public school education. By the age of eighteen he was said to sound more English than the English. He returned to America where he studied poetry at Yale University and developed a taste for breeding orchids, before joining the war effort with the OSS in 1943.

Philby taught Angleton all he knew, and after this London master class, in 1944, Angleton was sent back to Italy, where he was put in charge of the OSS counterintelligence operations as the Allies drove the Nazis out of the peninsula. The two men remained close confidants, and Angleton was pleasantly surprised when his English pal called in to visit him in Rome in September 1944 on his way back from a rather tricky case in Istanbul.

Despite his relative youth, and his ill-looking appearance which earned him the nickname 'The Cadaver', such was Angleton's intelligence and ability that he was utterly dominant in his section. Colleagues were exasperated by the way he wanted to control everything and suspected everyone of trying to undermine him to the extent that he would check his office for bugs each morning. He conducted his business from behind a desk piled high with papers, and would peer at anyone with whom he was conversing through a gap in the files. The feeling of his dominance was exacerbated by the sofa he insisted visitors sat on, which had broken springs that left a person sitting about two feet below his piercing gaze.

But whatever their personal thoughts about Angleton and his funny ways, his colleagues were united in admiration for his abilities as a spy. His boss, Colonel William Quinn, travelled through Austria, Italy and Switzerland with Angleton in early 1946 and was 'amazed at the breadth of his understanding and knowledge. I felt we had a real gem.' In the post-war period he got his feelers into everything in Italy, ensuring that the OSS had a network of informers all over the country. One of his major sources was the Jewish underground, which was busy finding ways to get those fleeing the Holocaust into Palestine, and one of his best contacts was Teddy Kollek, who stated 'I believe Jim saw Israel as a true ally'. That was correct, and their friendship was genuine, but more prescient was Angleton's assessment that the fleeing Jews might be a useful conduit for the Russians to sneak spies into Europe, the Middle East, and even America. And so it proved; Kollek's contacts were as anti-Soviet as Angleton, and were all too happy to share their sources with the OSS, which in turn gave the Americans some major successes against the KGB.

But for all his intellect and his obsessively suspicious mind, Jim Angleton didn't notice one of the most dangerous Soviet spies of all right under his nose. The end of the Second World War saw Kim Philby appointed OBE – one grade above Maurice Oldfield's MBE in the pantheon of these things – an indication of just how highly regarded he was in official circles, never mind social ones. He must have felt unassailable. In January 1947 it was Douglas Roberts, and shortly afterwards Oldfield, who took on R5, and their predecessor, the feted Philby, went off to become MI6's Head of Station in Turkey, with the official title First Secretary of the British Consulate, Istanbul. Philby, not a man renowned for over-praising his former colleagues, gave the following assessment of the new team at R5: '[Brigadier Roberts] took over from me in leisurely fashion, and questioned me more closely on the clubs of London than the work of the section. His firmest claim to fame, as head of R5, was his success in persuading Maurice Oldfield, an officer of high quality from SIME, also to join SIS. Within a few weeks of his installation as Roberts's deputy, Oldfield had earned the nickname "Brig's Brains".' While Philby's assessment of Roberts's capabilities is probably a little harsh, it fits with the sense of tweedy, bumbling gentlemen's clubbishness that prevailed in MI6 at the time, and wasn't entirely without merit. As Alistair Horne noted, 'When I met him [Roberts] in years to come the conversation went along the lines of "What clubs do you belong to? What cars are you running now, Horne?"'

It was left to Oldfield to get to grips with the brief and master the work they were taking over from Philby. This was one reason why Maurice liked to start his working week on a Sunday. With few people around and therefore fewer distractions he was able to turn his historian's brain to the files of MI6. This was a challenge in itself as masses of them had been destroyed, whether for lack of space, out of incompetence, or simply because officers weren't always encouraged to retain everything. As MI6's official historian,

Professor Keith Jeffery, reported when he was granted unprecedented access to the files up to 1949, it seemed as if the organization had no real sense of history until around the 1960s, and furthermore that documents would be routinely destroyed once they'd outlived their usefulness. Even taking that into account, the challenge in taking over from someone as clever and resourceful as Philby was always likely to bring its own problems for his unwitting successors. At that stage, Roberts and Oldfield only knew him by reputation as a well-regarded high flier. Philby was hardly likely to leave a paper trail of his entire body of work, just the bits he wanted them to see.

Maurice got to work, familiarizing himself with the organization he would one day head. This was absolutely the heart of the British Establishment, and the new deputy head of Section R5 was very much the outsider, finding his way. He studied what he could find about his fellow officers, their ways and their operations. The big challenge was dealing with the USSR when the official policy was not to have spies operating in the territory of wartime allies – at least insofar as they weren't allowed to have agents working in the Soviet Union from the British Embassy. They knew from the Gouzenko case in 1945 that the Soviets didn't take that approach, but the British sense of fair play (together with not wanting to stir up a conflict) meant other proposals needed to be considered.

Dick Ellis suggested staging burglaries of Soviet embassies around the world to obtain information, and his view found favour in some quarters; the fear in others was one of risks versus rewards: a bungled burglary could potentially cause a diplomatic incident far beyond the value of any intelligence retrieved and set back the gathering process exponentially. So other plans were agreed. Eastern European émigrés based in friendly nations would be trained and dropped by parachute or other means, dressed in local clothing, into remote parts of the satellite states – Bulgaria, Romania, Czechoslovakia and their like – just over the borders, to become embedded in the local communities.

From his base in Istanbul, Kim Philby was charged with organizing one such operation, Climber, an infiltration from the wild and mountainous border country of north-eastern Turkey into Georgia, a southern outpost of the USSR. The first Climber operation, in 1948, ended when the two men sent to try to cross the border disappeared in mysterious circumstances. The plan was then modified to be a slowly, slowly one. Two Georgian émigrés living in Paris, one aged forty-seven, one in his thirties, were recruited by MI6 and sent to Britain to train for their climbing expedition – in wild and mountainous Devon. Philby and an MI6 colleague, both dressed as Turkish sentries with fixed bayonets, travelled the seven hundred or so miles to the mission area to identify the best routes for their climbers to take. Quite what the immaculately coiffed Philby, with his gentlemen's club manners that made him more at home with a Martini in his hand than a set of crampons, made of his mission is a moot point; the fact remains that in August 1949 he declared that the time was right for the climbers to get to work.

The idea was that the Georgians would use army uniforms procured from the Turks to get to the border. Once they'd scaled the mountains, they would bury the uniforms on the other side and change into Georgian peasant clothing with their new false passports to hand. They would then get to know the locals and gather information on the area's infra-structure, the way of life, and any munitions factories and naval installations on the Black Sea coast. The whole process could take a year or more. The Georgians, however, had other plans, and insisted on cramming their mission into a mere five weeks, with the intention of laying down the foundations then going back to Paris before returning to Georgia the following year. Despite being apparently surprised by the suggestion, Philby agreed to it.

The journey into Georgia was a three-day challenge. The crew set off from the Turkish side by car, then transferred to a Jeep, before tackling the highest, most bleak and remote mountain passes for eight hours on horseback. As they reached an oxygen-thin 2,500 metres in altitude, it became clear that the summer days spent rambling on the hills of Dartmoor whose highest point is High Willhays at a breath-taking 621 metres were not entirely the best preparation. The elder of the Georgians, whose stated age of forty-seven might have been a misprint for nearer sixty, collapsed and had to be taken back to base. His colleague ploughed on for the last few miles on foot and managed to get over the border without further incident.

Once in Georgia, the climber did find out some useful information about the area, including some details of hydro-electric power stations, an assessment of living conditions, and the spotting of a couple of Soviet submarines in the Black Sea, so on one level the operation was considered a success. On the other hand, there were several elements that were demonstrably risky. The collusion with the Turks to get to the border was a potential risk factor, as was the fact that the hill village they used as a base was known to be watched by the Soviets. The climber also claimed to have been spotted by two Soviet troops, and to have shot the pair in self-defence. Then there was the possibility that someone was leaking from within.

All around the boundaries of what Churchill had described in 1946 as the Iron Curtain, small investigative missions of this kind were yielding the same results – limited success from taking disproportionate risks. A larger-scale plan was running concurrently: the infiltration of communist Albania, mostly using Albanians who had fled the country after the war and were seeking refuge in Greece, Turkey and Italy, to try to foment an anti-communist uprising. Operation Valuable, as it was called, was intended to capitalize on the fact that Albania was now isolated from the rest of the Soviet Bloc as Yugoslavia, under Marshal Tito, had split away from Stalin's control and that country now formed a buffer between Albania and the other satellite states of the USSR. Albania was also Europe's poorest country, and felt to be susceptible to rebellion. And, of course, once one of the satellite states abandoned communism, the rest would be sure to follow. Or at least that was the plan.

The OSS had been superseded by the CIA in 1947, and a joint project between the new organization and the older, long-established British MI6 was felt to be a positive step in the special relationship between Britain and the USA. The British had the expertise and the heritage, the Americans had the cash and the resources. British Prime Minister Attlee, Foreign Secretary Bevin and US President Truman were all in favour, and a joint group was formed to coordinate the effort. Led by the chairman of the Joint Intelligence

Committee, William Hayter, a British delegation including Gladwyn Jebb and Earl Jellicoe from the Foreign Office and Peter Dwyer and Kim Philby from MI6 headed for Washington DC to meet their American counterparts, who included diplomats Robert Joyce, James McCarger and Frank Lindsay, and their Head of the Office of Policy Coordination – a covert psychological operations and para-military group that was soon to be absorbed into the CIA – Frank Wisner.

The Anglo-American group agreed that they would train exiled anti-communist Albanians recruited from the Displaced Persons camps in Italy, Greece and Turkey as agents, and use the island of Malta – then still part of the British Empire – as a base from which to launch the campaign. As Wisner told Philby, 'Whenever we want to subvert any place, we find the British have an island within easy reach.'

Through 1949, six groups of agents working for MI6 were dropped into southern Albania by boat. One of the groups was wiped out, another was described as being 'location unknown', and three had fled across the border to Greece within two weeks. Just one group managed to bed in for about six weeks before failing to find a winter base and giving in. A planned second wave of infiltrations in 1950 was cancelled, and there were only sporadic attempts over the next couple of years, all of which ended in disaster, the Albanian security services intercepting the incursions each time.

Two friends of Maurice Oldfield based in Istanbul, Halsey Colchester and Head of Station Rodney Dennys – brother-in-law of Graham Greene – took over responsibility for training agents for Operation Valuable in 1950 and couldn't work out why every one of their men, all meticulously trained down to the last detail, was arrested on landing and executed. In all, over three hundred agents were killed; many more were rounded up and sent to labour camps. It was as if the communist regime had been tipped off as to exactly where and when the agents were going to be dropped, but at the time the assumption was that they were just up against a well-organized foe – an assumption that was shared back at Broadway.

In London, Maurice Oldfield's mastering of life in MI6 continued. He familiarized himself with all the operations around the world, and read up on the recent history. He took the opportunity to look into some of the cases that had vexed him during his time in the Middle East, cases he'd seen only one side of from his desk in Cairo. He studied the Vermehrens, the German couple whose defection had been leaked, and whose information had been used after the war by the Soviets to liquidate many anti-communists in Germany. He read the papers about Alexander Radó, the back-and-forth communications he'd had with London that kept producing the same response – 'release to Egyptian police for onward transit to Moscow' – until the wretched, suicidal man had gone. He spoke to Douglas Roberts about the Volkov case, the mysterious disappearance of that would-be defector from Istanbul.

Was there some connection between these cases? Or was it just a mixture of coincidence, misfortune, the murkiness of espionage and a bit of good old-fashioned incompetence?

He delved a bit deeper. Where was it the Vermehrens had stayed in London? Hadn't it been at the home of a helpful MI6 officer's mum? Who was manning the desk that kept sending unsigned requests about Radó? Who was the MI6 officer who had arrived in Istanbul before Douglas Roberts, but too late for Volkov? And who was the person 'fulfilling the duties of head of department' of an intelligence agency in London?

The answers were illuminating, but of no official use to Oldfield. The Vermehrens' case had been officially dealt with by Nicholas Elliott; the couple themselves had been the guests of a Mrs Dora Philby of South Kensington. There had been various desk officers on duty during the time Radó had been held in Cairo; one of them had been H. A. R. Philby. In the case of Volkov, it transpired, an officer had persuaded Sir Stewart Menzies that the matter was so important that he should fly out to investigate personally, before Douglas Roberts arrived. When he was asked why it had taken twenty days to get to Istanbul, H. A. R. Philby replied, 'Sorry old man, [to get there earlier] would have interfered with leave arrangements at the office.' As for the London spy, well, that could have been Guy Liddell, head of counterintelligence at MI5, and Establishment to the core – but it could have been his counterpart at MI6, H. A. R. Philby, also Establishment to the core. It was at this point, he told Anthony Cavendish, that Maurice thought he knew that Philby was up to no good.

What Oldfield didn't have was any direct proof that Philby had done anything wrong. Any smoking guns were safely back in Moscow. As a senior retired officer told me, 'Had Maurice made allegations of that kind against Kim on that basis, at that time, he'd have been laughed out of the Service.' The highly regarded former MI5 officer Jane Archer, known as a formidable interrogator, who had joined MI6 in 1944 bringing with her evidence about a young British journalist who had worked for Russian Intelligence during the Spanish Civil War, had been sidelined swiftly by a panicking Philby (the very same young British journalist) when she was 'pluncked [sic] down in my midst'. Oldfield was but two years into his job; he was only just becoming known and building his connections: Philby was already being mentioned as a future Chief. And in the old-school-tie atmosphere that governed MI6, Lady Manners Grammar and Manchester University carried far less weight than Westminster School and Cambridge.

To what extent Maurice let his suspicions be known can only be a matter of conjecture, though there is anecdotal evidence. He certainly told Alistair Horne later that he'd always suspected Philby, and he certainly told his family much the same thing once the matter had become public knowledge. In the mid 1990s the Oldfields' family solicitor, Vernon Colhoun, was working for a client in the Republic of Ireland when he met Philby's middle child, Tommy, working at a racing stables. It's a matter of record that, despite having been effectively abandoned by his father as a child, Tommy was a regular visitor to Kim's Moscow flat in the 1970s, and became something of a confidant. Talk got on to Bakewell, and mutual connections, which led Tommy Philby to tell Colhoun 'Maurice Oldfield was the only person my father was afraid of. He knew he [Oldfield] was on to him'. This contrasts markedly with most of Oldfield and Philby's contemporaries, who always claimed they never suspected a thing. People would recall occasions when something Philby had said or done struck them as a bit odd, and people who remembered the young communist from his Cambridge days expressed surprise at where he'd ended up, but these were isolated incidents that didn't at the time trigger any real concerns. Anthony Cavendish, who was later a regular dining companion of Philby's in Beirut, said that even when Oldfield had been proved right and he knew the full story about Kim, he still found the whole thing difficult to believe. People who knew the man of old found it impossible.

Given his remarkable memory, his analytical mind, his talent for the swift absorption of facts, and the fact that he was the person dealing directly with Philby's old job in R5, it would seem incredible if Oldfield didn't have the measure of the man, at least to the point of harbouring grave doubts about him. The question was how he would deal with the circumstantial evidence he had. To take the matter to the Chief would in all probability have been like signing his own resignation letter. Someone as cool, clever and well placed as Philby, who, as Maurice would have been aware, had originally engineered his way into what was then the job of head of Section IX (the immediate predecessor to R5) by working his charm on colleagues to ensure they dismissed the claims to the post of the even more old-school and theoretically better qualified Lieutenant Colonel Felix Cowgill, would find arranging the demotion or removal of an outsider like Oldfield a relatively straightforward matter.

The opportunity to do something presented itself to Maurice in the autumn of 1949. In the summer the decision was taken that Philby would be recalled from the Istanbul station and be made the MI6 Counsellor in Washington DC – the chief liaison with the CIA. The chance to get into the heart of Western intelligence was so great that Philby didn't even await confirmation from Moscow before accepting the post. He took instructions from Jack Easton, the then

London-based MI6 officer with responsibility for coordinating relations between MI5 and the CIA who was to be his immediate boss, and quickly became the most popular man at Broadway. As Philby put it: 'I was lunched at many clubs on business pretexts. The discussions over coffee and port covered many subjects, but all my hosts had one thing in common – the desire for a free trip to America. I did not discourage them. The more visitors I had in Washington, the more spies I got my finger into. That, after all, was my aim in life.'

As the excitement mounted in Philby's mind about how he might use and abuse his new position, Oldfield came into the possession of some information that he knew would, if used properly, cause significant discomfort for Philby. In early September 1949, Maurice learned from his CIA colleagues that the United States Signals Intelligence Service had, via what was called its Venona Project – a top-secret programme designed to decrypt messages being sent by Soviet intelligence agencies – uncovered a leakage of intelligence from the British Embassy in Washington during 1944–5, and one from the atomic energy plant at Los Alamos in New Mexico, one of the sites where the Manhattan Project (the US nuclear weapons programme) was being developed, over the same period.

At this stage there was nothing in the information to identify any individual directly, but Oldfield must have known that given the scale on which the operations in Eastern Europe had been afflicted by leaks, it was unlikely in the extreme that Philby (assuming he was involved) was working alone. Anyone involved would be virtually certain to know others involved, and to find that their espionage was on the verge of being uncovered ought to put the whole thing into a tailspin. Maurice wasn't a policeman. He couldn't arrest Philby and question him, even if he had firm evidence – which he hadn't. Besides, as someone who had spent the last seven years trying to turn agents, not merely stop them, his strength lay in the fact that knowledge is power. And the uncertainty he could foster in an enemy agent in terms of what he did or didn't *really* know only added to that power. If Philby was the genuine, impressive MI6 loyalist the hierarchy held him to be, then none of that would matter anyway.

So Oldfield briefed Philby, just hours before he and his family were due to sail out to take on the job that was supposed to propel him into the inner sanctum of the Western world's biggest and most prestigious foreign intelligence agency. The news rattled the normally unflappable Philby to a degree that he seldom let slip in his carefully managed autobiography: 'My briefing on the counter-espionage side aroused grave anxiety in my mind. This was given me by the formidable Maurice Oldfield, and included a communication of the first importance.'

The grave and anxious Philby set about finding out exactly what was known and who was involved. He knew perfectly well the source of the Washington leak, and a quick scan of the Foreign Office staff list confirmed that it was his old Cambridge friend Donald Maclean. Maclean had been in Washington at the British Embassy from 1944 to 1948; after a brief stay in Cairo where he'd become involved in drinking and fighting he had been sent back to London – something of a nadir for him after years of sending the detailed minutiae of British and American planning for the post-war settlement, especially in Europe, to Stalin's Russia. Back in the Foreign Office he was rebuilding his career quite quickly and had just been promoted to be head of the American Department. The nuclear spy was not an acquaintance of Philby's: it was Klaus Fuchs, a German-born physicist who had been granted British citizenship in 1942 and who had rewarded that welcome by passing details of the British and American nuclear programmes to the Soviets.

As he glugged away at the case of Moët et Chandon his 'disgustingly rich friend' Victor Rothschild had arranged to have delivered to the Philbys' cabin on the luxurious RMS *Caronia*, and chatted to his friend the *Daily Express* cartoonist Osbert Lancaster, the champagne communist's thoughts turned to how he was going to handle things on the other side of the Atlantic. Thinking it through logically, he knew that MI6 didn't operate in the United States, so any investigation into the leaks would be handled by J. Edgar Hoover's internal intelligence and security service, the FBI. Hoover was not someone held in great esteem by Philby, and the snob in him extended that feeling to the FBI generally.

An FBI representative was sent out to meet Philby on a motor launch, to save him the inconvenience of bothering with customs. The British spy greeted the American security man with a glass of Tio Pepe sherry, 'which he sipped unhappily while we made polite conversation. I was later to learn that the men of the FBI, with hardly an exception, were proud of their insularity having sprung from the grass-roots. One of the first senior G-men [FBI agents] I met in Washington claimed to have had a grandpappy who kept a general store at Horse Creek, Missouri. They were therefore whisky-drinkers, with beer for light refreshment. By contrast, CIA men flaunted cosmopolitan postures. They would discuss absinthe and serve Burgundy above room temperature.'

Philby drew comfort from his views on the FBI. History showed that if they were – and they surely were – in possession of the information Maurice Oldfield had shared with him, then the place they'd be looking for the leaks would be among the menial staff. The odd cleaning lady with a Latvian grandmother would be the subject of hours of FBI attention; it could be months before they even considered looking at the senior staff, never mind the senior diplomats. It was said that when an MI6 officer was sent on an overseas posting his wife would ask 'Will we have a chauffeur again?' while a KGB officer being sent to the West would be faced with resigned questions such as 'Will you be a chauffeur again?'

But even when he'd convinced himself of the FBI's likely course of action, Philby still had to watch his back and rein in – or at least be more careful with – his normally prodigious output of intelligence to his Soviet friends. He experienced another sobering moment when he was introduced to the Director of the CIA, Admiral Roscoe H. Hillenkoetter, at the agency's headquarters in Langley, Virginia. While making small-talk, Hillenkoetter mentioned to the new MI6 liaison officer the 'eminently satisfactory' discussions he'd held with some of his London colleagues when they'd visited Langley in the summer for 'wide-ranging talks', including discussions about the progress of Operation Valuable. Philby enquired who the colleagues were. The reply came that it had been a man from the Foreign Office, William Hayter, and an officer from MI6 named Maurice Oldfield. The man who had made Philby grave and anxious had not only beaten him to Washington, he'd got the ear of the chief.

The next item on Philby's agenda was to be introduced to the people he'd be dealing with day-to-day, and he was relieved to find that the man with whom he'd be doing most of his business was one of his closest friends in professional life, James Jesus Angleton. The two men quickly settled into a routine, with weekly lunches at Harvey's restaurant in Washington where the wiry Angleton astonished his companion with his capacity for food and drink – quite an achievement when Philby himself was known to be a very thirsty man, and one whose stress levels were making him thirstier by the day.

For Maurice Oldfield, though, the 1950s were about to bring an entirely different challenge. After three years becoming fully immersed in the work of its Broadway headquarters, MI6's CIA-endorsed rising star was sent for his first overseas posting. Just as Kim Philby was settling into Washington life, the man most likely to be able to expose him was sent just about as far away from the engine room as it was possible to get.

The longer I researched this story, the more feasible the possibility became that Philby encouraged that relocation for *that* officer at *that* time. He certainly had sufficient influence. Whatever the reasoning behind the move, the Far East was at the time one of the most unstable yet, for Maurice, enticing areas he could have hoped to visit. Back in Over Haddon he sat down with his four-year-old nephew John Pearce to talk about this latest adventure. The globe was brought down from the attic, and between them they calculated that Uncle Maurice would soon be 6,786 miles from home in distant Singapore.

7

Go East Young Man

AFTER A GRUELLING six-week trip on a troop ship, Maurice Oldfield sailed into the bustling port of Singapore on 18 April 1950. There, as part of the team headed up by the Commissioner General for South East Asia, Malcolm MacDonald – the son of Britain's first Labour Prime Minister, Ramsay MacDonald – he was to join the effort to rebuild British Intelligence in the Far East for the post-war world, in circumstances of communist uprisings in countries that had been occupied by Japan during the war and in the midst of what was dubbed the Malayan Emergency. It was a complex, multi-faceted situation, and aside from the nuts-and-bolts work of gathering intelligence, a key element was dealing with the relationships between MI5 and MI6 in what was known as Combined Intelligence Far East (CIFE).

The traditional demarcation between the two services meant that the homeland security service, MI5, would normally deal with British colonial assets – as they were then, Malaya, Borneo and Sarawak – with the overseas intelligence service, MI6, operating in the neighbouring, but foreign, Burma, Indonesia, French Indochina and Thailand. Joining together under CIFE enabled a sensible overlap of duties, unhindered by man-made borders in a time of fluid and changing politics. It was a neat way around the Attlee Doctrine, under which the agencies' geographical responsibilities had been reinforced. Operating across both MI6 and MI5 territory were the recently formed CIA, the French intelligence agency the Service de Documentation Extérieure et de Contre-Espionnage (SDECE), and, by the end of Maurice's first stint, the Australian Secret Intelligence Service. All of these were nominally on the same side in the face of communist guerrillas, but inevitably there were also overlaps, rivalries and inter-organization suspicions.

Leading the MI6 effort were the quietly diplomatic new Head of Station James Fulton – a former schoolmaster from Eton nicknamed Soapy Sid, with something of a reputation with the ladies: he kept a 'love nest in Mayfair' and liked his secretaries to accompany him on overseas postings – and his new deputy, Maurice Oldfield. The MI5 contingent was led by Keith Way, the main conduit to the Malayan Police. The changing status of territories in the region, with some being given independence or at least a measure of self-government, led to an unusual, virtual no-man's land for the services, and they had essentially to share their responsibilities. Headquarters was in Singapore, the cosmopolitan colonial outpost Britain had wrested back from the Japanese after their surrender in August 1945, and it was there that Maurice lived for the duration of his stay. Of all the postings and overseas visits he made over the next twenty-eight years, it was to remain his favourite.

Being so far from home, and without an official camp in

which to be billeted as he'd initially had in the Middle East on his previous overseas stint, Maurice took the deliberate decision to make a life in the Singapore community. For the first few weeks, as he got the feel of the place and his new job, he stayed at the Raffles Hotel, living between the colonial grandeur of that place and his new work base, the Commissioner General's office at Phoenix Park in Tanglin, a couple of miles away across the city centre. Most of the Commissioner General's staff lived within a mile or so of the office, but anywhere Oldfield was going to be staying for any length of time, and where he was likely to aspire to any kind of normal life, would demand the presence of a suitable church.

Most among the British diplomatic elite favoured the grandeur of St Andrew's Cathedral, where the Dean was the equally grand Robin Woods, later to become Domestic Chaplain to Queen Elizabeth II and a mentor to Prince Charles before being appointed Bishop of Worcester in 1971. This was religion as theatre, with the congregation as the cast, overwhelmingly drawn from the wealthy expat community – very much there to be seen. By contrast, Maurice's sort of church was about the people and the feeling, not the building. In Over Haddon, his childhood church was a small, simple limestone building with a close-knit village congregation and his family's graves in the steeply sloping plot out front. In Manchester, rather than the cathedral which was the preference of some of his contemporaries, Maurice was a regular at the campus chapel – nothing more than a wooden hut. He liked to be able to know a church and its people intimately, and be involved in its affairs. Anyway, as a Secret Service officer, being somewhere simply to be seen was fairly low on his list of priorities.

After a few weeks sampling the churches and services of Singapore, he settled on the twenty-year-old St Paul's Church, set at the sixth milestone on the Upper Serangoon Road out on the eastern side of the island, about eight miles from Phoenix Park. St Paul's had been built in the traditional colonial style by a successful Eurasian barrister and municipal commissioner named George Oehlers (later to become the first Eurasian in Singapore to be knighted) in memory of his son who had been killed in a motor accident in London in 1930. With a capacity of only sixty worshippers – the place was brimful every week – and enjoying a friendly, welcoming atmosphere, this was to be the focal point of Oldfield's private life in Singapore for all of his time there. It was professionally useful for him to be involved at St Paul's too. The congregation comprised a good cross-section of the Singaporean community, which fulfilled the diligent intelligence officer's requirement of letting him see how the people lived, what their motivations and opinions were, and building unforced local connections at grass-roots level.

Maurice's next priority was to find somewhere to live, and through a fellow member of the St Paul's congregation he found a house to rent less than a kilometre from the church. At the age of thirty-four, and having helped sort his family's living arrangements before his own, 8 Flower Road was the first home Maurice Oldfield had to himself, and he loved it. A typical Singaporean 'bungalow' – brick-built and white-washed, with a wooden floor raised four feet from the ground to give both ventilation and protection from the monsoon floods – Maurice's house was set in large gardens behind a hibiscus hedge, with tropical trees and a grove of bamboo plants providing shelter for the occasional monkey. The front of the house had a spacious veranda where Maurice would sit and read, shaded from the sun and enjoying a gin and tonic in the tropical breeze. What it didn't have was modern sanitation – but then even Mona View only had a rather sociable outside lavatory in a shed at the bottom of the garden with two seats, side by side, emptying on to a soil heap for fertilizing the vegetable patch. Visitors to Over Haddon were surprised by this arrangement, something Maurice found amusing as he monitored their reactions. It never bothered him one bit.

Maurice began to take on the trappings of the archetypal colonial British civil servant. He ordered his first tailor-made suit – a light cream tropical number, together with matching tie and brown leather shoes – but his glasses remained strictly of the Billy Bunter variety. Determined never to drive again, he hired a local chauffeur, Ahmed, to pilot his MI6-issue Vauxhall Velox, and to impress his new boss Ahmed would sport a starched white tunic with shiny metal buttons and a traditional Malayan velvet hat called a songkok, which looked like the sort of hat a bellboy might wear. Maurice also took on a couple to be his cook and housekeeper, and liked to entertain friends – whether local, British or American – to Sunday lunch at the house after church. The cook would produce his signature dish, foo-yong-hai – an omelette of crab meat and gourd, Maurice's favourite – and they'd wash it down with ice-cold glasses of Tiger beer. A Malayan gardener completed the ensemble and ensured that the grounds were kept immaculate.

His landlord, Mr N. I. Low, a Chinese schoolmaster

with a frail, housebound wife, lived in a smaller house, separated from Maurice's by a large monsoon culvert. The Lows hailed from Foochow (now Fuzhou) in southern China, and had come to Singapore before the Japanese invasion of 1941, as 'NI' (as he was always known) had a contract to teach English language and literature at Serangoon English School. He was a cultured Mandarin speaker steeped in the teachings of Confucius, and he coached his tenant in the wisdom of the Orient, including demonstrating t'ai chi, calligraphy, finger painting and meditation.

Maurice was the only Englishman living on Flower Road in 1950, but his open (for a spy) and easy-going manner meant he quickly made friends with his neighbours. These ranged from a Tamil family, the Pauls, who had two sons who raced up and down Flower Road on Norton motor-cycles, to the Ngiams, a poor family comprising a widow and her five young children, and the Gomes, an elderly Anglo-Indian couple who, Maurice was interested to learn, had a son who travelled extensively in his job with the Shell Oil Company. It wasn't long before MI6's Deputy Head of Station (Far East) was receiving information about movements in the oil industry from the helpful son of his new neighbours.

His immediate neighbour at No. 9 was a wealthy Chinese merchant who was keen to cultivate a friendship with Maurice. He had been warned at church about this man's formidable hospitality, but after a couple of courteous refusals the English guest succumbed to an invitation to a birthday celebration and headed next door with a gift and a slightly nervous demeanour. The warnings had not been exaggerated. The party was entertained to a full ten-course meal, its *pièce de résistance* an entire roast suckling pig. Drinks were full tumblers of either whisky or brandy over ice, and the host insisted on following the custom of yum-seng (meaning 'bottoms up') after each course. Maurice wasn't accustomed to imbibing on that scale. Very drunk indeed, he eventually made his excuses and left, saying he needed to trace the course of the culvert in his garden all the way to the Tampines River over a mile away. He proceeded to stagger off and do just that, before returning somewhat sheepishly to 8 Flower Road and handing over to his house-keeper a rather shabby light cream suit in severe need of dry-cleaning.

Maurice's own hospitality soon became well known, and one of the first people he tracked down and invited to dinner was the English botanist John Purseglove. One of Oldfield's most effective methods of securing intelligence was to use unofficial agents, or 'Friends', known to him personally, to back up (or occasionally contradict) what he was being told by his official salaried officers. While most of his professional network was reliable and their information trustworthy, there were instances when an ambitious officer would embellish a report to try to 'sex up' – in the modern parlance – the content to give his superiors what he (or she) thought they wanted to hear. In Maurice's view it never hurt to have intelligence checked, and checked again.

John Purseglove was one of these Friends. Born in the same parish – Youlgreave – as Maurice, in 1912, Purseglove had been three years ahead of Oldfield at Lady Manners School and was the distinguished scholar of his year. By 1950 he was already an eminent botanist, specializing in tropical crops, and had written on the subject having travelled in Kenya, Uganda and now Malaya, enjoying barely questioned access to the more remote areas of these countries. Over the next twenty-eight years, Purseglove's reliable reports added important local colour to Oldfield's assessments of life in the countries in which he worked, not least in the Caribbean, where from 1957 until the late 1970s Purseglove was Professor of Botany at the National Herbarium of Trinidad and Tobago, part of the University of the West Indies. Purseglove was to claim later that he'd 'never realized that Maurice was in MI6'. Maurice had merely asked him to provide informal reports for the Foreign Office, an arrangement that suited both of them and helped to assure that those reports were sober and calm – and also that he was able to, should he be questioned, plead ignorance of British Intelligence with total honesty.

This stint in the Far East saw Maurice, among other duties, involved in one of the most highly pressured and volatile conflict zones in the world at that time. In any other circumstances the Malayan Emergency would have been called a war – indeed the Malayan National Liberation Army, the military wing of the Malayan Communist Party against which the British were fighting, called the conflict the Anti-British National Liberation War – but for the fact that the tin and rubber companies operating in the area would not have had their losses covered by Lloyd's of London had the thing been deemed a war. The success (even though it lasted from 1948 until 1960) of the handling of the Malayan Emergency by the British side, including reasonable cooperation between MI5 and MI6, remains an exemplar of how a colonial war of its kind can be conducted and perhaps led the Americans into taking something of a rose-tinted view of their own prospects in Vietnam.

The Emergency arose amid the economic hardship caused by the Second World War, though its origins can arguably be traced back to the British taking control of the area in the nineteenth century. It can be distilled down to those most basic of human needs – food and money. Malaya was rich in supplies of rubber and tin, which provided a decent income for the Malayan population, albeit one that was at the mercy of movements in the world prices of those commodities. When the British took control of the Malayan economy they imposed taxes on the products of the rubber plantations and tin mines, which had a direct downward, though not insurmountable, pressure on local incomes. To cut costs, the business owners used cheaper labour in the shape of immigrant Chinese workers, which drove Malayan unemployment and poverty up and fomented tensions between the ethnic groups.

Japanese occupation of Malaya from 1941 made the problem far worse as production was reduced to serve only the needs of the Japanese economy – a major, if artificial, contraction in demand for the output of Malayan industry, and one that had the effect of restricting trade in both directions. Malaya was highly dependent on imports of rice, and the lack of trade led to a lack of food. The Malayan population, which was to a worrying degree untrained in agricultural skills, fell victim to famine as quickly as by 1942. To try to counter this, the British assisted and trained Malayan guerrilla groups to act as a resistance, and by 1943 these had combined to form the Malayan People's Anti-Japanese Army (MPAJA) and were working alongside the

Special Operations Executive and under Lord Louis Mountbatten's Southern Asia Command. The end of the war saw Mountbatten awarding British service medals to the MPAJA's leaders, and their fighters each being given S$350 as a demobilization payment to surrender their weapons.

The British now needed to reimpose their government of Malaya, so important was the trade in tin and rubber in terms of helping to rebuild their economy after the war; but there was still local resentment of the old colonial occupation of the region from before the war. These circumstances, and the enduring poverty, provided an ideal breeding ground for communist insurgency, and large numbers of the MPAJA fighters who had worked with the British to drive out the Japanese were recruited by the Malayan Communist Party to help form the Malayan National Liberation Army (MNLA), whose aim was to rid the place of what they now saw as their colonial oppressors.

In April 1946, Clement Attlee's Labour government introduced the Malayan Union, a colony created by amalgamating the provinces in the region that were under British control. The Malayan Union was the responsibility of Commissioner General Malcolm MacDonald, with Sir Edward Gent, a civil servant from the Colonial Office back in London, appointed Governor. As part of the formation of the Malayan Union, a generous policy on citizenship was created allowing anyone, including Chinese immigrants, to apply for citizenship. This proved unpopular with the native Malayans, was quickly suspended, and was one reason why in February 1948 the Malayan Union was replaced by the Federation of Malaya – still under MacDonald and Gent, though with the latter re-designated as High Commissioner for Malaya. The citizenship rules were tightened up, and the Federation of Malaya was to endure past independence in 1957 until the formation of Malaysia in 1963.

Soon after the formation of the Federation of Malaya, the MNLA – largely made up of ethnic Chinese people (who'd been employed under British rule and had the carrot of citizenship dangled before them under the Malayan Union only for it to be snatched from their grasp by its replacement), with smaller numbers of Malayans, Indians and Indonesians – increased their level of terrorist activity. They took advantage of the natural cover, holing up deep in the jungle, and their terror campaign involved sabotaging rubber plantations and targeting transport links and the region's infrastructure. In their jungle enclaves the MNLA fighters were schooled in Marxism-Leninism and encouraged to produce propaganda leaflets to drop into local communities. The MNLA was organized into regiments covering the geographical areas of Malaya, and even had their own secret service.

By contrast, the British response was, initially, woefully inadequate – at least until the state of emergency was declared in 1948. Commissioner Malcolm MacDonald had been, at the start of his tenure in South East Asia in 1946, sceptical about the level of the communist insurgency, and there was an air of complacency about the intelligence effort – mainly stemming from a lack of leadership, or understanding of the need for decent intelligence, from the likes of MacDonald and Gent. It didn't help that the two men were in disagreement over the threat posed by the Malayan Communist Party. Gent recommended that the MCP be banned, thus enabling legal action to be taken against the political masters of the terrorists. It had been banned before the war, and had only grown up again afterwards; Gent, the consummate official, saw no reason why the ban should not be reinstated. MacDonald's view was that in democratic Britain the Communist Party was tolerated and it was therefore unreasonable for the MCP to be treated differently in a territory under British control.

The intelligence system in Malaya prior to the Emergency amounted to the Malayan Security Service – which was just that, a security organization, not an organization equipped or trained for the collection of intelligence. The Director of the MSS, Colonel John Dalley, had not benefited from intelligence training, and neither had his senior staff. They were essentially policemen, perfectly competent at dealing with crime but not adept at gathering information. The intelligence they did receive came pretty much from one source, and this source was so vital that when it was lost to them, the MSS were left floundering. That source was Lai Teck, who was none other than the Secretary General of the Malayan Communist Party and a key figure in the MNLA. During the war he had provided intelligence to assist in the fight against the Japanese, and he'd continued this work in the aftermath, guiding the MSS to communist terrorist activity, which helped keep relative peace in the area until rumours started to circulate in the MNLA that one of their number was leaking information to the British. When one day in March 1947 Lai Teck failed to arrive at a meeting of the MNLA high command at which he was due to be quizzed about the leaks, and instead absconded with a substantial amount of Communist Party funds, his fate was more or less sealed. The British authorities' star spy went on the run via Singapore and Hong Kong to Thailand, where he was killed as Thai communists tried to apprehend him.

Internal arguments and a failure to fully grasp the seriousness of the threat from the MNLA meant that Lai Teck was never adequately replaced, and the terrorist attacks on the rubber plantations and tin mines intensified. John Dalley reported to MacDonald and Gent that the situation was worsening and that he needed them to secure extra help for the MSS from outside the Malayan establishment – which simply hadn't the resources in terms of either cash or manpower. The problem was exacerbated by the fact that the MSS knew the insurgents were obtaining supplies and finance via the borders with Thailand and Indonesia – largely provided by the Soviets, who were only too pleased to help a communist uprising – but could do little about it. MacDonald concurred with Dalley's view and lobbied London for more intelligence support; Gent, in a breathtaking display of bureaucratic complacency, felt it was more important to resolve the constitutional issues arising out of the formation of the Federation of Malaya. Even when terrorism reached such a pitch that the owners of the targeted industrial sites begged the Malayan government to declare a state of emergency, on 15 June 1948, High Commissioner Gent only declared that parts of two Malayan states, Johor and Perak, were in a state of emergency. He continued naively to believe that the threat from the communists was being overstated, and that tinkering with the constitution and the ensuing diplomatic effort would resolve the matter.

The following day, the *Straits Times*, the region's highest-circulation newspaper, led with the headline 'Govern or Get

Out', directly aimed at the High Commissioner. Like so many government decisions in more recent times, it took bad press to force action: Gent declared the start of the Malayan Emergency that very day. His credibility was now shot, and MacDonald recommended that the government in London take formal steps to rectify the matter. Gent was recalled to Whitehall where he was to be sacked by the Secretary of State for the Colonies, Arthur Creech Jones, but on 4 July he was killed when the military plane he was travelling in crashed into a Scandinavian Airlines flight over west London – the so-called Northwood mid-air collision. Gent was replaced as High Commissioner by Sir Henry Gurney, who had previously served in Palestine when the British were fighting the Jewish insurgency.

Maurice Oldfield arrived in the region as part of MacDonald's push to have an increased intelligence presence in South East Asia in response to the ongoing Emergency, and his work fascinated him from the start. He soon realized that while English and French would mostly get him by, he would only be fully effective if he learned the local languages, Cantonese and Mandarin Chinese, as well as familiarizing himself with the various dialects prominent in the region. Something that is often trotted out about Oldfield is the assertion that he was primarily a desk man. In his later career that was inevitably the case: a Chief of MI6 can scarcely be expected to crawl about in the undergrowth spying on communist guerrillas, or make dead-drops in war-torn cities. But in his early career, as acknowledged by his colleague Brian Stewart, whom he first encountered in this period while Stewart was an officer in the Malayan Police, Maurice was first and foremost a field officer.

From his base in Singapore, Maurice travelled extensively. His role was concerned with reporting on the flow of funds and materials from the areas he was covering – Thailand, Indonesia, Burma, the Philippines and French Indochina (notably Vietnam and Laos) – into Malaya, Singapore and Hong Kong. His passport stamps show that under the guise of 'Government Official' he was regularly on the move, spending time in Bangkok, Jakarta, Rangoon and Saigon; he was also occasionally in Iran and Iraq, where the local stations valued his wartime Middle Eastern experience and he was called upon to advise on situations developing there. He took a wide-ranging view of his responsibilities and understood that joined-up thinking, unconstrained by national boundaries, was essential if he was to get an overall picture of the global situation. Just because MI6 didn't officially operate in an area didn't mean that an officer passing through couldn't use his eyes and ears and build contacts.

From observing the movement of goods across the Thai border into Malaya in particular, Oldfield was able to report that while the Soviets were supplying the communist insurgents with weapons, these were tired and outdated, not of the quality being used by the British and their allies. His travels in Vietnam and Laos showed him that while the Soviets were supporting the communist uprisings, they were not directly behind them: they tended to be driven by smaller tribal factions which were more likely to fall out with one another than to unite and form a major concerted threat. These reports were fed back to London.

Another key role Oldfield had to play was in building a relationship with the CIA in South East Asia – an area where the Americans' later Station Chief Joseph Smith described his British counterparts as a 'bunch of supercilious snobs'. Maurice came to the region with a reasonable reputation among CIA officers from his visit to Washington in the summer of 1949, and while this didn't immediately build formal bridges between the agencies themselves, Oldfield worked on a personal level to forge strong and lasting relationships with individuals. He quickly became good friends with an officer at a similar level, the towering and burly Robert J. Jantzen, whose flaming ginger mane atop his six-foot-four-inch frame earned him the inevitable nickname 'Red' and who shared with Maurice a natural conviviality that was to benefit his work. Red Jantzen later became CIA Station Chief in Bangkok and delighted in taking Thai politicians and officials on marathon drinking sessions with a miniature tape recorder stuffed in his jacket pocket so he didn't have to worry about remembering what he was told. Jantzen's most notable achievement was to come in 1959 when he took the military Prime Minister of Thailand, Sarit Thanarat, for a serious drink and convinced him to abandon a planned invasion of Cambodia. Not for nothing did Jantzen's then boss, Desmond FitzGerald, describe him as 'the greatest single asset the United States has in South East Asia'. Whether Thanarat's sudden death from liver failure barely three years later was connected to his socializing with Jantzen can only be a matter for conjecture.

Red Jantzen had a rather sad British connection which helped Maurice to add depth to their friendship. His wife, Jane, had previously been married to a Briton, John MacGavin Hair, who had been working in the Philippines, where their son Gilbert was born in 1941. John Hair volunteered for the US Army and was captured by the Japanese in 1942, and his wife and son were placed in a prison camp. John died on a Japanese 'Hell Ship' and the conditions in the prison camp left the infant Gilbert with lifelong health problems. Upon liberation in 1945, Jane married Red Jantzen, and he raised Gilbert as his own. Maurice became friends with the whole family, and helped Gilbert to learn about his British roots. When Jantzen's Far East service ended, Gilbert went to the USA with his family, and Maurice remained firm friends with him, enjoying watching his career develop.

It was this kind of personal relationship, which Oldfield cultivated so well and so easily, that enabled him to transcend any official disagreements and suspicions between the CIA and MI6 and operate successfully on a one-to-one level whatever the circumstances. Red Jantzen went on to become CIA Station Chief in Canada in the 1960s, so Oldfield had a ready-made and trusted ally in place. Another key CIA ally with whom Maurice became friends at this time was Sam Halpern, later to be a prominent figure in the Cuban adventures of the 1960s. Halpern was of Jewish ancestry; his father had worked with future Israeli Prime Minister David Ben-Gurion prior to the First World War. Oldfield and Halpern's shared interest in Middle Eastern affairs gave them a connection – exactly the kind of little 'in' Maurice liked to exploit – and Halpern and his wife Kay became regular guests at Flower Road.

Oldfield began to share and exchange pieces of intelligence and opinions he had found and developed, not things that were unique to Britain's interests and which should therefore be kept secret but carefully verified information that he could use to build the confidence of his primarily American but also French counterparts. One area ripe for this was the smuggling of wolfram, the ore from which the rare and hard metal tungsten is obtained. Tungsten was in high demand by industry in both Britain and America, essential for engineering, X-ray machines and weaponry, and there were large quantities of wolfram in the hills of the British colony of Hong Kong. In the early 1950s supplies from Hong Kong appeared to be drying up, which in turn was driving up prices. Maurice's agents in the region found that smuggling of wolfram was happening to a far greater degree than had been thought, and vast amounts from illegal mining operations in Hong Kong were finding their way to Russia and China. This was an issue of mutual economic importance to both Britain and America, and sharing his verified intelligence with the CIA on this matter enabled much of the smuggling operation to be closed down, to the financial benefit of both countries, and to the benefit of MI6's reputation with the Americans.

It was just as well that Maurice was building personal relations with CIA officers, as over in Washington DC matters were about to take a sinister turn and trust between the CIA and MI6 was to be strained to a degree that could have destroyed their working relationship for good.

Kim Philby had, on the surface, enjoyed a smooth and successful start to his time working closely with the CIA as MI6's liaison officer. He'd moved effortlessly through the agency's highest social strata, his impeccable upper-class English manners and his cheeky, infectious smile winning friends with ease. The Philby family had moved into a large house, 4100 Nebraska Avenue, which soon became the location of hugely sociable and boozy dinner parties for anyone who was anyone on the Washington intelligence and diplomatic scene.

Within a few days of his arrival in the US capital, Philby had been promoted to joint commander of the Anglo-American Special Policy Committee, the main role of which was to coordinate Operation Valuable, the scheme devised to foment an anti-communist uprising in Albania. The man who had been sabotaging the operation from the start was now in charge of it. For the next few months Philby was able to supply his Soviet controllers with precise details of the numbers of Albanian guerrilla agents being sent in by the CIA and MI6, their movements and the timings of their attempts. All were doomed to end in failure as a result, and the number of deaths – when taking into account the reprisals wreaked on the families of the guerrillas – is thought to have run into the thousands. Similar, if smaller-scale, operations were being opened and bloodily thwarted in Soviet-held Armenia, Estonia, Lithuania and Ukraine, all of which had substantial numbers of exiled anti-communists who had been persuaded by the British and Americans to attempt insurrections. Initially the level of casualties was considered more or less normal for wartime (based on Second World War figures, not the newly developing circumstances of the Cold War), but when it became clear that things were going horribly wrong on every occasion, Operation Valuable and its like were quietly cancelled.

But beneath the confident, unflappable demeanour, Philby was becoming more and more agitated, fearing exposure. The news Maurice Oldfield had given him the previous September had been nagging away at Philby since his arrival in Washington. In February 1950, Dr Klaus Fuchs, the nuclear spy Oldfield had told Philby about, was identified and arrested in London, and on 1 March was jailed for fourteen years. In June the level of nagging increased horribly when news reached Philby that the Venona decrypts had revealed the presence of a further and 'particularly important' spy who had been working in Britain for the Soviets in 1945, codenamed STANLEY. The Washington spy, whom Philby knew to be Donald Maclean, was revealed to have the codename HOMER. STANLEY, Philby knew, was himself.

A trip to the US government decoding centre in Arlington Hall, Virginia, confirmed to Philby that the FBI and MI5 investigation into HOMER was still focusing on lower-level Washington embassy staff. This allowed him to draw breath, but he updated Moscow that the Venona team was closing in and began to prepare a self-preservation plan. He tried to persuade Guy Liddell of MI5 that MI6 should take on more of his outfit's role in Washington, and encouraged his own Chief, Sir Stewart Menzies, to keep him apprised of any breakthroughs in the Venona programme, ostensibly so he could look further into the matter. To neither of them did he mention that his real reasoning was to try to take control of the search for HOMER himself, and to give himself time to make good his escape should that search go rather too well.

Philby began to drink more heavily than usual, though he continued to put his brave face on and entertain his old friend and CIA colleague James Angleton at their weekly lunches in Harvey's. But just when he thought he'd got the measure of the situation and had started to plan a discreet escape route, even more worrying news reached Philby via the good offices of the US Mail.

'I have a shock for you!' announced the jovial letter from Guy Burgess.

Guy Burgess. A charming, rude, artistic, dangerous, intoxicating and intoxicated sometime Foreign Office official, full-time Soviet agent and colleague from his Cambridge days, Burgess had been posted to Washington. Fond though he was of Burgess, the prospect of this notorious loose cannon being let loose in the American capital where Philby was only just holding things together was the last thing STANLEY needed.

In normal circumstances two Soviet spies operating in the same city would be very unlikely to share the same digs. And in circumstances where the net was closing in on their treachery the logical thing would be for them to put as much distance between themselves as possible. In the summer of 1950, though, the idea of Guy Burgess carousing around the Washington cocktail circuit with his slack tongue and low morals was something neither Philby nor their Moscow masters could stomach. Philby would need to keep Burgess under his roof to have any chance of keeping him in order.

Aileen Philby was even more reluctant than her husband to take in Burgess as a house guest, but Kim assured her that it would only be for a few weeks. The Philby children, by contrast, were all too pleased to have Uncle Guy to stay. He was good company, made time for the children, and he was soon ensconced in the cellar of 4100 Nebraska Drive where his whisky bottles made ideal features in the loops of the Philby children's model railway.

Burgess's extended visit came to an unfortunate head on 19 January 1951 when Kim and Aileen Philby hosted a dinner party at their home where the guests included Jim and Cicely Angleton, the FBI's liaison officer with the CIA Robert Lamphere and his wife, and William King Harvey, a CIA man who had joined the agency as a counterintelligence officer after resigning from the FBI rather than be demoted for admitting to having arrived late for work one day due to sleeping off a hangover. Harvey, whose present job was flushing out Soviet spies, was accompanied by his wife Libby, and the couple were exactly in keeping with Philby's stereotype of the FBI officer rather than the urbane sophisticates that inhabited the CIA.

It had been a pleasant enough evening, and Aileen was clearing up the coffee cups as Kim was serving a whisky nightcap to their guests when Burgess arrived, steaming drunk after a busy night out. Kim gingerly introduced him to the party. One of Burgess's more endearing traits was his ability as a caricaturist; as a party trick he would dash off a quick and amusing sketch to present to a friend or acquaintance. Libby Harvey had heard of Burgess's talents and badgered the inebriated spy into producing a cartoon of her. The resulting picture was not entirely flattering; indeed a fellow party guest described her face as drawn by Burgess as being like 'the prow of a dreadnought with its underwater battering ram'.

If Libby Harvey was mortified by the sketch, her husband was furious, and swung a fist at the gibbering Burgess. Aileen Philby broke down in tears of embarrassment and shame as her guests left, Bill Harvey still fuming, Jim Angleton quietly brooding. Kim Philby, the unflappable Kim Philby, was in the same tearful, shaken state as his wife. It was to be the end of the beginning of Philby's downfall: the first time he had openly broken – and right in front of the very man who was seeking to expose STANLEY and HOMER.

It wasn't more than a few weeks later that Philby received news from Arlington Hall that the Venona team was closing in on HOMER. Decrypts showed that this spy's wife was both American and pregnant – too accurate a description not to be Melinda Maclean, wife of Donald. There was nothing, yet, to associate Philby with Maclean – the two men hadn't seen each other in years – but the pressure was now on Philby to get word to Maclean back in London that the time had come to get out. The answer, Philby felt, was to get their mutual contact Burgess back to London with a message. It may have been a coincidence – Philby would claim it all as a cunning plan – but Burgess contrived to make his passage out of America a forced one. By obtaining three speeding tickets in one day, and roundly abusing the police officers dealing with the matter, the undiplomatic Burgess tried to claim diplomatic immunity from his offences – actions that tested the authorities' hospitality and tolerance too far. He was recalled to London, and took with him instructions for Maclean – and one simple instruction for himself. 'Whatever you do,' Philby insisted, 'don't you go with him.'

It was 7 May by the time Burgess arrived in London and got word to his ring's controller, Yuri Modin, of Maclean's impending arrest. There was still a little time, while evidence was gathered, but the oxygen was diminishing. The Soviets consented to Maclean's defection, and astonishingly, given the man's instability and his as yet unrevealed links to Philby, allowed Burgess to coordinate the escape. Modin was aware that by day Maclean would be under constant surveillance by a team of MI5 'Watchers', ingeniously disguised as spies complete with raincoats and trilbies as they tried to catch him red-handed with his Russian contact. They'd follow him to and from the office, and back to the station for his train home. At night, though, and over the weekends, the Watchers would hang up their hats and coats and go back to their loved ones. A Friday night would be a cracking time for a defection, it was reckoned – it should give them a two-day head start on their pursuers – and on 28 May, after an evening meal at Maclean's house on the North Downs, Burgess and Maclean headed to Southampton docks. 'Back on Monday!' was Burgess's last call to the harbour staff as the car he'd hired was abandoned at the dockside and the two men sailed off to St Malo to begin their long trek to Moscow.

Monday, 31 May 1951 was a bad day to be an MI5 Watcher. The duty officers took their places to wait for Donald Maclean to emerge from his morning train at Victoria Station as usual, but he didn't. He wasn't on the next one either. Then a call came through to the Foreign Office from a rather agitated Mrs Melinda Maclean to say that her husband Donald had left home on Friday night with a man named Roger Styles and hadn't been seen since. It didn't take long for Special Branch to report that a car hired in the name of Guy Burgess had been abandoned on Southampton docks, and that Burgess and Maclean had skipped the country.

Immediately, telegrams were sent across the world to all British embassies and bases circulating descriptions of the 'missing diplomats' and demanding that they be apprehended by whatever means necessary. In Berlin, Anthony Cavendish was summoned to the MI6 office at the Olympic

Stadium where all the officers were given photographs of Burgess and Maclean and sent to various crossing points from West into East Berlin in case the fugitives attempted to pass through. In Singapore the news was scarcely relevant: it was hardly a likely target stop-off for two spies fleeing to Moscow.

In Washington DC, though, for one man who had spent the preceding months preparing to feign indignation at Maclean's treachery when the time came – not least since it became known he was wanted for questioning by MI5 – when an ashen-faced Geoffrey Paterson, MI5's main man in Washington, came to his office bearing grave tidings, the news could scarcely have been worse.

'Kim, the bird has flown.'

For a moment it looked as though it was mission accomplished.

'What bird? Not Maclean?'

'Yes, but there's worse than that. Guy Burgess has gone with him.'

Philby knew then that the game was up for him. Less than two years had passed since Maurice Oldfield had briefed him that the Venona project was closing in on an agent working for the Soviets in Washington DC after the war. In that time, on the face of it, Philby had been the model Soviet spy: cool, calm and collected, and with access to the highest levels of confidential information the American capital could offer. He'd continued to betray Operation Valuable, but the CIA was already aware that security around the operation was poor with or without Philby. It would have failed with or without him. In truth, the major successes of Philby's treachery had been accomplished before he ever set foot in the

States, and the unflappable spy had been secretly flapping like mad for most of the time he was there. When asked, years later in Moscow, not long before he died, for his view on Maurice Oldfield, Philby said, 'I described him in my book as formidable. And indeed he was.'

Oldfield himself felt that Philby's most successful time as a traitor had finished earlier even than 1949. 'One thing that Philby did for the Russians made his whole career worthwhile,' he said later. 'His single biggest service was to keep them informed from 1941 until 1945 of any British or American moves for a separate peace with Germany. This is why Burgess was so valuable to him. Philby knew the Service attitude, Burgess knew the political attitude.' In Oldfield's view, the war was the time of Philby's 'first pressings'; after that it was a case of diminishing returns and, like so many defectors in Oldfield's experience, he was left trying to justify his existence. This is perhaps why Oldfield, when it all became public knowledge, was less angered by Philby's antics than some of their colleagues.

It was Bill Harvey, a man still affronted by Burgess's insult to his wife, who first publicly aired the link between Burgess and Philby that led inevitably to Maclean and the defection. He later claimed the answer came to him as he was brooding at a red traffic light: the link between the Volkov case and the Maclean case, now confirmed by his friendship with the absconded Burgess, was Kim Philby; it must have been him who tipped off Maclean that it was time to fly.

Harvey and James Angleton were ordered by the then Director of the CIA, Walter Bedell Smith, to draft a report about what they knew of Guy Burgess. Both reports identified Burgess as an obvious security risk, an unstable but well-connected drunkard. Angleton's, however, treated Burgess's link with his friend Philby as more or less coincidental, unfortunate rather than conspiratorial. Harvey, on reading Angleton's notes, asked, 'Where's the rest of it?' The Harvey report was to the point. Philby was as guilty as hell. Bedell Smith concurred and, though there was no evidence that could be put before a court, the message was sent to C, Stewart Menzies, back at Broadway that Kim Philby was no longer welcome in Washington.

The Philby episode is of huge importance to this story, both because Oldfield's present and future work was almost inextricably linked to his relationship with the CIA, and because Philby's duplicity, and MI6's lack of action in dealing with it, so damaged relations between the CIA and MI6 that a good deal of Oldfield's energy had to be expended in rebuilding the inter-agency trust. To understand the magnitude of Oldfield's task it is necessary to understand the enormity of Philby's betrayal. And Philby's return to London was far from the end of the matter.

Back in Singapore, apart from the inevitable ribbing from his CIA colleagues when the story of the missing diplomats was making headlines from the *New York Times* to the *Straits Times*, Maurice Oldfield's work was fascinating him. As well as reporting on supply lines to the terrorists in Malaya, he was reading up extensively on the lives and motivations of people in China, and visiting Thailand, Laos, Burma and the Philippines, seeing how the people lived and getting a feel for what was driving the various communist uprisings. What struck him was the level of nationalism he found. While the insurgents were happy enough to take supplies and cash from the Soviets or the Chinese to support their campaigns, they no more wanted to be ruled by Moscow or Peking than by London or Paris. Their communism was a vehicle for nationalism and independence as much as it was an ideology.

That is not to say that Oldfield was in any way sympathetic to the communist doctrine; indeed one of his closest friends at the time was Robert Carew Hunt, a prominent expert on, and vehement critic of, communism. (Ironically, when Philby was really flying in MI6 it was Carew Hunt he hired to advise him on communism – another bit of colour to add to Philby's 'good egg' Establishment credentials.) Oldfield's understanding of the complexities and the actual rather than perceived threats posed by communism was to become one of his great strengths – one that would, in time, serve his country very well indeed.

Just as important as the threat posed by communists in the region was the question of what would replace them if they were defeated. Oldfield spent a good deal of time studying the secret societies of China, the Tongs and the Triads. These organizations, some of them honourable, some connected to such diverse activities as drug trafficking, counterfeiting and prostitution, were worming their way into every country in South East Asia, and it was feared that a dispersal of the communists might simply create a vacuum in which these societies could thrive. Maurice's view, having studied the operations of the Triads in particular, was that while they were in the main nationalists, more importantly they were generally opponents of any form of government, and were motivated solely by the acquisition of money. Members of the organizations were often keen to supply information to the intelligence services, but Oldfield was convinced that this was usually misinformation or mischief-making. He instructed his officers and agents to avoid any contact with secret societies, and, if contact was made, to treat any information given with the utmost suspicion.

Most of Maurice's personal collection of intelligence at this time came from open sources: travelling, seeing how people lived, studying local press reports and posters advertising events. He didn't confine himself to embassies and official meetings; he liked to get into the towns and villages and see people how they really were. He found, overwhelmingly, that most people wanted a quiet, ordinary life. In few places was there such unrest that the population was about to throw itself under the Soviet or Chinese juggernaut. People wanted to be governed by their own and to be left alone to forge a living. Those he met in the villages of Laos, Vietnam and Thailand weren't so very different from the people with whom he had grown up in Over Haddon. I recall as a boy asking Maurice, as he told me of his travels, 'But what are the people *like* in China?' His answer stuck with me: 'They're just people, Martin, just like you and I.' It was this ability to pare things down to the most basic level that led him to state in a Speech Day address at Lady Manners School in 1978, 'Intelligence is about people, and the study of people. To understand an enemy you must first understand his motivations, his aspirations and his beliefs. Or even if he has no beliefs.'

Cutting through complexity to get to the heart of a matter was one of Oldfield's talents. But it took time, extreme patience and commitment. At this period in his life, such focus was all-consuming. He spent his days travelling, making notes, watching and listening. His nights were mostly taken up with putting together reports – his own and those from agents – taking language classes and studying the *I Ching*, the voluminous Chinese Book of Changes. It was all part of becoming fully assimilated into the culture about which he was providing intelligence for the British government. The long letters home were to an extent replaced by picture postcards with occasional news updates but more regularly messages as simple as 'Hope all is well. See you soon. M.'

It was also exhausting work. Maurice became run down, for the first time afflicted by psoriasis, the irritating skin complaint thought to be brought on by such factors as stress, a change in climate, drinking, smoking and being overweight – all of which Maurice would cheerfully have put his hand up to, to one degree or another. It was a disease that was to trouble him periodically for the rest of his life.

As he approached the third year of this first stint in Singapore, Maurice was on hand to witness a turn in Britain's favour in the Malayan Emergency. On 6 October 1951, as High Commissioner Sir Henry Gurney was being driven in a convoy that included his Rolls-Royce Silver Wraith to the Malayan resort of Fraser's Hill to spend some time away from the stifling heat, he was assassinated by a gang of communist guerrillas. At the time Britain was in the middle of a general election campaign that was to see Clement Attlee's Labour government driven from power by Winston Churchill's Conservatives, despite winning nearly a quarter of a million more votes, thanks to the first-past-the-post system. Churchill returned to office determined to use his military prowess to resolve the Malayan situation – both politically and in protection of the vital rubber and tin supplies – and to retain what he could of the British Empire.

In February 1952 Churchill appointed Sir Gerald Templer, of Intelligence Corps fame, to become High Commissioner in Malaya – and Templer's stewardship, though it was to last for just two years, was held to be an exemplar of its kind when fighting insurgency. Churchill gave Templer unprecedented powers to deal with the situation, combining the role of High Commissioner with that of Director of Operations, a post previously held by Sir Rawdon Briggs until he retired in 1951, his health shot to pieces by his time in Malaya. According to Brian Stewart, who worked under Templer's regime, the man had 'more power than a Viceroy'. He took forward the plans started by Gurney and Briggs (known as the Briggs Plan) which entailed creating new villages, protected by the British military, where the resident population was forcibly re-housed out of reach of the communist terrorists. Templer also formed a government, taking in representatives of all strands of the Malayan population, and instead of simply flooding the jungle with ever more troops to try to bludgeon the terrorists into submission he based his strategy on obtaining good intelligence. Intelligence officers and agents were dispatched to the new secure villages to see how they were living and gauge how politicized they were; where their loyalties lay. This approach seems certain to have appealed to Oldfield enormously.

Templer decided the next key part of his strategy was to win the hearts and minds of the population, with the aim of discouraging them from being drawn into support for the terrorists. He wanted the British to be seen as the saviours, not the oppressors. He ensured the new villages were safe and well supplied with food – and to emphasize that, he clamped down on supplies that were sustaining the terrorists. When the terrorists became desperate and started to grow their own food, Templer arranged for the herbicide known as Agent Orange to be sprayed from the air to destroy the crops. He travelled around Malaya to see for himself what was happening, not content merely to sit in the splendour of his official residence, King's House in Kuala Lumpur. He would drop in on the new villages unannounced. If he found spirits low and the population restless, his local staff would be given a dressing down. He imposed curfews, which were relaxed in areas where the communist threat diminished and reinstated if the threat returned. All his activities combined to provide a comfortable way of life where his wishes prevailed, and tough love where they didn't.

By the time Templer left the region a couple of years later, eventually taking up the role of Chief of the Imperial General Staff under Anthony Eden, *Time* magazine reported 'the jungle has been stabilized'. Never one to be accused of complacency, Templer's response was 'I'll shoot the bastard who says that this emergency is over.' He left a much-improved situation, but was right to show caution. The emergency was to continue, to a lesser degree, for a further six years, but Templer's implementation of the Briggs Plan was a major factor in its eventual conclusion, even if ultimately it was the world increase in tin prices that ensured the hearts-and-minds policy was a success. The efficacy of Templer's methods, especially the use of an intelligent approach to intelligence, and appealing to people's basic emotions and needs to achieve the desired outcome, were not lost on Maurice Oldfield.

May 1952 saw the formation of the Australian Secret Intelligence Service, and the first ASIS officers arrived in

Singapore shortly afterwards. Maurice beat the CIA to it and cultivated the Australians from the outset – another potential ally in a vast corner of the globe – and was reported as having had 'a very strong influence over Australia's spymasters in Singapore' right from the start. This was a relationship, and a strategic connection, Oldfield was to build on in his next Far Eastern tour. His position there was helped by the fact that a predecessor at MI6's Far East Station, Charles 'Dick' Ellis, himself an Australian by birth, had been enlisted to help set up the new service.

As 1952 drew to a close, Oldfield's first tour of duty ended with it. His next posting was to be back at Broadway, with the official title of Assistant Secretary (Foreign Office). When he got back to England he found a Service still in total denial over Philby's treachery. The fall-out from the affair of the missing 'diplomats' was only just beginning to engulf MI6, whose long-serving Chief, Sir Stewart Menzies, had retired in the summer, tired, ill and apparently suffering from terrible nightmares. It was claimed they featured Kim Philby in a starring role.

8

To London – and the World

MAURICE OLDFIELD ARRIVED in London in December 1952, after a return journey which included week-long stops in Pakistan and the Lebanon, promising himself he'd go back to the Far East as soon as ever the chance presented itself again. He'd fallen in love with Singapore, and was fascinated by the history, culture and politics of the East. But now, nearly three years on, home soil beckoned, with carte blanche to travel as and when Maurice felt necessary in the course of his work.

But before that started he was called to see Sir James Easton, one of several officers to act as Chief of MI6 in the hiatus between Menzies' retirement and the appointment of Sir John Sinclair. Jack Easton was aware of the amount of work his thirty-seven-year-old colleague had been putting in over in Singapore and, conscious that the man was close to burning out, arranged for Maurice to take three months' leave – on condition that he rested. Before the 'Leave Granted' stamped in ink on Easton's note had dried, Oldfield was on the train to Derbyshire for a long-awaited reunion with his family.

He now had another nephew, Anthony Joe, whom he'd never met, and his elder nephews Richard Pasley, now aged eleven, and six-year-old John Pearce, both impossibly excited, were waiting for him at Mona View when he arrived at the farm with gifts of Chinese books and a collection of postcards with pictures from his travels. Once he'd visited his parents and his youngest siblings, been to see how the farm was doing, and called in at the Lathkill to hear the gossip from the locals, he settled into a couple of months' normal village life. He picked up his organ playing at St Anne's Church and attended a few meetings of the newly formed village hall committee – a hard-working band of locals, including his brother Joe and his father, who were pooling their skills to build a community facility in an era of post-war austerity, long before the availability of lottery money to help construct such things on the back of sharp business plans and risk assessments.

He also made a useful new contact: the editor of the *Manchester Guardian* (soon to be relocated to London and renamed the *Guardian*), A. P. Wadsworth, who had bought a house in Over Haddon. Or rather Wadsworth, who was an ill man and moving into his last years as editor, provided Maurice with two eminently useful contacts. The first was the newspaperman's daughter Janet, who lived in the village full-time and became close to Maurice, which fuelled some fairly useful speculation that the two might be embarking on a relationship as they went out for day trips and accompanied each other to functions. This speculation also benefited Janet, with homosexuality still illegal and also rather taboo in the more remote rural areas, as it meant her girlfriend was quite clearly just a lodger. The other contact was slightly more well known. One of the *Manchester Guardian*'s foreign correspondents was Alistair Cooke, who was introduced to Oldfield by Wadsworth during a visit by Cooke to his editor's country house. Cooke agreed to supply Maurice with occasional, more personally tailored Letters from America as he travelled around his adopted country.

Towards the end of February 1953, and this time knowing it wouldn't be for so long, Oldfield said his farewells and headed south. First, he took the train to Oxford, where he spent a week with Betty Kemp; then it was back to London to prepare properly for a life in the capital. He bought a flat, 18 Chandos Court on Caxton Street, a walk from Broadway shorter than the one he used to have from farmhouse to farmyard in Over Haddon.

He also decided, as was the norm for senior MI6 officers, to spend more time at the gentlemen's club he'd joined, just a five-minute waddle from home or office across St James's Park. Rather than one of the more political clubs, such as Brooks's or White's – the scene of Stewart Menzies' encounter with Douglas Roberts during the Volkov affair – he went for the more artistic, scientific and intellectually based Athenaeum Club on Pall Mall. Nominated by the author about communism, Robert Carew Hunt, and his old mentor Lewis Namier, Assistant Secretary (Foreign Office) Maurice Oldfield's membership had been confirmed on 19 January.

Even though at the time the Athenaeum was decidedly scruffy and struggling financially in the aftermath of war, with its eclectic clientele and stimulating company Maurice felt very much at home. Over the years the club had had such diverse members as Charles Darwin, T. S. Eliot and Kim Philby; the main requirement for membership was 'eminence'. Maurice valued the place for its quiet, discreet rooms where he could talk to people without fear of eavesdroppers, and whenever he was in London he would dine there most days for the rest of his life. There were a few occasions when his guests filled the leather sofas with large, aggressive-looking armed bodyguards, which led to the odd complaint to the committee, but in the main it was a happy arrangement.

The final part of his triumvirate, with the flat and the club, was, of course, the church. In London, typically, he eschewed the grand and went for nearby St Matthew's in Westminster, tucked away off Great Peter Street and again convenient for home and office. He was introduced to St Matthew's by one of his colleagues in MI6, Kate Fuller, whose husband was curate there, and to whose home Maurice would often go for a meal if not dining out – cookery was never his strongest suit.

From London, Maurice travelled into Europe. In Brussels he lunched with two of his colleagues from SIME days, Alistair Horne and Michael Wrigley. Wrigley was working undercover for MI6 at the British Embassy, Horne as a journalist on the *Daily Telegraph*. Also in the colourful group that met were Earl Jellicoe, then an embassy official, later to resign from the Cabinet in the midst of a sex scandal, and Group Captain Peter Townsend, who had been sent to Brussels as an air attaché after his emotional break-up with Princess Margaret.

After lunch, Oldfield took Horne to one side and asked him if he would do a little work for the office. The young journalist was astonished to be told that Maurice wanted him to spy on the West German government in Bonn. 'We're no longer allowed to spy on our new allies through officers in Germany, Alistair,' Oldfield explained, 'but as a journalist you'll have perfect cover and you'll be run from Brussels.' As Horne spluttered about what his boss might say, Maurice was ready with the answer: 'We'll talk to Pawley. He was an intelligence officer in the war. He's very cooperative. There won't be a problem.' Horne was still uneasy, but was convinced by Oldfield's argument that the war was barely eight years over, the Cold War was pretty hot, and nobody really knew how things would pan out. Oldfield wasn't prepared to risk British interests for the sake of a detail. Horne agreed, and was given responsibility for running three agents, Germans working as officials in the Bonn government. Judging when, and how, to spy on Britain's allies was – with a notable later exception – one of Maurice's strengths.

Broadway was, by most accounts, more or less out of control at times in 1953. From Philby's recall from Washington in the summer of 1951, the senior officers of MI6 had rallied round in support of their (in their view) badly-done-by colleague as he faced interrogation from MI5 as to whether he was the traitor who had tipped off Burgess and Maclean, and the man who'd been responsible for the disappearance of Volkov and the betrayal of Operation Valuable. Many of these senior officers were those known as the Robber Barons, obsessively patriotic men, independent of spirit and, in their minds, independent of the constraints of the laws of their or any other land. They favoured, and practised, intelligence almost as an end in itself, with their love of risky operations and covert action, and they liked nothing better than to mount the odd coup. They leaned more towards the James Bond image of the Secret Service than the more cerebral George Smiley incarnation. The lack of formal democratic accountability extended to MI6 by virtue of its official non-existence was extremely convenient to these Robber Barons, and the replacement of Sir Stewart Menzies by Sir John Sinclair had removed the one brake on their activities.

Menzies had been Chief of the Service since 1939 and had frequently held meetings with Winston Churchill to brief the Prime Minister – a big fan of intelligence gathering and deception – as well as overseeing Alan Turing and his team of codebreakers at Bletchley Park. He had a huge reputation, but was also the archetypal MI6 officer: an Old Etonian Grenadier Guardsman whose impossibly rich family had been friendly with King Edward VII. There was even a rumour that Mrs Menzies had been intimate with the King and that baby Stewart was the product. He was a Victorian-born man with Edwardian connections who simply could not believe that a gentleman like Kim Philby was a traitor and a Russian spy. So when the message came from the CIA that either MI6 got rid of Philby or the special relationship was over, it rattled every preconception Menzies had held in his long, distinguished career.

He sent his assistant, Jack Easton, along with Philby for his first interview with MI5, as a demonstration to the middle-class policemen (as they were perceived by many in the Secret Intelligence Service) of the Security Service that MI6 was right behind its man. Successive interviews by successive MI5 interrogators ranged right across Philby's career, starting with his time in Spain, initially as a supposedly impoverished freelance journalist before he got his job on *The Times* –

'So, Mr Philby, how did you fund your trip to Spain?'

(A nasty little question, Philby thought.)

'I sold some gramophone records.'

– but failed to get the man to crack, as he used his best stammer either to garner sympathy or to buy time. Or probably both. Philby's friends, including some of the Robber Barons such as his closest pal Nicholas Elliott, John Bruce-Lockhart and George Kennedy Young, stood firmly behind him as MI5 failed to extract a confession or make the circumstantial evidence stick. Some in MI5, including Deputy Chief Guy Liddell, became persuaded of Philby's innocence, while some in MI6 – including Jack Easton, who had sat in on the initial interrogations – went the other way and became convinced that the American view was correct and Philby was guilty. From being odds-on to succeed Menzies as Chief, Easton was sidelined for having the nerve to doubt one of MI6's most trusted officers.

Small wonder, then, that Maurice Oldfield, himself junior to Easton, and of a social class that was far more MI5 than MI6, kept his counsel on the matter. It would have achieved nothing except to stymie Maurice's ambitions to progress, not least because Philby left the Service. Even though Menzies and most of his senior colleagues were wholly supportive of Philby, his admission of a connection with the treacherous Burgess meant he had to go. The £4,000 pay-off – a substantial sum at the time – that Menzies granted Philby does not indicate an employee who was leaving with any kind of official blemish, and indeed in April 1952 an almost apologetic Menzies took Philby to lunch and asked if an advance on this pay-off would be a help.

The matter was not to rest there. Philby, who was still

being defended to the hilt by his MI6 friends in 1953 when Oldfield returned to Broadway, would cast a shadow over the Service and its reputation with the CIA for years to come.

Sir John Sinclair, nicknamed Sinbad, was Menzies' choice as his replacement. A tall, lean Scot, according to Philby Sinclair 'was not overloaded with mental gifts' though 'he never claimed them' either. He was known for his loyalty and integrity, and was exactly the champion Philby needed, even going so far as to write to MI5 accusing them of bias in their interviews with the now unemployed Soviet spy. The blinkered view of the Chief in regard to people of the right class was continuing untrammelled under the new occupant of the post. Sinclair also failed to exert any real control over the Robber Barons, who paid lip service by reporting trivia to him and didn't see the need to trouble him with serious matters. Not for nothing was Sinbad's tenure of the Chief's office at Broadway to become known as 'The Horrors'.

The Robber Barons' patriotism was beyond question, but it was quite literally of the Queen and country variety; the kind of devotion to the monarch of which Henry VIII or Charles I would have heartily approved. Hence their attitude of seeing themselves as above, or separate from, government when it suited. Oldfield's patriotism was equally sincere, but his loyalty to the monarch was beyond the personal and theoretical, it was in the shape of Her Majesty's demo-cratically elected government of the day. He was intensely politically aware but not politicized – unlike, for example, the Deputy Chief of MI6, George Kennedy Young, who later stood (unsuccessfully) for Parliament from his position on the far right of the Conservative Party. People's politics tend to be shaped by their parents, and the Oldfields were not party-political at all, though liberal in attitude. Where Maurice and the Robber Barons did agree wholeheartedly was in their loyalty to their country. In whatever he did, Maurice's aim was to do what was in his country's interests, even if that meant interfering in the governance of another. He was by no means a coup-monger, but he would use whatever means at his disposal to protect Britain, whether in terms of security or economics.

An operation that fitted this bill occurred in 1953, and its repercussions are still felt over sixty years later. In 1951, the Shah of Iran, Mohammad Reza Pahlavi, formalized the appointment as Prime Minister of Mohammad Mosaddegh, who had been nominated by the Iranian parliament following an election. One of Mosaddegh's first actions as Prime Minister was to nationalize the Anglo-Iranian Oil Company (AIOC), which had been providing both oil and healthy profits to the British Exchequer. This economic threat stirred Clement Attlee's government to place sanctions on Iran, supported by US President Harry Truman. Mosaddegh strengthened his position by holding elections seeking a mandate granting him greater powers to appoint his own Minister of War and Chief of Staff, positions that had previously been in the gift of the Shah. Meanwhile, negotiations at diplomatic level between the British and Iranian governments were going nowhere.

After the election of Winston Churchill's Conservatives in October 1951 Britain sought American support to overthrow Mosaddegh, something that was resisted by Truman. When the Republican Dwight Eisenhower won the US presidency by a landslide in November 1952, taking office the following January, the opportunity was ripe for a new

171

approach to the Americans, and this time the British found favour by adding to the oil problem as the reason for a coup the 'C' word.

Even though Mosaddegh was no communist, the British pointed out to the Americans that unrest in Iran – the people were suffering hardship under the sanctions – was potentially leaving the country susceptible to a Soviet invasion via their bordering satellite states of Azerbaijan and Turkmenistan. The thought of communists getting hold of the Iranian oil-fields was more than the Americans could bear to entertain. Oil made the overthrow of Mosaddegh an economic priority; the fight against communism made it an easier sell to the public. Not for the last time in history, an honest and perfectly reasonable argument about oil was not considered strong enough in itself to justify action. And despite the other two factors, the official justification for the proposed coup was that Mosaddegh was acting unconstitutionally by claiming the additional powers noted above. All that was needed was the Shah's approval.

The Shah was felt to be a pleasant man but a weak leader, and persuading him to fire Mosaddegh was no easy task. After a period of politicking during which the governments of both Britain and America tried to pursue a diplomatic strategy, a joint MI6 and CIA operation – codenamed TP-AJAX by the Americans and 'Boot' by the British – was agreed. The operation was to be headed up by Kermit Roosevelt – grandson of President Teddy – for the CIA, with Sinclair leaving George Kennedy Young, Norman Darbyshire and Monty Woodhouse as the main British officers involved. The aim was to stir up agitation against Mosaddegh and in favour of a candidate for his replacement as Prime Minister, one approved by the Western allies, General Fazlollah Zahedi. This unrest, the setting up by MI6 of a radio station to broadcast anti-Mosaddegh propaganda to the Iranian people, covert action against Mosaddegh and his supporters by the intelligence agencies, and the strong support of the Shah's domineering sister Princess Ashraf, all made it easier for the Shah to be convinced he should formally sack his Prime Minister.

The upshot was that the Shah's personal power increased (Zahedi was to last only two years as Prime Minister): he was to retain control of Iran until ousted himself by the coup by Ayatollah Khomeini in 1979. And the British regained control of AIOC – at a cost of giving 40 per cent of the company, which was eventually to become BP, to the Americans. It is generally accepted, with the benefit of hindsight, that while operationally successful, Boot was a major reason for the antipathy of people in the Middle East to the British and Americans and an early contributor to the level of conflict that prevails today. Another view, as put in 1997 by Monty Woodhouse – by then Lord Terrington and a retired MP for Oxford – was 'I've sometimes been told I was responsible for opening the door to the ayatollahs. But we delayed Khomeini's return by a quarter of a century.'

The reason for including this episode – the overthrow of a democratically elected leader by the intelligence services – in Maurice Oldfield's life story is not to suggest an over-inflated level of personal involvement on his part. His name has rarely been linked to Boot, but his passport records show that he was in Beirut and Cyprus – the locations of the planning meetings – on the dates when the operation was being arranged. His role, given his Middle Eastern expertise and his strong and growing reputation with CIA officers, including Kermit Roosevelt, was most probably as an adviser and facilitator. That he was a relatively minor applicator of oil to the cogs is a sensible assessment of his contribution.

Neither is the fact that the coup showed that the CIA and MI6 were capable of working together, operationally at least, in spite of the Philby, Burgess and Maclean affair, crucial to Oldfield's story. More important is that it was to be the start of a twenty-five-year personal relationship between the MI6 man and the Shah, one that was fruitful for most of that period. From the time of the overthrow of Mosaddegh, Oldfield became MI6's main contact with the leader, and the two men met regularly, often in Switzerland where the Shah had a residence, occasionally in Tehran. It was Maurice's aim to encourage the Shah to Westernize the Iranian economy. The Derbyshire farmer's lad and the hereditary sovereign of Persia formed a close bond: within a few years Maurice's bodyguard was impressed to report that his boss was the only person outside his immediate family the Shah would see without a security presence. It was also a relationship that was to have an unfortunate ending that Maurice considered to have been at least partially caused by one of his biggest mistakes, as we shall see.

Much of Maurice's time when in London in the period between 1953 and 1955 was spent networking, and building his credentials within the Service and with its political masters. As an outsider in terms of class and attitude, in order to progress his career would require friendships and connections in Britain as well as the useful ones he had already forged overseas. He became friendly with Conservative MP Julian Amery, a former soldier with an interest in foreign affairs whose marriage to Catherine Macmillan, daughter of the future Prime Minister, would open all kinds of ministerial doors to Amery, not to mention useful connections for Maurice. Philip Goodhart, soon to become the MP for Beckenham and later to serve as a minister in Northern Ireland, was a good friend of Maurice's from the 1950s, and another who had the benefits of a well-connected wife: Valerie Goodhart was a niece of the late John Winant, who had succeeded Joseph P. Kennedy as US Ambassador to London during the Second World War.

Maurice also travelled extensively beyond Europe during the period he was nominally a desk officer in Broadway. In September 1953 he took out visas for travel to Panama, Costa Rica, Mexico, Ecuador, Peru, Argentina, Bolivia, Brazil and Venezuela, and spent three months exploring Central and South America. But the main focuses of his visit were Panama, its canal the vital passage between the Atlantic and the Pacific, and Argentina, a huge country that had provided refuge for fleeing Nazi officers such as Josef Mengele and Adolf Eichmann.

The end of the war had caused the Panamanians to look again at the Canal Zone. This area, artificially created to ensure the security of the canal in 1903, cut the country in half. The Americans had control of the zone, which included land five miles either side of the canal (excluding Panama City and Colón) and took in the reservoirs that were created in wider Panama to control the water level. It was an obvious potential source of tension, and an area that Oldfield considered vital to British interests in terms of moving its fleet around the world. He remained in regular contact with MI6's man in Panama, Tony Mansfield.

Far to the south, Argentina was moving towards the end of the Perón era. Eva Perón, 'Evita', the iconic wife of the President and the woman who had given hope to the working people of the country, had died the previous year, and the country was just two years away from a military coup that would see her husband Juan swept from power. It was a country in transition; an ostensibly wealthy nation but one suffering from industrial unrest – and one that British Intelligence needed to learn more about.

As usual, it was down to grass-roots as a starting point for the Assistant Secretary (Foreign Office). Maurice had contacts in the agricultural sector in Argentina, farming friends of his brother-in-law Warren Pearce – people who had emigrated just after the war to take on a vast estate on the Pampas – and he used that connection as a stepping stone to build a network of contacts in Argentine business. He learned first-hand about the economics of the country and, in his established pattern, the way of life of the people and their political motivations during a period of uncertainty surrounding Perón's regime.

The possibility of finding oil in the South Atlantic, which scientists had hinted was feasible, struck Oldfield's antennae for economic intelligence from an early stage. In the light of the ongoing trouble in the Middle East, the strategic location of the British-owned Falkland Islands and its potential for oil exploration were part of the MI6 man's enquiries. Irrespective of any idealistically democratic reasons for supporting the islanders' right to remain British citizens, he identified the maintenance of British sovereignty as an economic necessity.

By 1955 the well-travelled Maurice Oldfield was

considered senior enough to be part of MI6's interviewing panel for potential new recruits. I have found a couple of examples of the work of these panels, the prospective spies having contrasting recollections. The first of the two happened in the summer of 1955. A young journalist with experience in the Far East, Neal Ascherson, was invited to meet a group of six or so MI6 officers at the Reform Club, apparently as part of an attempt to recruit him. One of the officers was 'introduced as being Maurice Oldfield'. Ascherson found them 'all upper class, middle-aged and tweedy', merry, if not drunk, and 'happily reminiscing about torturing Jews in Palestine after the war'. They made 'rather arch comments, such as "I hope you like eating dog, that's what they eat where you're going", and talked about sending me to Hanoi under the cover of writing about Ho Chi Minh: "You know, get to know the chaps around Ho Chi Minh, get them to see our point of view." It seemed to me to be a one-way ticket to the scaffold.' Ascherson was not impressed by the quality of the men's knowledge either: 'Some of them were not sure where Hanoi was. Annam? Cochin China? So we all had to go upstairs, clutching brimming glasses, and consult an old *Times* atlas.'

Ascherson says he was already 'revolted' by the foregoing, but not wanting to appear wimpish claimed not to speak Vietnamese. This was not a problem, he was told, and he was given the address in Holland Park of their Vietnamese expert, 'who will put you in the picture'. At the house, the door was opened by an Asian manservant who ushered Ascherson into a sitting room full of bamboo furniture and ferns in pots to meet the man in question – Donald 'Butch' Lancaster, one of the more flamboyant homosexuals in MI6 at the time and brother to Kim Philby's friend the cartoonist Osbert. Lancaster, about twenty years older than Ascherson, seemed a little tongue-tied but made some small-talk about his house in France, ignored his guest's questions about Hanoi, and then grabbed Ascherson firmly by the genitals. Ascherson leapt to his feet, burbled an excuse and resolved not to become a spy. To this day he does not know if it was all part of some test to see whether he was too wet and squeamish to join MI6, or whether that was genuinely what the officers involved were like.

I find this story interesting on a variety of levels, and must stress that I have no reason to doubt Ascherson's account, even though a retired MI6 personnel officer I ran it by said he had never heard of a recruitment being initiated in that manner. It would seem unlikely that someone of Oldfield's known emotional intelligence would seriously brag about torturing Jews, especially given that Ascherson was a socialist with Jewish ancestry, which lends credibility to the suggestion that it may have been a test.

What it illustrates more than anything is the chameleon-like quality of Maurice Oldfield. The officers concerned, 'all upper class, middle-aged and tweedy', certainly fit the stereotype of MI6 men of the era, as does the 'little Englander' part about the men not knowing where Hanoi was. But nobody ever described Oldfield as upper class, and he was still (just) under the age of forty at the time. Furthermore, he had travelled extensively in Vietnam and been to Hanoi many times. Whether or not he had been involved in torture in Palestine can probably never be proved; it certainly went on, but given Maurice's oft-stated views about the first pressings of an interrogation being the best, on a personal level it seems unlikely. But to a young outsider like Neal Ascherson, Oldfield clearly blended into a group of what sounds like a vivid description of the Robber Barons of the time. It seems little different, in fact, from when he was back in Derbyshire, where he would slip back into village life, dress and manner of speech. His ability to adapt to suit the company set him apart as much as it blended him in.

The second account of the selection panel in action varies in both execution and tone. The former MI5 and MI6 officer David Cornwell, who writes under the name of John le Carré, had a different experience when he was interviewed at a similar time with a view to joining the latter service. 'I was brought before five officers,' recalls Cornwell, 'but there was no way they were going to introduce themselves by name. It wasn't until much later that I realized three of them were Nick Elliott, Maurice Oldfield and George Kennedy Young. I still don't know who the others were. They gave me a fairly robust grilling, including things they knew about my private life. I'll admit it made me respond quite aggressively. They probably liked that.' Cornwell's was, to start with at least, a more traditional encounter – prearranged, and office-based. It mirrors more closely what I was told by the retired personnel officer: an approach to a potential recruit might have occurred in a club, but he had never heard of a formal interview being held in such surroundings.

In marked distinction to travelling the South Americas or upsetting Neal Ascherson, Maurice found time to blend himself back into Derbyshire as often as he could. In the summer of 1955, he went back to be part of the official opening of the new Over Haddon Village Hall. That was a real celebration, of community spirit and renewal ten years after the war, and the dancing went on into the night. The following day, Maurice joined a village trip to the Uttoxeter races, where he wasn't successful in his betting but did lead the bus in singing on the coach ride back to an evening supper at the village hall.

For Maurice Oldfield, the contrasting approach of the high-risk world of covert action as espoused by the Robber Barons, set against his own grounded, measured way of working, convinced him that MI6 had to move away from the former towards the latter. It simply wasn't credible for post-empire Britain to be blundering about as if she still ruled the world. In Oldfield's view his country was better served in the modern era by building relationships, gathering intelligence, and using that intelligence judiciously to support British interests. He was a man of secrets, certainly; in fact an associate going back to Singapore days told me, with a certain amount of awe, 'Maurice seemed to know everything and everyone. He used that bank of knowledge carefully, to the benefit of his work.'

It wasn't until 1956 that MI6 – or at least its political masters – came round to Oldfield's way of thinking, and by then failed gung-ho operations had brought embarrassment to the Service. Oldfield, whether by accident or design, managed to avoid being tainted by The Horrors, a period that would lead to the enforced retirement of C, John Sinclair, and George Kennedy Young's aspirations to succeed him as Chief being dashed. Though not part of their immediate circle, Oldfield was to retain the friendship and respect of people such as Young and Nick Elliott for life. After Maurice's death, Young was one of his stoutest supporters.

Oldfield was becoming increasingly highly regarded

during this period for the quality of his analysis of reports and his people skills, and crucially this was not limited to his superiors in MI6: the CIA, with whom Maurice had worked so closely during his first stint in the Far East, also began to rely on him. An opportunity to cement this relationship had come in October 1954 when the Chief, Oldfield and their colleague Fergie Dempster – Station Chief in Saigon, and the man who was the following year to recruit the author Graham Greene as an agent – flew to Washington for high-level talks with the new Chief of the CIA, Allen Dulles, and his Far East controller, Frank Wisner, with regard to attempting to subvert communist activities in the Far East. The outcome of two weeks of discussions was the Four Square Agreement, whereby the CIA would remain in primacy in the Philippines and the British would retain unique control over Burma, Singapore and Malaya.

This left Vietnam, Cambodia, Laos, Thailand and Indonesia. To Oldfield's delight, it was agreed that operations in those countries would be run jointly; better still, the two countries' ambassadors and intelligence chiefs could run those operations without constantly referring back to London and Washington. Oldfield's close CIA colleague in Singapore, Sam Halpern, who was privy to the talks, reported that Maurice and Dempster, who had previously been scornful of the British ambassadors who were content to 'stand under fans drinking G&T', were enthused by what amounted to 'a licence to wage war on communist agitation'. An inspired Halpern said, 'Fergie taught me there was intelligence and hard intelligence. Oldfield never made a statement without supporting facts.' Whether a stronger Chief than Sinclair would have ceded so much power to colleagues is a matter for conjecture; the fact is that power had been granted, and Oldfield couldn't wait to get back to Singapore to use it.

Sinclair had acquired a reputation for being rather soft, and his intellectual limitations were becoming well known. Officers recalled a week's visit he made to the German station at Bad Salzuflen, which in the aftermath of war was considered the most important territory to MI6 due to its pivotal location in central Europe. Sinclair was given detailed briefings on the operations that were running into Eastern Europe, the technical equipment that was being developed to eavesdrop, and the methods of penetration that were getting MI6 into Poland, Czechoslovakia and the Soviet Union. He spoke to numerous officers, assistants and scientists, and the only comment he made in summing up was that 'the drivers' mess needed smartening up'.

At least Oldfield and Dempster went to the trouble of getting high-level approval for their plans. The success of Operation Boot gave the Robber Barons a taste for mounting operations of that kind irrespective of the views of Sinclair. As Young made clear when interviewed years later, if it appeared the Chief might say no to an operation, they'd simply do it anyway and tell him afterwards. Trying to rein them in was Jack Easton, who in briefing Sinclair's eventual successor would comment, 'I've had to stop a lot of operations in the Middle East. Too many are suspiciously unsafe.' The period from 1954 to 1956 was to see them embroiled in misadventures that would taint MI6 operationally almost in the way Philby and his cohorts had contrived to do in diplomatic circles. And in 1955 that man Philby was back to haunt his old colleagues yet again.

9

The Horrors

T HE MIDDLE 1950s were pivotal times for MI6. It was then, under the inadequate supervision of Sir John Sinclair, that a concentration of failures left the government with no choice – in their view – but to appoint an outsider to try to bring discipline and control to the organization. It was that step that effectively opened the door to the possibility that Maurice Oldfield might one day become Chief, and established the principle that MI6 must be cleaned up in order to survive.

It was in fact to be nearly two decades before the Chief of the Service was appointed from within the ranks. A former colleague told me how a mixture of fortuitous circumstances saw Oldfield avoid becoming embroiled in The Horrors, which led to some of his senior contemporaries having their reputations tarnished and their careers curtailed. 'Even though Maurice was operating out of Broadway from 1953 to 1956, his main sphere of influence remained in the Far East, and so he was conveniently out of the way for more time than the record might suggest. He was also heavily involved in Central Europe, advising on the post-war situation around the Iron Curtain.'

Thus as the Service's reputation in Whitehall and Langley was being trashed, Oldfield's personal stock was rising. His work in both Europe and the Far East saw him liaising closely with the CIA and sealing a bond of trust with some of their senior officers. While the Robber Barons were planning ever more elaborate schemes and operations and bypassing Sinclair, Oldfield was taking a more diplomatic route. While neither the Robber Barons' nor Oldfield's concern about the threats posed by communism were in doubt, their approaches to dealing with them were different. For Oldfield, it was about accumulating intelligence to aid in understanding the problems, assessing the levels of threat, and trying to find ways of influencing opinion. Many of his colleagues preferred direct action – and it was this, along with the ongoing weakness in regard to the treacherous Philby, that was to bring the Service to its knees.

To understand the chain of events that led to the replacement of Sinclair it's necessary to take a look at those happenings as they set the context for what followed. It was inevitably the Middle East, and this time Egypt, that was once more the scene of MI6's agitations. In 1951 Egypt had withdrawn unilaterally from the 1936 treaty that had leased Britain its base in Suez – by the canal – until 1956. Thus from 1951 Britain was remaining in situ only by clinging to the terms of the treaty and by the fact that they had eighty thousand troops stationed there. It was clear that anti-British feeling was running high. In January 1952 anti-Western riots broke out in Cairo, yet despite this, the intelligence gathered by MI6 failed to predict the overthrow of King Farouk of

Egypt in July via a coup led by General Mohammed Neguib.

The real power behind the coup was the nationalist and anti-British Gamal Abdel Nasser, who began agitating against Neguib – and the Robber Barons of MI6 began agitating against both of them. Britain looked like being driven from Suez, which was not just a vital artery that carried two thirds of all European oil from the Middle East, it was, to many, a symbol of an empire they sought to protect. As Lord Hankey, part of the so-called Suez Group set up to speak up for Britain's interests in the area – and which contained many MI6 officers – put it: 'If we cannot hold the Suez Canal, the jugular vein of World and Empire shipping communications, what can we hold?'

Initially the CIA considered Nasser to be a man with whom the Americans could do business and resisted MI6 requests to join forces against him, leaving the British to plot alone, trying to motivate British sympathizers in the Egyptian army to oppose their new leader from within. Early in 1955, Winston Churchill retired as Prime Minister, to be replaced by his Foreign Secretary, Anthony Eden. Eden had been growing increasingly impatient to succeed Churchill almost since the war, and in the new Prime Minister the Robber Barons of MI6 found an ally in their moves against Nasser.

Before the Suez business reached its peak, two other incidents occupied MI6's time and saw the Service reveal its seamier side in public. In April 1954, a Russian diplomat named Vladimir Petrov defected to Australia, offering details of Soviet espionage in return for political asylum. Petrov revealed not only that Guy Burgess and Donald

Maclean were living in the Soviet city of Kuibyshev but that their defection had been triggered by a tip-off from a mysterious Third Man, a British diplomat. When the story reached the British press in September, speculation mounted as to the identity of this Third Man – and with this being but a few years since Graham Greene's film of the same name, public interest in the matter was feverish.

The Third Man himself was drinking more than ever, and financially on his uppers. His Russian handler, Yuri Modin, keeping an eye on his charge, arranged for Moscow to send £5,000 to help keep Philby sane as the traitor waited for the inevitable call to interview from MI5. By now Sir Dick White, one of Philby's interrogators from their previous attempt to flush him out, was Chief of MI5, and this time he was determined to get his man. 'Pure trade' was how the class-driven snobs in MI6 dismissed White as once more they rallied round to protect their man. Needing to do something, the government produced a White Paper in which it attempted to explain the Burgess and Maclean affair. The thing was fudged; it didn't even mention Philby and looked as though it might have been concocted by one of his friends, such as Nick Elliott. Which it probably had.

Instead of a further MI5 interrogation of Philby, the Foreign Secretary, Harold Macmillan, decided that MI6 should 'conduct a review'. Instead of being subjected to bright lights and 'nasty little questions' (as he'd referred to some of his previous interviews), Philby found himself having a rather cosy chat with some of his old friends, one of whom might easily have been Nick Elliott. They pronounced themselves pleased to announce that they had unanimously agreed he was innocent, to the utter disbelief of Dick White, who was listening in to the interview by wire at MI5 headquarters. In truth, Philby knew perfectly well that the single biggest thing in his favour was that he had not done a runner. For now, he felt, he was safe. The Robber Baron faction in MI6 had protected one of its number from the inconvenience of justice.

It wasn't to last. In America, the head of the FBI, J. Edgar Hoover, was as furious as White to hear that Philby had escaped scot-free again. And if the British couldn't be trusted to do something about it, then Hoover would. On 25 October, the New York Sunday papers named Philby as the Third Man. The British could whitewash it no longer. Or could they?

The law of unintended consequences was to come to Philby's aid, in the unlikely shape of a well-meaning Labour MP, Colonel Marcus Lipton, who used parliamentary privilege – the convention that enables MPs to raise matters in Parliament that would ordinarily be constrained by the libel laws – to ask Anthony Eden, in a formal question, whether he had decided 'to cover up at all costs the dubious Third Man activities of Mr Harold Philby?' The government was now obliged to answer, and given that investigations by both MI5 and MI6 had cleared him, the answer could scarcely contradict that verdict – Philby hoped and reasoned. He waited with bated breath to see how the government would respond.

It was decided that the Foreign Secretary would reply on 7 November, and further that he would be briefed on the matter by Tory MP Richard Brooman-White, who happened to have previously been an MI6 officer of the Robber Baron persuasion, an old friend of Nick Elliott's and one of the men who had recruited Philby to the Service back in 1939. On the 7th, the House of Commons fell silent as Macmillan rose to speak. The Foreign Secretary stated that 'Mr Philby had communist associates during and after his university days' but that there was no evidence to show he had tipped off Burgess and Maclean. He summed up: 'I have no reason to conclude that Mr Philby has at any time betrayed the interests of this country, or to identify him with the so-called "third man", if indeed there was one.'

By forcing the government to make a statement before it had legally sound evidence against Philby, Marcus Lipton had left Macmillan with little choice but to clear the man. The MP was later obliged to admit that he 'deeply regretted' making his accusations, and that his 'evidence was insubstantial'.

Philby, meanwhile, invited the world's press to a conference the next day at his mother's flat, where he agreed to answer questions. What followed was a tour de force in accomplished lying, the video of which is still said to be used as a training tool by MI6. Cool, polite – unflappable – Philby, the consummate English gentleman, said that the last time he'd spoken to a communist knowing him to be a communist was some time in 1934. He did admit to an 'imprudent' association with Burgess, but refused to be drawn on the subject of friendship. When asked outright 'Were you in fact the Third Man?', Philby answered firmly, 'No, I was not.' To everything else he answered 'no comment'. And with that he served the journalists tea and beer. Elliott and his friends were delighted with the outcome, which left Philby to rebuild his career as a journalist in Beirut – and also left open the possibility of resuming work for MI6, if only as an agent not an officer. Philby's controller, Yuri Modin, watched the performance on television with rapt admiration.

John Sinclair's tenure as Chief was soon to come to its well overdue conclusion; indeed it is now known that Anthony Eden had already decided to replace the man who was widely accepted not to be up to the job – and unsurprisingly it was a Robber Baron operation gone wrong that was to be the final nail.

In April 1956, Soviet leader Nikita Khrushchev and his Prime Minister Nikolai Bulganin arrived on a state visit to Britain. For Eden this was probably the most important official visit of his premiership, and he was anxious to emerge from Churchill's shadow on the world stage in his own right. The Prime Minister made it perfectly clear that as the Soviet leaders were coming as guests he wanted no nefarious spying activities going on in the background. To the Station Chief in London, Nicholas Elliott, though, this was too good an opportunity to miss. He prepared a list of suggested operations and submitted them to the Foreign Office for consideration – then, true to the world of the Robber Barons, interpreted the lack of a response as a green light.

The Soviets arrived in Portsmouth Harbour on a cruiser named the *Ordzhonikidze*, and British Intelligence wanted details of the vessel's keel, propellers and rudder. The man Elliott selected for the job was a diver of some celebrity named Lionel Crabb, nicknamed Buster after the celebrated American swimmer and actor. Crabb had a history of daring missions, before and during the war, including some successful operations for MI6. But history is exactly what they were. By 1956 Crabb had been out of action for some time and had tried a range of occupations from undertaker to salesman, but still hankered after his glory days. He would even take ladies out on dates wearing his wetsuit. The offer to take on another mission, at last, for Queen and country was one Crabb could not resist, despite being horrendously unfit and more than partial to a drink. Elliott had confidence in his man because of his historic track record.

Unsurprisingly, the entire affair was a disaster. After plunging into the murk of Portsmouth Harbour, Crabb was spotted by Russian crew members on the *Ordzhonikidze*, and disappeared. News of this leaked, eventually causing great embarrassment to Eden and launching a host of conspiracy theories as to Crabb's fate, which only served to boost the mystique of the Russians as a sinister force and to give the impression of incompetence in British Intelligence. In early 1957 a headless, handless corpse in a wetsuit was washed up in Chichester Harbour, just along the coast, and it was generally accepted that it was Crabb. The only vague positive in the story was that it was said to have inspired Ian Fleming to write the underwater scenes in *Thunderball*.

When Eden found out that not only had his orders been ignored but that Crabb was missing presumed dead – and worst of all that Khrushchev knew all about it – he was furious. He took the very unusual step of making a statement in the House of Commons blaming the officials – something virtually unheard of in British government: normally ministers take the rap; officials are protected. 'It would not be in the public interest to disclose the circumstances in which Commander Crabb is presumed to have met his death,' Eden said. 'While it is the practice for ministers to accept responsibility, I think it is necessary in the special circumstances of this case to make it clear that this was done without the authority or knowledge of Her Majesty's ministers. Appropriate disciplinary steps are being taken.'

To MI5 this was marvellous news: their sister service had been found wanting owing to reckless misadventure. The First Lord of the Admiralty tendered his resignation, and John Sinclair was forced into early retirement. The one man who should have taken the blame, Nick Elliott, claimed the whole thing had been 'a storm in a teacup'. He felt it unfair that MI6 had been discredited, and that Eden was at fault for how he had handled the matter.

In the normal scheme of things either George Kennedy Young, well known as a talented and imaginative officer despite his maverick tendencies, or Jack Easton might have been expected to be promoted to head of MI6, but both were too deeply connected to the *ancien régime*. It was entirely without precedent that the head of MI5 should be made to switch services; the rivalries between the two organizations and their entirely different roles and methods made such a move highly unlikely. But that is exactly what happened: Sir Dick White, interrogator of Philby, was appointed as Sinclair's successor, with a brief to calm the Robber Barons; Easton and Young stayed on as his deputies. The more measured Easton warned the new Chief, 'We're still cloak and dagger. Fisticuffs. Too many swashbuckling green thumbs thinking we're about to fight another war.'

One person who welcomed the new appointment, though no doubt he would have been too diplomatic to mention it to Young, Elliott or Easton, was Maurice Oldfield. White may have been privately educated, but it was at Bishop's Stortford College, not Eton, Harrow or Westminster. And while his background was by no means as humble as Oldfield's, White was far from being of aristocratic stock. The only inheritance in the White family was the ironmonger's shop in Tonbridge, Kent, that had passed through four generations and where the young Dick grew up. It may have been a forced situation, and he might never truly fit into his new surroundings, but White's arrival indicated to Maurice that background was no longer a barrier to advancement.

And in Dick White, Oldfield had the perfect firewall to the swashbuckling schemes of previous years. When Michael Wrigley, a great friend of Oldfield's from SIME days to whose daughter he was godfather, asked Maurice to sanction a £10,000 payment to an assassin for the proposed disposal of a troublesome Thai communist leader, Maurice was able to say, 'Forget it. We don't do that kind of thing any more.' And Wrigley's frustration was not aimed at his friend but at the Foreign Office who'd foisted White on to them. 'They've got no balls,' was Wrigley's comment. 'All they want to do is write history.' MI6 had been driven by people who wanted to make history.

White inherited the unfolding situation surrounding Suez, and also a proposed murder that had been planned by MI6 which was sanctioned at the highest level just days after his appointment. George Kennedy Young had been planning to overthrow Nasser since his takeover in Egypt. When, in July 1956, the Egyptian chief nationalized the Suez Canal, Anthony Eden was incensed and spoke openly about killing Nasser – and to a spy chief with an axe already in the process of being ground, this was all the authorization he needed. To Eden, the nationalization of the canal was an act of war, right up there with Mosaddegh nationalizing the oil company, even Hitler invading Poland. He saw Nasser as an Egyptian Mussolini, and the fact that he was being armed by Moscow as an indication that the Soviets planned to cut a swathe through the Middle East. This was a direct threat to Britain's sovereignty and her economy. Unfortunately, her biggest ally, the USA, didn't agree.

Dick White, newly in post and still an outsider, could scarcely go against his Prime Minister just a week into his job. He also noted the enthusiasm with which Young and his plans were met around Broadway. So whatever his misgivings – and he later claimed many – White took briefings from Young, engaged in talks with the CIA (who were broadly more supportive than their political masters), and generally tried to do the right thing without too much personal capital being expended.

At government level, Eden forged a plan with the French and the Israelis to drive Nasser from Suez, while in the background MI6 made plans to deal with the man himself. Things under discussion following suggestions by the technical equipment section, the quartermasters – normally known as Q Branch – included providing Nasser with an electric razor packed with explosives, pumping poisoned gas through the ventilation system of his HQ, or simply recruiting a highly paid local hit squad to take him out. In the end it didn't happen. No sooner had the British and French troops entered Suez than the US, the Soviets and the United Nations ordered a ceasefire. Nasser, for a period, had won, and the MI6 officers who'd been engaged in his proposed murder regretted not having done it anyway. It was a sure sign that times were changing.

The Suez Crisis was to cost Anthony Eden his health, his

job and much of his reputation: a twenty-five-year apprentice-ship ended with fewer than two years at the top. He was to live a further twenty years but would be forever tarnished by Suez.

In stark contrast, for Maurice Oldfield this period based in London was the one that took him from being a promising officer who was learning, assimilating himself into the ways of MI6 and creating his first circle of contacts around the world, to an officer who was marked for greatness. His return to Singapore began in September 1955, and his journey there was a steady progress. He called in at Tehran, where he met with the Shah and his new Prime Minister, Hossein Ala. Ala had previously been Iranian Ambassador to both London and Washington and had an understanding of Western lifestyles, which was important to the Shah's planning. Barely two months later, Ala survived an assassin-ation attempt at a funeral. From Tehran, Oldfield visited Bombay (as it was then), before proceeding to Australia for meetings with his colleagues at ASIS, and the Australian security service ASIO, where his friend Charles Spry, the head of the service who had orchestrated the Petrov defection, briefed him fully on the matter. Then it was off to Saigon, where on 16 November Maurice celebrated his fortieth birthday, and Thailand.

When at last he arrived in Singapore in readiness to take up the post of First Secretary and Head of Station, it felt in a way like coming home. Maurice was now officially at a senior level within MI6, and he was refreshed and ready to tackle his new job with confidence.

10

Return to the East

FROM THE BEGINNING of 1956 Oldfield was, as First Secretary and Head of Station, the de facto chief of CIFE, the combined MI5 and MI6 organization for the Far East operating from Singapore. He was due to move into a mansion on Fernhill Road in Tanglin, only a couple of miles from the High Commission, but this was not quite ready for occupation as the previous tenant had not yet left so he went to visit N. I. Low, and for the first six months rented his old house on Flower Road. He found his former chauffeur, Ahmed, was available and engaged his services once more, though this time the Vauxhall had been replaced by a rather more grand Buick limousine. He quickly reacquainted himself with old friends and neighbours, and was invited, again, to the home of the wealthy Chinese merchant that had been the scene of a trashed suit over five years earlier. Since then, Maurice had become a fixture on the London club scene and had acquired the unavoidable habit of good lunches and its associated weight gain – so he arrived at the dinner confident of a better outcome.

The welcome was effusive, the kind that might be extended to a prodigal son, and the drink flowed with even more generosity than last time. Again it was a ten-course meal, and again each course was followed by a full vessel of whisky downed in one after the yum-seng custom. And the traditional dinner had its traditional end – Maurice crawling home through the hibiscus hedge and cutting his clothes to ribbons. This time, though, rather than tracing the course of the culvert, the weary Head of Station found his way to bed, and claimed to have then slept for two days solid, only being woken occasionally by the housekeeper checking he was still alive.

Oldfield also resumed his association with St Paul's Church, and was once more a regular communicant and occasional organist at their Sunday services. Early in 1956 Maurice spotted a note at the church from the residential School for the Blind that had recently opened just off Upper Thomson Road (now the Lighthouse School), asking for volunteers to drive three pupils who wished to attend services. From then on, whenever he was in residence on a Sunday, Maurice would arrange for Ahmed to collect the three children from school in the Buick at 7.30 a.m., Maurice sitting up front with the driver while the children enjoyed the comfort of the limousine. He would then troop them into church where he'd arranged front-row pews close to the fan that kept the congregation cool during the hour-long service. One of the children, David Lim, now seventy years old, is still involved with the church in Singapore, and speaks of Maurice with great affection.

Oldfield also sponsored the education of several children he knew through the church. Some time after he'd moved into the Fernhill Road property he was approached by a friend of his former neighbour from Flower Road, Mrs Ngiam, with a plea for help. Her eldest son, Tong Dow, was said to be terribly bright but despite his mother's efforts working as a washer-woman to support her five children she could not afford to put him through the Sixth Form. Maurice went back to his old street to visit the family, and after talking through the boy's plans with him he agreed to fund Tong Dow's passage through his A Levels. It was to be many years before he found out how that investment had paid off.

His new posting saw Maurice inherit the Station Chief's secretary, who at the time was a vivacious twenty-one-year-old Scottish woman named Marion Laidlaw. Sixty years on, Marion still remembers her first encounter with her new boss. 'As he walked into my office he glanced around,' she wrote to me, 'and with a twinkle in his eye said, "Everything is very neat and tidy. Very neat and tidy! What are you escaping from?!"' Marion describes how Oldfield reminded her of the White Rabbit from *Alice in Wonderland* – always on the move and busy as a bee. 'Like quicksilver, he was full of energy and never still.' She recalls with fondness her time working under Oldfield in Singapore. 'Those were carefree, halcyon days and I remember them with much happiness.'

Though they only worked together for that brief period, Maurice and Marion remained in occasional touch, meeting up for meals or to go to concerts – but she was still surprised some years later when Maurice, stationed in Washington DC, sent her a programme from a production of *My Fair Lady* which he had seen in New York. Inside the cover he had written: 'Marion, I've grown accustomed to your face.

Maurice.' This affectionate gift 'somehow touched me very much', Marion said.

Oldfield's status as Head of Station opened more doors for him, and he cultivated relationships with political leaders in Singapore. The Chief Minister of Singapore, leader of the centre-left Labour Front Party David Marshall, was presiding over a rather shaky government which was felt by the British colonial authorities to be susceptible to communist influence, and under his leadership attempts to obtain independence failed for that reason. Oldfield understood the need to get to know opposition leaders in the countries he visited as much as serving government ministers, as such leaders were very likely themselves to take charge at some point, and in Singapore in 1956 the Leader of the Opposition was a thirty-three-year-old politician named Lee Kuan Yew – who also happened to be Maurice's local MP. Lee's rise had been meteoric; his centre-right People's Action Party was barely two years old and was running the government close in the polls. Lee himself was an English-educated lawyer, and while as keen as Marshall on independence for Singapore, his attitude, Oldfield judged, was more likely to be beneficial to British interests in the coming years. As was his wont, Maurice ensured he became firm friends with Lee. The two men discussed politics, Singapore's path to independence and her position in the world more generally.

It is not known whether Oldfield briefed Lee formally during his period in opposition, but it is known that soon after they met the kind of questions Lee began to ask of Marshall in the Legislative Assembly started to address issues that were edging towards a more Westernized society. He talked of the economy, jobs, sanitation and trade. A multi-party delegation to London in April, led by Marshall and the Governor, Sir Robert Black, failed to achieve the goal of independence, mainly due to concerns over the communist threat, and Marshall resigned. He was replaced by his colleague Lim Yew Hock, who mounted a campaign against the communists that was so aggressive it alienated the general population.

Over the next three years Lee's status as Chief Minister-in-waiting grew exponentially, and in the 1959 elections he romped home by a margin of forty-three seats to three. As he did with the Shah, Oldfield remained a trusted friend, adviser and confidant of Lee Kuan Yew for the rest of his life, helping to ensure that Singapore, even when independent, remained an ally and became a Western-style economy, irrespective of government changes in Britain and elsewhere. And as with the Shah, some of Lee's methods wouldn't have stood too much scrutiny in a Western democracy. But in terms of creating a prosperous, independent nation with which Britain could do business his legacy is formidable. He took a third world country and turned it into a first world country in one generation, served as Prime Minister until 1990, and remained a Cabinet minister until 2011. Tony Blair would call him 'the smartest leader I ever met'.

While keeping an eye on the situation in Malaya, where the Emergency was to run for four more years – albeit under increasing control – Oldfield's pressing concern was the developing situation in Vietnam and the surrounding nations. Maurice's work in this area was to be one of his most notable successes. As George Kennedy Young commented, 'His main achievement was keeping in perspective the fluid and turbulent situation in S.E. Asia after the French withdrawal, and stressing that personal ambitions and tribal loyalties lay behind the upsets, coups and intrigues and not the hand of either Moscow or Peking.'

Since becoming party to the Four Square Agreement, Oldfield was essentially operating without interference from Broadway, but this didn't mean he was about to start launching missions of derring-do to overthrow governments. His position as Head of Station meant he was in effect leading Britain's partnership with the CIA in the region, something the Americans appreciated as they had grown to value the Briton's reading of situations. As well as his existing associates, such as Sam Halpern and Red Jantzen, Maurice began to communicate with Ray Cline, who was at the start of their association a desk officer monitoring the USSR and China before going to Taiwan in 1957 and becoming Head of Station there the following year. Cline would describe Oldfield as being 'so unpretentious a man in both bearing and appearance that he looked as if he had been invented to deflate silly Ian Fleming caricatures of the British secret agent . . . somewhat like George Smiley and not at all like James Bond'. It was a description of which Maurice would have approved. The two men discussed their views on China, and Oldfield shared Cline's opinion that while in the context of the 1950s the Russians appeared the bigger threat, in the twenty-first century the more industrious Chinese might be the ones to watch. Maurice told a colleague, 'to understand the Chinese we really need to peer into the future to see what they will be like in 2017'.

On 26 May 1956, the Queen's Birthday Honours list was published. While the headline award was a knighthood for the Yorkshire cricketer Len Hutton, hidden in the small print of the Civil Service list was a CBE for 'Maurice Oldfield (Foreign Office)'. For Maurice it was good to be recognized for the useful, if secretive and sometimes potentially dangerous, work he was doing; for his family back in England, who had no real idea then of what that work was, it was good to see he was clearly doing something right.

Most of that work still involved travelling around South East Asia, looking at countries beyond the confines of the G&T brigades inhabiting the embassies and consulates and trying to work out what was really going on. Under him was a network of agents, all reporting their findings back to Singapore headquarters. Some of the agents were local, some British; some were recruited by other salaried officers, some by Maurice himself. He visited Vietnam (mostly), Burma, Laos and Thailand. His agents were everywhere, and they knew that as Maurice was also travelling and could easily see what they were seeing, their reports had to be accurate.

Each week he would get together with the Commissioner General for South East Asia, Sir Robert Scott – who had succeeded Malcolm MacDonald in 1955 – and the two would work out a report for dispatch to London. These reports on the situation in the region, at a time when the communist threat had already shown itself in Malaya and when the Russian bear was growling not so very far away, aiding the Chinese in their Five Year Plan to move from an agricultural economy towards world power status, needed to be timely and based on good intelligence. In Budapest in October 1956 MI6 failed to see the Hungarian rebellion against the Soviets coming, so distracted were they by Suez, and what might have been an opportunity to splinter a nation away from the USSR, as had been planned under Operation Valuable, was crushed by the Soviet Army. Ironically, the whole bloody matter was reported in the press by Anthony Cavendish, who had been working as a journalist since being 'let go' by MI6 in 1952. So to have an officer of Oldfield's calibre producing measured, reliable intelligence reports was absolutely vital.

When the reports were received from Oldfield and Scott, George Kennedy Young would ensure they were the lead item in the Yellow Box of intelligence estimates that were sent to the Prime Minister each week. They were to show their true value over the coming years.

But it wasn't all work for Maurice. In the mansion on Fernhill Road he had room to entertain properly and hosted parties that, one step down from the formality of High Commission events, enabled the guests to relax and talk. He would invite friends from the church – a conveniently eclectic bunch – and friends and colleagues from the office. All the time he was absorbing what he was told, and he encouraged his junior colleagues to do the same. Even at that level contacts, vibes and opinions could be as useful in intelligence terms as anything discovered by eavesdropping or interrogation. The place had numerous bedrooms and bathrooms, and guests would often stay the night. Some younger staff coming to work at the station occasionally lodged with Maurice until they obtained their own digs, and he valued the company. One person who arrived and introduced himself to Maurice during this period was Gerald Buss.

Gerald's Kentish farming family had not been willing to support him through university and he had gone instead, aged eighteen, to work in the City of London for a company that dealt in rubber. Seeking a room to let in the capital, he was given an address to try which turned out to be that of Sir James Easton, one of the Deputy Chiefs of MI6, and Lady Easton. He lived happily with the Eastons, about whom he knew little other than that when Jack had visitors from the office both he and Lady Easton had to leave the room. It was evident that whatever Jack Easton did, it was secret, and his wife hated it.

After about a year, Gerald's company posted him to Malaya, and he was to be based in Singapore. When he explained this to his landlord, Jack wished him well and wrote down a name and address which he handed over, saying, 'When you get to Singapore, look up this chap. He'll look after you.' The name was Maurice Oldfield.

As a young man on his own in the Far East, Gerald did indeed look up Maurice, and they hit it off right away. 'From the start,' Gerald told me, 'Maurice was like a father figure to me. He was about forty, I was about twenty, and he showed me warmth and a level of concern that I'd never had from my own father.' Then coincidence struck. It transpired, as they discussed their backgrounds, that as a boy during the war Gerald had been evacuated from Kent to rural Derbyshire where he'd stayed with a relative named Storrs-Fox who ran a prep school in Bakewell called St Anselm's. And while they were in Derbyshire the kids would go and help on a nearby farm. The farmer was a lovely man called Joe Oldfield. In the end Gerald's stay in Derbyshire was brief as he found Storrs-Fox a nasty old bully who hit the children, 'but not very hard – he was a poor shot'. Gerald decided he would rather risk Hitler's bombs than Storrs-Fox's fists and begged his family to take him back to Kent.

Gerald lodged with Maurice until he found his own place, and during the week he went up to the rubber plantations on behalf of his company. When he had been there a while, Maurice said, 'Next time you go up into the hills, I want you to write me a report about what you see there.' And that's what Gerald did. He gave Maurice his report, and was embarrassed to admit that there actually wasn't very much to say at all. The people were simply getting on with their lives.

'Good,' said Maurice. 'You haven't told me anything I don't know already.'

Gerald was rather surprised by this, until Maurice pointed out that 'sometimes when we send someone to do a report for the Foreign Office they like to make it sound exciting. I know that mostly it isn't.'

At that stage he didn't know the exact nature of Maurice's work, but Gerald was to remain a 'Friend' of MI6 until Maurice retired.

While he says he never suspected that Maurice was gay, Gerald and Maurice's MI6 secretary Marion Laidlaw, who was also regularly at the house, did privately discuss the fact that Maurice was not married. Marion similarly harboured no doubts about his sexuality, but according to Gerald they did make the odd joke about his bachelor status. 'I was quite brash and open then,' Gerald recalled, 'and one night I just asked him – "Why aren't you married, then, Maurice? Are you queer or something?" Maurice asked what I meant. I said, "So do you prefer men, or what?" He smiled, and said, "Not all men!"'

As they'd started the conversation, Maurice opened up to them about the matter. He explained just how many married couples in the Service ended up divorced, such were the pressures of travel, secrecy, and simply not being able to have a normal life: 'You'll have seen how the Eastons are? Jack's wife detests the way they have to live. [In fact, at Lady Easton's insistence, the couple were soon to retire to Michigan for that very reason.] That's quite common among Foreign Office couples.'

'But what about a family? Don't you want children?'

Maurice pointed out that he had ten brothers and sisters, and even at this stage he had four nephews; there were sure to be many, many more.

It was obvious to Gerald and Marion that he genuinely did dote on his family, and truly saw no need to have children of his own. Men and women in the Service did tend to have tense, pressured marriages, with children they seldom saw, stuffed into English public schools. The logic of Maurice's position made perfect sense when he explained it like that.

Not only did the house on Fernhill Road have plenty of rooms, it also had an outdoor tennis court. Maurice hadn't played tennis since his Manchester days, and he hadn't been all that accomplished then. In Singapore he picked up the sport again, and would play against junior officials. His puffing and panting attempts to charge about the court had the effect of disarming his opponents who invariably found themselves quite in awe of the Head of Station. It was a great leveller, a good way of cutting through hierarchies. If someone in Oldfield's position could make himself a figure of fun with his podgy figure sweating and bouncing about in tennis whites then nobody needed to be self-conscious.

One afternoon Maurice offered his tennis court to the Youth Fellowship from St Paul's Church. Fourteen members of the YF attended; they played a tournament and afterwards were treated to afternoon tea in the mansion. Unsurprisingly, Maurice made another friend. The president of the YF was a sixteen-year-old of Chinese descent by the name of Michael Chan. Michael's parents asked Maurice to sponsor their son's application for a passport as he dreamed of going to London to study medicine at Guy's Hospital. He of course agreed, and also wrote in support of Michael's application to Guy's. Maurice further promised that he would look after Michael as soon as he was posted back to London. He was as good as his word, and would be a friend and mentor to Michael as he made his way through medical school and into work, initially as a paediatrician. Michael Chan had a varied and impressive career, culminating in his being elevated to the House of Lords as Baron Chan of Oxton – only the second person of Chinese origin to sit in the Upper House.

Michael Chan was never used by Maurice as a 'Friend' in the MI6 sense, but many other people were, sometimes without their knowledge. What the Service needed aside from the official MI6 officers operating out of embassies and passport offices were agents who could get into places others couldn't, avoiding detection. It was in the late 1950s that Oldfield increased his use of journalists, for example. Tony Cavendish, of course, remained in touch, and his reports were useful. Other important journalistic 'Friends' included Sefton Delmer (known as Tom), the foreign correspondent of the *Daily Express*, Harry Boyne, political correspondent of the *Daily Telegraph*, and Ian Waller, the Labour-supporting political editor of the *Sunday Telegraph*.

Tom Delmer had been, before the war, the first British journalist to interview Adolf Hitler, and during the conflict had worked for the Political Warfare Executive, broadcasting black propaganda via radio stations in Germany with the aim of convincing Nazi soldiers that their political masters were fleeing to South America. When the Labour minister Stafford Cripps found out what Delmer was up to it offended his sense of fair play and he wrote to the then Foreign Secretary, Anthony Eden, to say, 'If this is the sort of thing that is needed to win the war, then why, I'd rather lose it.' Delmer's resourcefulness and worldwide travels on behalf of the *Express* provided useful intelligence for Oldfield. And the arrangement was supported by Max Aitken, later to become the 2nd Baron Beaverbrook, a director of Express Newspapers from 1946 – and a personal friend of Maurice's. The two would dine together in London regularly, and Oldfield took occasional holidays at Aitken's home on the Isle of Wight.

Perhaps slightly more surprising is his use of Harry Boyne and Ian Waller, because it seems they were essentially spying for Oldfield on British politicians, even if they didn't see it that way. As well-connected lobby correspondents these two journalists had access to the day-to-day dealings of politicians – their relationships and interests, all the rumours and gossip, and who was pulling the strings of whom. In the quest for intelligence and the management of it, knowing the minds of the political elite beyond his immediate masters was important to Maurice.

Another favourite target for recruitment was airline crew. Such people, with their easy access to any country they happened to fly into, were an ideal conduit for receiving intelligence across national borders. Maurice had 'Friends' in, among others, Singapore Airlines, British Airways,

Kenyan Airlines, KLM and Qantas. People travelling across the Iron Curtain were especially valuable and airline crew fitted this bill too, as did people in business. He even had contacts in the International Olympic Committee whom I shall not name as some are still alive.

Probably the most notable group in terms of the sourcing of agents by Maurice, though, was the clergy: in every country he travelled he would visit churches and get to know the priests and their assistants. Elizabeth Roberts, wife of Oldfield's old colleague Brigadier Douglas Roberts, recalled that on one trip to Italy, while ostensibly on holiday, she and Maurice visited thirteen churches in a single morning. In some of them he just looked at the architecture; in the more likely ones he exchanged contact details with the priest in charge for future use. These people had their own networks across their communities that tended to encompass a wide cross-section of society. When Gerald Buss had finished his time in Singapore, Maurice encouraged him to follow his initial plan to go to Oxford University and helped ensure his entry. Gerald first took a course in Cold War Studies before training to become a priest. As chaplain of Hurstpierpoint College, Gerald had the perfect cover for a 'Friend'.

The work Maurice did during this second period in Singapore laid the foundations for intelligence successes that would benefit Britain in the coming years, particularly when the Americans went to war in Vietnam. By 1958 the main reason for Oldfield's presence in the region, the Malayan Emergency, was in its final stages. The independence granted to Malaya in 1957 had removed one of the main driving forces of the uprising, and the Malaysian communist parties tried to initiate peace talks. The last major insurrection took place in 1958, though the final declaration was not to come until July 1960. Maurice had developed a deep understanding of the region, and would continue to visit the area – Singapore in particular – for the rest of his career. The presence of a Friend of MI6 as the perpetual head of government in Singapore would provide him with an ongoing insight into political movements in the Far East during the turbulent times ahead.

In September 1958 Maurice was posted back to London, still with the rank of First Secretary, where he prepared himself to take on the biggest job of his career so far, that of Counsellor at the British Embassy in Washington DC, which was due to become vacant at the end of 1959. This was Britain's main link with the CIA, and the very job Kim Philby had left in ignominy earlier in the decade.

11

The Tenant of Waterside Drive

O NE OF THE first things Maurice did on his return to London was touch base with his protégé Michael Chan to see how he was settling into life at Guy's Hospital. Chan, who was eighteen at the time, recalled that he visited Maurice's flat at 18 Chandos Court on Caxton Street on 23 September 1958. They had mugs of tea at the flat, where pride of place was given to a photograph of Joe Oldfield carrying a pail of milk across the farmyard, and then took a taxi to the Hong Kong Restaurant on Shaftesbury Avenue. Maurice ordered a bottle of wine for the two of them, not realizing that at that time Michael didn't drink wine. So the MI6 man drank the whole bottle, and became 'quite jolly', using his cigarillo to try to burst a balloon being carried by a passing girl as they wandered down Shaftesbury Avenue after the meal.

Oldfield also set about renewing acquaintance with some of the representatives of other intelligence agencies, including Mossad from Israel, and spent useful time milking one particular contact, Emir Farid Chebab, a Lebanese intelligence officer with vast experience of Middle Eastern affairs who had recently been vice president of Interpol. Emir Farid, great-grandson of the last ruler of Lebanon, Emir Bashir III, had just been appointed Lebanese Ambassador to Ghana, Nigeria and Cameroon, and Oldfield – whose interest in Africa was developing – shared some intelligence on those countries while gaining another valuable set of eyes and ears there in return.

Maurice had been selected for the Washington job not just because he was generally accepted as the rising star in the Service; in the context of the factions of MI6 he was also ideally placed as he remained in many ways an outsider, untainted by uncomfortable links with Philby and conveniently clean in relation to The Horrors. He had the trust of the old guard of Robber Barons and of the Chief, Sir Dick White, and not many people of his seniority were in that category. He knew the Service inside out, too, and had earned a sound reputation among the CIA officers with whom he'd worked. In readiness for his posting, Maurice had meetings with the CIA's senior officers in London, Tracy Barnes and Bronson Tweedy, who were also returning to the USA at a similar time. He was pleased to discover that several of his colleagues from the Far East were due for promotion to senior positions in the American agency.

Oldfield was well aware that his time in Washington would inevitably be clouded by the Burgess and Maclean affair, the damage done by Philby, and the perception (not entirely inaccurate) that British Intelligence had been penetrated to a great extent by the Soviets. He resolved to have all the answers ready, and studied every file to do with the matter. He explored the motivations of the traitors and the likely damage that had been inflicted by their activities. In short, he was comprehensively prepared to field every ball the CIA pitched at him – and, by also researching the Americans' own shortcomings, was ready to return every one with carefully calculated interest. He delved into joint MI6 and CIA operations of the past to get a feeling for the personalities involved, and where, if anywhere, security might have been compromised.

One major operation carried out jointly was Stopwatch, or Gold as the CIA called it. This had its origins in an MI6 operation dating back to 1949 called Silver, which involved tapping into communication cables going into the Soviet Army base in Vienna. This required the use of a building to act as a cover from where the intercepted communications could be read, and MI6 initially rented retail premises and opened a shop selling Harris tweed clothing, on the assumption that nobody in Vienna would be all that interested in Scottish fashion. In the event, tweed became a must-have item and the shop was thronged with customers, all of them served by frustrated MI6 officers. Once the tweed was sold and the communications centre switched to a private house, Operation Silver was judged a great success, allegedly helping Austria regain sovereignty, and ran until 1955.

The success of Silver encouraged MI6 to share the techniques with the CIA, both to build bridges and in the hope that the Americans would help fund a similar but much more ambitious scheme. This was to dig a tunnel from West Berlin into the communist East, to a position where it was known there was an intersection of buried telephone lines, with the aim of tapping the cables and intercepting communications between the Soviet Embassy in East Berlin and Moscow, and between Russian and East German officials. Despite it being on German soil, German Intelligence was excluded from the planning of the operation as it was thought to be riddled with spies; it was carried out in London with only high-level CIA and MI6 officers present, and documentary evidence was deliberately kept to a minimum ('as little as possible must be reduced to writing' was the instruction from the then CIA Chief, Allen Dulles). Only Cleveland Cram for the CIA and George Blake for the British kept notes.

Bill Harvey, he of Philby's undoing, was selected to run the operation, and construction began in late 1953 in the form of a huge warehouse with a vast basement being built to house the tunnel entrance. In September 1954, digging began. It was a mammoth and tense task that involved tunnelling a distance of nearly half a kilometre not many feet under the most heavily guarded border in the world. After five months, and at a cost alleged to have been more than $25 million, not to mention numerous mishaps including digging through an undetected cess pit, the British inserted the taps and the first intercepts were made in the spring of 1955.

Over the next year thousands of messages were intercepted, so many that it was to be 1958 before they were all decoded. Even when the Soviets apparently discovered the Berlin tunnel in April 1956 and started complaining about the British and Americans using gangster tactics and acting in an imperialist way, Operation Gold was still hailed as a massive success due to the sheer volume of intelligence it had generated. And Western newspapers applauded the audacity of the plan and the feat of engineering that had delivered the tunnel. Oldfield studied the papers forensically, noting the details and the names of those involved.

During this period MI6 arranged to have Oldfield's London flat bugged, with his approval, so that it could be used to interview people without it seeming to be in a formal situation. Even if people knew, or suspected, that their conversations were being recorded, the fact that the equipment wasn't visible would tend to relax them and put them off their guard. It was an advantage of his bachelor status that Maurice could allow his home to be exploited in such a way; a married officer's wife might just have had something to say.

In the run-up to Christmas 1959 Maurice returned to Derbyshire for the last time before heading over to America. He was delighted to be asked to present the prizes at the Lady Manners School Speech Day – the first time he had been back to the place since he was the main recipient of the awards a quarter of a century before. Maurice spoke to the pupils about moving on from their education. His former teacher and friend Reg Harvey took notes on Maurice's address. 'Life could be regarded as a series of concentric circles, moving from the individual at the centre, through the family to school, the district, and then outwards to the world,' he said. 'All should be governed by the same principles of honesty, enthusiasm and loyalty.' This description of life would seem a fair summary of how Maurice viewed the connections he made in his career.

The family held a large celebration dinner that Christmas at Mona View, knowing that Maurice's posting to the US was for four years and that there was no way they could be

Above: The Lathkill Hotel and Hall Hill Cottage, Over Haddon, as they are today. MO's father, Joe, was licensee of the pub in the late 1910s, and the large Oldfield family lived in the cottage until 1939.

Left: Family Christmas dinner, Over Haddon, 1974. From left: Sadie, John, Warren, Tom and Martin Pearce; Maurice, Annie and Renee Oldfield.

Below right: Joe and Annie Oldfield (*on the left*) at the wedding of their daughter Freda to Jack Naylor. St Anne's Church, Over Haddon, June 1955.

Below left: MO aged nineteen; his first passport photograph.

Top: The Kantara crossing on the Suez Canal. MO's first job in the Intelligence Corps in 1941 was in passport control at the crossing – classic cover for an intelligence officer.

Middle: MO's favourite house, in his favourite posting – 8 Flower Road, Singapore. Taken by MO in 1950, the picture features his house-keeper and his chauffeur, Ahmed.

Right: Teddy Kollek. Described as 'the greatest builder of Jerusalem since Herod', Kollek was mayor of the city from 1965 to 1993, having become close friends with MO in the aftermath of the Second World War as a leader of the Jewish Agency.

Right: Lee Kuan Yew. MO identified Lee as the man to do business with in Singapore when he was still a young opposition leader. An important Friend of MI6 in the Far East, Fred Lee (as MO called him) served as Prime Minister from 1959 to 1990 and stayed on as a Cabinet minister until 2011.

Above: James Jesus Angleton of the CIA. Initially close to MO and to Kim Philby, the American's relentless molehunt eventually caused the MI6 man to describe Angleton as 'a disaster'.

Right: Anatoliy Golitsyn, who defected to the West in 1961, with his wife Svetlana. Golitsyn's theories stoked paranoia in the CIA and MI6 and remain controversial.

Above: MO with the British Ambassador, David Ormsby-Gore (later Lord Harlech), and Foreign Secretary Alec Douglas-Home, in Washington at the time of the Cuban Missile Crisis in 1962. Ormsby-Gore had introduced MO to the then Senator John F. Kennedy in 1960.

Left: The leader of the free world with the hereditary ruler of Iran – JFK and the Shah. Both were to value MO's counsel, with varying results.

Below: There were protests on both sides of the Atlantic in October 1962 as the Cuban Missile Crisis saw the world gripped by a fear of nuclear war.

Left: Oleg Penkovsky at his Moscow trial in 1963. As Station Chief in Washington, MO was the conduit for Penkovsky's intelligence to the CIA – a crucial role in the Cuban Missile Crisis when, for a time, nuclear war looked inevitable.

Below: Rozanne Colchester. One of the Bletchley Park decoders, Rozanne and her husband, Halsey, were MI6 friends of MO with whom he stayed when they ran the Paris station from 1968 to 1971. Rozanne would describe Maurice as 'a soul-mate'.

Below left: Bruce Mackenzie, MI6's Friend in Jomo Kenyatta's government. Mackenzie was assassinated by Idi Amin's Ugandan regime for his role in the Entebbe raid.

Below right: MO visiting members of the UN Peacekeeping Force in Sinai in 1975.

Above left: Maurice arriving in Cairo, 1976, accompanied by British and Egyptian intelligence officers.

Above right: The Athenaeum Club, where MO dined and hosted guests most days when in London. He was occasionally ticked off by the staff when his guests' bodyguards got aggressive.

Left: Tony Cavendish, one of MO's oldest and most loyal friends, with his dogs at home in Hampshire in 1977. The picture was taken by Maurice.

Below: MO being awarded the KCMG in 1975, with his chauffeur and, left to right, his sisters Renee and Sadie, and his long-serving bodyguard, Ken Dyer.

Above left and right: Brian Stewart, an able intelligence officer who was MO's preferred choice to be his successor as C. Others in MI6 did not agree with that assessment and threatened mass resignations unless MO changed his mind. He backed down and the job went to Sir Arthur 'Dickie' Franks.

Right: Sir Robert (later Lord) Armstrong, who as Cabinet Secretary under Margaret Thatcher conducted the investigation into MO's conduct. He described the episode as 'the most miserable of my career'.

Below: David Owen and James Callaghan, Foreign Secretary and Prime Minister when MO retired from MI6. Despite the economic turmoil in the UK at the time, he found working under them a breath of fresh air after the paranoia of Harold Wilson's last years in office.

Above left: Former MI5 and MI6 officer David Cornwell, who, when he was writing as John le Carré, emphatically did not intend George Smiley to be based on MO. After seeing Guinness play Smiley as Maurice, however, henceforth the character was written with him in mind – and MO became Smiley in the public imagination.

Above: Kim Philby in Moscow, interviewed by Phillip Knightley in 1988. The traitor gave his reflections on his life – and on the 'formidable' Maurice Oldfield.

Above right: Alec Guinness based his portrayal of George Smiley on MO after the two hit it off over lunch with John le Carré in Chelsea.

Right: It took Maurice numerous attempts to get the look right for his official portrait on becoming Chief of MI6 in 1973.

Below: Betty Kemp, in retirement at St Hugh's College, Oxford. Her relationship with MO endured from their meeting at Manchester University until his death, and was the closest he came to marriage.

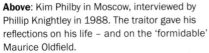

sure of seeing him in that period. For his part, Maurice promised that he would keep in touch, and his brothers, sisters, nephews and, by then, niece looked forward to receiving their regular letters and postcards. He was a meticulous correspondent and always remembered birthdays and anniversaries, and in return expected to be kept up to date with matters at home. As he left for London in January 1960, after all the farewells, for his final briefing before flying to America, he was not to know that it would be the last time he would see his father.

In Washington, Oldfield found a home through J. F. Begg (Realtors) Inc. at 2451 Waterside Drive, a handsome brick-built townhouse overlooking Rock Creek and only a ten-minute drive from the British Embassy on Massachusetts Avenue. As a way of integrating himself with his CIA counterparts, Oldfield took their advice on obtaining the essential services required by the spy about Washington: a tinker, a tailor (Thomas Saltz, 'purveyor of tweeds and worsteds to the traditionally tailored Washingtonian for half a century') and a dermatologist.

As Oldfield settled into life in the US capital, and his office in the British Embassy, which was fitted with one-way glass, he was aware that given the security issues in the light of the Philby affair he was not going to be allowed unfettered access to CIA information, or to the Chief. Even access to his official main point of contact, Richard 'Dick' Helms, was restricted, not least because of Helms's activities around the world: Vietnam, the Middle East and Central America were all occupying his time. So Maurice had to work his way in and build trust by other methods.

He busied himself with getting on friendly terms with

many of the contacts working in nearby international embassies, and became a well-known if enigmatic figure on the capital's cocktail party circuit. He got to know the CIA men near the top of the agency, accepting invitations to dine at their homes, and made a point of cultivating their wives – a lesson learned after Burgess's escapade with Libby Harvey. He became a close friend of Cicely Angleton and of Bill Harvey's new wife Clara, always known as CG. Janet Barnes, wife of Tracy, later remembered that 'Maurice loved to dance. In the summers he would come visit us in Rhode Island and dance under the trees at night.' People spoke fondly of this witty, gently mannered Englishman – but could never recall anything he'd told them. It was all part of his carefully managed persona.

He wasn't long into his posting when, on 11 April 1960, he received a call from his sister, Sadie, to say that their beloved father had died suddenly at home. He was seventy-five. Maurice was heartbroken by the news, doubly so when his work commitments meant there was no way he could return to Over Haddon for the funeral. He wrote a loving eulogy for Joe, which he posted to Betty Kemp in Oxford. Betty drove up to deliver it at the service, acting as Maurice's representative. He vowed not to be away when his mother died.

Much of Oldfield's early period in Washington outside social circles was taken up by painstaking talks with Angleton and other CIA associates, which were made easier by the personal friendships he'd built as he sought to re-establish trust between the Americans and his own MI6. He was a regular at CIA headquarters and also hosted meetings with their officers at his house on Waterside Drive. Tony

Cavendish was a frequent visitor and occasional lodger, and recalled these private meetings going on late into the night. An ongoing area of concern for the Americans was their British counterparts' supposedly lax vetting procedures, the very same that had allowed Burgess, Maclean and Philby to reach the highest levels of MI6, principally on the premise that they were 'the right kind of chaps', impeccably well connected and from the right schools. Even a cursory glance at Oldfield's credentials would have displayed a provenance entirely at odds with the CIA's standard profile of an MI6 officer – and this, together with Oldfield's well-informed and well-prepared critique of the failings that had allowed the traitors to prosper, and a robust amount of evidence to demonstrate that the Americans themselves were not without their communist infiltrators, enabled the British man to build useful relationships within the CIA remarkably quickly.

Oldfield found that he got along very well with Americans, and they with him. It also certainly helped that he had worked with the CIA's Ray Cline when both were Station Chiefs in the Far East. Cline was soon to return to Washington to become head of the Directorate of Intelligence at the CIA (where he and Oldfield would become closely involved in the Cuban Missile Crisis), but for now he was able to give his superiors the confidence that Oldfield was a man with whom they could work.

He didn't build these relationships in a superior, Foreign Office kind of way, though. Oldfield was, perhaps uniquely for one in his position, completely beyond pigeonholing by class. His shoulders were unburdened by chips. He could speak in a manner to suit whatever company he found himself in – a talent honed by the contrasts he'd become used to from the age of eleven when his life was split between the brusque, engrained agricultural ways of his village mates, the gowned correctness of his grammar school teachers, and the plummy tones of the parish priests.

The officer with whom Oldfield enjoyed the most success was James Angleton. Given that Angleton had been the man who'd felt Philby's duplicity the most personally, Dick White instructed Oldfield – in the very position once occupied by Philby – to target him as an important conduit for rebuilding trust. Angleton had been so stunned by Philby, a friend he'd trusted implicitly, that he was determined never to be fooled again. Even when a mutual friend of Angleton's and Oldfield's, Teddy Kollek, had visited the CIA during Philby's time and, remembering attending the man's wedding years earlier in Vienna, exclaimed, 'What's that communist doing here?', Angleton had remained emotionless. Maybe Philby's front had already so hoodwinked Angleton that he simply dismissed Kollek's warning due to the passage of time. Or, as he later claimed, he had suspected Philby all the time and was playing along with him until the time was right, except Bill Harvey beat him to it. Either way the effect was to engrain in Angleton a deep paranoia.

Oldfield and Angleton would lunch regularly at Angleton's new favourite restaurant in Washington, La Niçoise, or sometimes they would meet in the American's office at CIA headquarters in Langley, Virginia. And then there were the personal visits to the Angletons' home in Arlington. Oldfield listened to Angleton's theories about the moles in British Intelligence, and for now at least went along with them. The CIA's Cleveland Cram was to say that Maurice 'found a wedge into Langley. He played Angleton like a harp.'

Oldfield understood better than most of his MI6 contemporaries that background is no indicator of personal quality or intellect. He knew from his own brothers – all blessed with lively, enquiring minds and innate intelligence, and only held back from academic study by their need to keep the farm going and a shortage of school places – that he needed to treat people as he found them. No matter the company he kept he was entirely without pretension – something that was to benefit him when he was at a British Embassy party in the late spring of 1960.

As the guests mingled and chatted, Maurice was introduced by the Foreign Minister, David Ormsby-Gore, to a friend of his, a young senator from Massachusetts named John Fitzgerald Kennedy. At the time, Kennedy was trying to win the Democratic Party's nomination for the forthcoming presidential election, and was thus exactly the sort of person – like Lee Kuan Yew before him – with whom Oldfield liked to get on personal terms. In this case Oldfield had clearly done his homework in advance.

He enjoyed relating how, during the customary small-talk, Kennedy asked, 'So, what part of England are you from?', and when Maurice told him 'Derbyshire' the American replied, 'My sister's buried there!' Maurice told him, 'I know. My family lives only about five miles from the churchyard where she is buried.' Kathleen Kennedy, John's younger sister and the sibling to whom he was closest, had married William Cavendish, son and heir of the Duke of Devonshire. William was killed by a sniper in Belgium on active service during the war just four months after the couple married in May 1944; Kathleen died in an air crash over the Cévennes in France in 1948 aged just twenty-eight. It was the first incident of what became known as the Kennedy Curse. Kathleen was buried beside her husband in the churchyard at Edensor, on the Duke's Chatsworth Estate just outside Bakewell.

This gave Kennedy and Oldfield a connection – a small one maybe, but Maurice seldom needed much to work on – and from then, on the few occasions they met, generally at functions rather than one-on-one, there was more than average embassy chit-chat between them. Oldfield was thrilled to tell his sister that Kennedy had invited him to visit the family home in Hyannis Port, but as he never went on to describe such a trip it seems reasonable to assume any such invitation did not in the end lead to a visit. Maurice may have been discreet in terms of not disclosing the content of private conversations, but he was perfectly open about the contacts he had that were in the public domain. That he could relate any kind of friendship with Kennedy to a churchyard in Derbyshire was exactly the sort of link Oldfield not only liked to exploit but was happy to discuss. It was another example of his bringing things down to the most basic level.

Oldfield still needed to build a relationship with Dick Helms, then a Deputy Director of Central Intelligence, who was to be elevated to the top job under President Lyndon Johnson. Helms had been heavily involved in Project MKUltra to develop truth serums and other supposedly mind-altering drugs in the hope of weeding out moles and traitors. He was in the vanguard of the paranoia that had permeated the American intelligence services, and one of the most highly favoured weapons in his armoury was the polygraph, or lie detector – something he tried to foist on MI6.

Even though the obvious response to Helms's insistence would have been to consent to the suggestion in the hope of building the confidence of the CIA, Maurice Oldfield was steadfast in his scepticism about the effectiveness of the polygraph. He was known to be enthusiastic about techno-logical advances that could assist his officers in their work, and in particular those gadgets that made this work safer, but not at all costs. He was, as ever, using what he described as 'Over Haddon common sense', careful to be aware of the limitations and potential failings of emerging technology. In the case of the polygraph, Oldfield's line was that it was 'an easy way out for any scoundrel', and he urged the CIA to temper its inclination to rely on lie detector results with little, if any, question. He was aware that the KGB had a training section devoted to coaching its agents in how to beat the polygraph and how to lie in general, and encouraged the Americans to devote their energies towards learning the techniques involved. These were known to include con-trolled breathing, artificially raising the heart rate prior to the test, and using hidden implements to self-inflict pain at key points in the questioning to try to vary the readings.

Had a more pliable British officer been in charge of the Washington station at the time then it is plausible, given the gravity of the situation at what was the height of Cold War tension, intrigue and mistrust, that the CIA's pressure would have led to a recommendation being sent back to Whitehall that the polygraph be routinely incorporated into SIS vetting procedures. This could have provided a quick-fix to the rebuilding process. It is then equally plausible that the device could have become an established part of British official life beyond the realms of Jeremy Kyle's brand of exploitation in the name of entertainment. This would have been the easy decision, but Oldfield tended to think beyond the easy and get to the nub of a matter.

Oldfield's response came when the new CIA headquarters – which remained unnamed until 1999, when it became the George Bush Center for Intelligence – was opened in March 1961, and was as unexpected as it was effective. His chauffeur collected the British officer from his handsome townhouse and drove him for twenty minutes along the tree-lined George Washington Memorial Parkway alongside the Potomac River, through the security cordons to the new building at Langley.

Having been shown around, Oldfield surprised the agency staff by asking to be put through the CIA's security vetting procedures, including the polygraph. He was subjected to the usual round of questioning: seemingly irrelevant enquiries such as 'Did you have a coffee this morning?', designed to establish the likely effect of caffeine on the subject's pulse rate; the control questions that most people can answer but might feel uneasy about so doing, maybe 'Have you ever lied to get yourself out of trouble?', designed to establish a baseline of reactions; then, finally, the serious questions. Beyond the obvious need to assess a candidate's basic suitability for the job, such probing essentially establishes whether the subject may be susceptible to blackmail. The questions cover the subject's financial history, family background and political affiliations. They then move into a more intimate arena. Thus Oldfield was subjected to, as

Philby might have put it, the nasty little question 'Are you now, or have you ever been, a practising homosexual?'

Oldfield lied. He passed the test.

At a stroke, the situation was defused. The CIA was satisfied that the British now appeared to be taking the polygraph seriously, even if they were not about to recommend it for blanket operational use. Whatever technique Oldfield deployed to get him through the test is not known. To what degree he was concerned about the possibility of failure, or how he might have reacted to that eventuality, is similarly unknown. The episode does demonstrate that, despite the conservative image Oldfield outwardly portrayed, he was in fact a risk-taker of the highest order. At that point in history, what would have been the reaction of the CIA had the very man sent by the British government to repair the damage inflicted by the Cambridge Spies himself failed a lie detector test? As it was, Oldfield felt bold enough to tell Ray Cline: 'However heterosexual we may be, we bachelors today are always suspected of being homosexual just because we aren't married. Maybe they will now agree that I have no such problems.' From then on, whenever an occasion arose that required one of Oldfield's officers to be subjected to the lie detector, he himself would again take the test.

The episode was also useful to Oldfield in other ways. Firstly, he knew, privately, that the test could be beaten – indeed he had the real Q, Frank Quinn of Q Branch, make him a black box with red and green lights on it that were set up to flash randomly in response to people answering questions, and would gleefully enjoy their reactions when he tried it out on them. Secondly, he also knew, even more privately, that *he* could beat the test. It was something that would serve him well for the next twenty years.

That year, 1961, also brought a setback to Oldfield's work in rebuilding trust between the CIA and British Intelligence, and this came in the shape of two defectors. The first was a Polish triple agent, Michael Goleniewski, who had been providing information to the KGB, the CIA and Polish Intelligence since the late 1950s. In January 1961, under fear of detection, he defected to the USA, and in Britain this very quickly led to the arrest of what was known as the Portland Spy Ring, a group that had been sending details of British submarines from the Admiralty Underwater Weapons Establishment on the island of Portland in Dorset. The leader of the ring, Konon Molody – who had been using the identity of a Canadian named Gordon Lonsdale – Harry Houghton, Houghton's lover Ethel Gee, and an American couple called Morris and Lona Cohen were all jailed.

But the big one was George Blake. This was the same Blake who had taken notes of the plans for the Berlin tunnel, a man who had been in MI6 since he was recruited in 1944. Imprisoned by the North Koreans during the Korean War, Blake studied the works of Karl Marx during his captivity and became a convinced communist who volunteered for the KGB. Such was the scale of his betrayal he is sometimes referred to as the Greatest Traitor; indeed when he was interviewed he said, 'I don't know what I handed over because it was so much.'

That he has never claimed quite the level of infamy as the likes of Kim Philby can only be because he was never so much part of the Establishment as the Cambridge ring, and never reached the same levels in MI6. Born George Behar in

Rotterdam to a Protestant Dutch mother and an Egyptian Jewish father, Blake had joined the Dutch Resistance during the Second World War, and then the Royal Navy after his family fled to Britain and changed their surname. Also unlike Philby, MI6 didn't let the apprehending of Blake turn into a charade. At the time of their working out his identity, the spy was learning Arabic at a Foreign Office college in the Lebanon, and Dick White arranged for the Lebanon Station Chief, Nick Elliott, to ask Blake to report back to Broadway for discussions about his next posting. Suspicious, Blake asked his Soviet handler for clearance, and was told it was safe. For once, MI6 had not let anything slip.

Once back in London he was invited to discuss a few matters with Harry Shergold, Terence Lecky and Ben Johnson of MI6. It took three days for Blake to crack. As with Philby, although they knew they'd got their man, the evidence was circumstantial. Unlike Philby, Blake didn't have a phalanx of indignant friends refusing to believe his guilt. Even then, Shergold reckoned Blake was only half an hour away from walking free. It was only when the interrogator said 'Look, we know you spied for the Soviets, we just need to understand why' that the cracks appeared. 'When you were in prison in Korea, did they torture you?' Shergold went on. 'Did they blackmail you?' These aspersions being cast on his KGB masters caused Blake to open up. No, they hadn't blackmailed him. And no, they hadn't tortured him. It had all been of his own free will.

As well as revealing the identity of numerous British agents trying to penetrate the Soviet Bloc, Blake had betrayed Operation Silver in Vienna as soon as he'd been able to. As for the Berlin tunnel, he'd blown that from the start. The

Soviets took the decision not to close it down straight away because to do so would have been to expose Blake, one of the few people who knew the details of the operation – far too valuable an agent to lose. Instead they let the CIA pour millions into what was literally a money pit. They calculated, correctly, that such was the volume of traffic passing through the tap it could take years to decipher, and then once they accidentally on purpose discovered the tunnel and had it closed down in a flurry of righteous indignation, the CIA and MI6 could never be sure that the intelligence they'd siphoned off was even genuine.

Blake was jailed for forty-two years, reported in the press as being a year for each of the agents who had been killed after he'd betrayed them – something that is never likely to be proven. Aside from life sentences this was, until 1986, the longest sentence ever handed out by a British court.

These incidents did little to inspire confidence in the CIA that their view of British Intelligence being colonized by Soviet spies was anything other than spot on, but at least they enabled Maurice Oldfield to demonstrate to James Angleton that such matters were now being addressed properly and legal action was being taken. And when Dick White flew over to report personally on the matter to the incoming Chief of the CIA, John McCone, he found a sympathetic ear, and Angleton saying 'it could happen to anyone'. There were dissenting voices, notably Bill Harvey's, but in the main the Americans were appreciative that the Brits were now at least trying.

But the next defector would set in train a series of events that would fuel the all-pervading paranoia in the intelligence services of Britain and America and cause ructions between the allies for over a decade. A KGB major named Anatoliy Golitsyn switched allegiance in December 1961, bringing with him his wife, his daughter, and a host of information about Soviet agents operating in the West. Golitsyn took the train from Russia into Finland and flew from Helsinki to Stockholm, and there to interview him at the CIA station was James Jesus Angleton.

It's easy to see why Angleton became intoxicated with Golitsyn and his theories, and equally easy to see why the official historian of MI5, Professor Christopher Andrew, was to describe him as 'an unreliable conspiracy theorist'. Golitsyn began by confirming the identities of two Soviet spies the CIA and MI6 had known of but whose activities they had never been able to prove legally, and who were already safely in Russia: Guy Burgess and Donald Maclean. He then gave details of some spies who had not been unmasked, including the Briton John Vassall and a Russian double agent who had operated mostly in Germany named Aleksander Kopatzky. Vassall, a relatively low-level official at the Foreign Office, was later arrested, convicted and jailed. The case against Kopatzky was unproven and after a brief period seeking refuge in the Russian Consulate he braved it out and lived peacefully in Virginia for the rest of his days. Golitsyn also gave enough clues for the authorities, at last, to unmask Kim Philby – a spy who, having been effectively neutered a decade earlier, had arguably outlived his usefulness to the Soviets.

For Oldfield, the most relevant of the traitors was the largely anonymous Vassall. He had been the victim of the classic honeytrap, caught on camera by the KGB in homosexual trysts with a number of men. He was blackmailed into providing British secrets to the Soviets for about five years. The information he provided was disproportionate to the lowly status he held at the Foreign Office, and by betraying details of British radar, anti-submarine equipment and torpedoes he helped the Soviets to improve and modernize their navy. It was as a result of the Vassall case that henceforth MI6 vetting homed in more than ever on the question of sexuality. And the ongoing raft of information that flowed from Golitsyn was to add complexity and confusion to Maurice Oldfield's job as liaison officer in Washington at precisely the moment the Cold War was to reach its hottest.

12

Khrushchev – Kennedy – Oldfield

IN LATE JANUARY 1962, Maurice took a brief period of leave and went home to visit his family for the first time in two years, and for the first time since his father's death. Typically, though, he was not off duty for the whole time. Harold Macmillan's famous 'Wind of Change' speech in 1960, in which he'd spoken of the inevitability of the countries of the British Empire being given independence, had focused the minds of the intelligence agencies on the likely ongoing situations in the countries concerned. Both the CIA and MI6 were concerned that Africa was a prime target for the Soviets; after all it had all the hallmarks Lenin had identified as being essential for revolution – poverty, exploitation and colonialism.

During his time in England, Maurice had two interesting house guests come to visit Over Haddon. The first was remembered by the family as a 'bluff, whiskery man; a slightly tubby cartoon of a wartime RAF pilot'. Bruce Mackenzie exactly fitted that description. A South African-born farmer and adventurer, Mackenzie had served in the

RAF during the war and had come across Oldfield in Cairo. The men had kept in touch, and after the conflict Mackenzie moved to a farm in Kenya and served briefly as a minister in the colonial government, until 1961. As a guest on the farm in Derbyshire he proved popular, and like many a South African had a decent knowledge of rugby so happily discussed the sport with Maurice's nephew John Pearce, who was at the time due to take part in the final England Schoolboys trial. Mackenzie attended John's sixteenth birthday party, and enjoyed long talks with Maurice as they walked along Lathkill Dale, away from prying ears.

The second guest was already known to the family. Kenneth Skelton had been curate at St Anne's church in the last few years of the war. From there, the small, jovial Skelton had been a curate in Bolsover, a tutor at Wells Theological College and a vicar in Lancashire. At the time of his visit to Over Haddon he was an examining chaplain to the Bishop of Liverpool. Since leaving Derbyshire, Skelton had always kept in touch with Sadie Pearce by letter, and would occasionally visit for a break. During this visit, though, he would spend more time in discussions with Sadie's brother.

In February, Maurice went to London where he was updated on the case of an interesting Soviet double agent named Oleg Penkovsky, and listened in at meetings in Lancaster House where the terms of Kenya's forthcoming independence were being agreed. During this time he met the leader of the Kenya African National Union, who was thought to be odds-on favourite to become President in the post-independence elections. Oldfield described Jomo Kenyatta, who had been jailed in the Mau-Mau rebellion in 1952, as 'the most intimidating man I ever met. But it turned out he'd once worked as a farm labourer in Sussex, so we soon found some common ground.'

The family, except probably Sadie, thought little of these matters until much later. They were used to receiving interesting visitors during the course of Maurice's work at the Foreign Office, and to hearing about the personalities he met. They didn't even notice when, upon Kenyan independence, Bruce Mackenzie was appointed Minister of Agriculture by Jomo Kenyatta – it was hardly headline news. Mackenzie remained in post until 1970, for many of those years the only white face in Kenyatta's government. Under the Attlee Doctrine, MI6 was not supposed to operate in former British colonies, which were considered MI5 territory; nonetheless Oldfield ensured MI6 had a very useful Friend at the heart of the Kenyan cabinet.

The family were interested, though, when Kenneth Skelton was elected Bishop of Matabeleland within a few months of his visit to Over Haddon. 'It came as a bit of a surprise' was how the appointment was described in Skelton's obituary in the *Independent* in August 2003. It came as less of a surprise to Sadie Pearce. Skelton was a controversial figure in Matabeleland, speaking against racism and championing the rights of the black majority in his huge diocese which took in most of what was then western Rhodesia. As his obituary also records, Skelton 'threw himself into the work, driving (sometimes recklessly) around his 300,000-square-mile diocese . . . After a year he was fluent in the Sindebele language. He was deeply respected as a pastor, chairman of meetings and theologian, but clashes with the politicians became inevitable. Lardner Burke (the Law and Order minister) called him "The Devil's Advocate" for his defence of the rights of the ordinary people and announced that the government were watching him and would not hesitate to prosecute if he infringed the law. At the same time Skelton was keeping the Archbishop of Canterbury informed about the situation.'

It was suspected that Skelton was also keeping MI6 informed about the situation. That would have been impossible, as he knew that Prime Minister of Rhodesia Ian Smith's government were watching him. And as with Kenya, this was officially MI5 territory. But letters to old friends and parishioners were a different matter. For the whole period until he returned to Britain in 1970, Skelton sent coded letters to his old friend and parishioner Sadie Pearce, reporting on the unfolding political situation in Rhodesia, including the Unilateral Declaration of Independence in 1964 and, subsequently, sanction-breaking companies. It was Sadie, not Kenneth, who passed the intelligence on to MI6. It was Sadie who became the first family member to be told what her brother's real job was, and she never said a word until after the matter became public knowledge. From that point on she said even less.

Back in Washington, Maurice needed to get to grips with the Golitsyn matter, as it was to be further complicated by the intelligence being supplied by the defector's compatriot, Oleg Penkovsky. Golitsyn had gained the complete confidence of James Angleton, Oldfield's main contact in the CIA. His confirmation of what was known about Burgess and Maclean – information that was leading steadily to a denouement for Philby – and his exposure of Vassall accumulated to convince Angleton that Golitsyn's theories were infallible.

To get matters into context it is necessary to go back to early 1961, and a massive failure by the CIA. As had been the case for many of the coups and attempted coups of the previous decade, this one also came down to a new leader nationalizing assets to the detriment of a Western power. In this case, the takeover by the communist Fidel Castro as Prime Minister of the Caribbean island of Cuba in 1959 led initially to him deciding to use oil refineries in the country, owned by US companies Esso, Shell and Standard Oil, to process crude oil from the Soviet Union. When the companies refused, Castro nationalized their refineries and brought them under his control. The US retaliated by refusing to import Cuban sugar, so Castro immediately nationalized other US assets in Cuba, including banks and sugar mills.

Early in 1960 the CIA, then still under Allen Dulles, formulated a plan to overthrow Castro by fomenting unrest among the Cuban population and using exiled anti-Castro Cubans to restore the deposed Prime Minister, José Miró Cardona, to power. The plan was approved by President Eisenhower, and in April the recruitment of anti-Castro exiles began in Florida, where many of them had fled. This was the year of the presidential election in the USA, and both candidates, Vice President Richard Nixon and the Democratic hopeful John F. Kennedy, spoke powerfully about supporting the overthrow of Castro. Kennedy, though, at Nixon's request, was not fully briefed about the developing plans.

Kennedy won the election and was inaugurated in January 1961, with barely three months to go before the proposed operation was due to take place. The plan was to airdrop supplies for guerrillas in secret locations in Cuba, and for the invasion force including the trained Cuban exiles to land at the Bay of Pigs on the south of the island, shortly after a deception flight on 15 April. As far as Kennedy was concerned his hands would be clean as the whole thing would be carried out by Cuban nationals. What the CIA didn't know was that Cuban Intelligence had discovered the plot in Miami, and that Castro was well prepared. Moreover, according to David Ormsby-Gore, mutual friend of Kennedy and Oldfield, and soon to become ambassador to Washington, MI6 had also warned the CIA that they had found no major evidence of a popular uprising against Castro within Cuba. This warning had been discounted.

From where this intelligence had come – assuming Ormsby-Gore was correct – has never been stated. What is known is that Oldfield's colleague from Lady Manners School days John Purseglove was at the time Professor of Botany at the National Herbarium of Trinidad and Tobago, and in that role travelled extensively around the Caribbean, studying the horticulture of the region literally at grass-roots level. During these travels he visited Cuba. He would have met working people in the villages and farms, and he and Maurice were in regular contact. Also, in the spring of 1961, as the invasion was pending, Oldfield's passport shows he was travelling between Washington DC, Nassau in the Bahamas and Kingston, Jamaica, on a regular basis. As well as Purseglove, Oldfield had other contacts travelling around the Caribbean, not least his friend Shridath 'Sonny' Ramphal, who was then assistant Attorney General of the West Indies Federation. It could, of course, be entirely coincidental. Maurice may well have been enjoying two-day excursions in the region without gathering intelligence about what was going on – but given his record that would seem unlikely.

On the 15th, as planned, the deception flight over Cuba took place, and the Cuban Foreign Minister, Raúl Roa, tabled a complaint to the United Nations about the US using aggressive air tactics against his country. The US Ambassador to the UN, Adlai Stevenson, stated that any attacks had been undertaken by Cuban nationals and that no US military personnel had been, or would become, involved. The Bay of Pigs invasion started, again as planned, on 17 April, with CIA operatives assisting the Cuban exiles. Within three days it was thwarted by Castro's troops, to the intense embarrassment of the new President. A report into the matter identified shortcomings all along the line, including the CIA failing adequately to assess the risks, failing to involve the Cuban exile leaders, failing to foment a resistance within Cuba, failing to ensure there was sufficient intelligence on the Cuban forces, and a lack of contingency planning, including deniability. After a period trying to rebut the findings, early in 1962 Allen Dulles, his deputy Charles Cabell, and Deputy Director for Plans Richard Bissell were all forced to resign. Thereafter Kennedy was, if still committed to the removal of Castro, a good deal more cautious of which approach to take, and of the reliability of the CIA.

Colonel Oleg Penkovsky was an officer of the GRU, the Soviet overseas intelligence agency – the MI6 or CIA to the KGB's MI5 or FBI. He wanted to be, and should have been, a coup for the CIA. In June 1960 he had approached a group of American students as they walked across the Moskvoretsky Bridge near Red Square in Moscow and handed them a letter with instructions to take it without delay to the American Embassy. With more than a hint of nervousness, one of the students delivered the letter as requested. It gave details of how an American pilot, Gary Powers, had been shot down in his U2 spy plane as he carried out a reconnaissance mission over what was then known as Sverdlovsk in south central Russia, and captured, just the previous month.

Penkovsky stated in the letter that he would provide further information, but given the dangerous atmosphere on the streets of Moscow this would have to be done by dead-drop to protect the couriers from the all-seeing eye of the KGB. In this case the method would be for the CIA agent to make a chalk mark at a selected phone box when he was ready to receive the drop; Penkovsky would then deposit a package and make himself scarce, so there was no connection between the two. Of course this had all the hallmarks of a trap, or of the Soviets planting a false defector – but it was also too good an opportunity to miss.

Unfortunately there was a slight technicality: at that time the CIA had no operatives in Moscow. The first one they tried to get to work with Penkovsky failed. Codenamed COMPASS, the young officer found it difficult to cope with the pressures of the case and the intrigue of the city and turned to paranoia and drink. An attempt to link Penkovsky and an American businessman at a trade fair also failed. But at the same event the Russian did make contact with a British businessman named Greville Wynne – and luckily this was the same Greville Wynne, a Welshman with a carefully manufactured upper-class English accent for business purposes, who had recently been asked by Arthur 'Dickie' Franks of MI6 if he wouldn't mind doing his bit for his country on one of his trade visits to Moscow. When MI6 and the CIA realized they were both talking to the same man it was decided to run him jointly.

It was arranged that Penkovsky, who was going to continue officially working for the GRU, would suggest to his masters bringing a trade delegation to Britain as cover for some espionage. While at the delegation's hotel he would slip away to a pre-prepared room to meet the Allied intelligence officers. As a joint operation, with so potentially important an agent as Penkovsky to handle, it was decided that two officers from each agency should be involved in establishing whether or not he was genuine. For the CIA, two officers of Eastern European ancestry were selected: George Kisevalter, whose parents had come to America from Russia in 1915 to buy weapons for the Tsar and stayed when the Bolshevik uprising blew up, and Joe Bulik, a Russian speaker of Slovakian origin. MI6 selected a young officer named Michael Stokes to accompany the legendary Harry Shergold, fresh from his triumph over George Blake.

Now, with the CIA needing a result after the Bay of Pigs disaster and MI6 wary of a Soviet plant after Blake's imprisonment, the stakes were very high indeed. At the meeting, Penkovsky started by complaining that it had taken a long time for the British and Americans to meet him. After it was explained that it was simply down to ensuring the setting was secure, he said he would have about two hours before he was missed by his comrades. They started by trying to ascertain his bona fides, his ancestry and career path, and why he wanted to share intelligence with the West – to become 'a soldier of Queen Elizabeth and President Kennedy' as Penkovsky put it.

Having completed that procedure and established that he was a high-ranking military officer with supreme access to the most sensitive military intelligence at this most terrifying period of the Cold War, Penkovsky launched what amounted to a blitzkrieg of information at the four officers. The Western world had become convinced that a 'missile gap' had opened up with Khrushchev comfortably in the lead, and that he was hell-bent on world domination. According to Penkovsky this couldn't be further from the truth. The Soviet leader's glib comment that he had so many weapons that he was melting some of them down to make tractors was just bluster. In fact, according to Penkovsky the Soviets were way behind and in no position to start any kind of military campaign – though Khrushchev would certainly like to, and the West needed to act within the next two to three years to ensure he didn't.

For those two hours Penkovsky had to spare, and then a bit, the team was almost dumbfounded by what they heard. Only maybe a third of the millions of Communist Party members were active and committed, there was no appetite for war, and young Russians were disaffected and rioting for food. In other words the propaganda about the wonderful life in Mother Russia was just that, propaganda.

Penkovsky concluded this first meeting by asking to swear an oath of allegiance, but such things didn't carry an awful lot of weight in the world of international espionage. Instead, the following day, at the next meeting, he signed a contract confirming that he would be bound henceforth to betray his homeland. Two more days of interrogation followed during which the Russian was shown over seven thousand photographs from which he was able to identify around seven hundred GRU or KGB officers, some of them working out of the Russian Embassy in London. After that Penkovsky and his fellow 'businessmen' were due to head to Leeds for the next trade fair on their tour. Greville Wynne drove Penkovsky north and nearly lost the man, firstly by giving him a beer so cold it sent his kidneys into spasm, and then with an incident involving a revolving door and a confused Russian at the hotel.

Further talks followed in which it became clear that Penkovsky was dazzled by the trappings of Western capitalism. Michael Stokes was sent off to shop for suits and shirts at Harrods, the Americans agreed to pay $1,000 per month into an escrow account for the Russian, while Shergy, in charge of MI6 finances, gave Wynne the occasional £50 for himself and Alex from Belgrade (as Penkovsky was being introduced) to have nights out at clubs with dancing girls. The team also gave their star spy luxury goods, unavailable in Moscow, for him to take back to soften up his GRU chiefs – alongside the carefully vetted intelligence he was sent back with to ensure they could see his time was being well spent.

Penkovsky was keen to trade on his importance, and demanded to see the Queen, the Prime Minister or Lord Mountbatten. In MI6 it was a rare treat for a defector or even an officer to get as far as meeting the Chief, let alone royalty, but Dick White was wheeled out to meet Penkovsky and soothe his ego with platitudes about how pleased the Queen was with his efforts and how sorry Lord Mountbatten was not to be able to visit him. 'Alex' agreed to be that most valuable and rare of things, a spy who stays in his own country and continues to supply intelligence, so he was returned to Moscow with a tiny Minox camera and a plan arranged by Shergy to enable the flow of material to continue.

The Station Chief in Moscow, Ruari Chisholm, and his wife, Janet, would deal with the matter. The idea was that Mrs Chisholm would, at an appointed time and place in a Moscow park, stroll with her children, one of them in a pushchair. As Penkovsky wandered by, he would reach down to look at the youngest child and give it a little sweetie box – containing a film of intelligence gold. The first film was handed over on 2 July 1961, and by the 11th it had been communicated to JFK, so important was it considered to be. This happened time and again, sometimes in the park, sometimes at an apartment block. The risk to Janet Chisholm and her children was huge, not least because the Chisholms had known George Blake and, though they didn't know it then, had already been identified by him as spies.

On the 18th Penkovsky was back in London for a trade exhibition at Earls Court and another session with his inquisitors. He gave more details about the Soviets' planning and thought processes (it was all very well knowing about their military hardware, but what they planned to do with it was just as important in the Cold War poker game between Khrushchev and Kennedy). The information being provided by Penkovsky should have given Kennedy the advantage – if what he was being told was true.

The transcripts and recordings of the MI6 and CIA inter- views were sent to Washington by Dick White, together with the opinions of the team members. Shergold had told White that Penkovsky was unstable and motivated by vanity; White agreed, and added that he felt the star spy was neurotic, highly risky and crazy – but there was no doubt that the intelligence being provided was possibly the most valuable that had ever come their way.

And therein lay the problem. In Washington, Maurice Oldfield, with his highly tuned feeling for these things, was convinced that Penkovsky was absolutely the real thing – 'the answer to a prayer' was how he put it. The bluster and performance the Russian was putting on in terms of his wanting to swear fealty to the Queen and President Kennedy was clearly done as an attempt to prove himself, but Oldfield felt that while it was clumsy and over the top that didn't mean it wasn't genuine. This was a man who was impressed by trappings, titles and material goods and expected others to be the same. It was a bit gauche, maybe, but that didn't mean it was fake.

James Angleton, in contrast, believed that Penkovsky was a plant, and a dangerous one at that – one that could be trying to give the Americans a false sense of security that could inspire them to go to war with the Soviets. The Americans argued that Penkovsky should be made to take a lie detector test. Dick White felt that would just cause Penkovsky to mistrust his new friends, and added that he mistrusted the technique itself. Oldfield knew perfectly well the device's limitations and didn't disagree with his Chief. He was left in the position of having been given a brief to butter up Angleton and listen to his theories when he was already at odds with them.

The first test of how the President would react to the intelligence he was being given came in August 1961. In June, at a summit in Vienna, Khrushchev had told Kennedy that he intended to isolate West Berlin – something Penkovsky had stated in intelligence he had provided. The

Soviet leader added that if the USA interfered then he was ready for a war. Kennedy replied that it would be 'a cold winter of war' in that case. On the 13th, undetected by the CIA and MI6 and at a time when Penkovsky couldn't make emergency contact, the East-West border in Berlin was closed and work started with concrete and barbed wire to build the Berlin Wall. It was an intelligence failure, but Penkovsky's report, when it arrived, confirmed that he'd predicted what had happened – it had just arrived too late.

Another test came on 1 September when, despite having promised not to, the Soviets exploded an atomic bomb in remote central Asia. There were calls for America to retaliate, but Kennedy resisted, beginning to believe that Penkovsky was right and that Khrushchev's posturing was all a bluff to try to protect his own position. The Soviet threat was not as great as they liked to make out.

The biggest, most important test was yet to come, however, and Penkovsky's days as the so-called spy who saved the world were numbered. The Cuban Missile Crisis of late 1962 was probably the period during which the world at large became most acutely aware of what was happening in the Cold War. Such was the tension, fuelled by the media, that the general public really did feel as though it was on the brink of nuclear Armageddon. Even in schools in remotest Derbyshire it was the talk of the dinner queue, taking the pupils' minds off the Beatles. John Pearce remembered friends at Lady Manners School saying, 'Isn't your uncle in Washington? Doesn't he know what's going on?' People were convinced that nuclear war was inevitable.

John's uncle had as good an idea as anyone about what was going on. By the summer of 1962 Oleg Penkovsky had been codenamed HERO, and it was Maurice Oldfield's job to be the conduit for the voluminous intelligence HERO was providing. He was faced by scepticism on both sides, particularly from some American hawks among whom the received wisdom was that the Soviets were still well ahead in the arms race. And when the intelligence agencies were providing information that contradicted that received wisdom, telling their political masters what they didn't want to hear, it made Oldfield's job all the more challenging.

There's a near parallel here with the notorious Iraqi weapons of mass destruction episode and the so-called 'dodgy dossier' of 2002. In both cases the Western governments were convinced that their enemy had a vast arsenal of weaponry. In both cases there was a young, charismatic leader, the people surrounding them anxious to please. As a retired MI6 officer explained to me, 'If I was working for a government which appeared to be energized and had the popular mood and world opinion right behind them, can I honestly say that I wouldn't try and make my reports fit with what they wanted them to say? I can't be sure. Certainly colleagues who were working in the Blair era now freely admit that they were caught up in the excitement.'

The President had so far taken a cautious view, inclining towards believing in Penkovsky, but the Cuban Missile Crisis was to test that. The crisis had its roots in the fact that Khrushchev knew the balance of nuclear power was in the Americans' favour, even if they didn't. He had missiles that could reach the USA from Russia, but that basically amounted to the ability to wipe out Alaska; the political centres of the East Coast were way out of his reach. Furthermore there was the Berlin question, which as far as the British were concerned was at that stage still the issue Penkovsky's material was being used to assess. David Cornwell, stationed in Germany at the time, recalls Maurice Oldfield flying in from Washington to the MI6 station near Bonn to brief his team on an operation they were planning against the Soviets in Berlin. 'Maurice was by then already a legend in the Service,' said Cornwell. 'He talked us through the mechanics of the proposed operation with such clarity and precision that we all had total confidence. As it transpired the plan was never implemented – but there was nothing unusual in that.' Khrushchev had made his feelings clear on having the Americans and the British in Berlin – far too close for comfort. And then there was the fact that, unknown to most in the West, the US had missiles, albeit outdated ones, stationed in Italy and Turkey that were pointing straight at Russia.

What Khrushchev did have was an ally in the Caribbean by the name of Fidel Castro. Castro's Cuban Army had seen off one American invasion in the Bay of Pigs, but there was every chance that another might be mounted and that this one might be more successful. So Castro allowed Khrushchev to build nuclear missile sites on Cuba, ostensibly to defend his country; but of course from Cuba the Soviets could strike at the US from a strong position. Starting in June 1962, ships containing missile constructors and soldiers disguised as irrigation workers or machine operators started to arrive in Cuba; by July there were forty-three thousand troops on the island. Then the missiles started to arrive, and when questioned, the Cuban government stated that they were allowing the Soviets to station 'defensive missiles only'.

By now the CIA and MI6 had agreed to disagree over their ongoing use of Penkovsky. The CIA wanted to slow things down for fear the Russian might be detected; MI6 felt they had to run with him because of the volume and quality of material he provided. He thrived on it; to slow him down would be to lose him as an agent. The CIA favoured keeping him sweet with cash, gifts and platitudes; MI6 figured that an agent suddenly having funds beyond his status would attract the wrong kind of attention and wanted to keep the relationship low-key and professional. The courier Greville Wynne claimed the demands of dealing with Penkovsky were affecting his business and asked for more cash. The CIA felt he was the weakest part of the operation as he was a willing amateur, not trained in intelligence tradecraft.

But they continued to use the material their star agent provided. When it was noticed that the alignment of the defensive surface-to-air missiles was in the same pattern as the Soviets used to guard their inter-continental missile bases, they used Penkovsky's intelligence, collected by Janet Chisholm in a dangerous Moscow exchange, to identify the actual weapons present as medium-range ballistic missiles – not the defensive kind the Soviets had claimed were there, and not the inter-continental ones which were most feared, but with a potential range of 3,500 kilometres. The east coast of America was certainly under threat.

Before 1962 the US government had never truly believed that Castro would allow Khrushchev to station a missile base on Cuba, and consequently they had no real plan in place to deal with that eventuality. Now, in October 1962, they had to face the reality head on. They considered various options, ranging from doing nothing to a full invasion of Cuba. On the 18th, Kennedy met with Soviet Foreign Minister Andrei Gromyko, who when challenged claimed, again, that the missiles were defensive. Kennedy didn't need a polygraph to know that Gromyko was lying, but so as not to alarm the public he carried on with his normal business.

Kennedy's military advisers, the Joint Chiefs of Staff, were by now unanimous in their view that the only option was a full-scale invasion of Cuba. They simply didn't believe that when it came down to it the Soviets would try to stop an invasion, and furthermore they regarded the presence of the missiles on Cuba as tilting the balance of power in the communists' favour. It came down, in the end, to a choice between an invasion and instigating a naval blockade to prevent further shipments of missiles to Cuba.

The President favoured a blockade. He felt sure that an invasion of Cuba would lead directly to the Soviets invading Berlin – and, taking a world view, Berlin was more strategically important than Cuba, which would be more of an irritant than a threat if the missiles could be removed. The advice he was receiving from the CIA, after its analysis of Penkovsky's intelligence, continued to suggest that the Chiefs of Staff were wrong, that the balance of power remained on his side and that Khrushchev was trying to create a reaction that would enable him to take Berlin. What Kennedy needed was trusted intelligence to back up his own hunches.

It is here that there has been some controversy over Maurice Oldfield's involvement in the crisis. The biographer Richard Deacon stated in 1984 that 'it was his [Oldfield's] advice, his steady advocacy of Penkovsky, and his ability to get speedy answers to Kennedy's persistent questioning on technical matters which more than anything else enabled the Cuban threat to be dealt with in the most practical manner. Oldfield's own part in all this, how he not only obtained personal access to the President to stress the value of Penkovsky's evidence, but ensured that Kennedy had an independent scientific opinion and interpretation of the situation from the British side, was absolutely vital.' But this statement has been widely dismissed as an exaggeration, the fact that Ray Cline of the CIA initially let the British think that Berlin rather than Cuba was the Americans' priority a key justification for taking that view, along with the lack of documentary evidence for Kennedy speaking with Oldfield.

As is often the case, the truth would appear to be somewhere in the middle; Deacon was probably not entirely right, and the sceptics were not entirely wrong. Given Oldfield's adeptness at acting on a personal as well as professional level, his opinions were sought both privately and officially. To add a specialist view to back up what Penkovsky's evidence had been suggesting in September 1962, Maurice flew back to London for meetings with Geoffrey Wheeler and David Footman. Wheeler, a specialist on Central Asia, was widely used as a consultant on Soviet matters in the region; Footman was an acknowledged expert on Soviet communism. Oldfield was also in touch on a personal level with three of Kennedy's closest advisers. Dean Acheson, the former Secretary of State, and a notable hawk, firmly in the 'invasion' ranks, was one – but he was dispatched to Paris to try (successfully) to garner support from Charles de Gaulle for whatever action was decided upon, so is unlikely to have had the President's ear at the time. More interestingly, Oldfield's notes show that during these days he was in regular contact with Paul Nitse, the Assistant Defense Secretary – whose boss, Robert McNamara, was a supporter of the blockade proposal, the position adopted by those tending to believe in Penkovsky. By speaking directly with Nitse, Oldfield would have been able to bypass the sceptical Angleton and offer his view without having to compromise. And Ray Cline, despite the initial and understandable reluctance to be fully open with MI6, was both friendly with Oldfield and receptive to his interpretation of Penkovsky's material. Cline and his boss, John McCone, the main intelligence presence among Kennedy's advisers, were both supporters of the blockade. At the National Security Council meeting on 20 October 1962, by which time Oldfield was fully in the picture about the Cuban situation, the lead item on the agenda was Ray Cline's intelligence briefing – and the lead item in that briefing was pictorial evidence of the missiles identified using Penkovsky's material.

So through direct contact with some of Kennedy's inner circle, and as the official conduit of HERO's intelligence, Oldfield was able to reinforce his advocacy of Penkovsky and aid the thought processes that would lead to the peaceful outcome. But what of Deacon's assertion of Oldfield's *direct* access to Kennedy being the crucial factor? That is far from clear cut. Deacon may have had sources that are no longer available, so I can only relate what was told to the family by Maurice's long-time bodyguard, assistant and confidant Ken Dyer – a large, no-nonsense former soldier and Special Branch officer not given to hyperbole whose admiration for Oldfield was total – shortly after the crisis was resolved, and let readers make up their own minds. Dyer said that he had been bottling it up since returning from a spell working for Maurice in America in the autumn of 1962, but with the crisis now over, he felt he could speak. It was the one and only 'business' matter Dyer ever discussed publicly.

'It was Maurice,' Dyer said. 'He did that. It was on about 20 October, some time in the morning. We were in Maurice's office, and he took a call from the President. I knew they were acquainted, but I don't think even Maurice expected a personal phone call. The President asked Maurice to confirm whether in his view the intelligence they were receiving from the Russian [Penkovsky] was accurate. After giving a bit of detail, Maurice said that in his view yes, it was.'

What is beyond question is that Oldfield was the official conduit for the most important source of Soviet intelligence during the Cuban Missile Crisis, and that he executed that role with his customary skill. In the context of mistrust and tensions between the CIA and MI6 it was a juggling job that involved having to agree with the much-vaunted counter-intelligence expert James Angleton while disagreeing with him, and being considered the junior partner in the inter-agency relations. It was therefore quite an achievement. In terms of saving the world Maurice's role might have been small, but given the American Chiefs of Staff's overwhelming preference for an invasion of Cuba and the potentially terrifying chain of events such an action might have triggered, it was important.

At that National Security Council meeting on the 20th it was resolved to impose a blockade to stop further missiles reaching Cuba. Kennedy set up a smaller group to advise on the crisis, the Executive Committee of the National Security Council (EXCOMM), which was made up of people whose opinions ranged across the spectrum from all-out invasion to a more doveish approach. Even with an official position agreed, things were delicately poised and tensions continued to grow as Kennedy prepared to issue his ultimatum to Khrushchev.

On the 22nd, the President addressed the American nation to confirm that Soviet missiles had been deployed on Cuba. He called Harold Macmillan to apprise him of the situation and tell him he was proposing a blockade. He then wrote to Khrushchev, stating that though he was taking the minimum action required, he was 'determined that this threat to the security of this hemisphere be removed'.

For the men who had made Kennedy's actions possible, though, 22 October was not such a great day. Oleg Penkovsky was snatched from a Moscow street by KGB thugs and placed under arrest. Under extreme duress and begging for his life he gave up his accomplices. A few days later at a trade fair in Budapest, Greville Wynne was arrested, handcuffed and spirited to Moscow. He was tried and sentenced to eight years in jail, eventually being released in 1964 in exchange for 'Gordon Lonsdale'. Ruari and Janet Chisholm were deported for 'indulging in activities inconsistent with their diplomatic status'.

As for Penkovsky, despite knowing what his fate would be, the heads of MI6 and the CIA dismissed any suggestion that they ought to do the right thing by arguably their greatest ever spy and try to engineer a way out for him, even if by blackmail. As Dick White put it, 'The British always deny involvement in espionage. There was no reason for the Soviets to release Penkovsky, a Russian national, just as we would not release Blake.' In May 1963, Penkovsky was sentenced to death, and shot at Lubyanka Prison in Moscow.

Kennedy's blockade was imposed on the 23rd and, in an

important piece of semantics, swiftly renamed 'quarantine': a blockade could be considered an act of war, a quarantine could not. The following day Khrushchev replied with indignation: 'You, Mr President, are not declaring a quarantine, but rather are setting forth an ultimatum and threatening that if we do not give in to your demands you will use force. Consider what you are saying! And you want to persuade me to agree to this! What would it mean to agree to these demands? It would mean guiding oneself in one's relations with other countries not by reason, but by submitting to arbitrariness. You are no longer appealing to reason, but wish to intimidate us.'

By the 25th the Americans knew it was likely that at least some of the missiles on Cuba were operational, and given Khrushchev's belligerent riposte the world's press continued to hike the tension. The UN Secretary General, U Thant, appealed for Kennedy to allow a cooling-off period; the President refused as this would leave the missiles in place. The 26th saw Fidel Castro urge Khrushchev to strike first if the US invaded Cuba – but he suggested some conciliatory communication too. A member of the Soviet Embassy staff approached an ABC News reporter with a proposal, which was soon echoed in a rambling letter from Khrushchev to Kennedy offering to remove the missiles in return for the Americans lifting the quarantine and agreeing not to invade Cuba. The brinkmanship continued the following day as Khrushchev added a requirement for the US to remove missiles from Turkey as part of his demands, and an American U2 surveillance plane was shot down over Cuba.

The Americans decided to ignore the more aggressive letter and reply instead to the conciliatory one. The

President's brother, Robert Kennedy, met with the Soviet Ambassador in an attempt to agree draft terms for a settlement. On the 28th, it was all over. Khrushchev wrote to Kennedy accepting the terms. The world had stepped back from the precipice, and never again would the Cold War get quite so close to a terminal explosion. British Intelligence, and its representative in Washington at the time, had played a small but important role in ensuring the Cold War remained just that.

The facing down of Khrushchev was not, for Maurice Oldfield, the end of his interest in Cuba. After all, Castro was still in power, as was Khrushchev, and there was no guarantee that tensions would not be strained again; relations between the communist personalities were still potentially crucial. Maurice spent much of 1963 travelling between Ottawa, Washington, the Caribbean and Mexico City, taking soundings from his usual contacts including the spymaster John Starnes in Canada, John Purseglove in the Caribbean, and Sonny Ramphal in general.

In Mexico City, scene of Fidel and Raúl Castro's plotting with Che Guevara to seize power in Cuba four years previously, Oldfield's notes show him providing an agent identified only as 'Dick' with a James Bondesque, briefcase-sized device that was able to record conversations over a radius of five hundred yards 'or longer with an antenna', and dispatching 'Dick' to the Hotel Monte Cassino to listen in on an anticipated conversation between the communist leaders. Maurice followed this by liaising with a group of left-sympathizing American students – quite possibly without their knowing his role – led by activists Levi Laub and Vicki Ortiz and a thirty-seven-year-old Cuban architect, already well known in the country as Head of Design at the National Art School, named Ricardo Porro (whose wife, according to Oldfield's hand-written notes, was a suspected communist), who had been invited to meet Fidel Castro and Che Guevara. Hidden in the student group, which had to fly a tortuous route to Havana via Prague due to the limited air access to the Cuban capital, was a CIA agent, Barry Hoffman, who had been briefed by Oldfield.

That the students were impressed by Castro and Guevara is perhaps unsurprising (they were later charged with unAmerican activities even for going to listen to these revolutionaries). As regards Maurice Oldfield, Cuba in 1963 showed him sanctioning what would have been, if publicly known, controversial means in order to obtain crucial intelligence in a potential war zone – as would be the case in Northern Ireland years later. To Maurice's subtle mind, the important thing these well-meaning young activists found out was that by 1963 even Guevara was disassociating himself from the USSR. It was a symbol of a break in relations between this key island, so close and supposedly so threatening to America, and its previously belligerent Eastern European sponsor that was perhaps even more (if discreetly so) important than the end of the Cuban Missile Crisis.

13

Mesmerized by Moles

WHILE OLDFIELD'S TIME in Washington was supposedly being spent cultivating relations with the CIA, he also took the opportunity to extend his global network and find other ways to increase MI6's influence. One outcome of the CIA's and MI6's aggressive regime change operations, successful or otherwise, was to make it more difficult for the agencies to operate in certain areas, notably in the Middle East. So while working out of his Washington base, Oldfield didn't limit himself to CIA-centric activities; he travelled extensively, made wider friendships in the non-political world, and used imaginative means to get MI6 agents where they needed to be.

In terms of building friendships, as usual Maurice started in the church. He became involved with the Church of the Ascension and St Agnes on Massachusetts Avenue, not far from his home and office, and typically got to know all strands of the diverse congregation. He would host parties at his house on Waterside Drive, and, as he had in Singapore, allowed young people introduced by the church to lodge with him from time to time. Maurice had grown up in a tiny house, packed with young people, and was imbued with the Christian value of sharing as readily and naturally as he was taught walking, talking and manners. It was part of him, and he would have thought nothing of sharing a big house with people who needed it. Though no secret, and no surprise to those who visited Maurice and knew him well, his kindness was to cause trouble for him eventually.

Regarding his aims to improve the reach of MI6, Oldfield targeted the Canadian intelligence network, notably the intelligence arm of their Department of External Affairs. He built a range of influential links with the Canadians, who had better access in countries where the Americans and British were regarded with suspicion. His closest contact was John Kennet Starnes, who had a formidable track record in anti-Soviet counterintelligence, and who was at the time head of the Canadians' military mission in that most prominent of Cold War postings, Berlin. Oldfield's connection with Starnes and his colleagues gave MI6 a useful extra source of intelligence not just from the Berlin station, but from parts of the Middle East where, again, officials of Canada's Department of External Affairs were more welcome than their British and American counterparts. Oldfield would visit Ottawa on a regular basis to be kept apprised of developments.

Oldfield tried – but failed – to use his Canadian contacts to install an appropriate economist in the government of British Guiana (later Guyana), where the Prime Minister, Cheddi Jagan, was felt to have Marxist views that needed tempering. That problem was resolved when Jagan failed to win a majority in the 1964 general election and the British and Americans helped ensure that a coalition under Forbes Burnham took office.

On 8 May 1963, as the film version of *Dr No* was having its North American premiere and viewers were watching Sean Connery's James Bond have dinner with the CIA's Felix Leiter in a Jamaican harbourside restaurant, Maurice Oldfield was dining with the West Indies' Attorney General, Sonny Ramphal, in a Jamaican harbourside restaurant. Oldfield's influence was felt when Ramphal became Attorney General in Guyana in 1965 – a useful Friend in South America at the time of Guyana's independence. Ramphal was to go on to become Minister for External Affairs and then, when Maurice had become Chief of MI6, Secretary General of the Commonwealth from 1975.

A disproportionate amount of time, though, was spent dealing with James Angleton and the constant voice in his ear, Anatoliy Golitsyn. Golitsyn had come up with a number of leads on Soviet penetration of intelligence services in France, Germany, America and – of most interest to Oldfield – Britain. In Britain, according to the Russian, this conveniently backed up the belief of MI6 Chief Dick White that a ring of five British spies, all recruited at the same time and place, had been operating against their own country. Burgess and Maclean were two of them, and though Golitsyn hadn't identified him personally, White was more than a little suspicious that Kim Philby was the third.

John Vassall, the spy who had fallen for the homosexual honeytrap, was not thought to be one of the five (he had never even been for a day trip to Cambridge), and his very public arrest did not find favour with the Prime Minister. When the head of MI5, Roger Hollis, proudly revealed to

Harold Macmillan that Vassall had been arrested, the response was not what he expected. 'When my gamekeeper shoots a fox, he doesn't go and hang it up outside the Master of the Hunt's drawing room, he buries it out of sight,' the PM said. 'But you can't just shoot a spy as you did in the war. You have to *try* and catch him, but it's better to discover him, and then control him. But never catch him.' That approach would seem to concur with Maurice Oldfield's view of such matters: it was far better to control, and hopefully turn, a spy than to apprehend him. There was a kind of martyrdom associated with the Blakes, Burgesses and Macleans of the world, a sort of anti-hero status that brought endless media fascination. This was the era of the satire boom, and the end of any kind of reverence towards politicians. A Prime Minister like Macmillan, who seemed of a bygone age, had been ripe fodder for the likes of Peter Cook, and spy scandals gave programmes such as *That Was The Week That Was* endless material.

Over in Beirut, Kim Philby had forged a new life for himself, more or less permanently sozzled, with a third wife, Eleanor, and a few journalistic jobs to keep him in drink. He'd also renewed contact with the KGB and had started to feed them what snippets he could about life, politics and opinions in the Middle East. It was the journalism that was to be his final undoing. Writing for the *Observer*, Philby had produced some articles that were felt to be anti-Israeli in tone. Taking exception to this, in October 1962 Flora Solomon, a Russian-born Zionist who had known Aileen Philby since her Marks & Spencer days and who had in fact introduced Aileen to Kim, complained to a distant relative, Lord Victor Rothschild, that the *Observer* was using a known communist as a foreign correspondent. She went on to relate that she was fairly sure Philby and a friend of his, Tomas Harris, had been Soviet agents in the 1930s. Victor Rothschild had been at Cambridge with Guy Burgess and Philby, had served in MI5 during the war, and was a good friend of Maurice Oldfield's. No doubt embarrassed at having previously provided the Champagne for Philby's trip to America, Rothschild reported the matter to Arthur Martin of MI5, and Martin, Roger Hollis and Dick White, after interviewing Flora, agreed that this amounted, if not to firm evidence, then certainly to something new that could be put to Philby. The question was how. White had been expressly told by Macmillan to 'keep a lid on things'; the last thing the Prime Minister wanted was another spy trial and more foxes hanging outside his drawing room. The matter needed to be dealt with quietly, and away from London.

The Prime Minister agreed to White's suggestion that Philby be confronted in Beirut, and then Harris wherever he was. Harris was in fact to die in a car accident, in mysterious circumstances, the following year in Majorca, just before MI5 got to him. As there was no court-worthy evidence against Philby, there was no prospect of a conviction so it was agreed that he would be treated as a gentleman and offered immunity from prosecution in return for a full confession and complete cooperation. The original plan was that Martin of MI5 would travel to Beirut, but then it was felt that Philby would be more likely to unburden himself to a sympathetic friend than to someone he would see as a lower-middle-class policeman.

MI6's Station Chief in Beirut, Peter Lunn, who had met Philby from time to time in the city, set up the meeting. It was to be held at the flat of an embassy secretary not far from the beach – an informal chat with the carrot of a possibility of future work to appeal to Philby's wallet and his vanity. At four p.m. on 12 January 1963, Philby showed no surprise when rather than Lunn opening the door to him it was his old friend and stoutest defender Nicholas Elliott. 'I rather thought it might be you,' was Philby's cool comment. Elliott told the traitor that the game was up; they had new information and this had come from the KGB. The recent, highly publicized conviction of Blake and defection of Golitsyn convinced Philby that his old friend might very well be right. 'I once looked up to you,' said Elliott. 'My God how I despise you now. I hope you've got enough decency left to understand why.'

As Philby sat there showing little emotion, Elliott outlined the lifeline he was offering in terms of immunity. Then he detailed the sanctions his friend would face if he refused: his bank accounts would be frozen and any other bank he tried would refuse his business, he would be denied residency permits for anywhere in the Western world, and his newspaper contracts would be finished. Life for the urbane English gentleman would become extremely tedious if not impossible in any practical sense.

Philby agreed to the proposal. Elliott sent a telegram to Dick White, updating him with the news that Philby was broken. For the next few days elation reigned at MI6, and in Beirut Philby and Elliott talked, dined and drank. Philby swore that he had not betrayed any secrets since 1949. After four days, a couple of incidents when a smashed Philby had to be peeled from the floor after refuelling on whisky, and hours of Elliott listening to Philby without really learning very much, White felt confident enough to summon Elliott back to London and leave matters in the hands of Peter Lunn. Having listened in on the recorded conversations, White concurred with Elliott's view that having confessed, Philby would remain in Beirut for further questioning.

The reality of Elliott's departure and being left in the hands of Lunn gave Philby pause for thought. What did this 'immunity' he'd been offered mean in practice? For how long would his anonymity be protected? And once it was blown, then what? It didn't take long for Philby to do a personal risk assessment and set in train the escape route his Soviet controllers had in place for just such a moment. On 23 January, Philby told Eleanor he was off to meet a contact and would be home by six to change for dinner with a Foreign Office official. Within hours Kim was dressed as a Russian sailor on board a hastily departing freight ship, and a frantic Mrs Philby was phoning Peter Lunn to say 'Kim's gone'. Not long after that, Elliott was summoned from the Congo (his next stop after his prematurely triumphant return to London) and sent to Beirut to speak with Eleanor, only to find he'd been beaten to it by a KGB officer who'd failed to persuade her to follow her husband to Moscow.

As the headlines screamed about yet another missing spy, in Washington Maurice Oldfield was doing his best to calm his colleagues in the CIA and the FBI as they raged about the Philby affair. Oldfield contacted Dick White to convey bad news: the special relationship had been set back again, and J. Edgar Hoover of the FBI was particularly aggrieved. White flew to Washington to take the flak personally. It helped, but there was no escaping the Americans' conclusion: MI6 had more or less contrived to allow Philby to escape. The one saving grace amid all the press furore was that thanks to

MI6 not existing in any official sense, hardly anyone was aware of exactly how senior an officer Philby had been. It was a small mercy.

Henceforth, at White's insistence, Oldfield was told to ingratiate himself still further with the CIA, and with James Angleton in particular.

Thanks to Philby, Golitsyn and Angleton, 1963 would become known as the year of the mole – and the confusion and creeping paranoia generated by the mole hunt would infect the intelligence services for another decade. The unmasking of Philby only served to raise Golitsyn's currency, despite his not actually having named the man, and Arthur Martin of MI5 flew to Washington to join Oldfield and Angleton in analysing his theories. In the spring of 1963 Golitsyn was told of the Penkovsky affair, and after studying the files he declared that the West's super spy was a fake, a KGB plant that was part of a wider scheme of Soviet disinformation. Angleton, who had only been persuaded of Penkovsky's bona fides by the likes of Oldfield, saw this as vindication. Work began on analysing Golitsyn's list of suspected moles, about 150 of them, and agencies around the world turned themselves inside out instead of seeking intelligence. The sudden death of the moderate British Labour Party leader Hugh Gaitskell was in Golitsyn's view the work of the KGB's poisoning department. His replacement as Labour leader, Harold Wilson, was, by the same token, a KGB agent of influence. The Sino-Soviet split, which had been festering since Stalin's death ten years previously as Russian and Chinese differences became increasingly marked and had come to the point of a total break in relations when Chairman Mao criticized Khrushchev for backing down in the Cuban Missile Crisis, was dismissed by Golitsyn as a fake, a ruse to deceive the West. For now at least, Oldfield went along with these theories, whether sincerely swept away by Angleton's enthusiasm or because he needed to in order to improve Anglo-American relations.

Angleton was so committed to Golitsyn that he felt British Intelligence as a whole would benefit from a dose of his theorizing, and he persuaded Oldfield and Martin to arrange for the Ukrainian to be invited to London. Maurice was probably quite glad to see the back of the defector, who could sometimes be arrogant and unpleasant, and equally glad to be out of England at the same time, March 1963, when news broke of a tangled love triangle including a Russian naval attaché, an attractive twenty-one-year-old girl and a married Tory Cabinet minister.

The so-called Profumo affair might have fizzled out had the Secretary of State for War not lied in the House of Commons about his relationship with Christine Keeler. As it was, John Profumo's denial of any impropriety with Miss Keeler sent the media into a frenzy, which uncovered the whole sordid business and the potential security risk when it emerged that the Soviet, Yevgeny Ivanov, had been identified by Oleg Penkovsky as a GRU agent, and that Ivanov and Profumo had shared Keeler as a lover. Ivanov had been targeted by MI5 as a potential defector. The man who had introduced the trio, Stephen Ward, known as a 'society osteopath', had been cultivated by MI5 as a route to Ivanov, and had organized parties at Cliveden House, home of Lord Astor.

In a period during which spy stories were all over the papers, this one had it all. Russian spies, exotic girls, Cabinet ministers, class, glamour – it had scandal written all over it. By the end of the year the episode had cost Profumo his job and his reputation, and Ward his life – officially by means of a self-induced barbiturates overdose, though according to the espionage specialist Stephen Dorril it may have been murder. Ward, the fixer, knew too much about too many people and was said to have been poisoned by an agent working for MI6. The Profumo affair also contributed to bringing an end to Macmillan's premiership.

Amid the intrigues that were dominating British Intelligence in 1963, from Philby to Profumo, Golitsyn had an absolute ball. He was given unprecedented access to MI5's files in the hope of identifying the potential fourth and fifth men. While trawling the Philby case, one phrase stuck out: 'I rather thought it might be you.' To anyone studying the transcripts it seemed clear: Philby had been tipped off about Elliott's visit in order to allow him to prepare himself to fend off the inquisitor as he had done so often before. For someone to have tipped him off, that person must have been familiar with the case, and must be in MI5. It was MI5 who had investigated Philby in 1951 and 1955, and the only people who had the right access and the right knowledge that were still there were the Chief himself, Roger Hollis, and his deputy, Graham Mitchell. Could one of them be a Soviet mole? There followed an almost comical charade as, with Hollis's approval, Arthur Martin set up a project under which Mitchell was investigated and kept under clumsy surveillance. He was followed about, observed through holes drilled in his office wall as he picked his nails, and driven slowly mad as they found nothing to implicate him. Hollis was then told by Martin that he himself was under investigation. He remained under suspicion past his retirement in 1965 and his death in 1973 despite several investigations finding nothing to indicate any kind of treachery. Years later, the defector Oleg Gordievsky was to say that the KGB was utterly baffled by the allegations against Hollis. They were probably quite amused too. In fact, Hollis was too fixated on trying to manage his private life to have much time for spying. David Cornwell told me, 'When I was working as night manager at MI5 we were given a sheet of excuses to give Lady Hollis if she phoned trying to find Sir Roger. He was enjoying an affair with his secretary and we had to cover for him.'

On 22 November 1963, as Maurice Oldfield's third year in Washington was drawing to a close, an event that was to give rise to a host of conspiracy theories took place. As he was driven through Dealey Plaza in Dallas in his open-topped Lincoln convertible, President Kennedy was shot. He was declared dead on arrival at Parkland Hospital. The assassination, it's no exaggeration to say, stunned the world. On both a personal and a professional level, Maurice was deeply upset by Kennedy's death. In their conversations he had found the President both interesting and interested, and he felt he still had a lot to offer. After the initial debacle of the Bay of Pigs he had shown a growing assurance and was a decisive and charismatic leader who was, in Maurice's view, getting the political decisions right. The way he had handled the Cuban Missile Crisis had paved the way for a steady improvement in East–West relations.

Kennedy's time in office and the sense of optimism that had accompanied it was in marked contrast to what was happening in Britain, where the patrician aristocrat

Macmillan had just been replaced as Prime Minister by the 14th Earl of Home in a smoke-and-mirrors succession characterized by a lack of any kind of democracy. As Foreign Secretary and MI6 Head of Station in Washington respectively, Alec Douglas-Home (as he became on renouncing his peerage) and Maurice Oldfield had enjoyed a warm relationship. Despite the senior law officers having advised Douglas-Home that Kennedy's blockade of Cuba the year before was illegal, Oldfield's reassurance on the intelligence side of the matter helped Douglas-Home to remain calm and stoic when advising a nervous Macmillan to be supportive of the Americans' strategy. But in terms of finding a forward-looking Prime Minister, Britain would have to wait.

The search for moles continued unabated despite these political changes, and the next high-profile one uncovered would again be a Cambridge man. Despite the agitating and relentless driving of the hunt by Golitsyn and Angleton, the name was revealed by an entirely separate source. While accepting employment in a government post in Washington, a forty-seven-year-old American named Michael Straight decided to admit his communist past when questioned as part of a routine background check. He contacted a friend, Arthur Schlesinger – a former aide of President Kennedy – who passed the case to Bill Sullivan of the FBI. Sullivan liaised with his MI6 associate Maurice Oldfield, and Oldfield arranged for Arthur Martin of MI5 to fly out to interview Straight. Straight had been at Cambridge University with Burgess, Maclean and Philby, and his testimony led directly to his former friend who had attempted to recruit him to the Soviet cause in the 1930s – the much-hunted fourth man.

Anthony Blunt, the eminent art historian and Surveyor of the Queen's Pictures, had been interviewed by MI5 eleven times in the wake of the Burgess and Maclean affair as he was known to have been a friend of both. The formerly Marxist historian Goronwy Rees had already told MI5 of Burgess and Blunt's attempt to recruit him to the Soviet cause only to have his claim dismissed by Guy Liddell. Blunt had denied all knowledge, and until Straight's casual confession appeared to have got away with it. Now Liddell was dead and the mole hunt had gone beyond the political: the latest suspect was working at the heart of the very royal family he was accused of betraying. For Dick White, the allegations against Blunt were another personal blow: the two men had served together in MI5, where Blunt had been involved in processing the intelligence generated at Bletchley Park. The accused was another archetypal Establishment figure: before Cambridge he'd been at Marlborough College, he was the son of a vicar, and he was third cousin to the Queen Mother.

Arthur Martin visited Blunt at the Courtauld Institute in London in April 1964, and as soon as Michael Straight's name was mentioned, Martin claimed, Blunt's right cheek started twitching. It seems likely that Blunt would have been told by his Soviet friends of the offer to Philby, and knew that he was likely to be made the same. Unlike Philby, though, Blunt accepted immunity from prosecution and was guaranteed fifteen years' anonymity in return for a full confession. MI5 decided not to trouble Alec Douglas-Home with the matter of Blunt's immunity, officially so as not to compromise the Prime Minister in any dealings with Buckingham Palace, but more likely to prevent any awkward questions being asked about Blunt's long career as an MI5 officer and Soviet spy.

For Blunt, the trappings of his lifestyle were far too enticing to be countered by his communist ideals. He knew that life in Moscow would in no way match up to that which he enjoyed in London, and his commitment to art was stronger than his loyalty to any cause. After a period of silence and a stiff drink, Blunt admitted to his betrayal, and named Straight, Peter Ashby, John Cairncross, Bernard Floud, Jenifer Hart, Leo Long and Phoebe Pool as fellow spies. The immunity afforded to Blunt logically had to be afforded equally to those named by him, as to arrest someone on the word of this man would leave any subsequent case untenable. The prosecutors could scarcely bring a case against someone where the key witness was guaranteed immunity and anonymity.

Despite having gone along with the immunity policy, Arthur Martin was far from happy about the idea of MI5 taking the law into its own hands and acting as judge and jury on what was, in the light of the confession, a straightforward case of treason – historically an offence carrying the death penalty. Instead of even facing a court, Blunt would face fifteen years looking after the royal art collection safe in the knowledge that no one would bother him. By Whitsun of 1964 Martin's relentless pursuit of the mole had made him enemies in the Service, and Hollis suspended him for a fortnight because he was 'a focus for dissension in the Service'. After that he was quietly transferred to another department – though he remained in touch with the mole hunters.

MI5 investigated all those named by Blunt, and two,

Bernard Floud and Phoebe Pool, went on to commit suicide. They interviewed Blunt many times with the aim of extracting more information about his treachery and that of his comrades, many of these sessions undertaken by the new mole-hunter-in-chief Peter Wright in Maurice Oldfield's Caxton Street flat, with its state-of-the-art hidden recording system. Wright, a Chesterfield-born scientific officer in MI5, had become enthralled by the notion of Soviet penetration and took over Martin's role with all the gusto a 'disruptive and lazy officer' (as the future head of MI5 Stella Rimington would describe him) could muster. Hollis would become the focus of Wright's attention.

In America, unbeknown to Oldfield at the time, Golitsyn's position as Angleton's major influence and all-seeing guru had been threatened by another walk-in Soviet informer, who had first offered himself up to the CIA in Geneva in early June 1962, asking for $900 to replace KGB money he'd blown on drinking sessions in return for information. Making it a hat-trick of walk-ins after Golitsyn and Goleniewski, Yuri Nosenko claimed to be a Lieutenant Colonel in the KGB and provided intelligence that only someone with detailed KGB knowledge could have, thus convincing the CIA's man in Switzerland, Pete Bagley, that he could be genuine.

George Kisevalter came over from Washington to interpret Nosenko's statements, and the latest Russian would-be double agent described in detail how the KGB had bugged the American Embassy in Moscow, and also gave details that led to the British naval spy John Vassall and which tied in with what they'd learned from Golitsyn. But from there, the information divulged by Nosenko was markedly at odds with what had been supplied by Golitsyn. Crucially, Golitsyn's claim was that there was a mole deep inside the CIA – Nosenko was adamant there was not. James Angleton commented that 'Bagley thought he had the biggest fish of his life. I mean he really did. Everything I heard from him, however, was in direct contrast from what we had heard from Golitsyn.'

From quite early into his own defection, Golitsyn had let it be known that the KGB would be almost certain to try and set off a trail of misinformation through fake defectors to discredit what he was saying. Bagley went back to America, where Angleton gave him full access to the Golitsyn files and began to indoctrinate him in his own take on them and their importance. Angleton then gave Bagley access to Golitsyn himself, and after being questioned by the visitor from the Swiss office, Golitsyn laughed and said that Bagley had obviously met one of the KGB's fakes. When it was time to return to his post, Bagley remarked that 'Alone, Nosenko looked good' but that alongside Golitsyn 'Nosenko looked very odd indeed'.

Unless they were involved in the same dastardly plot, Golitsyn and Nosenko could not both be right. Small wonder that Angleton, the ultimate master of his genre, described what he was facing as being like a 'wilderness of mirrors'. Maurice Oldfield, the medieval historian, similarly enjoyed taking the pieces of evidence, some of them arcane, weighing them, assessing them and trying to build a picture. But while Angleton had become so utterly sold on Golitsyn that he was blinkered to alternatives, Oldfield retained an element of scepticism.

Nosenko agreed to remain in situ with the Russians and,

despite Bagley concurring with Angleton's assessment and letting it be known that the would-be agent must be assumed to be a Soviet plant, the CIA agreed to meet again with him on his next visit to Geneva. Sure enough, Nosenko arrived in the Swiss city on 20 January 1964, and Bagley and Kisevalter were soon there to talk to him. The matter he wanted to discuss caught them by surprise. Nosenko went to great pains to claim that Lee Harvey Oswald, Kennedy's assassin, was nothing to do with the KGB, despite his having approached them as a volunteer in 1959. Given the conspiracy theories that had surrounded the assassination, and coming at a time when the Russians had recently backed down in the face of Kennedy's ultimatum, this could not be ignored. If Nosenko was telling the truth, the CIA concluded, the KGB and the Soviets could be discounted as having been responsible. If, however, he was lying, then it would be reasonable to surmise that his disinformation was designed to disguise a connection between Oswald, the KGB and the shooting of the President.

The received wisdom was going against Nosenko, and when he completed his debriefing by saying that contrary to his previous proclamations he now wanted to defect to the US as he feared he'd been compromised – a suspicion fuelled by a telegram summoning him back to Moscow – a new plan was needed. The CIA granted his requests and agreed a schedule of payments with him: $25,000 per year, plus $15,000 for his work in identifying John Vassall. In short, the CIA convinced Nosenko that they believed in him. A polygraph test would be the final element to the agreement to help with his defection.

Nosenko was subjected to three tests, two of which he

failed when it emerged that he was lying about his rank – something he claimed to have done in order to make himself sound more important than he was – and about the telegram ordering him back to Moscow. Silly little lies catalysed the suspicions against him; he also claimed to have undergone one of the tests with a CIA officer's thumb stuck up his backside. He was taken to the USA in early February and subjected to a hideous regime as the CIA tried to break him. He was then put on a plane and told he was going to Moscow, but after several hours of screaming he was in fact taken to the CIA training centre at Camp Peary in Virginia, known as The Farm. There he was subjected to what can only be described as torture. He was confined to a concrete cell with no heating, constantly filmed, and deprived of pillows or covers. He claimed to have been drugged. Unbelievably, he was to be held for three and a half years, all the while sticking to his story.

Nosenko's nightmare wasn't all James Angleton's doing, but it was symptomatic of the messianic fervour he'd applied to every cranny of the CIA's counterespionage effort that such treatment was meted out to someone who dared to challenge the Golitsyn orthodoxy. Unsurprisingly, when Golitsyn was allowed to view Nosenko's file, he dismissed the man as a Soviet plant.

Maurice Oldfield was beginning to have doubts about Golitsyn and Angleton, not least when yet another defector arrived, this time directly to the British. Yuri Krotkov, a dramatist, broadcaster and KGB agent, came to London in September 1963, and in time his information would influence Oldfield's thinking considerably. For now, though, he continued to understand and respect the need to be seen to be going along with Angleton for the sake of MI6 relations with the CIA. By cultivating Angleton while building a personal fund of goodwill among other senior officers at Langley, and through his work in helping sell Penkovsky to the sceptics, Maurice had done a remarkably solid job in maintaining and growing British respectability. Oldfield would return to London in 1964 with a reputation as one of the top few officers in MI6. His place in Washington was taken by Christopher Phillpotts, accompanied by his assistant Stephen de Mowbray; it was down to Phillpotts now to take on the task of being the main receptacle for Angleton's theories. The mole hunt wasn't about to end any time soon, but at least Oldfield would be free to speak his mind.

14

Close to the Summit

ARRIVING BACK IN London in the spring of 1964 from what would be his last full-time overseas posting, Maurice decided to aim for the position of Chief of MI6. Only in that role could he hope to undertake the changes he felt necessary to continue the efforts being made to bring the Service respectability. Before Dick White's appointment – a desperate attempt to bring the organization under control by bringing in the successful head of MI5 – the chances of someone of Oldfield's background reaching that position had been less than zero. In fact, before White there had been more chance of Kim Philby becoming Chief than Maurice Oldfield.

Oldfield's return coincided with a more physical change for MI6: the Service was being relocated from the old, rambling Broadway buildings in the heart of St James's and a stone's throw from Parliament to a new, bland, twenty-two-storey tower block south of the river. Century House, on Lambeth Bridge Road, was conveniently located close to Waterloo Station and, remarkably, more or less on top of a petrol station, its utilitarian grey linoleum floors more in keeping with the popular image of austere Soviet design than the tweedy, oak-panelled tradition of the British Establishment. Though MI6 in theory still didn't exist, the move to Century House was a poorly kept secret, and for the next thirty years bus conductors would call 'spies alight' as their vehicle drew up at the stop outside. The building was said to be well known to every taxi driver, bus driver and KGB agent in London.

That year Douglas-Home's government spent heavily in an attempt to win the forthcoming general election. The next government, almost certain to be Labour according to the opinion polls, was sure to have to make cuts, and at that time it was not inconceivable that an organization such as MI6 with its deep links to the Tory Establishment might even face abolition. The move to Century House, away from the centre of power, was almost symbolic of a potential reduction in status. It was Maurice's job to make his organization indispensable.

At the end of his time in America, Dick White asked Maurice and two other senior colleagues to submit their written recommendations for the post of Deputy Chief. All three wrote in support of Maurice, including the man himself, and so, after a rubber-stamping from the new Foreign Secretary Rab Butler, from 1964 he was Deputy Chief of the Secret Intelligence Service and Director of Counterintelligence.

Despite White's undoubted decency and sound reputation, the Blunt affair and the ongoing mole hunt had turned attention back to MI5 and White was inextricably linked to the recent past in that place. His sincerity in wanting to expose the supposed traitor in its midst while repairing relations with the Americans had caused him to throw his weight behind the theories espoused by James Angleton and Anatoliy Golitsyn, almost without question. While White was playing an important role in restraining the Robber Barons and their penchant for risky special operations, he'd also appeased them by appointing George Kennedy Young as his deputy, then regretted it after the Suez episode. In truth, he'd never truly fitted into his MI6 role. The wider pressures that accompanied the job were things White found difficult to control.

White claimed that it was only his family life that kept him sane, and he liked to retreat to his country house in West Sussex where he lived with his wife, Kate, and their children, and was close to his brother and sister. He recommended that Maurice take the same approach, which he already did; but White's suggestion went further than that. 'Maurice was over-involved in his work, and obsessive. He needed a good wife like Kate to get a complete change of subject in the evening.'

Thoughts of marriage were stirred when Maurice heard that his protégé from Singapore, Michael Chan, had become engaged. Michael had graduated from medical school the previous summer, and on his return to London Maurice invited him over for supper at a steakhouse near his Caxton Street flat. Arriving a little early, the young doctor called in at the flat to find Maurice still busily studying paperwork at his desk – and, casually looking at what his friend from the Foreign Office was reading, he noticed that all the writing was in code. 'That was the moment when I was sure that Maurice was in security intelligence,' he said. Chan tried to hide the surprised look on his face and asked, 'Is decoding a tedious job?' 'It depends if one knows the key to the code, Michael,' came the smiling reply. It was over supper, for which Maurice insisted on sitting in a seat where he could see the windows to his flat because 'I know the place is under surveillance, and I'd like to see if I can spot anything', that Chan announced his engagement.

The two discussed the subject, Maurice mentioning his boss's advice, and they arranged a dinner at the Athenaeum where the forthcoming Mrs Chan, Irene, would be introduced. At that time women were still not allowed in the club dining room, so the trio dined in the basement on kangaroo soup and Maurice wished the couple well, giving them a colour photograph of Mona View Farm as an engagement present. 'He said, with some obvious sadness, that he felt he would never be able to marry, because of the nature of his work,' Chan remembered.

Dick White's analysis was clearly too simplistic for someone of such private complexity, but after his talk with Michael Chan Maurice did discuss the matter of marriage with Betty Kemp on a visit to Oxford. Betty turned the tables on him and, with 1964 being a leap year, proposed marriage. He considered the proposal seriously, not least because as they both left Washington to return to London postings a fellow Foreign Office diplomat, Denis Greenhill, had warned him that the FBI – which automatically kept visiting intelligence officers under surveillance – had raised the matter of the occasional lodgers Maurice had housed in Waterside Drive, some of whom had been young and male. It had only been his timely passing of the polygraph test that had prevented the matter being taken further. Taking a wife would help to dispel such speculation. Betty said that in the end Maurice told her that 'his job offered no life for a wife. I would get postcards from the oddest places, and he was often in danger.'

At the age of forty-eight, as he was at the time, a marriage would have in any event been a strange choice for someone in Maurice's position and with his plans. Normally the closer officers got to the top in MI6 the more they would be based in London, but Oldfield had no intention of stopping his travels with the increasing control he had over his movements. To marry at that stage, irrespective of more personal aspects, could potentially act as a brake on this freedom to roam. And having to consider another person yet not be able to share the details of what he was doing would put severe pressure on the relationship.

As a devout Christian, Maurice was also a firm believer in the principle that marriage was entered into for the creation of children, which was something he had no intention of doing. A marriage that consisted of one partner being an academic who was utterly engrossed in her work at Oxford while the other led a nomadic existence between airports, embassies, hotels and government buildings with no routine or structure was not a marriage as Maurice recognized it. Such a marriage could only be as a form of cover, and he saw no need for that, even supposing using the institution for such a purpose had been acceptable to him.

As a senior officer in overseas secret intelligence he still liked to see for himself what was happening around the world, while of course maintaining his contacts. Politicians, business leaders and fellow intelligence officers with whom he'd become friendly over the previous two decades were similarly reaching the pinnacle of their professions and their influence. To turn over those personal contacts entirely to other officers would be, in his view, to risk diminishing the sway he held.

Brian Stewart, a colleague going back to Malaya days, compared Maurice with Dick White and in his view the differences between the two were marked. 'Sir Dick White often said to me that he envied me my field experience. Despite the flamboyant title of his biography, *The Perfect English Spy*, he was fundamentally an intelligence bureaucrat, not an operator. Maurice Oldfield, on the other hand, after a short spell in academia, spent most of his career in the field and was the mandarins' favourite intelligence chief. Sir Dick did not have the same people knack and confidence as Maurice, or the personal contacts all over the world.'

With his new appointment, Maurice set about arranging his life around it. For the next fourteen years his trips to Derbyshire would become more frequent – generally about once a month, though endlessly variable – and he would use those times, as White had advised, to temporarily free his mind from his work. Sometimes he would bring guests back with him, colleagues usually, and he would always be accompanied by Ken Dyer. In those days he was able to move with relative freedom, usually arriving by train and being collected from Bakewell Station by John or Warren Pearce: their car was registered with the police as Maurice's official vehicle.

Betty Kemp was a regular visitor to Over Haddon, as was Tony Cavendish. Both appreciated the peace Maurice enjoyed there, and would continue to visit long after he died. He was often to be found in the Lathkill enjoying halves of bitter and spinning tales nobody could ever remember. A close friend in the Service said of Maurice, 'It was very obvious to us that his family and Derbyshire were what he lived for.' He enjoyed the seasons and the local life: the Bakewell Show, which he'd attend with his brothers and scan a knowledgeable eye over the prize cattle; Flagg Races, the point-to-point horse racing on bleak Flagg Moor that took place every Easter Tuesday come rain or rain; and Over Haddon Village Show, the horticultural event in which the overall winner is still given the coveted Joseph Oldfield Cup, named in honour of Maurice's father.

When the tenancy of the Royal Oak pub near Hurdlow, about four miles further into the Derbyshire wilds, became available, Maurice installed a former officer, Diane Phillipps, as landlady. She became another set of eyes and ears for him in the area – a source of intelligence from home when he was abroad. And if he needed somewhere away from prying eyes for a private meeting, Diane would simply close the pub. Not all MI6 business was dealt with in Century House, panelled offices or gentlemen's clubs.

As Director of Counterintelligence, Oldfield was now, if not equal in status to James Angleton in global intelligence, of equal rank in terms of their respective organizations. That meant that he no longer had to kowtow to the American's theories – though he was content for Chris Phillpotts and Stephen de Mowbray to do just that; they could continue sucking up to the CIA as much as Dick White liked. Phillpotts had gone to America with exactly the same brief from White, and arrived already converted to set about absorbing Angleton's doctrines like a desiccated sponge. It was not long before Phillpotts was reporting in and confirming to the Chief that the mole hunt was still vitally important.

The response was the setting up of a joint committee of MI5 and MI6, chaired by Peter Wright and given the code-name Fluency. Arthur Martin, though sidelined by MI5, was nominally taken on by MI6 and acted as an unofficial consultant to Wright's committee. Keeping the Wright/ Martin axis in the investigations indicated, astonishingly, that Dick White remained open to the suggestion that Roger Hollis – still head of MI5 – might be the mole.

As they pored over all the old files, the Fluency committee realized that they were looking back nearly twenty years to the Volkov and Gouzenko cases, and trying to work out, in the light of what Golitsyn was saying, whether the spy both had identified – now codenamed ELLI – was the same person or two people, and either way, was ELLI still at large? Had, as some suspected, ELLI been a disgraced MI6 traitor named H. A. R. Philby, who had recently disappeared to Moscow, or was ELLI in fact Hollis, as Wright and Martin desperately wanted to prove?

The committee members dug into everything, producing monthly reports that were analysed by Oldfield and his equivalent in MI5, Alec MacDonald, and then passed on to Dick White and Roger Hollis. Unsurprisingly given the constant pressure coming from Angleton, while not finding anything, the reports consistently stated that there was a high-level Soviet penetration of the intelligence services but without offering any proof. One file note hand-written by Hollis, addressed to Peter Wright, asked, with more than a hint of bewilderment, 'Why do you think I'm a spy?'

The complete lack of evidence beyond anything that could not be explained by naivety or complacency prompted Oldfield at last to question White about his slavish adherence to Angleton's strictures. He felt moved to tell his Chief that the American had become 'a disaster'. In Maurice's view, Golitsyn was, by 1964 if not before, showing all the hallmarks of what might be termed 'Oldfield's Law', the one that says defectors are like grapes – the first pressings are the best. Initially, Golitsyn's information had been good, if mostly because it did that most welcome of things: confirmed Angleton's existing theories. But now the defector was well into the dregs, trying to justify his own existence, coming up with ever more fanciful allegations that were difficult to disprove. He was being well paid and had a comfortable life and wanted to make sure that continued. Golitsyn's claim that he was living in fear of KGB assassination seemed a bit hollow when he was happy to carouse around New York's smartest restaurants which were well-known haunts of Soviet officers.

The other, more sinister explanation was that Golitsyn himself was the Soviet plant. After all, he hadn't really told the CIA anything they didn't suspect or couldn't find out by some other means. His more outlandish theories were either eventually proved wrong or impossible to prove either way. And the overall effect was to plunge the British and American intelligence services, and eventually the British government itself, into a spiral of paranoia, navel gazing and suspicion for well over a decade. Even if Golitsyn was genuine, his efforts must have been warmly applauded in Moscow.

At least part of the problem was that on a personal level the officers, including Oldfield, both liked and admired Angleton. Even Golitsyn could be good company when he wanted to be. Angleton made for an interesting night out, capable of drinking everyone under the table and appearing unscathed while all around him were dozing off, and knowledgeable on a range of subjects, not just his personal hobbies of orchid growing and fly-fishing.

For now, White was insistent that the policy of sticking with Angleton was correct and was going to prevail. Their disagreement caused White, for the first time, to lose confidence in Oldfield. Maurice studied the case of Yuri Krotkov, who had defected to the British the previous autumn. Krotkov helped to uncover a suspected Soviet agent of influence, the Canadian Ambassador to Moscow John Watkins, who died of a heart attack in October 1964 while being interrogated by the Royal Canadian Mounted Police and the CIA. Inconveniently for James Angleton, Krotkov also vouched for Nosenko, still languishing in his CIA hellhole.

For Oldfield, his interest in Krotkov went beyond the narrow confines of the mole hunt. The intellectual defector was a source of intelligence on life in Soviet Russia, and he spoke eloquently of the dissatisfaction with the communist regime among his peers. There was always the fear that if the Soviet people were really behind the regime then the leadership could mobilize them in support of any diabolical plans for world domination. Krotkov indicated that this was far from being the case.

Angleton flew in to meet Krotkov, and his response was predictable. 'The man's a phoney,' he told Oldfield. 'Lock him up for six months in a Scottish castle until he confesses, and in any case just shove him back to the KGB at Checkpoint Charlie.' In spite of everything, Angleton was advocating the exact remedy that was being applied to Nosenko. When Maurice told Dick White, the Chief was horrified. 'We'll never get another defector,' he said. He found the whole idea 'ridiculous, impossible and illegal'. The CIA sent over two Soviet experts to debrief Krotkov and check his bona fides. They found him credible, and Oldfield concurred. Angleton did not, and his acolytes Arthur Martin and Peter Wright went along with him. In spite of all the scepticism, and to the despair of Oldfield, White, probably still scarred by mistakes from the 1950s, stuck by Angleton and his mole hunters. Even when Golitsyn's claims that the Sino-Soviet split had been a cunning ruse to foil the West were comprehensively debunked – something that should have set alarm bells ringing – Angleton and his followers agreed that everything else must still be true. They'd invested their whole reputations in their pet defector.

Maurice was by now quite open in his scepticism about Angleton's theories, denouncing them as being both without substance and downright dangerous. He was gratified to find some in the CIA were in agreement with him, such as his friend Cleveland Cram, but the prevailing opinion was to give the Fluency committee its head and let it run its course. A practical step Oldfield could take, though, in his capacity as Director of Counterintelligence was to instruct his officers to rein in their aggressive pursuit of potential Soviet defectors. The carnage being wrought by the defectors they had already was, in Oldfield's view, not worth exacerbating by seeking more. This policy brought him into conflict with the officers who were taking a more proactive approach. Maurice favoured confining their activities to intelligence gathering, and for the moment his view prevailed.

The rampant paranoia of the mole hunt did not occupy

all of Oldfield's time, however. In October 1964 the 14th Earl of Home was defeated at the polls and Harold Wilson and his Labour government came to power, albeit with the thinnest of House of Commons majorities – a mere four. Maurice now had to get used to a new list of political masters, and a slightly odd appointment as Foreign Secretary. Patrick Gordon Walker, Wilson's preferred man in the Foreign Office, had unexpectedly lost his supposedly safe seat at the election, but despite having a seat neither in the Commons nor the Lords, the new Prime Minister appointed him anyway. It was to be three months before Michael Stewart was installed in Gordon Walker's place.

Wilson's early months were taken up with trying to deal with his relationship with America's new President, Lyndon Johnson, and Johnson's travails with the Vietnam War. There was no appetite in the Labour Party for Britain to go to war in Vietnam, nor, in the light of Suez, much appetite in the wider country. But as the US's supposedly strongest ally, President Johnson might reasonably have expected Britain to join the fray in support. This position was reinforced by the fact that Britain's balance of payments position was weak, and the country was depending on American support to prop up the pound. It was no time to be a new Prime Minister with a slim majority, having to stand up to the world's biggest superpower.

Wilson would complain in Cabinet that 'Lyndon Johnson keeps begging me to send even a Battalion of Bagpipers' in support of the American war effort. The Prime Minister needed sound, practical reasons to resist Johnson's overtures, and via his Paymaster General, George Wigg, sought the advice of the Secret Intelligence Service. Dick White arranged for Wilson to see his recommended specialist on Far Eastern matters, Maurice Oldfield, whose reports from the region had been required reading for much of the 1950s. The minister Richard Crossman, a man who had a sound war record in intelligence, sat in on the meetings.

When it became clear that Wilson was not going to cave in to Johnson's request, Crossman's Parliamentary Private Secretary, Tam Dalyell, congratulated his minister on the result. 'It wasn't me,' said Crossman, clearly impressed, 'it was the MI6 guy, Maurice Oldfield. He convinced Harold that the Vietnamese fighters were not being manipulated by Moscow or Peking, and that there was nothing to be gained by Britain going in. We would be bogged down for years.' A compromise was reached whereby Britain would provide intelligence to the American effort and guarantee to maintain its presence in West Germany and east of Suez, in return for continued US support for the pound. Also, several thousand British troops were allowed to de-list and sign up for the US Army at their own discretion.

As recently as 2003 and the Iraq debates, Tam Dalyell would cite Maurice Oldfield as an example of an intelligence man who helped prevent war rather than encourage it, as appeared to be the case at that time. The episode gave Oldfield an early boost in his relations with the new Labour ministers, and for his part Oldfield was impressed with Harold Wilson. 'He was very politically astute,' Maurice would say of him, 'and a politician that would always give you a decision.'

Oldfield continued to travel extensively, including visits to the Shah in Tehran, to Alexandria at the time of the Arab League Summit in 1964, and then, in early 1965, he was in

Jerusalem, where his friend from SIME days Teddy Kollek had just been elected mayor, a post he would hold until 1993. From there he went to Amman, using an introduction from Kollek to meet King Hussein of Jordan, who was at the time trying to forge friendly relations with neighbouring Israel.

Closer to home, Maurice was introduced by his journalist friend Sefton Delmer to the former head of the West German Intelligence Service Otto John. John's was a colourful career, and one Oldfield had studied for many years. He had originally come to notice as part of the 20 July Plot to assassinate Hitler; his brother, Hans, was one of the executed conspirators. Otto used connections in British Intelligence to escape to England, and worked for the BBC producing anti-Nazi black propaganda, and also for MI6, where his boss was Kim Philby. He was a witness at the Nuremburg trials, and was appointed Chief of the Secret Service in 1950. Four years later he apparently defected to East Germany and statements were issued in his name denouncing the West. In 1955 he defected back to West Germany, claiming that his trip to the East had been as a result of abduction by the KGB, who had then drugged and tortured him and forced him into his anti-Western pronouncement. The West Germans didn't believe his story and Otto John was jailed for treason. He was eventually released in 1958 and spent the rest of his life trying to prove his innocence. Oldfield and John became firm friends; Maurice absolutely believed his story. He became another fixture on Oldfield's annual travels: the visits to Innsbruck to see Otto and Lucie John were a favourite holiday.

Otto John's case attracted the attention of documentary makers, and in 1965 Oldfield heard that an Old Mannerian, the television producer and later Labour MP Phillip Whitehead, had nearly finished making a film about John, focusing on his work with the British Secret Service. The film ran the risk of making two MI6 agents identifiable, and when Oldfield was told he sought out Whitehead. In the crowds at Flagg Races on Easter Tuesday 1965, as Whitehead checked out the runners and riders under his umbrella, Maurice appeared at his shoulder and told him that if the film on John went out in its current form those agents were as good as dead. 'Don't put people at risk just for a TV programme,' Oldfield said. 'I'll tell you the best explanation about Otto John.' Before Whitehead had taken it all in, Maurice was gone, lost in the crowd. A few days later a note arrived at Whitehead's office with the promised explanation, and the documentary was edited and aired without causing any deaths.

By the end of 1965, Oldfield's position as Sir Dick White's successor seemed assured, the reforms promised at the time of White's appointment finally agreed, after consultation with the Cabinet Secretary Sir Burke Trend. Roger Hollis, worn out by the constant insinuations, retired as head of MI5, but not before one last, forlorn 'Why do you think I'm a spy, Peter?' to Wright. Wright would claim Hollis said, 'you've got your tentacles into me, Peter', but he was prone to exaggeration. To Oldfield it did seem there was cause for optimism if the prime target of the mole hunters was no longer in post.

In January 1966 most of the remaining Robber Barons were offered retirement, with only Nick Elliott, appointed Controller for Western Europe, hanging on for another two years. Among other appointments, the widely admired

Harold Shergold was put in charge of the Soviet Bloc, and a protégé of Oldfield's, Ellis Morgan, became Controller for the Far East. The Chief hosted a meeting where he stated that he could 'assure you that my successor will come from within the Service'.

The outsider – Oldfield's supposed competition – was Chris Phillpotts, whose early recall from Washington gave him the thought that White was trying to usher him closer to the controls at Century House. Phillpotts had the advantages of being tall, dark and handsome, and he had a 'dazzling' wife. He was also an avid Angletonite, and at the time White was still encouraging his officers down that route. Phillpotts's replacement in America, John da Silva – whose appointment Oldfield opposed – was told his relationship with Angleton was paramount as he was the expert on Soviet penetration.

But as Deputy Chief, and with a remarkable record of service and the confidence of the government, Oldfield remained in pole position.

15

Frustration

THE EARLY MONTHS of 1966 were dominated by Harold Wilson trying to reassert his authority in Britain by calling a general election, a plan that was vindicated on 31 March as his Labour government was returned to power with a thumping majority of 96 over all other parties in the House of Commons. It would not be long before the Secret Intelligence Service came under the control of a new Foreign Secretary with whom Maurice Oldfield would have a more challenging relationship than he enjoyed with any of the other holders of that post under whom he served. When George Brown challenged Wilson for the Labour leadership after Hugh Gaitskell's death in 1963, the minister Anthony Crosland had called it 'a choice between a crook and a drunk'. Others were heard to say 'better George Brown drunk than Harold Wilson sober'. Oldfield would have taken Wilson over Brown every time.

On the face of it Brown and Oldfield might have been expected to get along; both had reached the top from humble backgrounds, and both had strong Derbyshire connections.

Oldfield's roots were well known, and Brown had been the MP for Belper, twenty miles south of Bakewell, since 1945. But in fact theirs was a difficult relationship. Brown was said to find Oldfield 'donnish and severe'; and in spite of coming from an organization in which heavy drinking was de rigueur, Oldfield found it difficult to respect the fact that his boss could scarcely function without large quantities of drink. Not for nothing did his agent coin the phrase 'tired and emotional' to explain Brown's behaviour when disembarking from a long flight.

Maurice liked to tell a couple of stories, almost certainly apocryphal, to illustrate his opinion of George Brown. The first took place during the visit of the Soviet statesman Alexei Kosygin to London in 1967. Some of the Soviet officials were entertained at the Foreign Office, a function attended by Maurice and hosted by Brown. After a long lunch during which the Foreign Secretary matched his opposite number vodka for vodka and then some, the party left, blinking into the sunlight of Whitehall. Then, reaching for something in his pocket, Brown turned to the KGB man at his side, said 'hold these a minute', and handed over his office keys. An invention, possibly, but a story Maurice used to sum up Brown.

The other story became more well known. Its veracity, too, is dubious, though Maurice did claim to have been at the event concerned, which took place on a diplomatic visit to Brazil. The lunch at the Palacio da Alvorada in Brasília was, as usual for Mr Brown, long and moist. After the meal, the band struck up a tune and everyone rose to their feet, including a swaying Foreign Secretary, who spied a striking-looking woman in a flowing red gown across the room and staggered over to ask her to dance. Brown was embarrassed to be told: 'There are three reasons I won't dance with you, Mr Brown. Firstly, you are very, very drunk. Secondly, this is not a dance, it is the Peruvian national anthem and we are standing to attention. Finally, I am not a woman, I am the Cardinal Archbishop of Lima.'

The mole hunt, by now becoming an annoyance to Oldfield, was actually intensified by Chris Phillpotts's return to London, all fired up as he was by – and according to the CIA's Bronson Tweedy 'deeply attached to' – James Angleton. Inevitably, Phillpotts fell into the orbit of the Fluency gang and, egged on by Peter Wright and Arthur Martin, he identified several colleagues who were thought to be suspicious and urged Dick White to sack them. White went along with the sackings, against his better judgement, and this led to arguments between Oldfield – who was opposed to dismissal on the grounds of suspicion rather than fact – and Phillpotts. White's less than decisive verdict was to instruct Phillpotts to carry on hunting, yet he agreed with Maurice that the ongoing investigation would eventually leak out and become an embarrassment.

On 14 March 1966 Maurice was surprised, but not impressed, to receive a call from Angleton to say that he was arriving on a one-day visit and wanted to meet Dick White, the head of MI5 Martin Furnival Jones and other senior officers from both services – and that he was bringing Anatoliy Golitsyn with him. Angleton gave instructions that the visit was so secret that even his own CIA station in London did not and must not know about it. His brief, he claimed, was from Director Richard Helms, and it was to engage in talks about the problems of disinformation and penetration. In other words he was claiming top-level support for his mole hunt.

The first meeting was attended only by White, Furnival Jones, Alec MacDonald and Peter Wright; the second, that evening, saw Angleton and Golitsyn being entertained at Maurice's flat along with MacDonald and Wright. They talked late into the night, and Wright lapped everything up. MacDonald and Oldfield remained sceptical, though MacDonald admitted 'the whole performance was quite extraordinary, but then Jim and Anatoliy are quite extraordinary chaps'.

When Angleton swept into town yet again in April to try and sign up MI6 to his intelligence supergroup CAZAB, comprising the agencies of Canada, America, New Zealand, Australia and Britain, under his own control, Oldfield's tolerance of his friend reached a new low. The proposal was one of total disclosure between the agencies and the focus was to be on tackling Soviet penetration. Instead of being what an international intelligence agency should be, outward-looking and seeking information to benefit the countries involved, Angleton was advocating looking endlessly into his wilderness of mirrors.

The Angleton sceptics were becoming more numerous, and bolder; Harold Shergold had been encouraging White to sever the ties, and Oldfield was telling anyone who would listen that the American had become a nightmare. Angleton's repeated assertion that Penkovsky was a plant even drew White to say that the suggestion was ridiculous. However, the arrest and imprisonment for violation of the Official Secrets Act of a former MI6 man and Ministry of Aviation officer, Frank Bossard, the previous year, was all the justification the mole hunters needed to stick to their task.

The Fluency committee, predictably enough, decided that the new deputy head of MI5, Michael Hanley, was a prime suspect. A lengthy investigation and interrogation showed that suggestion up for the nonsense it was, and all eyes turned back to the bewildered Roger Hollis. Phillpotts investigated all of his MI6 colleagues, darting back and forth across the Atlantic to keep a delighted Angleton up to date.

A personal edge to the mole hunt came for Maurice at about this time. The former Station Chief for the Far East, Dick Ellis, whom Oldfield had known since the 1950s, was accused of selling secrets to the Germans before the war, and the Soviets after. Ellis was by 1966 long retired but was subjected to interrogation by Phillpotts, Theodore 'Bunny' Pantcheff from MI6 and Anne Orr-Ewing from MI5. Eventually the sixty-nine-year-old confessed to having sold some files on Nazis to the Germans in 1939, but vehemently denied having spied for the Soviets. Maurice was aggrieved at what he described as Phillpotts's 'Gestapo methods' in extracting what was in his view a dubious confession from his friend, and subjected his rival to a reprimand.

Whatever the truth about Ellis's treachery, Oldfield remained loyal to the man and they stayed in regular contact until Ellis died in 1975. Some, such as Peter Wright, used this as an example of what they considered Maurice's poor judgement of character. As Wright put it: 'Even though we had uncovered a traitor of major proportions, I sometimes felt as if it were I who was being blamed. Oldfield despised the climate of fear engendered by Phillpotts's vetting purge, and campaigned hard to change Dick's [White] mind. The fact that Ellis had confessed seemed to weigh hardly at all on his thinking.' Oldfield's view was that a confession extracted using Phillpotts's methods was likely to be unreliable, and that even if true it was 'all a long time ago, and best forgotten'. In such matters, Maurice was both pragmatic and forgiving. Ellis's 'confession' would not stand up in court, and so punishment for punishment's sake was not an option. Further, what happened, if it happened, was over twenty years ago – Ellis was thirteen years into his retirement and not harming anyone. In the search for a current and active mole, should one exist, the hounding of Dick Ellis was, in Maurice's opinion, barely more than a distraction.

The whole thing was getting completely out of hand; it was in danger of rendering MI6 work in the Soviet Bloc a virtual impossibility. Every officer who had any contact with a Russian was immediately put under suspicion and assumed to be a mole. A future Director of MI6, Gerry Warner, who had been based in Poland, suggested to Shergold, the Soviet Bloc chief, that he ought to give a seminar at the MI6 training camp at Fort Monckton about the desirability of officers visiting the Eastern Bloc to learn about how the people lived. Shergy shook his head and said that if Warner did that he'd be returned to London and earmarked as a dangerous subversive. Both men saw the sense in Warner's proposal; Shergold knew that in the dark paranoia engendered by Angleton, Phillpotts and Fluency such sense was off the agenda.

Enterprising officers found a way round the problem. Oldfield's solution came in the shape of his young friend Gerald Buss. Inspired by Maurice, Gerald had completed his degree at St Stephen's House, the theological college attached to St Catherine's College, Oxford, and as part of his course

he'd covered Cold War Studies. With experience of doing reports from his days with Maurice in Singapore, this time Gerald was sent across the Iron Curtain on the pretext of visiting friends in the Russian Orthodox Church. This was in the early days of Leonid Brezhnev's regime, and Gerald, with no official government links, was able to travel around in relative freedom and see for himself exactly how the people were really living.

A few years later Buss became chaplain at Hurstpierpoint College in West Sussex, and far from slowing down his Russian trips, he actually increased their number. Twice a year he would make the journey, once on his own as normal, the other in company. Some schools had trips to the Lake District, France or even Spain; Hurstpierpoint's sixth formers went to Moscow or Leningrad. 'The first year there was a bit of trouble,' Gerald told me. 'Despite my briefing before the trip about how things were over there, and how they needed to behave, some of the boys got absolutely plastered on vodka, and the Russian police got a bit heavy-handed about it. After that, each year I got the previous year's lower sixth, those who'd been before, to do the talk after me when I left the room. Peer pressure worked. I'd listen at the door and hear them say "what Gerald said is right". We never had any trouble again.'

The difference between his experiences alone or with the students was stark. 'There was never any problem going with the school,' Gerald found. 'The Soviets wanted to impress, and all the authorities were welcoming. Travelling solo, though, could be a different matter. You could tell which of the border guards were KGB, they could be very sinister. Once I was detained for ten hours while they checked me out. I did hear of people being sent to Siberia and, well, that being it. I used to just stick to my story that I was disillusioned with life in the West and wanted to sell their country to my friends. It seemed to work.'

After each trip, which took in towns and cities all over Russia, Gerald would telephone Maurice and arrange to meet to discuss his report, either at Maurice's flat or at the Athenaeum Club. No doubt the Fluency spies would have made a note in a file about Oldfield meeting a tall, dark, handsome man twenty years his junior.

The weekend of 21 October 1966 was one of Maurice's trips back to Derbyshire. He spent the Friday evening with his mother and sisters, and then on the Saturday went to watch John Pearce play for the Old Mannerians rugby team against the Old Baileans from Matlock – the big local derby. The Bakewell team won 48-0, and a lively night out was had around the pubs of the town. Late in the evening a group of the players managed to find a lift and joined Maurice, Warren Pearce and some other farmers for a drink up in the Peak District hills at the Royal Oak near Hurdlow, still run by Maurice's old colleague, Diane Phillipps.

Time raced by, and before they knew it closing time had passed, the lights were dimmed and they settled down to a good old-fashioned lock-in. Suddenly there came a bang at the door and a call: 'Police! Open up!' Panic set in among the drinkers. Thinking the place was being raided, farmers and rugby players started climbing out of the windows and running off over the dark fields. Maurice, who had taken a phone call an hour earlier, knew it wasn't a raid and sat in quiet amusement amid the pandemonium. Derbyshire Constabulary had been sent to make sure he got straight back to London. The jailed traitor George Blake had escaped from Wormwood Scrubs.

It transpired that Blake's escape had been masterminded by three sympathetic fellow prisoners – the events later inspired Simon Gray's play *Cell Mates* – but at the time it was widely suspected to have been the work of the KGB, a suspicion that seemed to be confirmed when he popped up in the Soviet Union. Even though MI6 had warned the Home Office that Blake was likely to attempt a break for freedom, and so could not be fairly held responsible, the association was there and it was seen by the CIA as another example of British incompetence – and by James Angleton as a very good reason to carry on weeding out moles, real or imaginary.

Perversely, the Blake escape may well have affected Oldfield's chances of succeeding Dick White, whose retirement from his post was looming. Not, of course, because he was in any way to blame, but as the most prominent voice of scepticism about the relentless mole hunt his view was not popular among those who considered the escape to have been another example of KGB infiltration. Oldfield's indirect criticisms of White regarding the Angleton matter affected their relationship too, and probably helped to diminish White's support for his deputy.

When the time came for Denis Greenhill, as Permanent Under Secretary at the Foreign Office, to nominate a successor in time for White's scheduled retirement in March 1968, he was unsure which way to go. Oldfield had been the expected successor for most of the time since he returned from Washington, an appointment that would have found little opposition from within the ranks. But recent disagreements with the outgoing Chief meant White declined to offer Maurice his formal support, and there was a feeling that he didn't delegate well – the Derbyshire man had his own way of operating. The other internal candidate, Chris Phillpotts, had the ability and the wife but wasn't wholly trusted among colleagues.

With hindsight, people have suggested that Oldfield's suspected homosexuality may have queered the pitch against him, given Greenhill's previous reference to the lodgers at Maurice's Washington home, but that seems very unlikely. Had such suspicions existed then, they would still have existed when he was eventually appointed five years later. A long-serving colleague from the time told me 'there was no indication to us that Maurice might be gay, and there were certainly no rumours in the Service'. Whatever the reasons, Greenhill didn't throw his weight behind either Oldfield or Phillpotts in his submission to George Brown; he simply let the Foreign Secretary decide. Phillpotts was dismissed out of hand, and Brown and Oldfield had a mutual antipathy. Brown really wanted MI6 to be brought under closer Foreign Office control and almost flippantly offered the job to Greenhill himself, before a completely unknown figure was plucked from the obscurity of the ranks of the deputy secretaries.

Ironically, Brown resigned from the government shortly after telling Dick White that his replacement would be one John Rennie, leaving his successor at the Foreign Office, Michael Stewart – back for a second stint – to rubber-stamp the appointment. Rennie was reckoned to be a decent if unexceptional time-serving diplomat whose sole experience of intelligence work had come when running the International Research Department, a Foreign Office propaganda vehicle, for a period in the 1950s. He had, though, served with both Oldfield and Greenhill in Washington and was known to be inoffensive to both. Jack Rennie was also known as an artist, whose paintings had been exhibited at the Royal Academy in the 1930s, and as a product of Wellington and Balliol College, Oxford, he was absolutely from the tick-box background. What seemed to clinch it for Rennie, however, was that he and his wife Jennie were known to be a pleasant couple with a lovely family who would go down well among the Establishment in the Foreign Office.

Oldfield's disappointment at being overlooked was genuine, but as he was appointed to carry on as Rennie's deputy there was no question of a demotion, and in the eyes of everyone in the Service he was now clearly the anointed successor – the power behind the throne. The devout and hawkish officer Peter Lunn told David Cornwell that he intended to 'pray to God that Maurice gets the job next time'. It was a view commonly held in the Service. Phillpotts, by contrast, despite his record of service, was clearly a busted flush. Two years later, despite a brief resurgence under Rennie, he would retire, disillusioned, aged just forty-five.

Later in 1968 Oldfield's profile took another unwanted boost, from an unlikely source. Kim Philby's KGB-edited autobiography *My Silent War* was published, and though the traitor claimed to wish to avoid naming names of serving officers, 'the formidable Maurice Oldfield' escaped the censor. The scenario was thus a strange one: the new Chief, John Rennie, had his anonymity protected by a government 'D' notice – the system used to prevent secret information from reaching the press – but his deputy, Maurice Oldfield, was the only serving MI6 officer to be publicly named. Oldfield was obviously a senior figure, and from then on the press kept a close eye on his progress.

When asked for his view on Philby's book, Oldfield averred that it was 'cleverly peppered with disinformation and mischief. He fudges dates and drags in names without reason. Why did he name me, for example?' Nonetheless, though obviously unimpressed by its existence and its naming of him personally, Maurice described it as 'largely true', so he was by no means entirely dismissive of its veracity.

16

A Waiting Game

THE RENNIE ERA in Century House, from 1968 until early 1973, was not bathed in a good deal of glory. It didn't take very long for the Foreign Office mandarins to discover that in their eagerness to appoint one of their own they had made a mistake. It seems a little harsh to describe a fundamentally decent man with such words, but 'hapless', 'dud', 'shy' and 'nonentity' are all terms that have been used in relation to John Ogilvy Rennie and his unfortunate tenure as Chief of MI6.

After Dick White had spent twelve years trying to steady MI6 following The Horrors of the early 1950s, this was a return to the amateurishness of the past. At an official dinner in Washington as the guest of Allen Dulles, Rennie was said to have sat in silence throughout. Maurice Oldfield would have got to know everyone present, the names of their partners and children, and given away absolutely nothing of himself. This lack of self-confidence on the part of the Chief was to usher in a period that featured too many unnecessary difficulties Rennie's successor would have to try and put straight.

Unsurprisingly, Maurice spent a good deal of his time on his travels; to foreign leaders and intelligence agencies he was the de facto Chief and the person with whom they wanted to deal. By contrast, Rennie stayed parked behind his desk in Century House. Britain was, in the late sixties and early seventies, trying to achieve membership of the European Economic Community, an aspiration of both major political parties – though in those days it was Harold Wilson's Labour Party that was the more divided. Twice during the sixties, once under Macmillan and once under Wilson, Britain's application for membership had been vetoed by French President Charles de Gaulle. Wilson and Leader of the Opposition Edward Heath were both committed to joining the EEC, a state of affairs not lost on Oldfield, who spent a good deal of time in Paris studying the politics and politicians of Britain's nearest neighbour.

When in the French capital, Maurice would stay at the home of MI6 officers and friends Halsey and Rozanne Colchester, who were stationed there from 1968 until 1971. Halsey Colchester had been a friend of Maurice's since his early days in MI6, and was previously known as an accomplished personnel officer for the Service. His wife, Rozanne, one of the Bletchley circle, first really got to know Maurice during this period in Paris. Writing about him recently, Rozanne said, 'I came late on to the scene, although Maurice and Halsey had known each other for years in "the office", and we clicked at once. Strange to say Maurice and I often felt like brother and sister so well did we fit in with each other! I still miss him – he was more than a friend – not a lover but a true "soul-mate". Knowing him was perhaps the happiest time of my life.'

On 17 April 1969 Oldfield travelled from Paris to St Moritz for one of his regular meetings with the Shah of Iran. He requested to be kept informed of a forthcoming movement back in England and Ken Dyer was asked to monitor the telephone while the two men had their discussion. At two p.m., Ken knocked and entered the room with a message. 'Your Imperial Majesty,' said Maurice, 'I have just become a great-uncle.' 'Then I shall now call you Great Uncle Maurice,' chuckled the Shah. When my brother, Tom, was born three years later, the Shah renamed Maurice 'Great Uncle Twice'.

Avuncular was a word that was often used in relation to Maurice, both personally and professionally, and in many respects that was accurate. His Christianity was entirely genuine. But to reach the top in secret intelligence does require a tough edge, and Maurice was not without that side to his personality when the situation demanded. During his period as deputy to John Rennie, an MI6 agent was captured by the KGB in the Eastern Bloc and was in danger of being tortured into betraying a large number of others, which could easily have led to their deaths. Word reached Maurice that an insider where the captive agent was being held could possibly smuggle a cyanide pill into his cell. It was a time for swift, decisive action, and in spite of all his deeply held beliefs, Oldfield agreed for the pill to be supplied so that the agent could take his own life and thus protect the many.

Rennie was perceived as weak and pliant as Chief, a trait the mole hunters were able to exploit. While Oldfield was Director of Counterintelligence he had been able, to an extent, to rein in their activities, and his scepticism about Fluency and the Angleton–Golitsyn axis was well known. Now, as C's formal deputy, he was travelling much more again and was thus conveniently out of the way for much of the time. Oldfield's former rival for the top job, Christopher Phillpotts, briefly enjoyed a new lease of life, and indoctrinated Rennie with the fears and paranoia that were his favourite subject.

Rennie was encouraged over to Washington, where he met with Golitsyn and Angleton and became fully immersed in their intoxicating theories. He returned eager and motivated, and Phillpotts was soon Director of Counterintelligence. Along with his assistant Stephen de Mowbray, he began purging away at everyone in the Service. He didn't unearth a single traitor but managed to orchestrate the removal or retirement of ten senior MI6 officers on the basis of historic connections, sexual misdemeanours or youthful flirtations with communism. Bearing in mind that the world of MI6 was, in contrast to the area it covered, a small, quite incestuous one where everyone knew everyone else, it really shouldn't have come as a surprise to the mole hunters to discover exactly that.

Everyone in the Service was fully investigated. Even someone as blameless as Sir Dick White, now intelligence coordinator for the Cabinet to top up his pension, was lamely accused of being the mole. Just about the only senior MI6 figure never to have such allegations, however spurious, thrown at him was Maurice Oldfield. After nearly a quarter of a century, at last, perhaps, Maurice's background was a positive advantage. He hadn't been to school with Kim Philby, or to Cambridge. He didn't have links to dubious financiers and there were no serious suggestions of sexual shenanigans. Even as close a colleague as Denis Greenhill would say of Maurice 'he's an enigma to me'.

There was another key practical factor in Oldfield's favour:

he had never been to Russia. Despite his global travels and his insistence on seeing things at first hand, he studiously avoided the Eastern Bloc. Professionally he had full trust in Harold Shergold and his team, and he was content that Friends such as Gerald Buss were providing him with an accurate picture of life behind the Iron Curtain. Whether by accident or design, the effect of Maurice's absence from the Soviet Bloc was that he was not tainted by association – the bewildering affliction that affected so many, such as Gerry Warner. Even though Oldfield was considered one of MI6's foremost opponents of communism, his manner of dealing with it was at more than arm's length. Though he was the conduit for Oleg Penkovsky's intelligence to the CIA, he never met the most important double agent to that date. He listened to the recordings, viewed the papers, analysed Shergy's reports and sold it as a package without ever engaging in direct contact. Given that in every other respect Oldfield was very much a hands-on roaming officer who liked to see things as they were on the ground, this would seem to indicate that Maurice was conscious of how the minds of the mole hunters worked.

Oldfield also understood the limitations under which MI6 was operating in the Soviet Bloc, which were at least partly financial. Under the Wilson government, the Service was asked to build more of a presence in African countries that were being freed rapidly from colonialism and where communism was considered likely to fill any voids – but without any commensurate increase in funding. So the MI6 budget did not run to building a bigger presence in the East, even had that been possible with the KGB so vigorous in policing its territory.

MI6 and other Western intelligence agencies were criticized for not having foreseen the August 1968 crushing by Brezhnev's Soviet Army of the Prague Spring uprising, which had been an attempt to liberalize life in Czechoslovakia that the Soviet leadership saw as a threat to its autonomy. The simple fact was that the West did not have enough of a presence in the East to be able to predict such things. Technical surveillance developments meant the West knew what military capability the Soviets had, but no access to the strategic planning of how that equipment would be used. While the trouncing of the rebellion was a reminder of the brutal capability of the Soviets, importantly it was also realized by the analysts that this wasn't an act that threatened any forthcoming invasion of the West. It was essentially, to the Soviet mind, a defensive action to protect the satellite states from Westernization.

With Rennie's blessing to keep hunting for moles, Golitsyn returned to Britain several times, and under de Mowbray's stewardship was given access to all of MI5's files prior to his defection. The Russian ranged across them, and rekindled his old theories about Hugh Gaitskell having been murdered in order to secure the premiership for the KGB's favoured Labour leader, Harold Wilson. It was an assertion without any kind of evidence other than Gaitskell's doctor having told Fluency's Arthur Martin that his patient's sudden contraction of, and death from, lupus erythematosus (the attacking of healthy tissue by a hyperactive immune system) was a mystery. People such as Peter Wright began to delve into Wilson's connections with the Russians on the mole hunters' assumption that anyone, particularly of the left, who had anything to do with the East was therefore also a traitor. In fact Wilson's trips to Russia were no secret. He genuinely believed that trade with the Soviets was no less desirable than trade with anyone else. That didn't make him a communist. Increasingly people such as Wright began to develop all manner of theories about Wilson, to the point where Harold Wilson Conspiracy Theories became almost an industry in their own right.

This was the time of Home Secretary Roy Jenkins's push towards a permissive society. Homosexuality between consenting adults had been legalized, *The Times* had stood up against the Establishment when Mick Jagger and Keith Richards of the Rolling Stones were convicted for possession of drugs, and the days when Harold Macmillan could proclaim 'you've never had it so good' in relation to a booming economy were long gone. After battling against the inevitable for three years, Chancellor of the Exchequer James Callaghan had been forced to devalue the currency, and Wilson's claim that 'the pound in your pocket' was still as valuable was widely derided.

On the world stage Britain's empire was now a subject for study by historians, and pride in the country was seen only in the work of such ephemeral entities as pop stars and footballers. The 1966 World Cup win was the most recent event that could be claimed as a national victory. In Northern Ireland, unrest had started to become more prominent in the mid 1960s with marches and confrontations on both sides of the loyalist and republican divide, and these exploded into violence in 1969 with the Battle of the Bogside in Derry, which resulted in the British Army being sent to intervene in what was the symbolic start of what would become known as the Troubles.

People on the fringes of politics, particularly on the right, became so concerned by the state of the country that they began to plan for an alternative form of government. George Kennedy Young, the former Robber Baron and Deputy Chief of MI6, became a Conservative prospective parliamentary candidate, but was in fact so concerned by left-wing infiltration, the rise of the trade unions and the degeneration of society that he reaffirmed his belief that it was people such as himself who needed to protect Britain from itself. The words of a paper he circulated in the 1950s, and which George Blake would use as an example of his disillusionment, perhaps best sum up the views of the likes of Wright and Young at the time:

In the press, in Parliament, in the United Nations, from the pulpit, there is a ceaseless talk about the rule of law, civilized relations between nations, the spread of democratic processes, self-determination and national sovereignty, respect for the rights of man and human dignity.

The reality, we all know perfectly well, is quite the opposite and consists of an ever-increasing spread of lawlessness, disregard of human contract, cruelty and corruption. The nuclear stalemate is matched by the moral stalemate.

It is the spy who has been called on to remedy the situation created by the deficiencies of ministers, diplomats, generals and priests.

Men's minds are shaped of course by their environments and we spies, although we have our professional mystique, do perhaps live closer to the realities and hard facts of international relations than other practitioners of government.

We are relatively free of the problems of status, of precedence, departmental attitudes and evasions of personal responsibility, which create the official cast of mind. We do not have to develop, like Parliamentarians conditioned by a lifetime, the ability to produce the ready phrase, the smart reply and the flashing smile. And so it is not surprising these days that the spy finds himself the main guardian of intellectual integrity.

It was against this backdrop that Wilson lost the 1970 general election, Edward Heath transforming a large Labour majority into a majority of 30 for his Conservatives in one go. This did not stop the agitations against Wilson, however, and despite Heath's pre-election talk of taming the unions and reaffirming traditional conservative values, many on the right considered his government to be little different from Wilson's.

On the face of things, Maurice Oldfield and the new Prime Minister had much in common. Both were self-made grammar school boys from humble backgrounds. Both were bachelors, and both were organists. Both had reached dizzy heights in their organizations, the Conservative Party and MI6, despite being in many ways atypical of their kind. And on a professional level they got on perfectly well; each could listen to and respect the other's opinion. Personally, though, they were different. While Oldfield was known for his sharp wit and gentle humour, Heath was never likely to be mistaken for a ray of sunshine. While Oldfield was gregarious and outgoing, his career forged on his ability to make and keep loyal friends, Heath was thought to be insular and reserved. People tended to assume that because of their backgrounds and interests they would automatically be friends; in fact their relationship was no more or less than a perfectly functional professional one.

The Northern Ireland problems soon became a vexation for Heath. As early as 1970 it was obvious that the security situation in the Province was being hampered by the inability of the organizations concerned, most notably the Army and the Royal Ulster Constabulary Special Branch, and to a lesser extent MI5, to work together and coordinate their intelligence about the dominant terrorist organization, the Provisional IRA. Despite Northern Ireland being home territory, and thus in MI5's domain, the Director, Michael Hanley, was reticent about his service becoming further entangled in the region.

When Heath instructed Rennie and Oldfield officially to take MI6 into Ulster, the two men were united in their opposition. They were being asked to take their Service into what was very much British territory, and such an incursion could only add to inter-agency rivalries. Prior to this, any MI6 presence had been on an advisory basis, offering a view on intelligence, and because the Soviet Embassy in Dublin had become proportionally overmanned and there were suspicions that the KGB was creating links with the IRA. Inevitably, though, the Prime Minister got his way and an MI6 team under Frank Steele was dispatched to Belfast in October 1971.

A feature of Rennie's tenure was that of MI6 officers slipping back into the bad old ways of risky operations, with the added complication of the use of mercenaries or criminals to carry out their work – which could then be denied if compromised. This was in part as a result of Rennie being what was occasionally deemed a Foreign Office stooge. Historically, the Chief would take a view on what matters needed to be referred to the Foreign Secretary for approval, which helped distance the politicians from anything controversial and maintained the convention of MI6 having a degree of autonomy. It was a system that, despite its obvious democratic deficit, generally worked, at least since the days of The Horrors. Almost *anything* that was brought to Rennie, however, was referred to the Foreign Secretary – who by 1970, once more, was the former Prime Minister Alec Douglas-Home.

So what was intended to have the effect of bringing MI6 under Foreign Office control in fact had the opposite result. If Rennie was going to take everything he was given straight to the politicians, then his staff would simply stop taking things to him. Officers were at liberty to engage their own sub-agents, or cut-outs, to keep them one step away from officialdom at one end and from operations at the other. During the Rennie era, the use of such people became extensive, with little or no quality control from above. An example was getting an agent to infiltrate, say, the IRA and orchestrate a bank robbery to raise funds for the organization. The person would claim to have a haul of, say, £10,000 from the robbery, but only £5,000 would find its way back to the IRA. All those involved would be suspected of having stolen the 'missing' £5,000 and, hey presto, the terrorist leaders would mete out punishments to their own men. The intention was to prime the terror cells to implode, and sometimes it worked.

An effect of this lack of control was that, just occasionally, apprehended villains would say they were operating with

MI6's authority, whether or not such a thing was true; and with this being difficult to prove, some escaped conviction. During 1971, a sometime armed robber and businessman named Kenneth Littlejohn came to the attention of the British government when Lady Pamela Onslow, an aristocratic divorcee who did some work with an organization dealing with ex-borstal inmates, related a tale told to her by one of those former inmates, Keith Littlejohn, about his brother. Kenneth Littlejohn claimed to have been shown Kalashnikov rifles in County Kerry which were said to have been smuggled in by Russian sailors. Lady Onslow arranged for Littlejohn to meet a Conservative MP, the Army minister Geoffrey Johnson Smith, to pass on what he knew. So far, so sensible. To some in MI6 the Littlejohns' willingness to talk represented an opportunity, and soon they were passing information to an MI6 officer who used it to help the security effort. Again, so far, so sensible. In September 1972 the IRA alleged that the British Army had used information from the Littlejohns to lure a young Catholic named Edmund Woolsey to his death via a bomb placed in his car, which he'd been called to retrieve after the police claimed to have found it abandoned. Things were now, if true, downright unlawful.

The big one came the following month. On 12 October, the most lucrative bank robbery to that date in the Irish Republic took place when £67,000 was stolen from the Grafton Street branch of the Allied Irish Banks in Dublin, after the manager had been driven to the branch while his family were held hostage. For the next few days the press in Britain and Ireland speculated that it was the work of the IRA; then, after reports of comments made by the robbers, the loyalist Ulster Volunteer Force was suspected. The effect of appearing to discredit the terrorists was not to last long, and after supposedly receiving a dressing down in Trafalgar Square for the robbery from their MI6 controller, code-named OLIVER, on the 18th, the Littlejohns were arrested the following day by the Flying Squad and taken to Edgware police station as the Irish Garda had requested their extradition.

There followed an embarrassing chain of events. The extradition hearing was held in secret after the Littlejohns claimed that not only had the robbery been approved and funded by MI6, but that MI6 had paid them to carry out assassinations in the Republic. Despite their claims of British government sanction, the brothers were convicted in Dublin at the Special Criminal Court of Offences against the State. The Littlejohn affair was to rumble on into Maurice Oldfield's time as Chief. Early into his tenure he felt obliged to summon all his staff to a meeting in the canteen at Century House and formally disown such operations, and to assure those present that there was no truth in the Littlejohns' allegations. If Maurice was already convinced of the need to clean up the Service, the Littlejohn affair and its like only served to reinforce that view.

The one major success of the Rennie era – and it was important – came from a joint MI5 and MI6 operation to monitor KGB officers working in London who might be susceptible to being turned. Oleg Lyalin turned out to be the man. He had been targeted after a surveillance team found that he was having an affair with his secretary; he agreed to share information in return for the affair being kept quiet and eventual formal resettlement in Britain. This was hastened when he was arrested for drink-driving in London. Lyalin's defection triggered what became known as Operation Foot, which resulted, effectively, in 105 KGB or GRU officers being expelled from Britain.

A sudden expulsion of that kind could have triggered a diplomatic incident, or caused inter-departmental rifts in Whitehall, but it was supported by both Rennie, who claimed the measure had the support of Britain's European allies, and the head of MI5, Martin Furnival Jones, who reported that there had been evidence going back over fifteen years of the Soviets penetrating government departments as diverse as the Foreign Office, the Ministry of Transport, the Board of Trade and the Ministry of Defence, as well as the Army, the Navy and the RAF. He claimed that at least thirty Soviet intelligence officers were running agents in the British government or industry.

Crucially, Operation Foot had the support of the Home Secretary, Reginald Maudling, and the Foreign Secretary. Heath's support was reluctant but, once granted, unequivocal. It became a matter of timing, and it was agreed that Douglas-Home would write to his opposite number, Andrei Gromyko, to outline the grievances prior to action. The Foreign Secretary cited the case of an officer named B. G. Glushchenko, who had been nominated to the post of First Secretary at the Soviet Embassy in London. Glushchenko had been out in the country ostensibly representing the air-craft industry at trade fairs: instead he was reported for offering bribes to a British businessman in return for details of British military equipment. Gromyko didn't reply. The expulsion went ahead. At a stroke, Operation Foot rid the country of more Soviet spies than the Fluency committee could ever have dreamed of. For the next twenty years, the

KGB's presence in Britain was effectively neutered. Henceforth, the intelligence their officers sent back to Moscow from the United Kingdom was almost exclusively from open sources – newspapers, television reports, political speeches and debate.

Jack Rennie may not have been popular among MI6 colleagues beyond the mole hunters, but nobody would have wished the manner of his retirement upon him, certainly not his replacement. On 15 January 1973, the Chief's eldest son, Charles Tatham Ogilvy Rennie, and his wife were arrested for being involved in an operation to smuggle quantities of heroin out of Hong Kong. Being the first Chief formally to take MI6 into Northern Ireland had made Rennie a terrorist target; the arrest of his son and daughter-in-law now made him a press target too. Not wishing to bring embarrassment to the Service or the government, he retired a year short of the official age, at just fifty-nine. Soon after-wards the German magazine *Stern* broke the story of Charles Rennie's arrest.

This time there was no jockeying for position, no shortlist of candidates, no question of the Foreign Office parachuting in one of its own. This time Denis Greenhill had no hesitation in recommending the new Chief, and Douglas-Home had no hesitation in accepting that recommendation and announcing his decision to Heath. Maurice Oldfield had, at last, acceded to the position of Chief of the Secret Intelligence Service.

17

M = C Part One

IT'S UNLIKELY THAT Maurice Oldfield expected that his elevation to become the fabled 'C' would allow him the anonymity that had been afforded to the majority of his predecessors. Kim Philby had seen to that in 1968 with the publication of his autobiography, even before the unfortunate publicity that precipitated Rennie's departure. It was the same magazine, *Stern*, that carefully reported Oldfield's appointment, making him the first Chief to be named in the press. The *Stern* report was picked up by the American magazine *Newsweek*, and the facts repeated. Once that had entered the public domain, the British press reported on that report, and Maurice's humble background and remarkable promotion gave all the daily newspapers a cracking story.

At that stage Maurice's home address – now a bigger, modern flat, 6 Marsham Court – was still listed in *Who's Who*, along with his mother's telephone number in Over Haddon. For the first time, too, a picture of the head of MI6 appeared in the press, though as it was a slightly blurred shot taken outside Buckingham

Palace when he was appointed CBE in 1956, featuring a dark-haired, unsmiling Maurice with round Billy Bunter glasses, anyone seeking out the man himself in 1973 wouldn't have found him easy to identify. For the next five years that was to be the photograph wheeled out every time his name was mentioned. It still features on any number of conspiracy theory websites.

The press descended on Over Haddon, expecting to find a host of locals wanting to spill their stories about the man who was by now almost casually being referred to as 'M'. Instead, the reaction caused one frustrated journalist to say to a villager, 'What's wrong with you people? Nobody will tell me anything!' A picture of Maurice's brother Brian, looking particularly agricultural as he carried a brush and a shovel across the farmyard, appeared on page three of the *Daily Express*, though typically Brian's comment was a simple 'my brother works for the Foreign Office, we never talk about what he does'.

His sister Renee, living at Mona View with their mother Annie, was doorstepped by reporters and said, 'For all I know he could be a vacuum cleaner salesman. All I know is when he uses my phone to make business calls he never pays the bill.' Only the landlord of the Lathkill, Pat Dougherty, offered a variation on the theme: 'Of course we all know what Maurice does. But we never talk about it.' Enquiries about Maurice to the Foreign Office were met with the statement 'Mr Oldfield is employed on extra-departmental duties'. The convention of disavowing MI6 was creaking under the weight of publicity about its new Chief, but Maurice had no intention of recommending a change to that policy.

Once the official round of congratulatory dinners and

drinks was done, Maurice went back to Over Haddon to talk through matters and gauge local reaction to the news reports. He was gratified to learn that nobody had said anything, and when he went to the Lathkill for his customary half of bitter, nobody treated him the slightest bit differently – even though he was now generally shadowed by a couple of plain-clothes protection officers as well as the perpetual Ken Dyer, who was almost as well known as Maurice in the village.

As Maurice was becoming established in his new job, in May 1973 the Parish of Bakewell with Over Haddon was also gaining a new vicar. Thirty-four-year-old father of two Edmund Urquhart was introduced to Maurice by his curate, Martin Leigh, after being warned 'Maurice is the head of MI6 and he worships at Over Haddon every Sunday. And by the way, he refers to the Holy Communion as "Mass".' Leigh himself was quite a character, a lovable giant of a man who would conduct Saturday weddings with his full rugby kit on under his robes, ready for a quick getaway, and who refused to swear until he crossed the parish boundary. When they met, and Edmund said, 'Good morning, Maurice', Oldfield replied to the man nearly twenty-five years his junior, 'Good morning, Father.' 'This made Maurice's Anglo-Catholicism obvious to me,' Edmund recalled, 'as I was "*un peu Catho*" myself.' The vicar and his new parishioner hit it off at once, and if the organist was ever indisposed Maurice would volunteer to step in. It struck Edmund that the fact religion was so important to Oldfield stood him in good stead in places as diverse as Northern Ireland and Israel. 'Maurice could understand and get alongside religious people. How much we need people with such wisdom today!'

Maurice wanted as normal a life as possible to be

maintained when he visited Derbyshire, both for his family's sake and for his own sanity. Since 1968 Bakewell Station had been closed. Maurice could have had a chauffeur as he did when abroad, but he insisted on taking the train and being picked up by John or Warren Pearce from Chesterfield Station. A call from Maurice to Derbyshire Police head-quarters at Ripley was enough to ensure that an unmarked police car would be there waiting at Chesterfield, and the Special Branch officers within would follow the Pearces back to Over Haddon at a safe distance. Maurice wished their presence to be kept as low-key and discreet as possible.

Still intending to potter around the farm and the village as ever he did, though with the two officers always lurking somewhere in the background, Maurice enjoyed wandering the lanes looking out over the limestone walls to Lathkill Dale, accompanied by the family's current sheepdog. One day in early 1973 he had ventured nearly a mile out of the village, scruffily dressed in a tweed jacket held together with baling twine, wellington boots and a rustic trilby, with Bob the dog, when he was flagged down by someone he recog-nized as a London journalist in a sports car. The man was obviously one of many looking for clues to his life in Derbyshire, but had not recognized Maurice in his civvies. 'I say, my good man,' said the impossibly plummy journalist, 'do you know the way to Over Haddon? There's a drink in it for you if you do.'

'Yes,' Maurice replied, and carried on walking.

Oldfield's appointment as Chief came just a few months before Roger Moore's screen debut as James Bond in *Live and Let Die*, and in the media hype leading up to the release of the film, finally being able to put a real name and face to the character of M was irresistible. The fact that the character's codename and Oldfield's first initial were the same was obviously no coincidence. From then on, in the press Maurice Oldfield was habitually referred to as 'the model for Ian Fleming's M', a tale that has persisted to this day. In fact Oldfield was only vaguely acquainted with Fleming, whose first book, *Casino Royale*, was written when Maurice was on his first stint in Singapore and barely known within Broadway, let alone without. There was even an article in one of the daily papers comparing Oldfield to the film actor Bernard Lee, who had played M on screen since *Dr No* in 1962. He played up to the association in his postcards home to his young nephews and nieces: instead of signing off the reports of his travels with his customary 'Maurice', henceforth he would finish with a very deliberate 'M'.

The media attention only served to add to the mystique surrounding Maurice and his position, and from the start of his time as Chief he kept one eye on the press. Previously, his main reason for cultivating journalists was what they could tell him; now it was at least as much about what he could tell them. He kept all the press cuttings about him personally and espionage matters more generally: as MI6 moved into the modern age, media perception was going to be important, and Maurice was determined to manage it as best he could. There had been the hint of a dig at MI6 – and possibly, he thought, at himself – in a 1971 Auberon Waugh 'HP Sauce' column in *Private Eye* in which Waugh referred to 'Ogilvy's bum boys' – Ogilvy being John Rennie's middle name. Only an insider would have worked out the intended target of the dig, but Maurice resolved to act. Henceforth he became friendly with Waugh, and the personal references became more favourable, if still irreverent, Waugh referring to 'my friend M' as his column prodded away at Harold Wilson – or 'Wislon', as the column preferred. Maurice even arranged for *Private Eye* to do a little cartoon and feature on his nephew John Pearce when John had to cry off a county rugby match after a cow he was milking sat on his knee and broke his leg.

Out of pragmatic necessity, Oldfield also formed a wary friendship with Harry Chapman Pincher. Chapman Pincher was one of the few Fleet Street journalists at the time to specialize in intelligence matters, and while appreciating the need to keep him onside, Maurice would surely have thought the title of his autobiography, *Dangerous to Know*, entirely appropriate.

In his first few weeks occupying the top-floor office at Century House, Maurice set about imposing his new regime on the place. As a chairman of directors, Oldfield was found by his colleagues to be if not exactly dictatorial then not very collegiate either – a very dominant presence. He knew MI6 from top to bottom and intended to run the place from top to bottom. Weak leadership had cost the organization dear, and as most of Oldfield's closest friends were outside the Service, he didn't feel the need to become embroiled in office politics. He wasn't allied to any particular faction in the service, though was liberal in outlook. Importantly, he was also on good terms with both the Prime Minister and the Leader of the Opposition, and many of their senior colleagues. Oldfield understood that keeping the trust of the PM was essential to the Service, and essential to him personally.

Though he'd been in the Service for the better part of three decades, and was the first member of the post-war intake to reach the top job, Oldfield was still in many ways an outsider. He'd seen first-hand the problems faced by his three immediate predecessors – all decent men, but for different reasons not right for the job. John Sinclair, widely accepted to have been incompetent, was forced out in the wake of The Horrors. Dick White, brought in from MI5 to clear up the mess, was, despite his long service, never fully accepted by MI6 and found himself drawn into the spiralling paranoia of the mole hunt, trying to look six ways at once. John Rennie, a man who had never aspired to the job and was out of his depth before being sidelined in unfortunate circumstances, should probably never have been appointed.

In Northern Ireland, Oldfield's accession came soon after the imposition of Direct Rule on the Province under Secretary of State William Whitelaw and the Permanent Secretary in the new Northern Ireland Office, Frank Cooper. MI6 and MI5 contributed to what was known as the Northern Ireland Assessment Staff, from their base on the top floor of Stormont Castle. Initially the group was led by an MI6 controller, Allan Rowley, who would in 1974 be succeeded by Denis Payne of MI5 – a prime mover of what was to become the Clockwork Orange operation, of which more later.

A key officer of the time was Frank Steele of MI6, operating under the official title of Political Adviser, who used MI6 techniques to forge a relationship with the leadership of the Irish nationalist party the SDLP which was to pave the way for the Sunningdale initiative, which led, briefly, to a power-sharing arrangement from December 1974. When Steele's tour of duty was completed he was replaced by Michael

Oatley, who used the hand left to him by Steele to get more deeply into the diplomatic effort, beginning – unofficially at first, as such activity was strictly forbidden – to develop back channels to the IRA itself. Once he had established his connections, Oatley informed Frank Cooper and MI6 about what he had been doing. Oatley recalls that when he visited Oldfield in London, his Chief listened very carefully to what he was told, and said, 'You do whatever Frank wants you to do and you have my blessing.'

Oatley was under an enormous amount of pressure, meeting with IRA Council representatives alone then travelling through the night to report back at Stormont at nine o'clock the following morning. Some in the Northern Ireland Office were supportive of what he was doing; others were not. Denis Payne chipped away at Oatley 'negatively and endlessly' and Cooper's support waned, leaving Oatley having to argue the merits of the case personally. He found himself on the verge of exhaustion and having to remain entirely focused in order to retain his objectivity and avoid bonding emotionally with the people with whom he was fraternizing – a recognized phenomenon known as Stockholm Syndrome.

I asked Oatley about Maurice's influence at this time. 'I don't know about the general picture and his impact upon it,' he said, 'but from a personal point of view I found him very helpful. When I was handling the secret dialogue with representatives of the IRA leadership on my own I was in a very exposed position. The political situation was highly delicate and it was natural that I should be subjected to very firm interrogation after each meeting, not all of it friendly. The MI5 Director of Intelligence [Payne] was openly hostile to the whole exercise. But over the following months, whenever I went to London, Maurice had left instructions that I was to go and see him. I was under a lot of pressure, as I am sure he could see, and he was as kind and supportive in those interviews as could be. I remember feeling encouraged and strengthened in keeping my end up when, later on, I found myself under quite hostile questioning by colleagues who were all older, and senior to me, and some quite sceptical about what I had got us all into. I remember thinking, "However much these people may pick at me I know that I have the complete and personal support of my Chief." It helped me very much. I was very grateful to Maurice at the time and I remain so to his memory.'

The connections made at that time were to be described by Sinn Fein's Martin McGuinness as 'the worst thing that ever happened to the IRA', as the work done deprived the terrorists of much of the popular support they'd previously enjoyed. Even after the Sunningdale Agreement collapsed and the situation in Northern Ireland deteriorated in a terrifying way in the late 1970s, the work done by the likes of Frank Steele and Michael Oatley paved the way for the Good Friday Agreement in 1998, with Oatley's contribution in particular leading a journalist and expert on the Troubles, Peter Taylor, to describe him as 'the most important British agent to have worked in Northern Ireland'. Oldfield's unwavering support of his beleaguered officer at that crucial time may only have been a small part in the nascent peace process, but it is conceivable that without that top-level support in the mid 1970s the process might never have happened at all.

The fact of Oldfield being associated with taking MI6 into Northern Ireland made him a direct target for the terrorists for the first time. The security presence around him became more visible, and from 1973 on there was a security officer on permanent duty at Maurice's Marsham Court flat, which was also, like the one on Caxton Street, bugged. Gerald Buss was one who noted the changes. 'Previously, while there was usually a policeman or security officer somewhere in evidence, it wasn't too intrusive. When Maurice became Chief, all that changed. There was always a protection officer sitting just inside the door to the flat, and the officer would only allow access to people who had been thoroughly vetted. It was really quite stifling.'

The most serious threat to Maurice's life – of which he was aware, that is – came on the evening of 13 October 1975. The biggest bomb yet found in Britain in peacetime was discovered by the Special Branch officers hanging from a railing outside Lockets Restaurant, directly beneath Oldfield's Marsham Court flat. Just a short walk from the House of Commons, the restaurant was popular with politicians, so it is probable that Maurice was just one of a host of potential targets the terrorists hoped to wipe out with their deadly nail bomb. The device was disabled by a bomb disposal crew, but its proximity to his home gave Oldfield cause to tell his family it had left him with a real sense of his own mortality.

In America, politics at this time was dominated by the Watergate affair – the scandal that launched a thousand 'gates' – after Republican President Richard Nixon's aides tried to cover up a break-in at Democratic Party headquarters. The scandal eventually led to Nixon's disgrace and resignation, and two of Oldfield's CIA counterparts were also brought down, directly or indirectly, in the whirlwind. At about the same time as Maurice was appointed Chief, his old colleague Richard Helms was sacked by Nixon for refusing to block the Watergate investigation. He was replaced by James Schlesinger, a man with no intelligence experience, who was only in post for five months before being appointed Secretary of Defense.

It was Schlesinger's replacement, William Colby, who instigated the other high-profile CIA departure. By 1974, James Jesus Angleton had added to his list of potential Soviet agents not just Harold Wilson but Swedish Premier Olof Palme, West German Chancellor Willy Brandt, and two Canadian Prime Ministers, Lester Pearson and Pierre Trudeau. Colby, not before time, decided that Angleton needed to be reined in, not least for the man's own sanity, and began the process of sidelining him; even Angleton – oh, the irony! – found himself accused of being a Soviet mole. At the end of the year Angleton retired, saying he had outlived his usefulness. He spent the rest of his life in relative peace, orchid-bothering, fly-fishing and smoking until he eventually succumbed to lung cancer in 1987.

So far as the ongoing mole hunt in Britain was concerned, Oldfield nominally allowed it to continue, but Phillpotts was retired and Maurice had already sent a reluctant de Mowbray off to a post in the southern Mediterranean – conveniently out of the way. The exiled mole hunter would never let go of his beliefs, despite eventually conceding that Roger Hollis and his deputy Graham Mitchell were not spies, though operating at such a distance it was difficult for him to do anything practical. The matter became largely an MI5 concern.

In order to reform MI6, Maurice decided to streamline the Service, and laid down his ground rules. Special operations of the Crabb, Suez or even Littlejohn kind were out. The new regime was going back to old values: the Secret Intelligence Service was going to be focused on collecting intelligence. To some of the young, thrusting officers of the time, brought up on the fables of the past, this was anathema. Upon reflection, most accepted it was also right.

One of the schemes Maurice favoured was a proposal brought to him by a colleague, and named Deep Chat. The idea was a development of the use of Friends but using officers, and was intended to allow MI6 to speak to sources without their interlocutors knowing they were speaking to the Secret Service. In theory this circumvented the need to obtain clearance from the Foreign Office for communicating with people where the situation might include political risk, or indeed danger, and negated any potential embarrassment for both parties – it was essentially taking a 'cover' story to a new level. Because the interlocutor was not aware he was being pumped for secret intelligence, in theory the officer's training and interpersonal skills would enable a deeper level of communication than would normally be achievable by diplomats. To Maurice, this was a low-risk, high-reward proposal. To many in the Service it was a no-go. A few simply enjoyed the kudos of letting people know they were in MI6, others were sceptical about how any information gained from this method could be described as 'secret' intelligence given that the source would presumably have divulged the information freely to anyone who asked nicely. It was effectively 'open source' rather than 'secret' intelligence.

Gerry Warner was in the latter camp, despite being an officer Maurice favoured, and said so in the seminar when the Deep Chat proposal was raised. He quickly found himself being dispatched to Malaysia, with Oldfield's instruction 'just keep an eye on the tin prices' ringing in his ears. The Deep Chat initiative was officially shelved, though Oldfield remained convinced of its merits and would encourage certain officers to use the techniques.

Particularly to those who had no rivalry with him, the avuncular persona of the man they affectionately nicknamed 'Moulders' behind his back was well known. One of Oldfield's great strengths was his ability to treat his staff with decency and respect no matter what their level. Though as Chief, when at Century House, he was inevitably operating in his office or the boardroom, and some of the more junior members of staff seldom saw him, those who did spoke warmly of his personal kindness. In researching this book, and meeting a range of retired officers, I was surprised by how many of their wives would wait until their husbands left the room before saying to me, 'I was one of Maurice's secretaries', and then relating a story of a personal gift or a pleasant comment that they remembered.

One such lady, whose identity I have promised to protect, recalled that she had to retire from the Service at a young age when she married as her husband-to-be was in a sensitive job and there might have been a conflict of interests. Though Maurice had previously had little to do with this lady beyond the usual pleasantries, when he heard she had to retire he called her up to his private office and promised to personally ensure that all her pension arrangements were in place and that she was being looked after. Forty years on, his kindness has remained with her.

Despite being the Chief of MI6, Oldfield continued to

travel, to a far greater extent than has been documented in relation to any other holder of that post. Early in his tenure he visited the Shah, in Iran this time, and told him that under his leadership he would not allow MI6 to operate in Iran, or to negotiate with the radical Islamic leaders. Maurice had worked closely with the Shah's intelligence agency, SAVAK, and had helped that organization forge links with Israeli Intelligence. He hoped that his connection to the Israelis via Teddy Kollek would continue to provide a back channel to the Iranian intelligence agency, and that by keeping his word to the Shah he would be able to help encourage him to rein in his more authoritarian ways. This was, as Maurice admitted, against his better judgement, but while he was C his personal relationship with the Shah enabled this situation to prevail. What was to happen in Iran in 1979 illustrated the drawback of so much of MI6's work at that level at that time being based on Oldfield as an individual.

Maurice made a point, too, of visiting his favourite station, Singapore, a number of times while he was Chief. The personal and the professional, as usual, were closely intertwined. On his first visit, in 1975, Maurice was here at the invitation of Lee Kuan Yew – who was still, of course, Prime Minister – to join in the 10th Singaporean National Day celebrations. Lee's real first name was in fact the very English 'Harry', but as the two became more familiar, Maurice jokingly insisted on calling him Fred Lee, because he thought his friend looked more like a Fred than a Harry. As they enjoyed their small-talk, Lee called over a smartly dressed civil servant. 'I know that you are a very perceptive man, Maurice, as head of MI6, and you can spot talent easily. But I take my hat off to you for spotting a future Permanent

Secretary while he was still at school and running around in short trousers.' The Permanent Secretary in question was Ngiam Tong Dow, the son of Maurice's neighbour on Flower Road, whose education he had funded some twenty years before.

A more upsetting reunion came on Maurice's next visit, the following year. A message reached him that his former chauffeur from the 1950s, Ahmed, was dying of cancer. Oldfield ignored all security advice and asked his current chauffeur to drive him to a hut in the crime-ravaged Lorong Tai Seng slums where he found Ahmed lying in great pain. On hearing Maurice's voice, the dying chauffeur opened his eyes and the two sat quietly, Ahmed's wasted hands in Maurice's. Ahmed's family reported that he died comforted by the knowledge that his important 'tuan', or master, had come from England to be at his side. When the time came, Maurice settled the funeral expenses.

Liaison with the CIA was, as always, an important role for British Intelligence. Maurice was on good terms with the new Director, William Colby, and also became friendly with Colby's successor, George H. W. Bush, the future President. Something that preoccupied the two agencies at this time was the radical Labor government in Australia, and its new Prime Minister, Gough Whitlam. Whitlam was not considered especially left-wing, but he was regarded with suspicion by the British as he drove through measures to distance his country from its British-inspired traditions; he replaced the British honours system with the Order of Australia, and was no lover of the national anthem, substituting for it 'Advance Australia Fair'. The Americans were suspicious of his links with the People's Republic of China, and displeased that he had withdrawn all Australian troops from Vietnam in 1973.

What united MI6 and the CIA in particular, though, was their concern that Whitlam might close down the joint satellite tracking base at Pine Gap, near Alice Springs in the Northern Territory. Pine Gap had only been operational since 1970 but was of huge strategic importance as it controlled satellite surveillance for nearly a third of the planet, including China, eastern USSR, and the Far and Middle East. In 1974, Whitlam ordered a Royal Commission on Intelligence and Security after he became the first Australian Prime Minister to discover that his country was party to the Western intelligence agencies' joint arrangement known as CAZAB, which had been pioneered by James Angleton. Until then it had been assumed by government that Pine Gap was an Australian-only installation, so the news that it was being run by the CIA did not fill Gough Whitlam with unparalleled joy.

The Royal Commission was put under the chairmanship of a senior judge, Robert Marsden Hope – with whom Oldfield communicated regularly; he even had the judge's home phone number. He also had the ear of one of the other commissioners, Judge Edward Woodward. When Hope let Oldfield know that the Commission was leaning towards cautioning against the Australian intelligence agencies having such close ties with their British and American counterparts, which might well involve losing their access to Pine Gap, the MI6 man informed Bill Colby. As it was Whitlam who'd been driving the matter, in the view of the intelligence agencies something needed to be done.

Luckily for the CIA and MI6, the adventurous Whitlam

government was running into difficulties and the astonishing chain of events that followed might have happened anyway, but according to the investigative journalists John Pilger and Joseph Trento, working separately, Colby and Oldfield were heavily involved. The opposition, under Malcolm Fraser, was blocking the financial bills necessary for Whitlam to fund his programme as they controlled the second chamber, the Senate. It was as if the House of Commons was having its agenda vetoed by the House of Lords: technically correct, but unsustainable. The Queen's representative in Australia, the Governor-General Sir John Kerr, who theoretically had the right to intervene – as does the Queen in the United Kingdom – indicated to Whitlam that he wouldn't. The usual result would be negotiations and the second chamber allowing the government's agenda to pass through with amendments. The Governor-General would continue as the nominal figurehead, handing out gongs, drinking gin, shaking hands and waving at people. But for the first and only time in Australian history, that didn't happen. Instead, Kerr sacked Whitlam. The democratically elected Prime Minister was turfed out by the Queen's representative. According to Pilger and Trento's CIA sources, Bill Colby and Maurice Oldfield discussed the matter and 'our man Kerr did what he was told to do'.

The Dismissal, as it became known, is still recalled with astonishment in Australia. But from the British and American intelligence agencies' point of view the outcome was exactly what they wanted. The Hope Commission didn't report until 1977, by which time Whitlam had been heavily defeated when he attempted to stand again – and Pine Gap remains a key asset of Western intelligence. Whitlam's parting shot was 'Well may we say "God Save the Queen" because nothing will save the Governor-General.' It didn't bother the Governor-General too much. He completed his day by reinstating the national anthem.

On the political level at home, Oldfield continued to have amicable relations with Ted Heath and Alec Douglas-Home, but felt equally comfortable with the Labour politicians. At the time, the mid 1970s, there wasn't, from Oldfield's point of view, an awful lot of difference between the two potential governments. The same preoccupations – Europe, the trade unions, the Cold War, the struggling economy – faced both parties, and the differences were more of emphasis than substance. Both parties operated so-called incomes policies as a means of trying to control inflation, were committed to membership of the EEC, and were trying with limited success to manage the unions.

In terms of the EEC, Oldfield's work in providing intelligence to the government about the personalities, motivations and foibles of its European allies was important. His long-held strategy of finding ways of spying on those you really shouldn't spy on was used more than ever before in the run-up to British entry. The trade unions, and the fears of their possible infiltration by the KGB, were more of a job for MI5. The Cold War, though, was very much an MI6 matter. Since the mass expulsion of 1971 there had been less of a problem of KGB officers infiltrating Britain, but equally there had been little success in getting access to Soviet thinking from within. Oldfield's policy of calming the aggressive search for Soviet officers who might be willing to turn had helped reduce the number of flaky defectors with dubious motivations of the Golitsyn kind, but he was aware that they could, ten years on, really use a new Penkovsky – someone with top-level access to Soviet policy, and a genuine commitment to assisting the West.

The second 'answer to a prayer' came in 1974, on Oldfield's watch, with the recruitment in Copenhagen of a KGB Colonel named Oleg Gordievsky. Gordievsky had joined the KGB in 1963, just after Penkovsky's execution, and risen swiftly through the ranks. It was the 1968 invasion of Czechoslovakia and the crushing of the Prague Spring that disillusioned Colonel Gordievsky, and he made his feelings known to MI6 while stationed at the Soviet Embassy in Denmark. While Oldfield was Chief, Gordievsky operated as a double agent, remaining in the employ of the KGB while feeding vital intelligence to the British.

The information he provided was in this second half of the Cold War as important as Penkovsky's had been in the first. It showed that the expulsion really had done its job. The KGB residents in Britain were few in number and they were primarily getting their material from open sources. Sometimes they'd jazz it up a bit to make it look more secret, but that's mostly what it was – jazzed-up open material. Their reading of the political situation in Britain was inaccurate, and they were convinced that the West would strike first in a nuclear exchange. What was particularly noteworthy was the fear Moscow had of the growing EEC. Unlike some of the more naive residents of the constituent countries, who had been sold EEC membership as a trading arrangement, the Common Market, and believed it, the KGB analysts saw it as a political union not unlike the Eastern Bloc – but richer and more threatening.

The reports Gordievsky was feeding to Oldfield showed

that the Soviets were convinced the EEC would have a joint defence policy and joint offence capability, and would be every bit as committed to expanding its reach as was the ailing Brezhnev. They also worried that the EEC was trying to formalize trade agreements with China, and draw that country and its vast market and military capability into an unhealthy alliance with Western Europe. To Moscow, it felt as though they were being ganged up on from all sides. The paranoia being felt in the East was every bit as strong as that in the West. What Oldfield also knew, from agents such as Gerald Buss, was that in real, everyday Russia there was no appetite whatsoever for the invasion of territories and world domination. 'It was an entirely different atmosphere in the Russian cities in the seventies than in the sixties,' Gerald told me. 'The aggressive edge of the Khrushchev days just wasn't there.' That isn't to say the Cold War was over, but the intelligence Oldfield was receiving showed that with calm, rational analysis, outright conflict could be avoided.

Oldfield remained fortunate in terms of the Foreign Secretaries with whom he had to deal. When Heath called a general election in February 1974 challenging the country to decide whether he or the unions governed Britain, the answer was a resounding 'we're not sure' and a hung Parliament saw the Prime Minister unable to form a government. Harold Wilson was returned by the ash in his pipe. The new Foreign Secretary, in succession to Douglas-Home, was James Callaghan, and as usual Maurice found he got along well with the new boss. Callaghan had held both of the other great offices of state, having served as Home Secretary and Chancellor of the Exchequer in the previous Wilson government, but had little experience of foreign affairs. He summoned the head of MI6 to his office and said, 'Tell me, Maurice, what, exactly, is it that you do?' Oldfield replied, 'My job, Foreign Secretary, is to bring you unwelcome news.'

In the early weeks of this second Wilson government, Oldfield was a regular visitor to Downing Street. A new face in Number 10 was the Head of the Policy Unit, a young academic named Bernard Donoughue. One Monday morning as Donoughue was walking along a corridor in Wilson's official residence, he saw a stocky figure coming towards him with a distinctive waddling gait. Donoughue recognized Maurice Oldfield, but as a complete stranger had no reason to expect the MI6 Chief to have heard of him, let alone recognize him by sight. So it came as something of a surprise when Oldfield smiled and said, 'Good morning, Dr Donoughue', and even more of a surprise when he added, 'Did you enjoy your football game yesterday?' 'I used to play football every Sunday morning on Hampstead Heath,' Donoughue told me, 'and I assumed Oldfield perhaps lived nearby and had just happened to see me play as he walked through the park.' When told that in fact Maurice lived in Marsham Court, just a stone's throw from the Houses of Parliament, nowhere near Hampstead Heath, Donoughue realized that 'the man knew everything. He'd obviously done his homework on all of Harold's staff and left nothing to chance.'

There were good reasons for Oldfield to know all about Wilson's staff. Ever since Golitsyn claimed that Wilson was a Soviet agent of influence, Peter Wright of MI5 and his team had been digging into his connections, whether friends, political contacts or employees. There had been talk of a right-wing coup involving the newspaper tycoon Cecil King (who wanted Lord Mountbatten installed as an emergency leader in place of the Prime Minister) dating back as far as Wilson's first term, and George Kennedy Young had formed what he named the Unison Committee for Action, a group of businessmen, barristers and bankers who were ready to step in when the supposedly inevitable collapse in law and order came about.

In Northern Ireland, the Army psychological warfare expert and intelligence officer Colin Wallace was involved in a black propaganda campaign called Clockwork Orange during 1973 and 1974, which started out spreading mis-information about the terrorist groups in the territory – but Wallace became dismayed when, he claimed, the operation turned its attention to smearing senior politicians. Wilson, of course, was a prime target, but so, among others, were Edward Heath, Liberal leader Jeremy Thorpe, Northern Ireland Secretary Merlyn Rees, and the fire-and-brimstone Unionist the Reverend Ian Paisley. Wallace also became if not the first then certainly the most prominent person working in the security services to bring the matter of abuse at the Kincora Boys Home in Belfast to the attention of the authorities.

All of the above factors, along with a fear of the trade unions with their growing propensity for damaging strikes and their alleged links to the Soviet Bloc, served to stoke the feeling of paranoia surrounding Harold Wilson. And it seems the circle around the Prime Minister didn't do an awful lot to calm the situation. Bernard Donoughue says that Wilson's long-term aide, private and political secretary Marcia Williams was a significant figure in fuelling the problem. She told Wilson that the security services were not to be trusted, and was said to have had a disproportionate influence on the honours system, which saw Wilson accused of handing out peerages to friends and associates of dubious character. Until 1966 the award of honours was, by convention, arranged by the government Chief Whip, keeping patronage, nominally at least, away from the executive; the early days of Wilson saw responsibility for dishing out the gongs moved directly to Number 10.

Following on from the guilt by association that the security services were shovelling on to their own people who had been in contact with the Eastern Bloc even in the legitimate execution of their jobs, it should have come as no surprise that those around the Prime Minister would be examined and their connections explored. In the dark and mistrustful circumstances of the early to mid 1970s, Wilson's choice of friends, however innocent he may have thought them, left him wide open to accusations of harbouring Soviet sympathies.

The Conservative MP Winston Churchill, grandson of the wartime leader, wrote to Wilson late in 1974 to warn him that one of his closest associates, the Lithuanian-born businessman Joe Kagan (formerly Juozapas Kaganas), was having KGB officials as house guests. Churchill may or may not have known that in fact Wilson had been warned by MI5 about Kagan's connections as early as 1968, and that, as his Principal Private Secretary Robert Armstrong later revealed, Wilson had been interviewed, at his own request, by MI5 about the matter in 1972 when it emerged that at least one of Kagan's associates was among the KGB agents excluded from Britain under Operation Foot. Wilson asked the Security

Service not to speak to Kagan directly but agreed to warn him personally about his contacts. In a pointed note, lest anyone thought him naive, Wilson added, 'for the record, I always assume that Russians I speak to may be connected to the KGB'.

An investigation into Kagan found that the KGB had been trying to use him as an agent of influence, but effectively cleared him of being a conscious agent himself. Given the prevailing sensitivities of the time it would be reasonable to assume that, even if only for appearances' sake, Wilson might have tried to distance himself from Kagan and his like. In fact the reverse was true: Wilson continued almost defiantly to associate with controversial business leaders with Eastern Bloc connections such as Kagan and the industrialist Rudy Sternberg, proudly wearing Gannex raincoats from Kagan's West Yorkshire factory while puffing away on his pipe. Sternberg was elevated to the Lords in 1975; Kagan followed in Wilson's resignation honours the following year, as part of what became known as the Lavender List as it was alleged to have been hand-written by Marcia Williams on her lavender-coloured notepaper, though she has always denied having any influence on its content. Bernard Donoughue was even more sceptical of such businessmen than the investigators who begrudgingly cleared them. 'There's no doubt in my mind that Kagan and Sternberg were KGB agents,' he told me.

Sections of the press in 1974 and 1975 were quite blasé when it came to talking about Wilson as a would-be traitor. Auberon Waugh's 'HP Sauce' column in *Private Eye* would say that it had long suspected Wilson of being a KGB agent and tell convoluted, jokey stories about his connections with the Siberian timber industry. The same column reported that Wilson was planning to merge MI5 and MI6 into a 'super' intelligence agency, with Maurice Oldfield as its Chief – a thread that was picked up by Chapman Pincher in the *Daily Express*. A report in the *Daily Telegraph* in late 1974 noted that 'Maurice Oldfield, named by the American magazine, *Newsweek*, as being the real-life "M", has not so far been awarded the knighthood that has come to be associated with being elevated to his post'. In fact Dick White had been knighted while he was still in MI5, and John Rennie when he was still an under secretary at the Foreign Office. The story bubbled away in columns in several other papers.

Whether or not Maurice propagated the issue will probably never be known; his elevation was in all likelihood inevitable. But when the New Years Honours list for 1975 was published, on the same day that Gary Sobers was knighted for services to cricket and Rudy Sternberg was elevated to the Lords for reasons unknown, Maurice Oldfield was appointed Knight Commander of St Michael and St George, usually abbreviated to KCMG. He liked to deploy the usual response when asked what the initials stood for. 'Kindly Call Me God,' he would say, beaming. I remember asking him, 'But now you're a sir, Uncle Maurice, what do you *actually* do?' and being told, 'It's rather boring, dear boy. I'm a kind of security guard at embassies.' On the day of his investiture, his sisters Sadie and Renee and bodyguard Ken Dyer were proud to be asked to join Maurice in the photographs outside Buckingham Palace.

Oldfield remained on good terms with Harold Wilson on a personal level. Of all the Prime Ministers with whom he had direct dealings – Eden, Macmillan, Douglas-Home, Wilson, Heath, Callaghan and Thatcher – Maurice would happily say he got along best with Wilson. He found it genuinely upsetting in the dying days of his government that the Prime Minister would cross the street rather than encounter him face to face, presumably – assuming Donoughue is correct – owing to the suspicion he had developed about the security services generally. Such was the level of paranoia that had enveloped Wilson's relations with the security services – possibly via Marcia Williams's influence, possibly because of MI5's investigations into him, possibly because of the smears that were quietly emerging from Clockwork Orange – that he began to see conspiracies wherever he looked.

Maurice told his sister Sadie, who would sometimes accompany him to lunch with Wilson or his ministers, that he rather missed the talks he had with the Prime Minister. He related how, freed from the flashing lights of the paparazzi and the need to put on a public face that suited his 'man of the people' image, Wilson liked to put away his pipe and draw deeply on a large, opulent cigar. Despite being offered a large Havana, Maurice preferred to stick to his chain-smoking of cigarillos – but then he didn't have a public facade to maintain. The two grammar schoolboys of similar age would discuss Oldfield's intelligence reports and the MI6 man appreciated the Prime Minister's ability to come to a swift policy decision.

By the summer of 1975 things were changing. Waugh's stirrings in *Private Eye* were becoming yet more brazen, even suggesting that Wilson 'will spend the autumn of his days in the miserable loneliness of an official flat in Pushkin Sq.

Moscow', and there was talk of a communist cell in Downing Street.

Peter Wright of MI5 wanted to confront Wilson with what he considered to be evidence of the Prime Minister's 'treachery', such as his connections with the Soviets (which amounted to some trade contacts) and his dubious associates such as Joe Kagan – all of which were encompassed in what was known in MI5 as the Henry Worthington File. Wright hoped that by confronting Wilson with everything he had he could convince the Prime Minister to resign. He claimed that Oldfield and Victor Rothschild talked him out of it and told him instead to take his proposal to his own chief at MI5, Michael Hanley.

When he heard what Wright was proposing, Hanley, according to Wright, went 'as white as a sheet'. Allegations of the kind contained in the Henry Worthington File, when combined with the long-standing Angleton-, Phillpotts- and de Mowbray-inspired reports of the Fluency committee about Roger Hollis, could easily have prompted Wilson to rid MI5 of its Chief and orchestrate a purge of the organization from top to bottom. By some means or another Wilson did get to hear of the machinations against him in MI5, and in his own words 'I sent for Oldfield'. After being asked directly by Wilson if he had heard of any, for the want of better words, MI5 plots against him, Oldfield was as diplomatic as he could be but confirmed that 'there is a section of MI5 that is unreliable'. In saying this, it seems likely that Oldfield was referring to Wright and his mole hunters.

The second Wilson government was only to last a few more months. Anthony Cavendish was convinced, from things Maurice told him, that his friend of thirty-odd years was somehow involved in the Prime Minister's unexpected resignation the following spring. At the time, Cavendish wasn't sure what that involvement was, other than it was something sudden. Forty years on, things appear to be getting clearer.

There has been speculation more recently that by March 1976 Wilson was already aware that he was afflicted by early-onset dementia and wanted to quit before he visibly deteriorated. Some, including the academic and writer Stephen Dorril, have suggested that the Prime Minister, whose intellectual capacity was never in doubt, wanted to return to academia and had planned to do that irrespective of what was happening to his premiership. Those things may well have contributed to his departure, but if so it seems more likely that an orderly departure, with a planned leadership election to decide the succession, would have been Wilson's style. What seems more plausible now is that Wilson's business connections had finally caught up with him and that Oldfield helped him to take a dignified way out.

In August 1975, at around the same time as Peter Wright was proposing to present Wilson with his range of theories in the hope of forcing him to resign, Maurice called round to a neighbour of his in Marsham Court, the barrister Desmond de Silva, and related how the Prime Minister's offices had been burgled the previous year, and that documents stolen in the raid were about to be sold to magazines in Holland and West Germany. At the time de Silva assumed his friend was joking when Oldfield said that he expected him to be called upon to represent the burglars in court in due course.

The burglars were arrested in March 1976 and, sure enough, Maurice arranged for de Silva to represent them in court. The barrister recalled that there were no state secrets among the stolen documents but that there were messages from a business associate of Harold Wilson's, a developer named Eric Miller who had helped fund Wilson's private office, advising the sale of shares in a company called Peachey Property Ltd. In the hands of the wrong barrister, the defendants could have embroiled the Prime Minister in an embarrassing story including allegations of insider trading. While there were no direct accusations of wrongdoing against Wilson, had de Silva encouraged his clients, when facing committal, to disclose full details of what was included in the documents they stole, the revelations could have brought huge embarrassment to the Prime Minister and to the government. This could have been Britain's own Watergate – 'Peacheygate', perhaps. Miller would go on to be knighted in the Lavender List – and then to commit suicide when facing charges of siphoning money out of Peachey Property Ltd.

Whether or not Wilson had been planning to resign, when Oldfield presented him with evidence that was potentially about to be brought before a court on 15 March, something certainly concentrated his mind. He resigned on the 16th, managing to hold intact his record of being Labour's most electorally successful Prime Minister, with four victories, and his reputation for being politically astute by going, publicly at least, at a time of his own choosing.

The portrait painter, Michael Noakes, recalls a sitting with the Queen on the day of Wilson's resignation, and commenting to Her Majesty, 'Gosh ma'am, that was a surprise!'.

Noakes was further taken aback when the Queen replied that she wasn't particularly surprised as Wilson had told her eighteen months previously that he'd most likely be gone by then. Given that the eighteen month timescale referred to by Elizabeth II in her conversation with Michael Noakes coincides remarkably with the burglary at the Prime Minister's private office, it seems more than feasible that Wilson would have been aware of the potential explosiveness of what had been stolen – and that it could somehow lead to his departure from office.

Much has been written about the so-called Wilson Plot. The official history of MI5 concludes that there wasn't one; the conspiracy theorists maintain that there was. From researching Maurice Oldfield's story, and coming to the 'plot' as a by-product with no preconceived ideas, it seems to me that the truth lies somewhere in the middle. There is little evidence of a coordinated, managed, top-down MI5-sanctioned plot against Wilson, but there is plenty of evidence that individual officers, or groups of officers, were genuinely concerned about Wilson, or more precisely the company he kept, and the effect that might have on the country. Equally, with the company he kept, and by his reliance on certain key advisers, Wilson did little to offer comfort to those who already regarded him with suspicion. The evidence would seem to suggest that Oldfield helped to find a tired, paranoid Prime Minister a respectable way out, and his country a respectable way forward.

18

M = C Part Two

THE SUDDEN RESIGNATION of Harold Wilson on 16 March 1976 left the Labour Party having to elect a new leader, and by default the new Prime Minister of the United Kingdom. Maurice Oldfield would be gaining a new political master, and the Foreign Secretary, James Callaghan, was favourite to be that person. The final ballot was between Callaghan, the left-winger Michael Foot and the liberally minded Roy Jenkins. In the few short days of the campaign Oldfield made it his business to get to know Foot and Jenkins, and entertained both, separately, with lunch at Lockets. His sister Sadie acted as his consort on both occasions. He told her, 'I find having a lady present encourages my guests to speak more freely about matters beyond their work. It helps me to get a better understanding of them if they aren't just "talking shop".'

In the event, Callaghan won the election, and he appointed Anthony Crosland, the MP for Great Grimsby and later to be revealed as having been a boyfriend of Roy Jenkins in their student days, as Foreign Secretary. Oldfield found

Callaghan to be a canny politician, but not as decisive as Wilson. Callaghan had to be canny though: he was trying to manage a majority of one in the House of Commons after some by-election results, and within a year this majority was wiped out and he was forced to enter into a pact with the Liberal Party in order to stay in power.

Despite Oldfield's personal warmth towards Wilson, he considered his replacement by Callaghan a positive thing. With Wilson gone, James Angleton gone, and Roger Hollis dead, even though Britain was still in an economic trough, the darkness and paranoia that had been dominating the intelligence services for so long appeared to be lifting.

As well as dealing with the ongoing information coming from Oleg Gordievsky, much of MI6's time during the Callaghan years was spent gathering intelligence on other European countries. An important area for Callaghan personally was trying to encourage the EEC to allow Greece to join. The left wing in his own party wanted Greece in as a reward for her success in ousting the right-wing military regime, but the country was considered by the European Commission to be too poor and too far behind in economic terms to be allowed into the community as an equal partner. There were concerns that Greece's unemployment problem would result in mass economic migration to the more prosperous nations, and that cheap supplies of such things as Greek olive oil being allowed to enter the Common Market would have an adverse impact on other olive-oil-producing countries, notably France, Italy and Spain.

For those reasons, the Greeks' initial application for membership was turned down. Callaghan was downhearted as he now faced having to explain to the Labour Party his failure to negotiate Greek entry. Notwithstanding the economic issues, which were – and remain – difficult to refute, the intelligence services could see very good reasons for letting Greece join the European party. The country's location directly next to the Eastern Bloc countries of Albania and Bulgaria, and with a gateway to the Middle East via Turkey, meant there was considerable potential benefit in making that place part of the European community.

A retired MI6 officer described how his organization used its human intelligence to influence the process in Greece's – and Callaghan's – favour. According to the officer, Maurice Oldfield, knowing the Prime Minister's position – and agreeing that it was in Britain's political and security interests to allow the Greeks to enter – visited Callaghan at Number 10. Oldfield gave Callaghan the contact details of a specific and important French official, and suggested that the PM call him directly to seek his support in getting the Commission's decision to exclude Greece set aside. More in hope than expectation, Callaghan made the call, and was amazed to find the official – previously hostile to the proposal – warmly supportive. The joint effort between Britain and France saw wider opposition in the community melt away and the process towards Greek entry was formally confirmed, with accession to take place in 1981.

Callaghan, delighted but puzzled, sought out Oldfield to ask how he knew that the French official would change his mind. 'It may be,' Oldfield told the Prime Minister, 'that a certain patriotic Greek lady had been denying the pleasures of her bed to a senior French official unless and until her country's application was accepted.' The intelligence proved correct. In the long term, the impact of Greek entry showed that the economic sceptics had a point, but in 1976, Oldfield's use of intelligence to serve a beleaguered Prime Minister had the desired effect.

At the end of June that year an incident occurred in which MI6 as an organization had no direct official involvement, but Maurice Oldfield's personal influence was brought to bear in helping to turn what was for those involved a terrifying experience into one with as positive an outcome as might have been hoped. On the 27th, an Air France plane carrying 248 passengers from Tel Aviv in Israel to Charles de Gaulle airport in Paris was hijacked by Palestinian terrorists and diverted to Entebbe airport in Uganda. The Ugandan dictator, Idi Amin, supported the hijackers, and provided military back-up. The non-Israeli passengers on the flight were released and sent on to Paris; the Israelis and cabin crew were taken to a disused terminal building and kept hostage.

The terrorists demanded a payment of $5 million and the release of around fifty Palestinian prisoners to secure the freedom of the French plane and the hostages, and a frenzy of diplomatic efforts began, with even Yasser Arafat of the Palestine Liberation Organization offering to try to negotiate a settlement. Behind the scenes a quick and effective intelligence effort was required, and the Israeli intelligence agency Mossad was the prime mover in what was called Operation Thunderbolt. What the Israelis didn't have was access to a place within easy reach to use as a base for their operation, which is where Oldfield came in. He put his contacts in Mossad in touch with his friend Bruce Mackenzie, the former Agriculture Minister in neighbouring Kenya, and, after being briefed by Oldfield, Mackenzie persuaded Kenyan President Jomo Kenyatta to allow the Israelis access to Kenyan airspace and to use Nairobi airport for refuelling and as a base from which to mount their intelligence work.

Having studied the plans of Entebbe airport and established where the hostages were being held, the Israel Defence Force was ready to strike, and at 2300 hours on 3 July the raid began. Of the 105 hostages, 102 were rescued, at a cost of one Israeli soldier's life. As well as three of the hostages, all seven hijackers and forty-five Ugandan soldiers were killed, and around thirty Ugandan fighter planes were destroyed. In terms of cooperation between intelligence services the Entebbe raid was a success, though Idi Amin was less impressed by the outcome and quietly planned his revenge. Over the next couple of years Bruce Mackenzie tried to build relations with Amin, and became a regular visitor to the dictator in the Ugandan capital Kampala.

Two years later, in late May 1978, Maurice Oldfield was sitting at the breakfast table at his mother's house in Over Haddon when he took the call that told him Mackenzie had been assassinated, killed as he returned in his private plane from a trip to Uganda by a bomb hidden in an ornament, a porcelain lion's head given to him as a present by Amin. Oldfield's sister Renee reported that her brother became visibly upset as he took the call, and just said quietly, 'That was for Entebbe.' Chapman Pincher – who was a friend of Mackenzie's, and a neighbour in Berkshire where Mackenzie had a house – later claimed that it was he who broke the news of their mutual friend's death to Oldfield, and that Maurice merely asked, 'Did he leave any papers?' In fact Oldfield was well aware of the assassination before Pincher called, and in asking about the papers was probably trying to ensure that the mischievous journalist hadn't got his hands on any. The Chief of Mossad, Meir Amit, arranged for a forest in Israel to be planted and named after Bruce Mackenzie.

The summer of 1976 saw Oldfield travelling widely in the Far East. Starting in Australia, as well as his visit to Singapore he went to Thailand, Burma and the Philippines before finishing in Hong Kong. One of the senior officers at the Hong Kong station vividly remembers the Chief's visit, and that the staff found him to be a kind man who could be fun to be with.

> Maurice joined in a game of 'Murder' after a staff supper. Maurice was to be the murderee, the place was plunged into darkness, and when the lights went up there he was stretched out on the floor, eyes closed, with a flower between his clasped hands. I remember thinking at the time that you would not find many permanent under secretaries or even (or particularly!) ambassadors willing to let their hair down with their, mostly junior, staff to that extent, but there was no loss of dignity; at that moment he was a kindly uncle whom we had not seen for some time. I also remember that he decided against the programme which I had carefully drawn up for his day off during that visit, preferring to spend it touring alone in the care of the station's young male Chinese driver whom he had encountered on a previous visit.

A few weeks later, a secretary at Century House told another officer about an occasion when she had overheard

Maurice engaged, quite openly, in 'an extraordinarily affectionate conversation with a young male clerk'. The officer discussed the matter with a senior colleague. Neither of them had any inkling that Oldfield might be gay, and neither had they heard rumours to that effect. As the exchange had been so blatant, they concluded it must be innocent of any physical element – and anyway, the personnel department must have been perfectly well aware of it. Nothing more was said or done at the time.

And then in September, in a couple of national daily papers and *Private Eye*, a little article appeared, without a by-line, saying that the head of MI6, and model for M of the James Bond films, was rumoured to be on the verge of marriage. It was said that MI6 staff had nicknamed the mystery woman 'Dorothy'. Nobody has claimed responsibility for these articles, but there remains the possibility that it was Maurice himself allowing rumours of a marriage to get about to deflect any whispers that may have started after incidents such as those just described. Within a few weeks other, similarly anonymous articles appeared, stating that the wedding was now off.

For all his warm personal qualities, Oldfield was also capable of being ruthless – and on occasion unnecessarily so in the view of some senior colleagues. One officer related how, when he was still Deputy Chief to John Rennie, Maurice insisted on sacking an officer who had got into a spot of trouble overseas thanks to a problem with alcohol. This officer, an otherwise capable man, had seen his positive vetting certificate withdrawn as a result of a complaint from the ambassador at his station – but at that stage he could have been rehabilitated and kept on. Colleagues were quite taken aback at just how hard-nosed Oldfield had been in that case, especially when others with drink problems were known to be tolerated.

There were also rare examples of Maurice being involved in the departure of certain officers who had been identified as a security risk because of their homosexuality. One in particular, who cannot be named, found support from other directors in relation to his being gay. They felt that a warning as to his future conduct would have been sufficient, but Oldfield insisted on the officer leaving the Service. For someone who was generally renowned for his Christian goodness, tolerance and liberalism, to see Maurice treating a colleague in so draconian a fashion came as something of a shock.

It seems that he had his favourites, and did enjoy being surrounded by good-looking colleagues. As one retired officer told me with a smile, 'I was a favourite for a period. But then I was also considered a pretty boy at the time!' There was never any hint of any impropriety in relation to these favourites, but sometimes there was a suggestion that Maurice was not always the best judge of character. Quite early on he decided that he wanted Brian Stewart to succeed him as Chief, and he set about engineering the process by trying to install Stewart as his deputy. Stewart's abilities as an officer were not in doubt, and he had a sound reputation dating back to his service in Malaya. But as much as Oldfield was warm, colleagues found Stewart to be chilly – with a streak of arrogance. And while Oldfield's character made him popular, Stewart's had the opposite effect. In an unprecedented move, senior MI6 officers agreed that they would resign en masse if Maurice insisted on pushing the appointment through. This show of strength by colleagues against the man who was so utterly dominant in MI6 saw Maurice back down and normal service resume.

Normal service saw Oldfield working closely with the new Foreign Secretary. His relationship with Anthony Crosland, a minister for whom he had a good deal of respect, was a strong one until Crosland died on 19 February 1977 after collapsing six days earlier, quite suddenly, with a brain haemorrhage while writing a speech on the subject of détente, the name given to the slight thawing of tensions with the Soviets that had occurred since the Cuban Missile Crisis had been averted. That speech ended up being delivered a few days later by the new Foreign Secretary, at the age of thirty-nine the youngest person to hold that post in a generation, Dr David Owen.

As a young Foreign Secretary, Owen appreciated the sound counsel his Chief of MI6 offered. Early in his tenure, Owen suggested to Oldfield that MI6 ought perhaps to consider assassinating Idi Amin. Twenty years earlier Maurice had told his friend Michael Wrigley 'we don't do that kind of thing any more' when he asked for £10,000 to pay a hit man to take out a communist leader; now he told his boss much the same thing. 'We prefer more cerebral solutions these days, Foreign Secretary,' was Oldfield's reply.

One area in which Owen found Oldfield to be particularly strong was in his use of 'raw' intelligence, as in information that had found its way to him before it had been looked over by the analysts. 'Maurice had the knack of showing me a piece of information and explaining what weight he would put on its veracity in the light of what he knew of the source, the background to the case, and the context in which we hoped to use it.' This talent – backed up by vast experience

– enabled intelligence to be used more quickly than would normally be the case, as usually sources would be checked and double-checked before being presented to the Foreign Secretary. It was, of course, inherently risky, but given Oldfield's combination of personal knowledge and analytical skills those risks were reduced.

David Owen was initially keen to see MI6 formally acknowledged, or 'avowed', to bring the organization under proper democratic control. Oldfield, while sympathetic to the principle, urged caution. The idea that he or his colleagues might be called in front of some parliamentary committee to account for themselves, and then be grilled by MPs who might not fully understand the issues, was not something Oldfield would agree to lightly. In the shady world inhabited out of necessity by the Secret Intelligence Service, to come blinking into the daylight in that manner was potentially dangerous to agents in the field and thus to British interests. Oldfield didn't claim that the convention of operating in an inherently contradictory manner – his organization was well known and the subject of many films and books yet officially did not exist – was in any way ideal. In fact the very nature of the secrecy only added to the media fascination and gave the likes of Chapman Pincher licence to publish without fear of contradiction.

That is not to say that Oldfield was opposed to being more open in terms of communicating with the public. He would, as we have seen, use the press to the benefit of the Service or for his own personal reasons. The journalist and author Phillip Knightley, who interviewed Maurice, told me that he was surprised, almost disarmed, at just how helpful the MI6 Chief was in answering his questions – albeit he was on the cusp of retirement when he spoke on the record to Knightley.

To try to get round the democratic deficit, Oldfield arranged with James Callaghan for the first time to give formal intelligence briefings to the Leader of the Opposition, who by then was Margaret Thatcher. Maurice had always understood the importance of getting to know politicians who were likely to rise to power and had a good eye for spotting such individuals, but by putting this on an official footing, opposition MPs could no longer claim they were being kept in the dark on intelligence matters. Chapman Pincher would later claim that it was he who orchestrated the talks between Thatcher and Oldfield; in fact Oldfield already had a direct contact with Thatcher via the politician and former MI6 officer James Scott-Hopkins, who was the Oldfields' local MP (for West Derbyshire).

In his private life, too, Maurice, while not exactly advertising the fact – he scarcely needed to – dropped the charade of being no more than 'something in the Foreign Office'. He visited Hurstpierpoint College at the request of Gerald Buss and gave a talk on his work to the Sixth Form, even taking part in a question-and-answer session. Once they got past the giddy excitement of questions such as 'Do you know James Bond?' and 'Is Gerald a spy?' the session was useful and the students got a feel for the reality of the secret world and how, for Maurice, it all came down to people and the study of people. The pupils at his old school, Lady Manners in Bakewell, were more than a little surprised to find the head of MI6 addressing them at a careers fair.

The publicity surrounding Oldfield was not, even in 1977, universally helpful. His identity was well known among the intelligence agencies of the world, and when his niece Jane, having finished school, planned an InterRail trip, Maurice gave her a briefing on where to go and where to avoid with a name like Oldfield. All was well until he received a panicked call from his brother Joe to say that Jane had telephoned from Berlin and was planning a day out on the eastern side of the Brandenburg Gate. As Jane queued at Passport Control she was surprised to be apprehended by an officer on the Western side and taken to a side room. 'Wait here,' the officer said, 'there's a phone call for you.' When she picked up the receiver a familiar voice was at the other end, a concerned Uncle Maurice warning her 'not to be so bloody stupid'.

More frightening still was the threat to his own life, and potentially those of his family, posed by being the head of MI6. Also in 1977, Maurice visited St Matthew's Church in Westminster, where he was a regular communicant and occasional organist, with his sister Sadie. Even when the church was empty, if he wasn't playing the organ Oldfield would sit at the back where his security guard could see him. People knew this. As he and Sadie opened their hymn books on that spring Sunday, the pages fell open on a note reading 'THE IRA WILL GET YOU'. That same spring, the church was fitted with a new £5,000 organ, partly funded by Maurice, and in May the building was burned virtually to the ground by a fire that had started near the organ, which was destroyed. Despite this, the church continued to hold services among the ruins, and Maurice continued to attend.

On the other hand, the Oldfield name could be quite useful. One night – or, more precisely, in the early hours of a Sunday morning – Maurice's nephew John Pearce and a teammate, Tony Robinson, were being driven back to Bakewell from a rugby game in Nottingham by John's wife Carolyn when the car was stopped by the police on the bleak Derbyshire moors. The constabulary wanted to know what the group were doing out in the wilds at that time of night, where they'd been and where they were going. John and Tony were amply refreshed after their game, and, getting bored and needing the loo, Tony boomed from the back seat, 'Do you know who I am?' He'd heard John say that the car was registered as an official vehicle of Sir Maurice Oldfield and decided, in his haze, to test the story. 'Call your headquarters!' Tony boomed. 'John, get his number!' The policeman duly called Derbyshire Police HQ at Ripley and came sheepishly back to the car. 'On your way, Sir Maurice. Sorry to have bothered you.'

During a phone call home in May 1977, Maurice was told by his mother that his old form teacher from Lady Manners School, Olive Faber, who was by then in her nineties, had telephoned to ask after Maurice and happened to mention that she had come from her home in North Yorkshire to stay with her niece, Patricia Fuller, and her husband, who lived in the village of Baslow, only six miles away from Over Haddon. Maurice was going back to Derbyshire the following weekend, and when he arrived at the station he had John first take him home, where he clambered into the attic and fetched his school exercise books, and then drop him at the Fullers' house in Baslow, where Mrs Faber was staying. Maurice stayed for dinner, and the long-retired teacher and her former pupil spent hours reminiscing about Lady Manners days and discussing the comments that had been made on Maurice's work – including that obligatory encouragement to try harder.

Mrs Faber was both surprised and thrilled that Maurice had made the time and effort to come and see her in person, and went off to bed a happy old lady. Maurice stayed until midnight talking to the Fullers – without once letting on that he knew full well that Patricia's husband was the son of his former colleague from the 1950s Kate Fuller. Even when Patricia asked, 'Perhaps you know my mother-in-law, Kathleen? She used to work in the Foreign Office,' Maurice feigned no knowledge. Kate later teased him about it, saying, 'Didn't you know Kate was short for Kathleen?' Maurice simply replied, 'I didn't want to cause them or you embarrassment in case they didn't know the Foreign Office was just your cover.'

In those years, 1976 and 1977, the issue of the Argentine junta and its potential threat to the South Atlantic became a major concern for the British government and the intelligence services. To this day, Maurice Oldfield's role in seeing off the threat remains a matter of controversy. In December 1976 it became known that an Argentine Air Force party had landed on the uninhabited British island of Southern Thule in the South Sandwich Islands and built a small base, officially for scientists. The British Foreign Office made official protests to Argentina about her occupation of the territory, but the talks made little progress.

By November 1977 the Prime Minister had concluded that diplomatic actions were having no effect, and a nuclear-powered submarine, HMS *Dreadnought*, together with a small number of supporting vessels, was sent to the South Atlantic in anticipation of further Argentine aggression in the region, including a possible attack on the Falkland Islands, whose sovereignty had long been disputed. It is here that the politicians' versions diverge. The Foreign Secretary, David Owen, maintains that the presence of the British fleet in the area was secret, and remained so, there just for back-up in case the diplomatic effort ultimately failed. The Prime Minister, by contrast, claimed that he told Maurice Oldfield he 'wouldn't be disappointed' should the spy chief use his contacts in Argentine business to let the junta know, unofficially, that a British nuclear submarine had been dispatched to the South Atlantic to defend British territory.

Though the Argentines didn't immediately vacate Southern Thule, there was to be no further threat to the other British islands, including the Falklands, until 1982, by which time Callaghan's task force had long since departed. Thus the Argentine threat was, by late 1978, considered to have been thwarted, and the diplomatic negotiations continued. David Owen told me he remains convinced that Oldfield did not go against his wishes, and that the British task force remained a secret, probably being spotted by Argentine Intelligence. 'Maurice was so dedicated a public servant that he would not have gone against the orders of the Foreign Secretary,' Owen says. In his autobiography, James Callaghan was equally convinced that Oldfield had followed his wishes and that it was that action which prevented an invasion of the Falklands in 1977. Oldfield had achieved the feat of convincing both his political masters that he had followed their orders while simultaneously deterring the Argentinians.

Colleagues of Oldfield tend to subscribe to the Prime Minister's version. One told me, 'Maurice not only got word of the task force to the junta via his contacts in Argentine business, he also let them think it was far bigger than it really was.' Lord Armstrong, formerly the Principal Private Secretary to the Prime Minister, later to be Cabinet Secretary, also backs up this version. He told me the British government 'continued to talk with the Argentines after Maurice retired, and after the Conservatives came to power, and because we were talking to them we tended to think that they wouldn't invade. We were rather naive. I rather wished that Maurice had still been around in 1982. The war might have been avoided.' The Franks Report into the 1982 conflict found little evidence either way in relation to the 1977 incident – which would seem to be exactly as Oldfield might have wanted it.

The last year of Oldfield's time as Chief was largely taken up with a tour of the world – something of a tradition for retiring Chiefs but especially so for Maurice, given his propensity for travel. He visited Stansfield Turner, by then head of the CIA, whom he'd known since Washington days in the early 1960s, and heads of other agencies around the world. By 1978 he had become one of the most revered figures in global intelligence, as illustrated by the collection of medals, ceremonial daggers, hand-written letters and awards he had acquired. As usual he went to the Far East, and took in Australia, New Zealand and India en route to the Middle East, where in Tehran he met with the Shah of Iran.

By early 1978, Oldfield's promise to the Shah that he would not allow MI6 to spy in Iran on his watch was already looking like a mistake, even if few were to predict the enormity of what would happen a year later. The reason for Oldfield's promise had been, by showing trust, to encourage the Shah to move the Iranian economy towards a more Western model – and to an extent that happened. But the Westernization of the economy did not extend to improving democracy, and as early as the mid 1970s the regime was trying to brook opposition to the changes, and the jails were slowly filling up with political prisoners.

The economic changes began to alienate the conservative Shi'a Muslims led by the Ayatollah Ruhollah Khomeini, exiled in Iraq, and though there was no war, the rumblings of unrest were heard. Another Muslim leader, Ali Shariati, who had served eighteen months in jail for his preaching, died unexpectedly in June 1977 from a heart attack in Southampton, to where he had fled to avoid further persecution by the Shah's authorities. In October, Khomeini's son Mostofa also died unexpectedly from a heart attack. Rightly or wrongly, the anti-Shah protestors blamed the Iranian intelligence service SAVAK, which had been oppressing left-leaning and liberal political movements, for both deaths.

With that and a resurgence of the feeling that the Shah was a puppet of the West, the unrest continued to grow into 1978. Even then things might have been averted had the Shah taken steps to rein in his behaviour and court the more liberal-minded Muslims. Instead the Shah urged the then vice president of neighbouring Iraq, Saddam Hussein, to drive Khomeini out of his country. Rather than solving the problem, this subsequent exile of Khomeini with Saddam's support – this time to Paris – merely made the canny cleric a kind of living martyr, and he used the world's media to portray himself as a victim of the Shah's oppression.

Oldfield told Anthony Cavendish that by the time he reached the Shah he found his old friend ill from cancer and unwilling to listen in any meaningful way. By October 1978, with Oldfield in retirement, Iran was gripped by strikes, inflation was raging and the Shah was forced to grant amnesty to his political opponents, including Khomeini. The following January, the ailing Shah was driven from office and exiled, first to Egypt and then to Morocco, where he was welcomed by a mutual acquaintance of his and Oldfield's, King Hassan II. He sought medical treatment in the USA, consented to by President Jimmy Carter, and died in Cairo in July 1980.

Ayatollah Khomeini's regime was to last for ten years in which time he did his level best to eradicate all the Shah's Western-style changes. Sharia law was introduced, women were forced to cover their hair, and many symbols of Western decadence were banned, including alcohol and most American films. It would be ridiculous to blame Maurice Oldfield for any of the events surrounding the Shah's departure, but that did not stop him feeling it personally. He would say to Anthony Cavendish and to Sadie that his promise not to spy on Iran in the Shah's time was one of his greatest regrets. Clever use of sub-agents could have offered early warning as to the grass-roots and religious reaction to the Shah's reforms, and might have enabled Oldfield to encourage him to behave differently. After all, Oldfield was not averse, before he was Chief, to spying on European allies in the aftermath of war and in the run-up to the formation of the European Community. But when he had the power, and could have acted, his word to the Shah was worth more than his better judgement.

Oldfield's retirement, in April 1978, coincided with his being awarded the Knight Grand Cross of the Order of St Michael and St George – known as a GCMG – in the Queen's Birthday Honours of that year. This, he enjoyed saying, meant 'God Calls Me God'. It was the highest honour ever bestowed upon a Chief of the Secret Intelligence Service, and was only equalled in 2015 by Sir John Sawers, after his retirement. It has never been surpassed. Just as Sawers's award was in great measure for his efforts in making the Service respectable again after the 2002 and 2003 debacle over the so-called 'dodgy dossier', so was Oldfield's in no small part for his work in building the Service's reputation in the wake of Philby, Blake and the disasters of the past.

A long-serving former senior MI6 officer told me of Maurice, 'His exceptional intelligence, intellectual power and other personal qualities made him by far the most respected Chief of SIS in modern times, a respect recognized by his Whitehall colleagues with the unprecedented award of a GCMG on his retirement from the job. And that performance, in turn, opened the road to SIS's full recognition as a department of government to be accepted on equal terms with the others. Maurice's career spanned the whole period from the disasters and mismanagement of the forties and fifties, via the clean-up under Dick White, to the Service's integration with the rest of the government machine, including a happier relationship with the Security Service and an always sound collaboration with CIA – which also valued him. Intellectually he stood out. He was an outstanding Chief and the Service was better placed and in better shape at the end of his tenure than it ever had been before, or so I think.'

A retired Director of MI6 went further: 'The pressures of Maurice's professional life were entirely different to those of his private life; unique, very complex and difficult to navigate, to restore and preserve the Service's reputation after the disastrous post-war years, and to deal with the turmoil caused by Chris Phillpotts, the Director of Counter-intelligence, who was a believer in James Jesus Angleton's theories. Maurice was clearly very successful in both areas, and most notably in gaining and keeping the trust of successive Prime Ministers. That, he must have seen as his most important priority, and he was quite right.'

A profile in the *New Statesman*, written anonymously by a fellow Lady Manners School alumnus, the MP Phillip Whitehead, under the title 'The Honourable Grammar Schoolboy' was not well received by Oldfield. Whitehead agreed to show Oldfield his draft for approval prior to publication, which drew this response when his secretary passed it to Maurice: 'Despite its "human" side, I don't like it and I shall tell him I would prefer to suppress it.' Whitehead published anyway. And lest anyone thought Oldfield was going to let retirement get in the way of his continuing to serve MI6, a little note appeared in *Private Eye* saying that he was going to carry on advising the Prime Minister on an ad-hoc basis. Quite what his replacement, Sir Arthur 'Dickie' Franks, thought of having a back-seat driver is not recorded, but it's unlikely he had so much of an eye on the press as his predecessor. It wasn't until a decade later, when Gerry Warner became a Director and was given a licence to talk, that MI6 would become formally engaged with the media to any degree.

The Whitehead profile concluded with the words 'Oldfield is retreating towards All Souls with his personal probity intact.' It was to be barely two short years until that comment was challenged, but for a good eighteen months Maurice enjoyed a happy, if frustrating, retirement. Of course, he spent a lot of time in Over Haddon, visiting Betty Kemp in Oxford and staying with the Cavendish family in Hampshire. In May 1978 he became the first head of MI6 to date to speak at the Old Mannerians RFC annual dinner at the Maynard Arms Hotel in Grindleford, five miles from Bakewell, where he was only third on the bill behind the Wales and British Lions rugby star Cliff Morgan and, standing in for club captain Mick Nicholls, a young player named Bryn Thompson. According to Thompson it was he who stole the show, leaving the distinguished guests in his wake. By the time Morgan stood up to talk he was amply refreshed with the local ale thanks to the generous pouring arm of John Pearce to his left, leaving the field clear for Thompson.

Maurice Oldfield's speech went down nearly as well, and included his favourite intelligence story. He related how a Russian peasant was walking along on a bleak Siberian winter's morning when he came across a wounded bird, struggling to survive in the cold. The peasant spotted a steaming heap of recently deposited cow dung and, thinking of the bird, picked up the poor thing and placed it in the heap so it might get warm and recover, before going on his way. After a while the bird began to feel better, and started to chirrup, loudly. Next along was a fox who, hearing the bird's song, fished it out of the dung and ate it. 'The moral of the story is this,' Maurice concluded. 'He who gets you into the shit isn't necessarily your enemy. And he who gets you out of the shit isn't necessarily your friend. Most importantly of all, if you are in the shit, keep quiet.'

Oldfield marked his retirement by granting a rare interview to the author Phillip Knightley, and their talks ranged around many subjects. Maurice admitted to a grudging professional admiration for the success of the KGB's penetration agents, and surprised Knightley by discussing the case of Rudolf Hess, Adolf Hitler's deputy, who had flown to Scotland in May 1941 in an attempt to start peace talks – and who was, at the time of Oldfield and Knightley's discussion, still incarcerated in Spandau Prison, with guard duties shared between Britain, France, the USA and the USSR. Without disclosing his source, Oldfield told Knightley that Hess had his own intelligence service, and that the chief of that service was a KGB agent. Maurice considered that it was possible this KGB agent was behind Hess's flight, and that this was the reason why the Soviets were so keen to keep the German in jail. It is now known, from files released in 2007, that by the early 1970s it was only the Russians that were insisting on Hess being maintained as Prisoner 7, the sole inmate in Spandau.

There were at least two possibilities for why it would have benefited the Soviets to keep Hess locked up. Firstly, when he flew to Scotland, Russia and Germany were not at war – they were still bound by the Molotov–Ribbentrop Pact. It's feasible that had Hess been successful, his KGB agent hoped that the pact would have been maintained and a truce declared with Hitler. This would have given the lie to the Soviets' claims that the pact was merely to buy them time to prepare to fight the Nazis. An alternative theory was based on the fact that Hess's agent – the KGB man – did not warn Stalin about the German invasion of Russian positions in Poland that occurred barely a month after Hess's flight. It is also, therefore, feasible that the KGB agent in Hess's employ was a double agent. Either scenario could have brought embarrassment on the Soviet regime had Hess been allowed to speak.

Oldfield left Knightley pondering these intrigues, and with the thought that the spymaster knew more than he was letting on. Nothing more was said until 2013, when a buff file of documents described as 'perhaps the most important wartime archive ever to be offered for private sale' turned up in an auction house in Maryland in the USA. On the front of the file were the words 'Most Secret' and 'Hess'. The auction house is maintaining the confidentiality of the owner of the documents – which failed to reach their reserve of $700,000 – but it seems the files were removed from MI6 archives by Maurice Oldfield before he retired and passed to someone he trusted, as he feared that whether by accident or design they could be lost to history.

Experts in the field agree with that assessment. Professor Scott Newton, a modern historian from the University of Cardiff, said of the matter, 'Like many historians, Sir Maurice believed the Hess affair still holds great secrets. Unusually, he had the chance to take action to stop the archives being "weeded" before they were opened to historians.' The military surgeon Hugh Thomas, who treated Hess in hospital, added, 'Sir Maurice removed the file without the intention of permanently depriving the government of it, because he was concerned it could be destroyed . . . and the truth about Hess's captivity concealed.'

It would fit with Oldfield's character that he would, if necessary, take unorthodox steps to protect what he considered to be important historical documents, though the full truth of this episode is only likely to become clear when the files are once more offered for sale.

Throughout his career in MI6 Maurice was very much against most, though not all, of the literary and screen depictions of the Service. He saw the James Bond series as harmless fun, however. I remember sitting with him to watch *Goldfinger* on our new colour television. It must have been around 1976, and he chuckled steadily all the way through without commenting on it very much. As Sir Gerry Warner told me, 'James Bond is our greatest ever recruiting sergeant'. The darker, seemingly more realistic portrayals, though, were a different matter.

When Graham Greene, himself a former MI6 officer who served under Kim Philby, published his novel *Our Man in Havana* – which teased the intelligence services, and especially MI6 – it was Oldfield who took Greene to task for it. Henceforth, Greene's espionage novels would start with a disclaimer, stating that the contents were entirely fictional. Despite their disagreement, Oldfield and Greene remained friends, and during Philby's Moscow years Greene was a kind of unofficial go-between between the traitor (who remained a friend of Greene's) and Oldfield. When asked about his relationship with Philby, Greene said, 'Kim knows that anything he tells me I will pass on to Maurice Oldfield.' The historian Sir Alistair Horne says he remains convinced that Oldfield 'played' Philby until the end, dangling the possibility of a return to Britain. 'It would be absolutely up Maurice's street to do that,' Horne told me. 'He liked the idea of Philby, the upper-class English traitor, being stuck in a dismal Moscow flat, powerless because the KGB knew of his communications with MI6 via Graham Greene and was thus never sure he could really be trusted. It was a more effective punishment than any prison.'

Phillip Knightley considers it very likely that Greene was acting as a conduit for messages from Oldfield to Philby, in the knowledge that Philby's communications would be read at both ends. In discussing the effects had Philby bitten at the bait of a return to Britain in return for a confession and immunity from prosecution, Knightley wrote, 'SIS would have won a propaganda round. Imagine the headlines: "British defector chooses freedom", "Can't stand Communism, says former traitor".'

Oldfield's equivalent at the head of the East German secret service, the Stasi, Markus Wolf, supported Knightley's assessment. 'Philby came to East Germany for a couple of visits,' Wolf told Knightley. 'I was responsible for his security arrangements and I entertained him – we did a bit of cooking together at my place in the country. He had a KGB escort, and I think now it was him rather than Philby who told me about the offers for Philby to return to Britain.' Wolf's eyes gleamed with appreciation of the cunning of the British ploy. 'I thought the offers must have come from British journalists,' he said. 'I believed, wrongly, that Philby saw a lot of them. I never thought of Greene, but it does make sense.'

Either way, Oldfield won. If Philby stayed in Moscow, Oldfield knew he was pining for the *Times* crossword on the day of publication rather than weeks later, cricket scores as they happened, English life and English voices. If Philby returned, tail between his legs after fifteen years, it would have been a huge coup for MI6. Oldfield admitted to Knightley in 1978 that he had received an indirect message from Philby, presumably via Greene. 'He said that he would welcome a word or two from me to wish him well. I won't give him that. On the other hand I won't do anything that will harm him in any way. I don't want him to get six years in the salt mines. Some of my colleagues would happily cut his throat. I don't feel like that.'

Oldfield and Greene's final run-in came just before the former's retirement with the publication of the latter's novel *The Human Factor*, which featured the supposed amorality of the top people in MI6. Oldfield objected to this portrayal and told Greene so. Whether the fact that one concern was that the main character was widely assumed (though this was denied by Greene) to be based on Kim Philby while having the name Maurice Castle, which could be construed by an insider as an amalgam of Oldfield's Christian name and Anthony Cavendish's original surname, remains a matter for speculation. Yet after having words at the time of publication, shortly afterwards, with Oldfield in retirement, Alistair Horne was surprised to witness his friend embracing Greene warmly at an event in Oxford. 'I asked him why he did that,' recalled Horne. 'He told me there was no point in bearing a grudge. I really think Maurice was incapable of hatred.'

Given his known antipathy for literary representations of his Service, it's perhaps a little surprising that Oldfield agreed to meet with David Cornwell and Sir Alec Guinness when the television adaptation of Cornwell's John le Carré novel *Tinker Tailor Soldier Spy* was being planned in the autumn of 1978. Cornwell considers that the reason for Oldfield's objections to such portrayals was personal as much as professional. 'It always seemed to me that Maurice thought of the Service as being like another family to him,' he told me. 'Like a family, for all its faults, he absolutely loved MI6 and was utterly loyal to it. The idea of it being, in his view, denigrated by the likes of me did not impress him.'

David Cornwell, giving an immaculate impression of Guinness's distinctive voice, explained to me how the meeting came about, and how the association between Oldfield and his lead character, George Smiley, evolved. 'We really wanted Alec to play Smiley, but he was a bit "Eeyoreish" about it. He was quite nervous, and didn't feel that after the surprise big hit of *Star Wars* he had another television series in him. He said to me, "But I've never met a spy; I don't know how to play one." I still had Maurice's telephone number, so I said I would call him and see if he would meet us. "But what shall I wear? Do we have to dress to blend in?" Alec asked. I told him, "Wear anything you bloody like."'

In the run-up to the lunch it's unclear which of the main players was the more excited, the spymaster or the Oscar-winning actor. Guinness had made it clear that he was intrigued by the prospect of meeting an actual spy, while Oldfield confessed to Cornwell that he'd been a long-time admirer of Guinness's work. He'd occasionally seen Sir Alec on a train, but despite being at home talking to heads of state, international terrorists and government ministers, Oldfield claimed he'd always been too nervous to approach his hero. Now, given the chance, not only did he gladly agree to meet, he suggested a venue for the meal.

Cornwell made the reservation at the restaurant in Chelsea and arranged to meet his guests there.

I was a little late arriving, and when I stepped inside there was no sign of Maurice or Alec. I told the maître d' that I was due to meet Sir Alec Guinness and Sir Maurice Oldfield. He looked furtively around, put his finger to his lips, shhhh'd, and said, 'Follow me.' I was led to a small room, obviously somewhere Maurice had used before, and there were Maurice and Alec, getting on famously.

As I sat down to join them, Maurice peered through his glasses and said to Alec, 'I think young David here has been getting a bit carried away with all this spying nonsense.' Alec nodded and said, sagely, 'Oh, I quite agree, Maurice.' For the next couple of hours I was given a dressing down by these two famous knights of the realm, and they still expected me to pay for lunch.

As the three men dined and discussed the television project, Guinness studied Maurice, absorbing every detail. When Maurice said he had to go, the trio agreed to keep in touch, said their farewells, and Guinness and Cornwell stood and watched as Maurice disappeared down the street. 'Do they all do that?' said Guinness, referring to Maurice swinging his umbrella as he went. Cornwell explained that they didn't. 'And what about the cufflinks? Do they all wear those garish cufflinks?' Again, the response was no. 'And I studied how he held his glass. I've seen people swill the dregs; it's a sign of being pensive. As is rubbing a finger around the rim. But I've never seen anyone wipe round the inside of a glass like that with a finger. Do you suppose he was checking for poison?' 'Well, if he was, he's dead,' Cornwell replied.

The actor and the author went back inside, and at last Guinness felt he was ready to take on the role of George Smiley. Until that moment Cornwell had never thought of Smiley as being Maurice Oldfield. Insofar as he was anyone, Cornwell told me, Smiley was based on a man named John Bingham, a former MI5 officer and later the 7th Baron Clanmorris. But Guinness turned him into Maurice – the look, the mannerisms, everything. Oldfield had turned up at the Chelsea lunch wearing a pair of orange suede desert boots: Guinness even got the costume department to buy him an identical pair. So *Tinker Tailor Soldier Spy* saw Guinness play Smiley as Maurice. Cornwell so liked the result that from then on he wrote Smiley with Alec Guinness playing Maurice in mind.

For his part, Guinness, without naming the spy he'd met, told the *Guardian* journalist Tom Sutcliffe about the meeting. 'I was told he [Oldfield] would be extremely reticent, very, very shy, and might be almost completely silent over lunch,' the actor recalled, but in fact 'I've rarely met a more garrulous, informative, unshy person as it turned out. He was very good fun.'

19

A Lonely Man in Stormont

IT MAY APPEAR strange to start a chapter about the bleakest period of a person's professional life with a reference to a popular television series, but the debut of *Tinker Tailor Soldier Spy* on 10 September 1979 unexpectedly thrust Sir Maurice Oldfield into the headlines right when he didn't need it. The best part of a year earlier, when he'd lunched with Sir Alec Guinness as the great actor was trying to bring George Smiley to life, Oldfield was in quiet retirement, and quite flattered to be asked to meet a man of whom he was a fan. Speculation about his being the true model for Smiley might have been quite entertaining to Oldfield at that time, freed as he was from the responsibility of high office, but when it coincided with his taking up a new post in Belfast it just added to all the publicity.

David Cornwell himself went to great pains to stress that Oldfield was emphatically *not* the Smiley he wrote, but Guinness's portrayal, and the three men's lunch together, meant that to the viewing public that's exactly what he was. From being an unassuming academic at All Souls College,

Oxford, Maurice was suddenly the most high-profile civil servant in the country, this link to popular culture making him as well known to readers of the tabloid press as to followers of current affairs and politics. He was arguably the first 'celebrity' civil servant – from a tradition where such people only became famous when they defected to the Soviets.

The background to Oldfield taking up his lonely, ultimately thankless residency at Stormont Castle on 8 October 1979 was mired squarely in the Troubles that had brought terror to the Province and the British mainland throughout the previous decade, and had culminated most recently in the Warrenpoint Massacre (eighteen British soldiers dead) and the assassination of Earl Mountbatten of Burma. A stark and horribly timely example of what the country was dealing with came on the very day Oldfield started work, when the murder of a twenty-four-year-old Catholic man on the Albert Bridge in Belfast was balanced out by the assassination of a plain-clothed British soldier in the west of the city.

The former Labour Northern Ireland Secretary Roy Mason chose that same day to make a statement about his own security, and his comments rang true to Oldfield's family and friends. It must be borne in mind that Mason had ceased to be Secretary of State some six months earlier, and while no doubt he would still have been a major target for the terrorists, the biggest scalp they could have claimed would have been that of the newly appointed Security Coordinator. Member of Parliament for the mining town of Barnsley, barely thirty miles from Over Haddon, Mason described how an 'assassination competition' between the

Irish Republican Army (IRA) and the Irish National Liberation Army (INLA) for ever more prestigious targets had grown up, and how he continued to face death threats, couldn't travel freely, and lived in what amounted to a 'mini fortress' at his South Yorkshire home. If the out-of-office, out-of-power Mason was still considered to be at constant risk, then the threat posed to Oldfield, who had just been the subject of major press coverage not only as the spy who was going to fight the IRA but the public face of both Smiley and M, was potentially far greater.

Things had changed decisively for his home village the previous week. On 28 September it was the same quiet agricultural backwater it always had been. On the 29th it was home to England's biggest security presence outside London. A police caravan was stationed in the orchard at Mona View, an alarm system formed a continuous ring around the property including the garden and orchard, and Annie (who was by now beginning to show signs of dementia) and Renee Oldfield were given a panic button to be pressed – in the words of the Chief Constable of Derbyshire Police, who came to give the family a briefing – 'in any emergency'. All the home telephone numbers of the family were changed and made ex-directory. Checkpoints were placed at both entrances to the village, and all the residents were interviewed, assessed, and their sheds and outbuildings searched. Car registration plates were recorded and checked. There was a permanent presence of at least six Special Branch officers based in the antennae-covered caravan, with two policemen on twenty-four-hour guard in the street outside Mona View.

As Special Branch were doing their rounds, they spotted

an estate car with Northern Irish number plates parked outside the Lathkill. There was nobody in the car, but in the rear, under a blanket, flashing lights were visible. The road was immediately cordoned off, then officers called in on pub landlady Hermenia Dougherty and asked her to tell her staff and customers to stay inside. The bomb disposal squad was soon on hand, and they gingerly approached the vehicle. Closer examination found the car boot to be full of traffic cones. The bomb squad was stood down, and an inspection of the inside of the Lathkill found the hotel bar to be full of drunken Irishmen who had stolen the traffic cones from the M62 as a prank on their way to a walking holiday in the Peak District.

On Monday, 1 October, Maurice arrived in Over Haddon to see his family for the last time before relocating to Stormont Castle. He shared his official Rover with the faithful Ken Dyer and two further bodyguards; one police car travelled a few minutes ahead to ensure a clear path, and another two accompanied Oldfield's car, one in front and one behind. A police helicopter hovered above for the entirety of the visit. Maurice spent an hour with his mother and Renee, then took a last walk around the village, calling on other family members and friends, spending a few moments standing by his father's and his two youngest siblings' graves, and praying in St Anne's Church, before calling at the Lathkill for a half of bitter with his brother Joe along with John and Warren Pearce. As he bade them farewell, John recalled that his uncle said, sadly, 'It may be some time before I see you all. I don't want to draw the fire.' Many of the family, though they couldn't know it then, would never see him again.

For the children of Over Haddon, the novelty of living in a police village was short-lived. For the previous few years any visit from Maurice had been quite an occasion. His status as head of MI6 had been well known since 1973, and for a generation brought up on James Bond and living in a village far removed from oak-panelled offices, Aston Martins and gadgets, this was about as exciting as life got. Even with his public profile Maurice had been able to spend his time in Over Haddon in relative normality and without affecting village life in a negative way. But with the stroke of Margaret Thatcher's pen on his letter of engagement, that was over.

It was, of course, entirely coincidental, but the fact that Oldfield's change in circumstances from one of quiet glamour to one of darkness, fear and anxiety happened just as a gloomy autumn was taking hold added to the slightly sinister feel that enveloped the village. Maurice had always enjoyed kicking a football in the street with the village children while telling sanitized but, to the kids, utterly thrilling stories of his travels. Now, on the day of his last visit, when the children arrived with the football, the resigned look on Maurice's face told its own story.

Once Oldfield was safely back on the road to London, the football resumed, and the policemen on duty outside Mona View joined in the games. But a hint of how things were now came when Robert Pocock, then aged nine, and playing with James Bentley, Jason Lally and me, sliced a shot and sent the ball over the high wall into the Oldfields' garden. Without a thought, and as he had done numerous times before thanks to his shooting not being what it might have been, Robert scaled the wall and was about to clamber down the other side when alarms sounded and he was hauled down by two

Special Branch men. That incident, more than any other, brought home to the village exactly how life was going to be for the foreseeable future.

The following morning the village cows ran amok as a police helicopter landed in an adjoining field and the sirens of two police cars signalled that something was amiss at Mona View. Sadie Pearce hurried down the street, fearing the worst, and was let into the house by a policeman. She returned home to report that all was well, and that 'Grandma Oldfield had pressed the panic button because she wanted a cup of tea'.

Another teething problem for the Over Haddon security set-up came in the darkness of the same night. As the Special Branch officers settled down to a cup of tea and a game of cards in their caravan, they heard rustling in the bushes between the apple trees in the orchard and spotted a shadowy figure in a balaclava crawling towards the house. As they'd been trained to do, one officer covered the area with his gun while the others targeted their quarry. The figure turned sharply towards them and one officer instinctively went to shoot, only to find his weapon knocked from his hand by a colleague. 'Stop! It's Derek!' And it was. The head of Bakewell CID, Inspector Derek Stoneleigh, had taken it upon himself to test the security at Over Haddon. On the positive side, the security had been effective. On the negative, he'd nearly got himself shot.

The official, rushed-through announcement of Oldfield's appointment on 3 October overshadowed two others that were also important in Northern Ireland. The two leading figures in security in the Province in the autumn of 1979 were the Chief of the Royal Ulster Constabulary (RUC), Sir

Kenneth Newman – whom Maurice had previously encountered over thirty years before in the Middle East – and the General Officer Commanding (GOC) of the Army in Northern Ireland, Lieutenant General Timothy Creasey. As the government was committed to making the security effort one that was police-led, for the obvious reason that making it Army-led would give the impression that the place was being run under some kind of martial law, it was important for Newman to be the lead partner. Newman, though, was a rather nuanced, enigmatic character who was felt to have done a good job of streamlining the RUC since starting as Chief Constable in 1976 but who was also notable for keeping a low profile. By contrast, Creasey, called 'The Bull' by his troops, was a leader who lived up to that nickname, one who felt that if only the Army could be given a more leading role then progress in the fight against the terrorists could be achieved more quickly. According to the *Irish Times*, relations between the Army and the RUC had ranged from cool to downright hostile, with the more forceful Creasey pushing for the Army's influence to be increased. The Warrenpoint Massacre was the final straw for Creasey, who, when Margaret Thatcher visited the barracks in the days after the attack to boost troop morale, pushed the Prime Minister to give the Army primacy over the police and basically allow them to declare war on the IRA. He also recommended that a Security Coordinator be assigned to take overall control of strategy – and thought the ideal man for the job would be one Lieutenant General T. M. Creasey. Newman's wish-list was easier to get through both politically and in terms of selling it to the public. He simply requested that he be given an extra thousand men.

In terms of Creasey's recommendations, Oldfield's appointment was at least partially successful in keeping the Army happy. It was clear, though, that for things to improve, despite the high regard in which both Creasey and Newman were held as individuals, new faces were needed in their posts. John Hermon, one of the Deputy Chiefs of the RUC and – crucially – an Ulsterman, was appointed to take over as Chief Constable, and Richard Lawson, who had been dubbed 'Dick the Lionheart' by the *Daily Express* for his exploits in the Congo in the 1960s, was to become GOC in the Army. The timings were important here. Creasey was to stay on until 1 December, when he was to be promoted to Chief of Land Forces, while Newman stayed until the end of the year before returning home to become Her Majesty's Inspector of Police.

This meant that Maurice Oldfield started work with two possible antagonists already lined up to move on to bigger things, and thus potentially more pliant in terms of accommodating Oldfield's agenda. It also meant that Oldfield's proposals would be in place before the new men took up their posts. Though essentially he would be bringing his formidable reputation to bear on plans that were already under way – a figurehead intended to give the public confidence as much as anything new he might add – Oldfield got stuck into his new job with his customary level of humour, intellect and common sense, and typically cut through the complexities with speed and precision.

Before he left for Stormont, though, Oldfield sought a brief from Brian Stewart, the man he had hoped to anoint as his successor at MI6 and who had a strong reputation from his time in Malaya in particular. Stewart recalled later that he was 'horrified when Oldfield told me that he had accepted this poisoned chalice; I could not see how Maurice, despite his many talents and wide experience, could do a "Templer" in Northern Ireland.' To Stewart, Maurice was not being given enough clout to make a real difference in the Province. 'In Malaya, General Templer was not only High Commissioner but also Director of Operations and had more power than a Viceroy. Maurice would have no power. [The situation in Malaya] was a far cry from the situation that Maurice was about to face as a Coordinator who was, in fact, only an adviser. The job killed him.'

Despite Stewart's misgivings, Maurice wasn't deflected from his task. He spent his first week meeting everyone with whom he'd be dealing, talking and absorbing, getting to know the tensions and internal motivations. One of his colleagues of the time recalled his first encounter with the new Security Co-ordinator, and his impressions were not of the kind of commander he was used to. He found Maurice 'small and scruffy, with an enigmatic smile, and twinkling eyes behind glasses that appeared to defy the laws of optics – being heavily scratched. His suits never seemed to fit, but that didn't seem to be a matter of great concern to him.' But beyond the first impressions, Maurice's abilities were quickly apparent. 'Very few did not fall under his spell. Maurice was a very good listener and interrogator; charming, considerate, human – and had the knack of probing to extract truth without being exultant when he had. He obviously had a brilliant mind, with a great aptitude to absorb complexity – but reduce it to essentials. Maurice was genuinely non-partisan and therefore it was hard for others to be offended by his enquiries.' He quickly became a popular figure among the staff at Stormont, and within a week he was ready to present his initial report to Northern Ireland Secretary Humphrey Atkins. Entitled 'But Me No Buts', it's worth recording a few snippets of these notes as they demonstrate some of Oldfield's characteristics:

BUT ME NO BUTS

This might be regarded as a light-hearted title for a paper on a serious subject – and it might also be considered presumptuous for one who has been in Northern Ireland for exactly one week to make such a comment. I have however found the same refrain going through all my talks at all levels and in all departments. It goes something like this:

'Our personal relations are very good, <u>but</u> . . .'

'We have no difficulty agreeing at operational level <u>but</u> there are matters of higher policy.'

'Of course the task is clear, <u>but</u> . . .'

I suggest that while recognizing the valid reasons for these reservations, our aim should be to convert the conjunction 'but' into 'and'.

In his second paragraph, Oldfield reported on the religious conditions in Northern Ireland: as always, the need to understand people's beliefs and motivations was important to him. He knew that the religious issues had been 'argued and re-argued almost interminably' but had not realized the extent of the theologies, or how dogmatic they could be. He felt it was important to 'produce a framework of practical measures to ensure the quick and effective exploitation of opportunities and to resolve disputes before they hamper action'.

Oldfield was always aware that his role as a civil servant was to implement the policy of the government of the day – something that had put him at odds with some in MI5 in the past – and his stated aim was set out in paragraph three of his report:

There can be no controversy about the aim which is set out in the Secretary of State's statement in the House of Commons on 2 July:

'It is the government's firm policy that we should continue in Northern Ireland to do our utmost to defeat terrorism, and to extend the pattern of normal policing throughout the whole Province. The implementation of these policies rests in the hands of the Royal Ulster Constabulary, assisted by the Army.'

There was certainly no ambiguity in that as a brief. Whatever power struggles had bubbled away around the RUC and the Army, government policy was clear, and the Security Coordinator was going to do his damnedest to implement it.

Oldfield then detailed, in his typically concise fashion, how he felt his input ought to be used to get a system in place that would give quick and effective results. He didn't propose to introduce a Joint Operations Staff, which was one suggestion officials had mooted, as he saw that such an organization would merely duplicate, or even triplicate, the command structures of the RUC and the Army. Rather, he set up the Planning Staff, a group of officers nominated by the RUC, the Army and the Civil Service which was intended to work on a bottom-up basis, advising at a local level to ensure the right balance between the police and the Army was in place to suit the specific needs of each area in the Province. Somewhere between them all sat MI5 – not mentioned in the official records, but their presence was confirmed to me by Sir Kenneth Newman. MI5 had been marginalized in Northern Ireland since Harold Wilson's day when – not coincidentally – MI6 under Oldfield had been given a bigger role. The Planning Staff would have investigatory and advisory roles, and would act as a kind of 'Court of Appeal' between the services to ensure that issues that might arise were swiftly dealt with. The whole premise was to get people working together rather than becoming bogged down in the inter-service disputes over power and responsibility that had plagued the security effort until then. Oldfield's group would be answerable to the Secretary of State, so there was no danger of it becoming another faction.

He set out the four areas in which he proposed the Planning Staff would be crucial in terms of offering advice: firstly, Operations of the Security Forces, secondly, Intelligence. It was, in Maurice's opinion, impossible to detach intelligence or counterintelligence from operations, since 'all Operations have a direct or indirect Intelligence interest'. Third was the matter of Public Relations, the importance of which Maurice had learned in MI6; and finally the coordination of, and support from, other Northern Ireland departments whose actions would impinge directly or indirectly on operations against the terrorists.

He signed off his report with a reference to an old colleague and former Director of the CIA, maybe to reinforce the sort of hinterland he was bringing with him, but also to give a no-nonsense envoi: 'I tell a story of Allen Dulles, who kept a card on his office desk. This card faced his visitor and it read: "Do you come with a solution to your problem, or are you yourself part of it?" Let's hope we can together find our solutions.'

And with that he set about his task. Despite suggestions that Oldfield's staff be located elsewhere, he insisted they remain at Stormont. Again, mindful of public perception, he felt that the need to be seen to be close to the Secretary of State was paramount.

A fortnight later, in answer to an enquiry about how Maurice Oldfield was doing, the Permanent Secretary at the Northern Ireland Office, Sir Kenneth Stowe, was able to write to the Prime Minister and describe how, at a recent security meeting, Timothy Creasey had asked for it to be recorded that Oldfield's proposals had the '100% backing of the Army – and that Ken Newman agreed'. This was, given the recent history, a substantial achievement.

Oldfield himself was involved, directly or indirectly, in all four of the areas identified above. In terms of the operations of the security forces, his advice started with a need to tighten up border security. He found that there were over four hundred places where roads led from Northern Ireland into the Irish Republic, yet only twenty had security controls. This was a matter that was relatively easily overcome with the deployment of some of the additional staff secured by Kenneth Newman. The official meetings between the RUC and the Army, which had traditionally been chaired by each in turn, were now Planning Staff meetings chaired by Oldfield. This led to each side being able to air its own views without a chairman who would instinctively veer one way or the other, and a more streamlined approach to the decisions that emerged and the actions that followed. Rarely was there a need to refer a matter to Humphrey Atkins.

The intelligence and public relations areas were places in which Oldfield involved himself personally; they were, after all, what he knew best. As he had found constructive so often in the past, he called upon his ability to use the clergy effectively. His time as a historian and a lifelong association with, and deep understanding of, religion had left Oldfield able to talk to Catholics of every shade in language they understood, and argue theological points with them as part of his dialogue. In Ulster he found a province riven by religious divisions and dogma, but also one where people were still, nominally at least, in thrall to their priests. In as discreet a manner as a man in a helicopter with a coterie of armed guards could, he would almost literally drop in and hold talks with Catholic priests. These talks started by giving him a genuine feel for the realities of life on the ground in the area, how people lived and what might be possible to achieve. This was traditional Oldfield intelligence gathering.

It was Oldfield's good fortune (if good fortune there was in Northern Ireland at that time) that the population, even those most committed to sectarianism, was in great measure tiring of the endless violence. Fear of recrimination had been a major factor in limiting the information on terrorists being given to the police – and understandably so. Oldfield's attitude to this was to set in motion a longer game. Tightening up the security systems; roadblocks; more effective coordination of the RUC and the Army; a more careful use of intelligence – these were all things that could produce relatively quick results. But improved use and cultivation of informers would need thoughtful and measured planning.

The usual way of obtaining information, other than by simply paying for it or by interrogating captives, was to infiltrate a terrorist group with agents. In some places this worked well; in tight-knit communities such as were found in Ulster the process was both more difficult and more dangerous. Using the contacts he was building in the Catholic Church, Oldfield began to develop internal informers, ones who from within would be able to build knowledge and pass on the names of those who were still engaged in violence. It was painstaking work, and it would be some years before the results would be seen – and even then some students of the situation in Northern Ireland have been reluctant to offer too much credit to Oldfield for any improvements that could be argued to have come under his watch. A former colleague who served in the Province in various postings told me, 'I don't think Maurice achieved that much. He simply wasn't there long enough.'

Oldfield's situation in Northern Ireland was complicated by his involvement there earlier in the decade, and further complicated by his background in intelligence – at least insofar as the local media were concerned. The press briefing authorized by Margaret Thatcher that was sent to the ambassadors in Dublin and Washington – where questions were sure to be raised – stressed that Oldfield had been hired for his 'outstanding qualities of mind, personality and integrity'. If asked why the post had gone to a former Chief of MI6, the answer they were to give was that 'Any particular past experience he may have had is incidental to this appointment. The appointment is based on the man's outstanding personal qualities, not because of any particular expertise and experience that he might have acquired in the past.'

The Irish press didn't buy that line for one minute. Even before he'd moved into the fortress at Stormont the speculation had begun. An article exploring the complex tensions between the RUC and the Army that had resulted in Oldfield being parachuted in, and questioning the strength of Humphrey Atkins given that he apparently needed such assistance, finished with the statement: 'We'll have to wait and see whether Sir Maurice Oldfield's job is to tinker with the police, tailor the Intelligence Services, soldier with the Army or spy on the whole lot of them.'

It was Oldfield's policy in Northern Ireland not to be seen in public, and not to speak to the press – the latter a significant change from his time as Chief of MI6 when occasional and careful use of the media had been one of his tactics. Now, he was determined, was a time to ensure the spotlight was on those whose job it would normally be to speak for the authorities – the Secretary of State and the Chief Constable. But so public had been his appointment that again this policy served only to fuel speculation that, given the secrecy surrounding Oldfield, could never be publicly contradicted. An example of this came when an Irish journalist claimed an IRA source had told him that Oldfield had been seen walking alone near the seaside resort of Bangor in County Down. It was one of those stories that was, at first reading, just about plausible – as was a later one that would have far more sinister repercussions – and it enhanced the mystique. Rumours ranged from one that Oldfield had never even been to Northern Ireland and the whole thing was just a ruse to tales of him striding along a beach in plain sight. In the paranoid, tense world that was Ulster in 1979, this was all grist to the mill.

The wider complexities that accompanied his job tended

to vindicate the press scepticism. It was known that Colonel Gaddafi's Libyan regime had been supplying the IRA with arms since the early 1970s, and it was suspected that the Russian Embassy in Dublin had become populated by KGB agents who used it as a base to spy on Britain and to show support to the terrorists in the North. The IRA and INLA were also known to have links to the Palestine Liberation Organization (some of the Irish terrorists were trained in the Middle East as was confirmed by both the Irish Garda and the Israeli Embassy in London in February 1978) and to give mutual support to the Basque separatist group ETA.

So, despite the official narrative, Oldfield's background in MI6 was without question directly relevant to his work in Northern Ireland, not just a happy coincidence. He knew how embassies and diplomatic postings worked, and was able to rein in the more gung-ho elements in the security services that might previously have been expected to take matters into their own hands. An example of this came when he was advised that an official from the Polish Embassy in London had been to Belfast, in contravention of the rule that visiting diplomats couldn't travel more than thirty miles from the embassy without notifying the Home Office. Much excitement was generated among Maurice's staff, but he was able to tell them to remain calm, and just watch the man's movements. Oldfield was more interested in where the spy was going from Belfast, where he'd been before, with whom he'd spoken; it was those facts he could use. To apprehend the Pole just for breaking a rule would have been pointless and probably counter-productive.

This manner of patient intelligence work was to pay off in 1981, when Sir Colin Figures, by then Chief of MI6, was able to recommend to the Prime Minister that a Russian official based in the embassy in London, Viktor Lazin, be expelled on the grounds of 'activities incompatible with his status as a diplomat' – a popular euphemism for spying. Lazin had arrived in London in 1977 and come into Oldfield's orbit in late 1979 when the Soviet had been reportedly travelling between Dublin, Liverpool and Belfast, and had been spotted with a known IRA man on Merseyside. The Oldfield policy of watch, listen, report bore fruit only after Maurice's death, but the careful timing and measured approach meant that not only did the British know exactly where Lazin had been, what he'd seen and who he'd spoken to, his expulsion was completed without creating any kind of incident. It was the first public exposure of a Russian spy since the mass expulsion of 1971, and the method of the project's execution gave a credibility boost to Figures's early days as Chief.

Reining in the more enthusiastic members of the security services like this was one of the key, if unspectacular, elements of Oldfield's work in Northern Ireland. Work in recruiting informants and cultivating sympathetic local knowledge had begun before he arrived, but had been hampered when over-eager Army officers went, with the best of intentions, free-range and sent in units to react to information received in an all-too-public way that sometimes left the source of that information exposed. At best, potentially good informers would retreat into silence; at worst, the recriminations could be fatal. Oldfield's policy of encouraging the RUC to be the public face of the security effort with the Army as the lower-profile partner may have been less than a headline grabber, but it was important and effective.

On Christmas Eve 1979, the Prime Minister and her

redoubtable Press Secretary Bernard Ingham arrived in Belfast to be given a security briefing by Oldfield and the chiefs of the RUC and the Army. If Mrs Thatcher was expecting a high-octane report on massive and decisive progress, she was to be disappointed. Oldfield was, more realistically, able to report on the painstaking work being done to build trust in Catholic areas, stressing the difficulties with this, particularly in the rural areas where strangers were easily recognized and ostracized. They were gradually getting more information about crimes, but the problem was that the evidence was in many cases simply not good enough to gain a conviction. Links with the Garda were improving, but the Garda didn't have the expertise to extract the necessary information from the willing when the opportunity arose.

After nearly three months in the job, the only extra resource Oldfield requested was not additional police or soldiers or weapons, it was more, and better, lawyers. Working within the framework he'd set up there had already been more arrests, but he felt there had also been too many suspects freed on bail that shouldn't have been. In such a volatile situation that kind of result was far from helpful, both in terms of propaganda for the terrorists and what the released suspects might get up to while at large. Overall, though, his report was one of steady, calculated progress and of improved cooperation between the services.

It's worth considering that once the post of Security Coordinator had been quietly phased out – or 'mothballed' as Sir Robert Armstrong put it – in 1981, it was surely more than coincidental that over-zealous, out-of-control state security units began to cause trouble again. In fact 'trouble' may be considered an understatement. In late 1981,

intelligence of a loyalist threat to murder a Republican solicitor, Patrick Finucane, was received by the RUC Special
Branch. They declined to act, despite the head of Special
Branch identifying it as a 'very real and imminent threat', on
the grounds that to warn Mr Finucane, or offer him protection, would jeopardize the source of the intelligence. Mr
Finucane was murdered in February 1989, shot in front of
his wife and children by two masked gunmen. The murder
led to the arrest and conviction of one William Stobie, a
former member of the Ulster Defence Association (UDA),
who, it emerged, had been recruited as an agent of Special
Branch in 1987 and then re-infiltrated this loyalist terror
group. In 2001, Stobie himself was shot dead by his former
UDA comrades. A series of inquiries by Sir John Stevens,
later Commissioner of the Metropolitan Police, found that
there had been widespread collusion between the RUC, the
Army and loyalist terrorists in the murder of Irish nationalists. Stevens also reported that he had been 'obstructed in
his work throughout' by elements within the RUC and the
Army. A further report, this one by Sir Desmond de Silva
and commissioned by the Coalition government in 2012,
upheld all the findings of the Stevens reports, and concluded
that there had been a complete lack of coordination between
the various agencies charged with providing security in
Northern Ireland from the mid 1980s. It was acknowledged
that many members of the RUC and the Army had been killed
or maimed during the Troubles, but also that individuals
and groups within those services had taken matters into
their own hands by way of vengeance, and had resented the
controls that were put on them by their superiors.

Clearly the events described above post-date Oldfield's

time in Northern Ireland – and I make no claim that things would necessarily have been different or better had he stayed in his post. But these reports, which cover the past thirty years in some shocking detail, lay bare the complexity of the situation in the Province. Stevens and de Silva demonstrate vividly and with a tangible sense of dismay the tensions that existed between and within the various security services, and how individuals weren't beyond taking enormous liberties with their positions – to the point of colluding in murder.

His time in Northern Ireland was, without question, the saddest and loneliest of Maurice's life. Geographically it was his closest posting outside London, but in terms of quality of life it was a million miles away. The constant, relentless but entirely necessary security presence brought on a feeling of claustrophobia for someone who had always been a sociable, outgoing person. He did manage the occasional, highly coordinated trip away from Stormont. In Northern Ireland he would dine at friends' homes, and sometimes stay with Robin Dixon, the former Olympic bobsleigh gold medallist and later Baron Glentoran, and his family at their home, Drumadarragh House in Ballyclare. There was the odd visit to Marsham Court, and to his close friends Tony and Elspeth Cavendish in Hampshire, where Maurice could wander in the gardens with the Cavendishes' dog Abdullah while Special Branch prowled the perimeter fence.

He also tried to keep some sense of normality by attending church as often as he could, and surprised the Buss family by making it over for the confirmation of their daughter – Maurice's goddaughter, Celina – at Hurstpierpoint College Chapel in East Sussex. Vivian Buss remembers that he 'arrived in the most amazing armoured car, bristling with aerials, with a team of bodyguards and a helicopter flying overhead. The college boys were fascinated.' Gerald also reported how the officers swarmed around the chapel before allowing Maurice to enter the building. 'They crawled all over the place,' he said, 'under the pews, in the vestry; every inch of the place was scrutinized. The pupils, quite innocently, asked me what they were looking for. "Bombs," I replied, to looks of sheer horror.'

But to his family, Oldfield became a virtual stranger. His first attempt to visit was aborted when police intercepted a car laden with ammunition heading to Over Haddon; the second, ramped up with additional security and the obligatory helicopter lurking over the village, was only a brief call at Mona View to see his mother, and those sisters and brothers who had been able to get there quickly enough. Annie Oldfield, by then eighty-two years old, was thrilled to see her eldest son, and beamed throughout his visit. Sadie recalled, 'Mother was getting so forgetful at the time. She had taken to wandering, saying she was looking for Maurice. When he came home it was as if all those memories had come flooding back.'

Maurice's loneliness extended into a feeling that he was being personally threatened – not in the physical sense, but in terms of a whispering campaign about his private life. Irrespective of the facts of his sexuality, he had always been aware that his bachelor status laid him open to speculation. In the sinister, febrile and dangerous atmosphere of Northern Ireland during the Troubles, with multiple potential enemies, it was probably inevitable that this would start to be used against him. Nothing actually appeared in the press, probably for fear of libel action, but the threat that it might hovered over Maurice from early March 1980 onwards.

Oldfield was also beginning to feel unwell. Initially he complained in a letter to his sister that the meals at Stormont weren't agreeing with him. He felt there was too much fried food, which irritated his stomach, and that he wasn't getting a very well-balanced diet. He went to see an Army doctor at Stormont, who diagnosed incipient diverticulitis, or inflammation of the colon – an unpleasant enough complaint, but not life-threatening. Maurice wasn't convinced, and the illness combined with the omnipresent threats led to a real sense of gloom descending. He tried to call his old mentor and friend from wartime days Douglas Roberts, but Roberts was also ill. His wife, Elizabeth, who took the call and spoke at length to Oldfield, reported that he had sounded 'very depressed'. He told Mrs Roberts, 'If they don't get me one way, they'll get me another.' He didn't specify who 'they' were.

Work on his brief continued regardless, and he produced reports and recommendations for each of the areas of Northern Ireland, taking into account the individual characteristics they displayed. This included the religious make-up, the attitude of the population to the authorities, and the physical geographical features, all of which influenced how the security issues had to be addressed. On 2 April 1980 he produced a report for the Prime Minister on the security situation in East Tyrone following a meeting of the Planning Staff. The area had been identified by the Northern Ireland Office as being 'particularly difficult from a security point of view'. Parts of the review give a flavour of how Oldfield felt his work in the Province was going. The first paragraph is particularly telling, in terms of the slow but steady progress Oldfield believed was being made:

The first point which was striking, particularly when compared to the first briefing I had, on South Armagh, also in Portadown, some 5 months ago, was the remarkable unanimity of approach and appreciation between the Police and the Army. Not to use too strong words, it would have been well nigh impossible to have such a conversation in such an atmosphere last year. It is fashionable to say that this is largely a matter of personalities. I think that is only partly true. It arises from a new feeling of cooperation not competition, and also equally important, a sense of direction in that the people on the ground see some progress. That this progress may be more in improving our own machinery than in tangible successes against the terrorists in the area does not belittle its importance.

Most of the report dealt with details of striking a balance between the services to achieve the desired aims, and Oldfield concluded by trying to answer the question 'Are we winning?' His opinion was not yet, though things were getting better:

While recognizing the difficulties and dangers of the area and of the continuous possibility of spectaculars and other incidents for which the terrorists have both personnel and equipment to hand or on call, there was a cautious optimism, particularly among the senior officers at the presentation. Some of those in the RUC had long service in the region and felt there was a new hope born largely from more effective intelligence and operational arrangements between RUC and Army. One or two of the younger ones advocated strengthening the specialist units in the area and all paid particular attention to the need for concentration on disrupting terrorist organizations by sustained harassment and, hopefully, convictions.

Perhaps I can best summarize the feeling after this initial look at the area by saying that there is no euphoric claim to be winning in East Tyrone yet, but there is a sense of general confidence stemming from an agreement that we have a firm platform from which we can go forward.

The words he used gave no indication that Oldfield considered his work done; rather, by describing it as an 'initial look' and referring to 'younger ones' advocating the strengthening of certain units, the impression given is of a man who saw a continuing need for an experienced hand at the tiller. But that hand was not to be Maurice Oldfield's. Within weeks of reporting on his progress to Margaret Thatcher he was writing to her asking to be relieved of his duties on the grounds of ill health. Correspondence between the two showed their mutual respect, and behind the scenes officials debated whether the post of Security Coordinator should be continued, and if so, who should take it on. Perhaps surprisingly given his recent report, Oldfield's view was that there was no need for him to be replaced, and that he would continue to be available to offer advice on an 'honorary' basis.

There was some sympathy for this point of view among politicians and officials. The marquee announcement had been that of Oldfield's appointment the previous autumn, and it had never been intended that this would be a long-term role. The feeling was that Oldfield had put structures in place that had facilitated a quick and effective improvement in the coordination of security, and that this could now be overseen by the Secretary of State. But stronger than that practical assessment was the presentational message that would be sent out if Oldfield retired and was not replaced. Mrs Thatcher was adamant that not only should the Security Coordinator's post be continued, but it should be filled by someone of considerable seniority. This, to the PM, was fundamental from a public relations point of view. She was perfectly content that the appointment could be for an initial six months and then be quietly phased out, but no appearance of weakness at the time of Oldfield's departure was to be sanctioned.

On 15 May, the Prime Minister's Principal Private Secretary, Sir Clive Whitmore, wrote to John Chilcot, then an official at the Home Office, to set out the official position. Sir Maurice Oldfield's health, Whitmore related, was 'becoming increasingly a matter of concern, and he should be replaced as soon as possible'. Their favoured candidate was Sir Antony Duff, a senior former intelligence officer and ambassador who was then a Deputy Secretary in the Cabinet Office, and who would go on to become a highly rated head of MI5; in reserve they had Sir Arthur Hockaday (who had been mooted prior to Oldfield's appointment) and Sir Francis 'Brooks' Richards. Richards was another Deputy Secretary at the Cabinet Office, acting as intelligence coordinator, and had a distinguished career in intelligence going back to the Second World War when he was a director of operations in the Special Operations Executive. The value added by Oldfield's background in intelligence had been duly noted, and there was little attempt to manoeuvre a traditional diplomat into the role beyond the cursory mention in dispatches of a couple of ambassadors.

A quick recruitment process saw Duff decline the role,

Hockaday's candidacy vetoed by the Ministry of Defence as he had become 'indispensable' there, and Sir Brooks Richards appointed to succeed Oldfield. The decision was approved by Foreign Secretary Lord Carrington, Defence Secretary Francis Pym, Northern Ireland Secretary Humphrey Atkins, and Sir Maurice Oldfield himself. Having seen what Oldfield had been through in terms of security concerns taking over his life, Richards had made it clear that his time at Stormont would be limited to no more than three days a week. Content that he would essentially be continuing to facilitate the security services working to Oldfield's established framework, the Prime Minister was happy with that. Richards's other request was that his appointment should not be formally announced. With public perception being so important, however, Thatcher didn't consider that to be an option.

It was decided that the transition from Oldfield to Richards would occur on 16 June, the announcement coinciding with the new Coordinator starting work, but again the inevitable leaks and speculation in *The Times* brought that forward to the 12th. Oldfield said his formal goodbyes to the Stormont staff on 6 June and returned to London, riddled with pain, frustrated at a job not finished, and with the prospect of facing a kind of strange purgatory where the reason for his stifling security protection had been taken away but the need for it remained. Margaret Thatcher wrote a personal letter to Maurice, thanking him for 'how effectively you have established a coordinated security team in the Province, boosted their morale, and achieved significant progress'. She finished by hoping that 'you will now enjoy to the full a second retirement richly earned'.

How sadly wrong that hope was to be.

20

Anatomy of a Smear

*H*ANSARD RECORDS THAT on 23 April 1987 the Conservative MP for Blackpool South, Sir Peter Blaker, asked the Prime Minister, Margaret Thatcher, 'whether she will make a statement on the recent allegations concerning Sir Maurice Oldfield in relation to the security of the United Kingdom?'

The Prime Minister gave the following written answer:

Sir Maurice Oldfield became Security Co-ordinator in Northern Ireland in October 1979. Subsequently reports were received which caused his 657W positive vetting clearance to be reviewed. In March 1980, in the course of that review, he made an admission that he had from time to time engaged in homosexual activities. His positive vetting clearance was withdrawn. By this time he was already a sick man; he finally ceased to serve as Security Co-ordinator in Northern Ireland when a successor took over in June 1980; he died in March 1981.

There was a lengthy and thorough investigation by the Security Service, which included many interviews with Sir

Maurice Oldfield himself, to examine whether there was any reason to suppose that he himself or the interests of the country might have been compromised. The conclusion was that, though his conduct had been a potential risk to security, there was no evidence or reason whatsoever to suggest that security had ever been compromised; indeed, he had contributed notably to a number of security and intelligence successes which would not have been achieved had there been a breach of security. That conclusion stands.

By the time of Thatcher's reply to Blaker's question, Maurice Oldfield had been dead for six years. The effect of her statement was to stir Maurice's former colleagues and his friends into an immediate and robust defence of the man, and to bring deep sadness to his family. Uniting the personal friends, the colleagues and the family was the vicar of Bakewell and Over Haddon, the Reverend Edmund Urquhart, who maintained his vigorous support for Maurice and his family in the face of a raft of allegations, speculation and innuendo that besmirched the memory of a person who was fondly remembered by many for his kindness, devotion to duty and friendship.

The ambiguity of Thatcher's statement allowed the press to have a field day with Oldfield's reputation, safe from the fear of libel action. Over the last three decades Maurice Oldfield's name has been dragged into the press every time an Establishment sex scandal has been reported; the facts have been long forgotten, and were mostly never properly examined. With Maurice dead, and having no right of reply, it was, and remains, an easy story for any journalist – especially when their reporting follows the received wisdom.

The conspiracy theorists continue to weave their elaborate webs, and the power of the internet, with its endless capacity to pass off conjecture as fact without scrutiny, has almost glibly, and definitely painfully for his family and friends, associated his memory with almost every form of deviance imaginable. Perhaps the most hurtful allegation, which still does the rounds on the conspiracy websites, is that Maurice was 'a misogynist who could only bear female company if it was his elderly mother'. That is possibly the most ridiculous and offensive statement in the whole sorry business: Maurice was utterly devoted to his sisters and his wide circle of female friends including Betty Kemp, Rozanne Colchester, Janet Wadsworth and Marion Laidlaw.

In researching this book I determined to explore every possible aspect of the story, and to report my findings honestly, however uncomfortable they may be. I must, of course, declare an interest as a relative of Maurice with fond memories of him, but I have not shied away from the possibility that some, or all, of the allegations about him may be true. In studying the matter I have spoken to many of Maurice's former colleagues, MI6 officers who had few if any direct dealings with him, MPs, other politicians, civil servants, journalists, Special Branch officers, and of course family and friends. I have had access to his surviving papers and have studied the newspaper reports of the time, and various archives.

Despite repeated requests under the Freedom of Information Act to see the official report on which Thatcher's statement was made, access was refused on the grounds that 'it relates to a member of the security services'. It seems there is more chance of Maurice coming back to life than that ever being made public, so it falls to me to relate what I have been able to discover and hopefully provide an accurate summary of what was by any standards a tragic end to a remarkable career and life.

The best starting place for explaining the circumstances that led to Thatcher's answer in April 1987 would seem to be the last days of Maurice's time in Northern Ireland in 1980. The story that was to bring Maurice down began when journalists were told of a rumour that in late March he had slipped away from Stormont Castle and his twenty-four-hour Special Branch protection team and made his way to the Highwayman public house in Comber on the outskirts of Belfast. According to the story, he had whiled away the afternoon in the pub, and then followed a man into the public toilets, where he propositioned him for sex. The man had complained to staff at the pub, who reported the matter to the police, and as a result Maurice was questioned by the constabulary.

Someone allegedly reported the matter to Sir David McNee, Commissioner of the Metropolitan Police, and, according to Chapman Pincher, McNee passed the report to William Whitelaw, the Home Secretary, and Sir Robert Armstrong, by then the Cabinet Secretary – head of the Civil Service and the Prime Minister's adviser on security matters. A swift investigation followed, and Armstrong summoned Oldfield to Whitehall to answer questions. Armstrong described the meeting to me as 'the most miserable episode of my entire career. I was utterly aghast to be having to question Maurice on such matters – he was the ultimate loyal civil servant.'

I asked Armstrong what allegations he had put to Oldfield. 'It was very strange,' he replied. 'The allegations were generated in Northern Ireland, but there was absolutely nothing relating to Northern Ireland in the allegations that were presented to me. What the investigation found were reports of Maurice having questionable friendships in his overseas postings.' I then enquired what the nature of the allegations was. 'There were no suggestions of impropriety in any physical sense,' Armstrong told me. 'There was, though, incontrovertible evidence that he preferred the company of men. Maurice made no attempt to deny it; he just sat, sad and broken, and apologized for having lied on his positive vetting forms when they homed in on sexuality.

'We agreed that, subject to an interrogation by MI5, he would return temporarily to Northern Ireland, but would then resign on the grounds of ill health. There was no lie in that; Maurice was clearly unwell. At that stage there seemed no need to inform the Prime Minister, provided the MI5 check came back clear. Maurice had been a loyal and valued servant, and I felt we owed it to him to be able to retire with dignity.'

That evening, Maurice summoned Anthony Cavendish to his Marsham Court flat, where his old friend found Oldfield sitting in a darkened room with an ashtray overflowing with spent cigarillos and a bottle of whisky that was definitely half empty. Cavendish sat down and drew up a glass, and Maurice opened up to him. 'Tony, I have been lying in my positive vetting. I have been to see Robert Armstrong, and I have resigned from my post.' He then explained about his youthful peccadilloes and how they had now come back to haunt him. He said the only people with whom he would discuss the matter were Cavendish and Victor Rothschild. 'I have never before considered suicide,' Maurice said. 'Today I have, and I need to speak with you.' By now his flat was under constant surveillance by the press, who were desperate to catch a rent boy entering the premises so they could break the story. The waiters from Lockets who delivered his meals, the porters in Marsham Court, the Special Branch officers on duty, all were badgered to sell their stories on Maurice. The pressure was relentless.

There followed two formal grillings by Cecil Shipp, MI5's top interrogator, who delved into every one of the allegations. Shipp accepted Oldfield's position that any physical acts of homosexuality had occurred from time to time in his student days, over forty years before. Since then, for all his time in office, Maurice had confined himself strictly to the closet.

In 2016, while answering questions to the Historical Institutional Abuse (HIA) Inquiry, MI5 would claim to have interviewed Oldfield no fewer than thirteen times, right until January 1981. The new head of MI5 at that time, Sir Howard Smith, reported that Oldfield admitted to 'relationships with hotel stewards in the 1950s' – but there was no reference to physical activity. MI5 concluded that Maurice may not have admitted to 'the full extent of his activities', an assumption that would help to drag the Oldfield name through the tabloid gutters in years to come.

My research indicates that there were two interrogations; MI5 would later claim there had been thirteen. Given the deteriorating state of Maurice's health (he was dangerously ill in hospital on some of the occasions when these supposed extra interviews would have had to have been held), and the exchange of letters in the Thatcher Foundation Archive, the former still seems more likely.

The important thing, though, is that despite being

subjected to a thorough investigation, no evidence of impropriety was found against the frail, weakening Oldfield.

The displays of affection witnessed by some (possibly including friendships with hotel staff) may have indicated a preference, but that was all. Alistair Horne considered that Maurice's weakness was, for a spymaster, a tendency to be too trusting. Some of those to whom Oldfield had shown kindness in Singapore or Washington had reported that they felt him to have shown homosexual tendencies. No action was ever taken because nobody had made any accusations of physical incidents, and Oldfield had consistently passed his vetting – and the CIA's lie detector.

With the Shipp investigation over, Maurice's positive vetting certificate was withdrawn due to his having lied on the forms, and he returned to Stormont to complete the reports on which he was working and to prepare to vacate the post. Had there been any suggestion whatsoever of impropriety on Maurice's part, or that he was a security risk, there would have been no way he could have carried on reporting to the Secretary of State. The termination would have been quick and sharp. When Maurice finally left Northern Ireland in June 1980 there were tears among the staff at Stormont Castle: as had happened at Century House, he had, in his short stint, become a much-loved and respected figure. It was a sad end to a notable career, but Oldfield returned to England with his reputation publicly intact, to fight his last battle.

He came, briefly, to Over Haddon, where he saw as many of his friends and family as he could. Carolyn Pearce remembered that he called in on her family, and found John working on the farm and the others out at school. 'What are you doing?' Maurice asked. Carolyn said that she was about to go shopping to Buxton, and was surprised to find the former head of MI6 asking if he could come along. Maurice struggled getting into the car, and was wheezing and sweating. Noticing Carolyn's concern, Maurice told her, 'For over thirty years I've been expected to have a heavy lunch and dinner almost every day, with rich food and plenty of drink. It's been part of my life.' She also knew that he smoked quite heavily. He then changed the subject to talk about medieval history, and how he hoped to return to All Souls to carry on his studies.

On reaching Buxton, they found nowhere to park, so Maurice said he'd wait in the car – left on double-yellow lines – while Carolyn did the shopping. She was dismayed when she emerged laden with bags to find her car surrounded by policemen, and was preparing her defence when she realized that in fact Maurice was holding court with the officers; though ill, his skill as a raconteur had not deserted him. Not for the first time, but for the last, the police's words for Carolyn were 'On your way, Sir Maurice'.

Having said his goodbyes to the family, Maurice visited Rozanne and Halsey Colchester at their vicarage in Bollington, Cheshire, and then returned to London. He had a regular list of visitors, Cavendish, Julian Amery, Victor Rothschild and Betty Kemp among them, and managed a trip himself to the Cavendish family in Hampshire, where he found some peace walking in the gardens with the family dog.

Another appointment Maurice had taken on in 1979 along with his Northern Ireland posting was as a governor of Lady Manners School, by then a state comprehensive, where he served alongside Edmund Urquhart, who was chairman of the governors. Edmund recalls that Maurice attended one meeting but was then dispatched to Ulster and found it difficult to get back. The chairman remembers being bemused that despite the practical problems associated with Maurice getting to meetings, the other governors resolved to write to him as there was an attendance rule. He called to say, 'I had no idea they wanted an active board', and henceforth, despite his illness, telephoned the headmaster regularly to offer his input and seek news of the school.

By the end of 1980 Maurice's previously full figure had begun to diminish. When Dr Michael Chan visited in December he noticed that his friend's shirt had become loose around the neck – a sure sign of illness. Whereas he was usually very assiduous in his sending and displaying of Christmas cards, Maurice's flat was conspicuously non-festive. 'I'm not bothering much this year,' Oldfield told Chan, but wrote out a card for him there and then. Chan wrote that despite Maurice not having mentioned it, he could tell that he was seriously ill. 'I never expected that this would be the last time I saw him, though,' Chan added.

Early 1981 saw Maurice's sisters taking it in turns to stay at Marsham Court to care for their brother, and in late January a visit by a concerned Tony Cavendish convinced Oldfield to seek further medical advice. He was examined by Queen Elizabeth II's own physician, Sir Richard Bayliss, who quickly diagnosed a case of stomach cancer, and Maurice was admitted to King Edward VII's Hospital for Officers in Westminster. The Oldfield family continued to maintain a constant presence at Maurice's side, and a stream of visitors came to spend some time with a man who was clearly dying.

Someone who claimed to have visited at Oldfield's personal request was Chapman Pincher, but a recently unearthed letter from one senior CIA officer to another indicates that this may not have been exactly in accordance with Pincher's description. Writing in late March 1981 to his colleague, Oldfield's old friend Cleveland Cram, John Leland Hart relates how on his last visit to Maurice's bedside; 'Who should be there? Chapman Pincher. Maurice was beside himself. I'm not sure that this coincidence was one a doctor would have prescribed.'

It seems from this reaction that even as he lay dying Maurice may well have suspected that Pincher's salacious muck-raking had somehow contributed to his resignation from Stormont. Certainly Hart's letter to Cram, which coincided with the publication of Pincher's *Their Trade is Treachery*, expressed concern about the veracity of the journalist's material, in which he was effectively a mouthpiece for Peter Wright in what amounted to an early version of *Spycatcher*. Hart had sent Cram a copy of the *Sunday Times* coverage of Pincher's allegations about Roger Hollis in the book, referring to 'the Hollis problem, which once affected me somewhat'. The CIA man was clearly exasperated by the way Pincher blended fact and fiction in his drive to sell books, and went on to comment that 'Such background as I have helps me to discriminate sense from nonsense, but I pity those without such background. They must be totally bewildered'. This view is reinforced by the experience of Hollywood film-maker William Tyrer, who set about making a film about Roger Hollis and got to know Pincher well when the journalist was in his nineties. 'I liked him very much,' Tyrer told me, 'but I abandoned the film project when I did my own research into Pincher's thesis'.

A regular and welcome visitor was Gerald Buss, who recalled that Maurice never lost his sense of humour. 'I said to him, "You must have a lot of secrets, Maurice. Is there anything you'd like me to tell the Queen?" Maurice fixed me with a stare, and said, "Not the Queen, Gerald, not the Queen."' Anthony Cavendish was generally at his friend's bedside, too. Alistair Horne, working in Washington, was saddened not to have been able to get back before his 'mentor and guru' died.

In early March, Maurice received an unexpected visitor in the unmistakable form of the Prime Minister. Maurice's brother Joe told me, 'We were all sitting around talking to our Maurice when two policemen knocked and entered the ward – followed by Margaret Thatcher. We stood up and she said "no, stay, stay", and spent half an hour talking with us all. I thought well of her for that. After a while she asked if we would leave the room, as she needed "to speak privately with Sir Maurice".'

When Mrs Thatcher bustled out, the family went back into the ward and found Maurice, who had previously been relatively calm, agitated and, for the first time any of them had seen, crying. Joe asked him what the matter was. 'Mrs Thatcher asked me if I was homosexual. I had to tell her.' As the light was fading on their eldest brother's life, this was the only time his family had ever heard any suggestion of that kind in relation to him, and it had come from the Prime Minister.

From that day, Maurice's condition deteriorated quickly. He made his siblings promise not to tell their mother he had died before he passed away, peacefully, on 11 March. He was sixty-five. As Maurice had requested, his mother was not told of his death; she would herself die the following year, still unaware that her eldest son had gone before her. The Northern Ireland Secretary Humphrey Atkins issued a statement that 'Britain has lost a great and valued servant'.

The Oldfield family sat cheek-by-jowl with politicians and spies, all crammed into the tiny church in Over Haddon to pay their respects to MI6's most decorated Chief in an emotional service conducted with customary dignity by Edmund Urquhart. The service was relayed by loudspeakers to the crowds gathered outside, and television news cameras filmed the burial. The occasion was not without drama. A plot was uncovered to blow up Maurice's coffin as it arrived at the church. Rumours circulated that an empty coffin was buried in place of the real one, to ward off any incidents. Though she had not been able to get to the funeral, many years later Oldfield's secretary from Singapore days Marion Laidlaw sought out his grave and left a posy of white roses and white Scottish heather. Marion was comforted by the beautiful setting with the fallen dry-stone walls and sheep grazing nearby. 'I felt that after all Maurice's adventures he had at last come home to where he really wanted to be and had found peace.'

A second service followed a week later, in open air amid the ruins of St Matthew's Church in the heart of Westminster, and then on 12 May a memorial service was held at the chapel of the Royal Naval College at Greenwich. This last one, a grand affair about which Maurice would have probably felt a little self-conscious, was led by the Reverend John Oliver of the Royal Navy and Maurice's long-time friend Halsey Colchester, with a tribute to Maurice being read by Sir William Deakin, a former colleague and Winston Churchill's literary assistant. Deakin's address ended with the words 'Maurice Oldfield was both a man of charity, and one of the most human of human beings whom those of us who have gathered here this morning to pay tribute to him may have ever known'. They aren't really the kind of words one might expect to be levelled at a formidable spymaster.

There can be few people who have been effectively 'outed' twice, let alone both times by a Prime Minister. Of one thing we can be absolutely certain: Maurice Oldfield did not want to be 'outed'. Whatever the truth of Maurice's sexuality – and it is by no means as clear as 'gay' or 'straight' – to go to the lengths he did to keep his private life exactly that must have been a full-time commitment for over forty years. In fact, evidence of Maurice being gay amounts to a supposition from student colleagues dating back to the early 1930s, an admission of the same from Maurice to Anthony Cavendish and to Robert Armstrong over forty years later, and then admissions to Armstrong and Cecil Shipp of what seem to have been no more than flirtations over the next few decades. Vitally, there was never any suggestion that any of the foregoing meagre occurrences had at any time prejudiced Maurice's work or British interests more generally.

Throughout the twentieth century there are examples of gay people being outed, actors and politicians among them, but none that I have found were outed by a Prime Minister after being vetted on that very matter and having been cleared of being a security risk by a top-level MI5 investigation. The first outing, on Maurice's death bed, after which he was so upset that he described what had happened to his siblings, was one thing. It was at least private, and neither Margaret Thatcher nor the Oldfield family said any more about it for six years. The second, in Parliament, was quite another. Given his lifetime of service, the stated lack of any security issue, and a politician's usually second-nature way of couching things, Maurice's wish for his private life to be respected ought to have quite easily led to a different form of words being used.

Had the Prime Minister's written answer stated simply that Oldfield's conduct had been thoroughly investigated and no security risk had been found, that could have been the end of the matter and thirty years of innuendo and smears need not have happened. The same outcome could have been achieved by a full and detailed answer. The response that actually came was, for Oldfield's family and friends – but not for the muck-raking journalists – the worst of all worlds. Phrases like 'from time to time', 'engaged in homosexual activity' and 'potentially a risk to security' were pounced upon and exploited. The bit about there being 'no evidence or reason whatsoever to suggest that security had ever been compromised' was seldom reported during the ongoing scandal.

For six years Maurice had rested in peace, his family content that his death bed outing by Thatcher had gone with him into the grassy Over Haddon hillside. Then whispers about the late spymaster's private life had begun to gain currency, resulting in Peter Blaker's question in Parliament and Margaret Thatcher's answer. Such was the vagueness of Thatcher's statement that the press had carte blanche to print whatever salacious versions of the story they saw fit. On 26 April the *Sunday Times* led with a huge article by the Northern Irish journalist Chris Ryder that expanded on the Highwayman pub story, reporting it as fact. Having been tipped off that the story was about to break, Anthony Cavendish sped up to Derbyshire in the early hours of Sunday morning to buy up every copy of the paper in Bakewell so that he could personally explain the story to the Oldfield family before they read the news.

The way the story was reported, from the Thatcher statement to the smears that followed, left Maurice's family feeling that his memory and all he had done for his country had been utterly betrayed. They could see absolutely no reason why the Prime Minister, whom they thought had enjoyed a relationship of mutual respect with Maurice, should have felt the need to make that statement in that way at that time. She had spoken to them personally to say how much she admired Maurice; it was even noted later, in the October 2008 *Times* obituary of his successor as Chief of MI6 Sir Dickie Franks, that Thatcher 'did not mention him [Franks] in her memoirs, *The Downing Street Years*. Given her views on the importance of secrecy, this may not be entirely surprising; but there can be little doubt that she had been favourably impressed by Oldfield, who had been authorized to brief her while she was still in opposition, and to whom she was to turn for help in Northern Ireland.' Oldfield was in fact mentioned in *The Downing Street Years*, without the smears, and was the only MI6 Chief to feature.

Sir Tam Dalyell, no lover of Thatcher it must be said, told me he felt her statement was 'utterly political and wholly unjustified'. It seems to have been done – admittedly driven by officials, not the Prime Minister herself – to distract attention from the *Spycatcher* affair that at the time was causing embarrassment to MI5, the Civil Service and the government.

Further insult was added by Maurice's supposed friend Chapman Pincher, who embellished the Ryder story for a book called *Traitors: The Labyrinths of Treason*, at the same time adding astonishing and entirely unsubstantiated stories that associated Maurice with rent boys and a liking for so-called rough trade. The inclusion of Maurice Oldfield's name in a book about traitors was too much for his supporters to bear. Anthony Cavendish challenged Pincher about his statements, and was told with a wink, 'You may have a pension, Tony. I need to look after mine.' The main allegation in support of Pincher's 'scoop' centred on an alleged incident at Oldfield's Marsham Court flat, where a security officer claimed to have seen Maurice with a young oriental man, looking as if he'd been beaten up.

Enquiries within Special Branch led nowhere, but then I stumbled on the answer in some papers left by Michael Chan (who died in 2006) dated 1981, just after Maurice died and six years before Pincher's 'exposé'. Chan related how he visited his friend some time in early 1978 just as the duty protection officers were changing, and just as a former MI6 officer he recognized was leaving, agitated. Maurice explained how the officer had arrived inebriated and turned aggressive as he had been dismissed from the Service for drunkenness. Suddenly, it all made sense. The dismissed officer would have been known to the protection team and thus allowed in. Michael Chan was known to the protection team and would have been allowed in. It seems almost certain that what the new officer saw was Maurice, looking a bit dishevelled, with a young oriental man – the future, and very married, Lord Chan of Oxton. Had there been any sexual activity, it would have been picked up as Maurice's flat was bugged. As it was, the drunken, disgruntled spy was gone, never to be seen again. Neither Oldfield nor Chan had thought any more about it at the time.

The timing of the stories, with Oldfield six years in his grave, and the nature of the allegations beg a good deal of scrutiny. As for the timing, this was the era of the MI5 mole hunter Peter Wright's controversial book *Spycatcher*, with its revelations that MI5 had 'bugged and burgled its way around London' – not exactly displaying the Security Service in a blameless light. In late March 1987 the headlines screamed about MI5 having been involved in a plot against Harold Wilson. Is it entirely coincidental that the bad publicity surrounding MI5 should be so quickly followed by a sex scandal involving the long-dead Chief of its sister, but rival, service MI6, which took the attention off the deficiencies of MI5 for a period? At the time Maurice's friends thought not, and sought to get to the bottom of the matter.

Channel 4, under the investigative journalist Robert Parker, looked into the Highwayman allegations and managed to track down the manager and staff of the pub, which had since closed down. All of them denied that any such incident had occurred. I contacted the journalist who broke the story, Chris Ryder. I asked him when he had first become aware of the Highwayman allegations; he said that it was in 1980, just after the supposed incident occurred. I asked Ryder why he hadn't reported the incident at the time. He told me that it was because even then, a few days after the 'incident' was alleged to have taken place, he 'couldn't verify any of the rumours to enable publication'. He told me his source was 'someone in the Northern Ireland Office'.

It is possible that Oldfield was not even in Northern

Ireland at the time. From appointment details I have I know he spent a considerable amount of time in England in March 1980. He was in Oxford for a period, including attending the annual dinner at All Souls, of which I have dated photographs. The few days he was in Northern Ireland that month – while it's not specified precisely when they were – appear, according to files released by the Thatcher Foundation, to have been spent writing reports and communicating with Whitehall. The opportunity for illicit liaisons would have been limited indeed.

Notwithstanding the complete lack of evidence, it is necessary still to consider the matter of opportunity beyond the simple availability of time slots, if one supposes that Maurice had decided to prise himself away from his security detail to try to find a man to proposition in a toilet. He was, at that time, the most protected non-royal person in the country. He couldn't leave a room without being followed, and his guards had to account for his every movement. He could only be alone with a third party if that third party had been thoroughly checked out. A Special Branch officer of the time told me 'it is simply not credible that the principal [Oldfield] could slip away from his twenty-four-hour protection'.

An army officer who worked closely with Oldfield in his Stormont posting, right when the alleged incident was said to have taken place, remembers that Maurice would sometimes come to his house for meals, play with the children and was great company. 'My wife and I discussed his sexuality then and felt that he was similar to others we had known who, while perhaps having latent homosexual characteristics, certainly had no sexual inclinations in any direction.

From our observation he particularly enjoyed the company of bright young people of either sex and found their conversation and challenges intellectually stimulating.' Turning to the scandal, this officer believed that 'the allegations . . . were either mischievous or delusional. Knowing the life he was living, with severe security constraints they would have been impossible. I suspect they started with loose gossip and were then exploited either by factions within the intelligence community or by the IRA propaganda machine.'

A member at the Athenaeum noted how Maurice had been in the club with his guards, bemoaning the suffocating security presence under which he had to live. Even had he managed to escape, how would a sixty-four-year-old some way from the peak of fitness have got to a pub several miles away undetected? Taxi drivers would have recognized him; he could scarcely wait at a bus stop, even assuming he knew the routes. Had his own driver taken him there then he and Oldfield's guards would have had to accompany him in, and thoroughly check the place out in advance. It is a matter of fact that even churches in England were carefully searched before Maurice was allowed to enter. The idea that a pub in Belfast would have been an exception is laughable.

Then there is the matter of the pub's location. There are dozens of pubs in Belfast and its environs. Why would Maurice have chosen that one, in a quiet suburb just outside of the city that a local resident and historian told me was known to be a particular haunt of off-duty Special Branch and RUC officers? The Highwayman at Comber was absolutely the last place someone who was trying to shake off Special Branch would have chosen.

It's difficult to resist the conclusion that whoever started the Highwayman story did so in order to be mischievous, given the place's connections with the constabulary – maybe even to give a journalist the chance to spot a flaw in the story.

It seems very clear that someone wanted Oldfield out of Belfast, ensuring that a rumour about his conduct reached the government. Whoever started that rumour must have had a reasonable idea of what an investigation into his private life might throw up – but rooting the trigger for that investigation in Northern Ireland immediately threw up any number of potential sources. The IRA, for one. As Gerry Fitt of the SDLP put it some years later, 'The IRA knew within five minutes of his arrival at Stormont that Maurice Oldfield was gay.' But if that is true, it seems very unlikely that the IRA played any part in the smearing of Oldfield. If they wanted rid of him then planting that allegation in the press would have been a simple matter and one that could have been achieved a good deal more quickly.

According to the intelligence officer Colin Wallace, he first heard whispers in Northern Ireland about Maurice Oldfield as far back as 1972, when Edward Heath sent MI6 into the Province. 'Oldfield was seen as a Mr Clean in Northern Ireland,' Wallace told me, 'and a threat to some of the more disreputable activities the various security organizations were utilizing. The smearing against him really got ramped up after he arrived as Security Coordinator in October 1979, and although at the time no newspaper published anything, the journalists were all well aware and were sniffing around.' Wallace, who was one of the prime movers in trying to expose abuse at the Kincora Boys Home in Belfast, also expressed surprise at attempts to link Oldfield to that scandal. 'The suggestion that Maurice was in any way involved in Kincora is just ludicrous,' he told me. 'He would have had no reason to go there, and there is no credible allegation that he ever did.' Wallace's view was backed up by Robert Armstrong, who told me 'there was no suggestion whatsoever that Maurice had anything to do with that children's home'.

The MI5 investigation into Maurice had the, probably unintended, side effect of propagating and prolonging the myth that he was somehow involved with Kincora. MI5's conclusion that Oldfield may not have admitted to the full extent of his homosexuality, almost unbelievably, meant that they didn't dismiss the possibility of a connection to Kincora. Britain's security service, supposedly the elite of homeland intelligence and seething with intellectual vigour, had basically conflated homosexuality with paedophilia. More than thirty years of misinterpreting files led, in the words of an MI6 officer involved, to documents being 'imperfectly drafted,' and Maurice being erroneously linked to Kincora.

It wasn't until the publication of the report of the HIA Inquiry, led by Sir Anthony Hart, in January 2017, that Maurice Oldfield was fully exonerated of any involvement in the Kincora scandal. The inquiry looked in detail at every aspect and concluded not only that Oldfield had not been to Kincora – he hadn't even been to Northern Ireland until his appointment in 1979. As we have learned, he had officers and agents in the province from the early 1970s – but had no reason to go there himself. It was simply impossible, and establishing this at an early stage could have saved Oldfield's family and friends years of upset. It is worth repeating, verbatim, the final sentence of Sir Anthony's report as it refers to Maurice.

'Having reviewed all of the evidence we are satisfied that the allegations about Sir Maurice Oldfield's connections with Kincora have no substance.'

In *Spycatcher*, Peter Wright refers to MI5 officers saying 'Bloody Maurice, interfering again' in relation to Harold Wilson asking him about the allegations of a plot and Oldfield confirming that there was 'a section of MI5 that is unreliable'. Whatever success or otherwise Maurice had in Northern Ireland, his reputation for doing away with dirty tricks and insisting on a clean approach to security is not in question. It is easy to see how, on hearing superiors moan about 'Bloody Maurice', a well-meaning subordinate might see that as a wish on the part of his boss to be rid of the man.

Anyone with a passing knowledge of Maurice's bachelor status could have found a willing press for an allegation of homosexuality, then quietly sat back and let the matter develop. Anyone involved with the notorious mole hunt that had been given access to MI6 Service files could have seen references to Maurice's questionable lodgers, and could have, so to speak, shaken the tree to see what fell out. Even if the investigation didn't lead to any falling fruit, it would inconvenience Oldfield, and the mud would, inevitably, stick.

Then there is the allegation made by Chapman Pincher, and verified by Colin Wallace separately, that Pincher was briefed about the allegations against Oldfield by David McNee and the Attorney General Michael Havers, independently, as early as 1985 – but that Pincher decided to sit on the stories until he was ready to put them in a book. If this is proved to be true – and as time has crept by most of Wallace's information has been, despite the Establishment rather wishing he'd go away – then the Commissioner of the Metropolitan Police and the Attorney General briefing against a dead Chief of MI6 would be scandalous. Reading around the case, Havers in particular seems to be somehow mired in the aftermath of Kincora, to the point where his sister, Baroness Butler-Sloss, had to resign from the government commission set up to investigate that and other matters in 2014. It seems feasible that Havers had reason to hope Pincher would besmirch the dead to protect the living.

I'm perfectly willing to believe this was not part of a coordinated, top-down conspiracy against Maurice by an individual organization. I am even willing to believe that whoever wanted Maurice out enough to smear him didn't anticipate the scale of the furore that was to follow. As well as Edmund Urquhart, whose campaigning on behalf of Oldfield's distraught family was tireless and included responding to all the scurrilous reports in the press and lobbying politicians and journalists, Anthony Cavendish wrote a book, *Inside Intelligence*, in his friend's defence. Both Cavendish and George Kennedy Young appeared on television to denounce the smears, as did the former manager of the Highwayman. Young told the *Daily Telegraph* that with his smears 'Chapman Pincher has done the KGB's work for them'.

Having seen Cavendish appear on the television news defending Oldfield, the former MI6 officer Kate Fuller, who was by then in her ninety-third year, wrote to him to say 'I want to thank you for what you are doing for one of the most "lovable" men I have ever known. I use that word instead of the word "intelligent" because everyone loved him, and as well as remembering his clear and active brain, I remember the way he treated the lowest member of his staff.' Other notable supportive letters came from Sir Kenneth Stowe, who was the Permanent Under Secretary at the Northern Ireland Office during Maurice's time there, retired colleagues such as James Fulton, and the then Chief Constable of Derbyshire Alan Smith, who wrote of his deep admiration for Oldfield.

MPs from the 'awkward' end of the spectrum such as Tam Dalyell and Ken Livingstone tabled questions on the matter in the House of Commons. Betty Kemp gave an interview to a *Sunday Telegraph* journalist – who genuinely tried to be supportive and it's difficult to avoid the conclusion that Betty would have preferred to dictate the interview – and would claim in a letter to Renee Oldfield after the article was published, 'Well, it *almost* said what I told him. It's not too bad I suppose.' Alistair Horne was slightly more abrupt in his attitude to Chapman Pincher's 'revelations': 'He was a self-serving, disreputable man. If he wasn't dead I'd still like to punch him.' Even Kim Philby, when the allegations about Oldfield went public, said, 'I never had any indication that Maurice was gay. If indeed he was.'

Reading the correspondence received by Urquhart and Cavendish in response to their lobbying, which was passed on to Maurice's sisters, what is striking is the uniform closing of ranks by the Establishment. Lengthy, well-argued letters generated brief, almost patronizing responses along the lines of 'Terribly sorry, but there is nothing I can add to the Prime

Minister's statement'. This included MPs, ministers, civil servants and senior journalists. As Cavendish pointed out, 'though Maurice was *in* the Establishment, he was never *of* the Establishment – though he always knew he'd be judged *by* the Establishment.'

Even thirty years later I have encountered this instinct in the Establishment to close ranks to protect their preferred version of the truth. The very mention of Colin Wallace's name, for example, will send the Establishment into a nervous frenzy that invariably leads to him being dismissed as a 'Walter Mitty character'. Even a close family friend who served as a highly ranked officer in the Army in Northern Ireland, and whom I would trust unreservedly, came back with the Walter Mitty phrase from his former colleagues when I asked him to look into Wallace's story. Deliberately not having any prior knowledge of Wallace's case before I met him, I found not only that he was remarkably calm about all that has come his way, but also that he could verify everything he told me. Bit by bit, Wallace is being proved right, in a long-running example of how the Establishment doesn't always know best. Indeed, by 1990 Margaret Thatcher was forced to admit that several statements she had made about Wallace were incorrect – and Armed Forces Minister, Archie Hamilton, admitted that several of Wallace's consistently made allegations were in fact true.

An MI6 officer who felt himself, like Oldfield, something of an outsider in terms of background was Sir Gerry Warner. His elevation to Director of Counterintelligence and Security in May 1986 gave him responsibility for a bundle of security and personnel files handed to him by his predecessor, Sir Christopher Curwen, which corroborated what Robert

Armstrong told me about Maurice's homosexuality – about which he had previously known nothing. After the story broke, it was clear that many, if not all, of the staff would be deeply shocked. Sir Gerry wrote to all the Service pensioners and called a staff meeting to announce that the Prime Minister's statement was broadly true. 'I have never seen so many suddenly white faces in one room,' he told me, 'but you have to remember that in the Service, Maurice was still respected and admired.'

Among the allegations that were to lead to Maurice's downfall – the Highwayman story having been roundly dismissed by nearly all concerned as no more than a trigger, a device to open the files – was the suggestion that Maurice may have engaged in improper behaviour with lodgers in his home on his overseas postings, but nobody has come forward with any claims of the kind. I have found several people who were present at the time, and none has made any allegations of physical contact. Anthony Cavendish (with the caveat that he was a close friend) stayed with Maurice for much of his time in Washington and was adamant that there was never any impropriety. Gerald Buss, who stayed with Maurice in Singapore, remains even more insistent that nothing of the kind occurred. 'Absolutely not,' he said, 'the suggestion was total rubbish. It just never happened.'

What people will concede, though, is that Maurice could be flirtatious, and that his choice of young friends could leave him open to speculation by those with a suspicious mind. David Owen, who described himself as being 'utterly shattered' by Margaret Thatcher's statement about Oldfield's private life, said he found nothing unusual about Maurice, though he noted a sense of loneliness, and sometimes a slight reluctance to leave at the end of an evening meeting. Owen considers that if Maurice did indulge his sex life then it was probably in the brief period between his retirement from MI6 and his appointment in Northern Ireland. 'I can imagine that, freed from the responsibilities of office, such a release may encourage a person to at last let himself relax.'

That said, Maurice's flat remained bugged until it was sold to Sir James Goldsmith after his death, and he retained the services of Ken Dyer, as his status as a target didn't go away the moment Dickie Franks took over C's desk. To the public, Maurice Oldfield was still the Chief, and, as a former MI6 officer told me, 'he remains our most famous Chief to this day'. At the time of his first retirement in 1978 he was sixty-two years old and a lifetime of good living was already taking its toll. For him suddenly to get an urge to make up for lost time in such circumstances would seem a little unlikely, though of course it is possible – and if he did, then I think most people would say 'Good luck to him!' Nobody has ever come forward claiming to have been a lover or a partner of Maurice's. Even the seemingly dubious characters who have come forward with questionable allegations against such people as Edward Heath, Lord Bramall and Leon Brittan have only ever said they 'think they recognize Maurice Oldfield from somewhere' – presumably a website full of conspiracy theories.

This aspect of Oldfield's life has become an unfortunate distraction from his life and his work, a view that was shared by senior colleagues. 'Maurice's stellar career was disproportionately overshadowed by his short stay in Northern Ireland after his retirement from SIS, and the opportunity which that, and the revelation of his homosexuality, gave rumour-mongers to suggest that he was in some way involved in covering up paedophilia in the Kincora Boys Home,' one told me. 'Maurice may have been a closet gay but there is no evidence that he was a paedophile or in any way sympathetic to such. And you see here, already, the unfortunate effect of these suspicions and gossiping is that I find myself drawn into mentioning them when the quite dramatic importance of his career was that his exceptional intelligence, intellectual power and other personal qualities made him by far the most respected Chief of SIS in modern times.'

And so, again, to the source of the smear. The view of people such as Anthony Cavendish, Colin Wallace and George Kennedy Young, and various historians with whom I have discussed the matter, is that it most probably came from within MI5. There were suggestions during the 1970s that Maurice would be moved sideways to become head of MI5, or head of some combined organization – something that would have been met with dismay at that time due to his objections to the mole hunt and his reputation as Mr Clean, not to mention opposition to the very notion of amalgamating the services.

People in MI6 have said that Maurice's time as Chief was like a breath of fresh air after what had gone before. There is less certainty that MI5 was ready for that. In Northern Ireland in the early 1970s, even though MI6 went in with MI5's formal agreement, the rivalries at a personal level were well known. By the late 1970s and his second coming, Maurice's presence was doubtless unwelcome to some at operational level. I would tend to agree with the assessment that the smear probably came from within MI5, but with the caveat that I think it very unlikely to have been officially sanctioned. More likely it was some variation on the Thomas Becket model: for 'Will nobody rid me of this troublesome priest?' read 'Bloody Maurice, interfering again.' I suspect that someone started the rumour rolling thinking it was what their superiors might want.

Ultimately, though, it wasn't his sexuality or even the smears that brought Maurice's career to such a sad end, it was the fact that he lied in his positive vetting. This leads to a consideration of whether the lie itself should be considered reason enough for such an outcome. Had the smears never happened but the lies remained, nobody would have been any the wiser and this book would be a chapter shorter. It was a case where the *fact* of breaking a rule was deemed more important than the actual *effect* of breaking that rule. To a mind as intelligent and disciplined as Maurice's it was probably evident that the only real harm being done was to the rule itself. Had he been honest from the start, Maurice may well have remained a successful officer, but in the light of such as Vassall, Burgess and Blunt, it's unlikely he would have progressed to such dizzying heights.

I suspect that Maurice felt he had no choice but to lie – he was probably able mentally to set aside his youthful flings to the extent where he could sail through a lie detector test – and there came a point when he could not suddenly change his story. He was also probably so confident in his own intellectual capacity that he knew he was not a security risk, however theoretically possible that may have been. Robert Armstrong's and Cecil Shipp's investigations would tend to bear that out. The price of greatness is sometimes the ire of smaller men.

A senior officer told me he felt that if there was one positive outcome from the way Maurice's reputation was torn apart after his death, it was that it was probably the first step in allowing openly gay people to serve in the armed forces. The idea that someone who is homosexual may be vulnerable to blackmail goes away if that person is openly gay and allowed to be so. Someone unmarried, such as Maurice, would no longer have to hide his preferences, whatever they were, should he wish to be open. That wouldn't, of course, help those who maintained their homosexuality as a secret. As David Cornwell put it to me, 'There were always gay people in the Service – it was the married, closeted ones that were vulnerable. And even then, the fear was more that their wife would find out than the Soviets. The wives of Tunbridge Wells were more terrifying than the communists.'

What I will not do, though, is finish a book about Maurice Oldfield with a negative. Even Margaret Thatcher's almost wholly disingenuous statement included the line – something of an understatement – that he 'contributed notably to a number of security and intelligence successes'. In talking about a Service that never discussed its work, and which at the time didn't officially exist, that line amounts to a ringing endorsement.

People find it difficult to pinpoint exactly the qualities which made Maurice the legend of MI6 that he remains. Some refer to his formidable intelligence, others to his astonishing memory. Some identify his Christian decency in a dark world and his understanding of other religions and cultures, which helped him to predict the actions of foreign governments – or even terrorists; others his rapid absorption of the complex. Even those who note Maurice's shortcomings

– his occasionally poor judgement of people, his desire to control the Service from top to bottom, his lack of delegation, and his tendency to trust too much on a personal level – acknowledge that without him MI6 would probably have been in a far worse state than that in which he left it.

Some former colleagues and friends consider that given the ending to his life and the tragic aftermath, Maurice might have been better served, on a personal level, by following his originally ordained path into academia. I am not convinced by that argument. Notwithstanding the global events he in some small way helped to shape, I do not think that forty years in academia would have been enough for Maurice. He loved the travel, the wide variety of people he met, the churches he went to around the world, and then coming back to tell his family about it all. His intelligence and self-control meant that despite what must have been a tremendous inner struggle with his sexuality he was able to compartmentalize that part of his life. As Betty Kemp explained, he would never have allowed his private life to compromise his professional life 'because he had an almost overpowering sense of duty'.

Researching this book has led me to look in some depth at the subject of the intelligence services, and I make no claim to have all the answers; it remains to me a dark and enigmatic world in which some of its practitioners saw, probably still see, 'The Game' as an end in itself. There will be things Maurice Oldfield did that will never be known, and different writers can put different slants on the same subject in the secret world in a way like no other. It was a world Maurice understood particularly well. As his boss for his last posting, Humphrey Atkins, told a BBC interviewer, 'Maurice Oldfield was wise in the ways of the wicked.' David Owen described to the same interviewer the almost boyish and awestruck excitement he felt upon being appointed Foreign Secretary when he realized he 'would get to meet Sir Maurice Oldfield'.

As with the gathering of intelligence, discovering Maurice's story has been a case of gathering together bits of evidence and trying to build a reliable picture. Despite my family connection I have tried to give a balanced view of Maurice and his life, taking into account his intellectual strengths, his people skills and capacity to forge friendships with kings and cleaners, his ability to take the most complex of world events and ground them in the reality that people are just people – the combination of characteristics that made Maurice unique. Alistair Horne described working for Maurice as being like having a series of dazzling tutorials, but most of what made up Maurice as a person was innate; it couldn't be taught. That, I believe, accounts for why he tried to control things as much as he could when, as Chief, he was trying to save his beloved Service from its past.

In summing up Maurice, the words of his Manchester University contemporary Professor Ronald Reed seem prescient. 'When, in the post-war world, Maurice saw that Russia and the United States of America would tend to dominate the scene, he never faltered in trying to maintain the former glory of <u>his</u> country as a world power. No wonder the spy Philby, and other would-be destroyers of this country, found him a formidable adversary. He deserves more of our thanks than our condemnation.'

A study of what has been written about the other Chiefs of MI6 reveals that all had varying strengths and weaknesses, skills and foibles. Thanks to his singular mixture of intellectual talents, his humble background, his genuinely held Christian faith, his position as an outsider at the heart of the most secretive and class-dominated part of the Establishment – all set alongside keeping the biggest secret of all, his own sexuality, until the end of his life – Sir Maurice Oldfield, my Uncle Maurice, seems to me to have been the most remarkable man ever to have held the post.

Acknowledgements

I first thought about writing Maurice Oldfield's story almost twenty years ago, and I must thank David and Georgina Oulsnam, who probably don't remember suggesting it as we walked through Bakewell Square in the early hours one morning after quite a lot of refreshment in the late, lamented Aitch's Wine Bar. More recently, the project has been encouraged in various ways by Mark and Marge Elliott, Sarah Doole, Mike and Sandy Dabell, Lord Owen, Alan Judd and Andrew Lycett.

The SIS 'alumni' whom I cannot mention know who they are and that their contributions are valued and appreciated. The professionals' in various fields I can mention, and to whom I wish to offer thanks, include Sir Gerry Warner, Sir Alistair and Lady Horne, Lord Armstrong, Lord Donoughue, Sir Tam Dalyell, Lord Waldegrave, Michael Oatley, Colin and Eileen Wallace, Gerald and Viv Buss, Rozanne Colchester, David Cornwell, Michael Smith, Ralph Erskine, Stephen Dorril, Robin Ramsay, Sir Desmond de Silva QC, Samantha Newbery, Neal Ascherson, Phillip Knightley,

Amanda Ingram, Michael Noakes, William Tyrer, Chris Ryder, Richard Davenport-Hines, Michael Wheeler, Garry Hemming, Nigel West, Marian Yeomans, Sir Kenneth Newman, Oleg Gordievsky, Christopher Andrew, David Gioe and Bryan Dutton.

There are many family, friends and neighbours who have been generous with their time and support in so many different ways: James and Alison Bentley, Elspeth Cavendish, Cath and Chris Clennell, Sue Stones, Patrick Thurlby, Roger Whitehead, Paul Hudson, Richard and Michelle Sherwood, Edmund Urquhart, Oonagh Pocock, Noreen Pearce, Anita Land, Anita Mallon, Jayne Sarnecki, Joe Oldfield, J. M. J. Oldfield, St Angela of Chichester and the Wednesday Night Supper Club, Laura Davis, Karin Wragg, Paul and Marie Wildgoose, Lisa and Dave Marshall, Vernon Colhoun, Anna and Darn Beresford, Emma and Gary Muse.

The guidance of my agent, Andrew Gordon of David Higham Associates, in turning my ideas into a proposal worthy of submission is hugely appreciated, as is his commitment to finding the right publisher. The fact that Doug Young and Bill Scott-Kerr at Transworld Publishers were willing to put their faith in this novice remains a source of amazement to me, and Doug's support and encouragement, particularly after the death of my father, have been stoic. The wider team at Transworld has been fantastic, especially Patsy Irwin, Helena Gonda and Helen Edwards. I'm still rather in awe of copy editor Dan Balado's calm reaction to my manuscript and his impressive capacity for positive suggestions and spotting things I'd missed despite numerous reads. I'm also grateful for the support of the Authors' Foundation.

Acknowledgements

Finally, and most importantly, I want to thank my family for their unstinting support over the many years the research and writing of this book have taken up. My sons Joe, Adam and Thomas have discovered a good deal of their family history from doing bits of reading for me, as has my brother Tom. My parents, John and Carolyn Pearce, provided a vast amount of information and background colour from their many conversations with Maurice – I'm just deeply saddened that Dad died so suddenly before he had a chance to see the finished article. Most of all I want to thank my partner, Marie, who launched herself into a new career so that I might be able to afford the time to complete this book. The work she has put in has been phenomenal, and I just hope her copy of the paperback has a happier ending than the hardback, which had an unfortunate reaction to being poolside reading!

Picture Acknowledgements

All images have been supplied courtesy of the author unless otherwise stated. Every effort has been made to contact the copyright holders. We apologize for any omissions in this respect and will be pleased to make the appropriate acknowledgements in any future edition.

Page 2: Kantara crossing, Suez © Popperfoto/Getty Images; Teddy Kollek © Fritz Cohen/GPO via Getty Images
Page 3: Lee Kuan Yew © Michael Stroud/ Getty Images; James Angleton © Diana Walker/Getty Images
Page 4: JFK and Shah of Iran © Pictorial Parade/Getty Images; Cuban Missile Crisis © Getty Images
Page 5: Oleg Penkovsky © Sovfoto/UIG via Getty Images; Rozanne Colchester © Karen Robinson/Guardian News & Media Ltd 2016; Bruce Mackenzie © Kenya Yearbook Editorial Board
Page 6: Athenaeum Club © David Williams/Alamy Stock Photo
Page 7: Brian Stewart © Heathcliff O'Malley, reproduced by kind permission of the Stewart family; Robert Armstrong © PA Archive/ Press Association Images; David Owen and James Callaghan © Rolls Press/Popperfoto/Getty Images
Page 8: David Cornwell © Kirsty Wigglesworth /AP/Press Association Images; Alec Guinness © BBC Photo Library; Kim Philby in Moscow, reproduced by kind permission of Phillip Knightley; Betty Kemp, reproduced by kind permission of the Principal and Fellows of St Hugh's College, Oxford

Sources

W HEN I SET about researching Maurice Oldfield's story, it soon emerged that even though the events in which he was involved happened at least thirty-five years ago, unearthing any facts beyond those already in the public domain was going to be more challenging than I ever anticipated. Requests under the Freedom of Information Act 2000 were met with a blanket refusal, as personnel of the Secret Service are covered by a level of security that is exempt from disclosure under the Act. The so-called Thirty Year Rule which governs the release of government papers does not apply to matters of secret intelligence.

My initial approaches to the Secret Intelligence Service itself, via inside intermediaries, were also met with a blanket refusal. The only officer of the Service whom I know to have been authorized by SIS to speak with me was Sir Gerry Warner. I am grateful to Sir Gerry for his assistance and for persuading his former masters to allow him to discuss Oldfield with me. Many other former SIS officers, secretaries and agents have spoken to me, but on the strict understanding that they are not identified. Any references to

SIS officers by name are thus in relation to matters that either involve the deceased or are already in the public domain.

When the historian Keith Jeffery wrote his authorized history of MI6, he found that even though he was given access to more files than any previous author, these were still weeded and strictly limited to matters before 1949. And since the Service began, officers have been encouraged to commit little to paper, and to destroy much that is not immediately relevant. Unsurprisingly, Jeffery found that there were many gaps in the archive. It is likely that historians won't be granted access to post-1949 files until outside my lifetime.

The advantage I did have, I found, was that as a relative of Oldfield, surviving officers who served with him were willing to speak with me perhaps more freely than they have spoken to others. Or at least that's what they told me! I have tried to respect these officers' requests for anonymity – by necessity, therefore, I have not named a number of sources – and as far as possible I tried to establish the truth of what they told me. I have erred on the side of caution, and sought to omit those pieces of information that couldn't be verified.

For their recollections, on which I have drawn freely, I am indebted throughout to both friends and family. Much of the information, particularly for the introduction and early chapters, has been gathered from discussions over many years, most recently with Maurice's brother Joe and sister Sadie. A substantial amount is derived from personal recollections. I have also had access to various notes, letters and postcards between Maurice and family members and friends, and of course to Maurice's notebooks, address books and day diaries. In the wider world, the books/articles listed in shortened form at the head of each chapter's notes (and more fully in the bibliography) were of great help to me during my research, as were archives at the Thatcher Foundation, St Hugh's College in Oxford, Manchester University, the National Archive at Kew, the CIA, the John F. Kennedy Archive in the JFK Library in Boston, and those of the following publications: *Daily Mail, Irish Times, Sunday Times, Guardian, Daily Telegraph, Sunday Telegraph, Independent, Independent on Sunday* and *Sunday Express*.

Chapter 1

Philby, *My Silent War*
Judd, *Quest for C*
Stewart and Newbery, *Why Spy?*
Routledge, *Public Servant*
Jeffery, *MI6*
Deacon, *'C'*
Cavendish, *Inside Intelligence*
Irish Times archive material

David Owen's recollections were communicated to me via email, and during a discussion in Lord Owen's office. Notes and letters from Anthony Cavendish to Renee Oldfield and others are in my possession. Letters and notes from the Thatcher Foundation archive: correspondence between Sir Frank Cooper and Sir Brian Cubbon; letter from John Coles to Sir Clive Whitmore; letter from Brian Mawhinney to Whitmore; letter from Sir John Killick to Whitmore; letter from Whitmore to Sir Kenneth Stowe; letter from Sir Frank Cooper to Stowe; correspondence between Mike Hopkins and Whitmore; Whitmore notes for the record; letter from Sir Robert Armstrong to Margaret Thatcher; letter from Whitmore to John Chilcot. The 'M Returns' headline was the *Daily Mail*'s on 3 October 1979.

Chapter 2

Jeffery, *MI6*
Harvey, *Story of the School of Grace*
Pearce and Dabell, *Unreliable Memories*
Morris et al., '50 Best Country Pubs' (*Independent*)

The 1881 Census was consulted, and the family genealogy by Carolyn Pearce. The school report quotes are taken from the actual Lady Manners School report books. The details about MO's teacher, Mrs Faber, are from the reports, and from a letter from Kathleen Fuller in 1988. The *New Statesman* quote is from a May 1978 profile written by Phillip Whitehead.

Chapter 3

Taylor, *Personal History*
Manchester University archive material

From St Hugh's College archive, Oxford: letters between A. J. P. Taylor, Betty Kemp and James Crompton; Taylor's obituary on Namier. Ronald Reed's recollections are taken from *Maurice Oldfield: A Retrospective*, written by Reed and held in the Manchester University archive, as are the recollections of John Robinson. Vic Smith related the story of MO's driving licence to Joe Oldfield. MO's notes on James Klugmann featured in a letter to Sadie Pearce and are mentioned in 'C' by Richard Deacon. I have, in addition, numerous documents relating to MO's time in Manchester.

Chapter 4

Roberts, *Storm of War*
Horne, *But What Do You Actually Do?*
Cavendish, *Inside Intelligence*
Andrew, *Defence of the Realm*
Deacon, 'C'

Irvine Gray's recollections were given to Sadie and Renee Oldfield. The David Petrie quotes are from the National Archive. Monty Trethowan's remark was in a letter to Richard Deacon. The 'Oh Dear' song was hand-written in a collection of MO's papers from the war, and was also used in 'C' by Richard Deacon. The Alistair Horne quote features in his memoirs, and was related to me in an interview. The Radó interrogation snippets and MO's reply to the Radó requests are in the National Archive.

Chapter 5

Andrew, *Defence of the Realm*
Hinsley et al., *British Intelligence*

The Alistair Horne recollections were told to me during an interview. The Anthony Cavendish and Alistair Horne quotes come from their memoirs. MO's 'funnies' quote was told to Horne. Jack Granatstein's description is from a 1984 edition of the Toledo, Ohio daily the *Blade*. Guy Liddell's diary extract is from the National Archive. MO's remarks on the official history of the Intelligence Corps's contribution to the war effort were made in an interview with Phillip Knightley.

Chapter 6

Martin, *Wilderness of Mirrors*
Verrier, *Through the Looking Glass*
Knightley, *Philby*
Macintyre, *A Spy Among Friends*
Cavendish, *Inside Intelligence*
Corera, *Art of Betrayal*
Dorril, *MI6*
Jeffery, *MI6*
Philby, *My Silent War*
Horne, *But What Do You Actually Do?*

Some of the direct Philby quotes were given to me in interviews with Phillip Knightley and others who can't be named. Graham Greene's comments on Philby were reported to Alistair Horne, Anthony Cavendish, Knightley and others. Horne discussed Douglas Roberts with me, and covers him in his memoirs. Philby's 'Sorry old man' quote has been reported various times; MO confirmed its veracity to Cavendish. 'It was at this point, he told Anthony Cavendish, that Maurice thought he knew that Philby was up to no good' was confirmed to MO's family by Cavendish in 1981.

Horne confirmed to me that he and MO had discussed MO's suspicions about Philby on a number of occasions over many years.

Chapter 7

Bower, *Perfect English Spy*
Philby, *My Silent War*
Deacon, *'C'*
Kauffer, *Histoire Mondiale*
Lownie, *Stalin's Englishman*
Macintyre, *A Spy Among Friends*
Martin, *Wilderness of Mirrors*

The comments by Brian Stewart come from unused parts of the manuscript for *Why Spy?* and are included by kind permission of Samantha Newbery. The comments by J. W. Purseglove are related in *'C'* by Richard Deacon, and have been confirmed by local friends who knew Purseglove. The dinner party tale, with its 'prow of a dreadnought' remark, has been told various times, including in the books above. MO discussed his views on Philby with Cavendish, Horne and Knightley; the latter two discussed this with me in interviews.

Chapter 8

Horne, *But What Do You Actually Do?*
Philby, *My Silent War*
Knightley, *Philby*
Bower, *Perfect English Spy*

Monty Woodhouse comment reported by Robert Fisk in the *Independent* (15 March 1997). The account of Neal Ascherson's 'interview' by MI6 was given to me in an email exchange with Mr Ascherson. David Cornwell's account of his encounter with the interview panel was related to me during a meeting at Mr Cornwell's home. The Singapore associate comment comes from a letter in my possession.

Chapter 9

Dorril, *MI6*
Bower, *Perfect English Spy*
Macintyre, *A Spy Among Friends*

The 'former colleague' quote comes from an interview between me and a former MI6 colleague of MO's who wishes to remain anonymous. The Lord Hankey quote is from the National Archive. Lipton/Macmillan/Eden comments from *Hansard* (June 1955).

Chapter 10

Allison and Blackwill, *Lee Kuan Yew*
Deacon, *'C'*

Marion Laidlaw's recollection comes from a letter from her to me. George Kennedy Young's comment comes from his foreword to Anthony Cavendish's *Inside Intelligence*. The Ray Cline quote comes from a letter from Cline to Richard Deacon, a copy of which was given to Renee Oldfield and is in my possession. MO's assessment about 'China in 2017' was confirmed to me by a former colleague, and was first told to Deacon. Gerald Buss's recollections came from discussions at his home and on the telephone, and from various email exchanges. The various journalist, airline crew, IOC and clergy contacts are taken from MO's personal address books and notebooks in my possession.

Chapter 11

Stafford, *Spies Beneath Berlin*
Murphy et al., *Battleground Berlin*
Thomas, *The Very Best Men*
Saunders, *Who Paid the Piper?*
Bower, *Perfect English Spy*
Hermiston, *Greatest Traitor*
CIA archive material

Michael Chan's recollections come from a detailed, unpublished 'memoir' he wrote about his relationship with MO, which he gave to the family in 1981, just after MO's death. Janet Barnes remained a close friend of MO's after the death of her husband, and some letters between the two are in my possession. MO described his views on the polygraph to various colleagues, and it was separately confirmed to me by Brian Stewart that MO 'swore blind he had beaten the CIA's lie detector'. MO's comments to Ray Cline on sexuality were noted in the letter referred to in the chapter 10 section.

Chapter 12

Bower, *Perfect English Spy*
Corera, *Art of Betrayal*
Obituary of Kenneth Skelton (*Independent*)
Massie and Logan, 'MI6' (*Sunday Express*)
John F. Kennedy Archive (Kennedy-Khrushchev quotes)

The family description of Bruce Mackenzie was given to me by my father, John Pearce, who met him with MO in the early 1970s. MO's comment on Jomo Kenyatta was given to John Pearce at a similar time. The fact that 'Kenneth Skelton sent coded letters to his old friend and parishioner Sadie Pearce' was related to me by Sadie on numerous occasions; the letters were passed on by Sadie to MO. MO described Penkovsky as an 'answer to a prayer' to Anthony Cavendish, who was visiting MO in Washington at the time. David Cornwell's recollections were given to me in a meeting at Mr Cornwell's home. The information about September 1962, when MO flew back to London for meetings with Geoffrey Wheeler and David Footman, together with the fact that during these days he was in regular contact with Paul Nitse, is new information I discovered in MO's notebooks. Ken Dyer's recollections were shared with the Pearce and Oldfield family just after MO died.

Chapter 13

Summers and Dorril, *Honeytrap*
Costello, *Mask of Treachery*
Carter, *Anthony Blunt*

Boyle, *Climate of Treason*
Andrew, *Defence of the Realm*
Rimington, *Open Secret*
Macintyre, *A Spy Among Friends*
Knightley, *Philby*
Philby, *My Silent War*
Straight, *After Long Silence*
Martin, *Wilderness of Mirrors*
Bower, *Perfect English Spy*
Obituary of Michael Straight (*Daily Telegraph*)
National Archive material

Macmillan's comments on Vassall have been widely quoted and are in the National Archive. Stephen Dorril expounded on his theory about Stephen Ward's death to me in a meeting. David Cornwell's comments on Roger Hollis were also shared with me in a meeting.

Chapter 14

Bower, *Perfect English Spy*
Stewart and Newbery, *Why Spy?*
Martin, *Wilderness of Mirrors*
Dalyell, *Importance of Being Awkward*
Wright, *Spycatcher*
Deacon, '*C*'
Obituary of Betty Kemp (*Daily Telegraph*, *Guardian*)
MacManus, 'Spymaster's Fall' (*Sunday Telegraph*)
Tiley, 'Britain, Vietnam' (*History Today*)
St Hugh's College archive material
National Archive material

Michael Chan's recollections are from the document referred to in the chapter 11 section. Betty Kemp's recollections about her relationship with MO were shared with his sisters, Renee and Sadie. She told the *Sunday Telegraph*'s James MacManus that MO had told her his job offered no life for a wife. Harold Wilson and Richard Crossman's comments were related to me by Tam Dalyell in a telephone conversation.

Chapter 15

Wright, *Spycatcher*
National Archive material

MO made his comments on George Brown and Harold Wilson to John and Carolyn Pearce, and no doubt others. Brown's opinion of MO was disclosed to Richard Deacon. Bronson Tweedy and Alec MacDonald's comments are in the National Archive. MO's reference to Christopher Phillpotts's alleged 'Gestapo methods' was recalled by Sir Dick White to Tom Bower, and Sir Gerry Warner shared similar views of Phillpotts's methods with me. MO remained in close touch with Dick Ellis until the latter's death in 1975, and with his family after that; he told friends including Cavendish that anything Ellis may have done was a long time ago and best forgotten. Gerald Buss's recollections were shared with me in a meeting and in telephone calls. Peter Lunn's comment was given to me by David Cornwell, who had been a colleague of Lunn's.

Chapter 16

Dorril, *MI6*
Corera, *Art of Betrayal*
Chapman Pincher, *Their Trade is Treachery*

Rozanne Colchester comment taken from a letter from her to me. Denis Greenhill described MO as an enigma to Dick White.

Chapter 17

Pilger, *Other People's Wars* (documentary)
Pilger, *Secret Country*
Wright, *Spycatcher*
Leigh, *Wilson Plot*
Dorril and Ramsay, *Smear!*
Hennessy, *Secret State*
Cavendish, *Inside Intelligence*
Chapman Pincher, *Dangerous to Know*
Callaghan, *Time & Chance*
Thatcher Foundation archive material

I enjoyed several meetings with Edmund Urquhart, and there was much email correspondence between us too. The Rev. Urquhart also allowed me access to his files of correspondence about MO. Michael Oatley's recollections were relayed to me via email. Gerald Buss's comments are taken from numerous emails with me. The Lee Kuan Yew quote was related to Michael Chan by MO. The exchange with Callaghan was described by MO to his sister Sadie, and has been documented by Callaghan and others. The Bernard Donoughue material is from a conversation between Donoughue and me. MO liked to tell the story about Wilson and his cigar as an anecdote he felt able to share; it was related to me by Sadie and John Pearce. The Harold Wilson letters about the KGB are in the Thatcher Foundation archive.

Chapter 18

Chapman Pincher, *Dangerous to Know*
Campbell, *Roy Jenkins*
Cockburn, 'Secretary' (*Harper's Magazine*)
Knightley, 'A Spymaster Recalls' (*Independent*)
Milmo and Rosthorn, 'Revealed' (*Independent on Sunday*)

MO's comment to Sadie about their lunches with dignitaries was related to me several times by her. I also recall specific lunches being described, including with Harold Wilson, Michael Foot, Anthony Crosland and Sir James Goldsmith. Renee Oldfield told John Pearce about MO's call regarding Bruce Mackenzie's death. Chapman Pincher's assertions about MO and Mackenzie remain unverified. The story related by the Hong Kong station officer, and that about the secretary, are from MI6 sources who cannot be named. David Owen's recollections were related to me during an interview in his office. Phillip Knightley's views on MO were shared with me via emails and telephone conversations. The anecdote about MO's niece Jane has been verified by several family members. John Pearce, Carolyn Pearce and Tony Robinson all recall the police anecdote. The Kathleen Fuller

anecdote is from a letter in my possession from Mrs Fuller
to Anthony Cavendish. The quotes from Lord Armstrong
are taken from a meeting with me at the House of Lords; the
'colleagues' referred to in that context are MI6 officers who
cannot be named. The comments made by MO to Cavendish
on the Shah of Iran were in draft notes of a book proposal by
Cavendish for a biography of MO – again, in my possession,
courtesy of Edmund Urquhart; it was also a subject about
which he spoke freely and frequently to Sadie. The Scott
Newton and Hugh Thomas quotes are from the *Independent
on Sunday* article listed above: Professor Newton confirmed
their accuracy to me. Gerry Warner's comment on James
Bond was made during a meeting with me. The Graham
Greene anecdotes and quotes were shared with me by David
Cornwell and Alistair Horne; they also feature in Knightley's
interview with MO. The meeting between MO, Alec
Guinness and David Cornwell was described to me by
Cornwell.

Chapter 19

Deacon, 'C'
Stewart and Newbery, *Why Spy?*
McKittrick, 'Oldfield's Job' (*Irish Times*)
Thatcher Foundation archive material

John and Sadie Pearce's recollections were commonly known
in the family, and formally confirmed during the research
for this book. Brian Stewart's comments are from the unused
parts of the *Why Spy?* manuscript. The 'But Me No Buts'
document (along with the Whitmore letter, Thatcher's letter,

and all MO's briefs and reports to government) was in the Thatcher Foundation archive. Kenneth Newman's confirmation regarding MI5's involvement in Northern Ireland came during a telephone call with me. Vivian and Gerald Buss's recollections are taken from interviews and email exchanges with the Buss family. The Elizabeth Roberts quote was in a letter from Mrs Roberts to Richard Deacon, which was shown to Sadie by Deacon in 1983.

Chapter 20

Cavendish, *Inside Intelligence*
Chapman Pincher, *Traitors*
Foot, *Who Framed Colin Wallace?*
Callaghan, *Time & Chance*
Thatcher, *Downing Street Years*
Horne, *But What Do You Actually Do?*
Knightley, *Philby*
Ryder, 'Pub Incident' (*Sunday Times*)
Obituary of Betty Kemp (*Guardian*)
Thatcher Foundation archive material (see chapter 19 section)
St Hugh's College archive material
Manchester University archive material

Robert Armstrong's comments on the matter of MO's departure were told to me during a meeting at the House of Lords. Anthony Cavendish's recollections feature in his book and were also described personally to the family, and in letters that are in my possession. Carolyn Pearce related details of her trip to Buxton with MO to me. MO's visit to the Colchesters' is detailed in a letter from Rozanne Colchester to me. Edmund Urquhart's information has been shared in emails and conversations. Michael Chan's comments were written in the 'memoir' he produced after MO's death. Gerald Buss's recollections were shared with me during a visit to the Buss home in Sussex. Joe Oldfield's comments were made during various chats I had with him. Marion Laidlaw's quote comes from a letter to me. Tam Dalyell discussed the matter at length with me on the telephone. Chapman Pincher's comment to Anthony Cavendish about his pension was one of many things that enraged Cavendish about the matter: he wrote letters to several newspapers, copies of which are in my possession. The information from Chris Ryder came to me via email exchange. The quotes and information from Colin Wallace were passed on during a meeting between him and me at the Wallaces' home, and via numerous emails: Wallace was always able to verify the things he told the author. The Kate Fuller letter was written to Cavendish and is in my possession. Betty Kemp's letter was sent to Renee Oldfield and is also in my possession. Alistair Horne's comments were made to me during a meeting at the Hornes' house. The Philby quotes come from Phillip Knightley's interviews with Philby in 1988, just before Philby died. David Cornwell's comment about homosexuality in MI6 was made to me during a meeting. The Ronald Reed quote is the final part of the summing up in his retrospective about MO.

Bibliography

Allison, Graham, and Robert D. Blackwill, *Lee Kuan Yew: The Grand Master's Insights on China, the United States and the World* (MIT Press, 2013)

Andrew, Christopher, *The Defence of the Realm: The Authorized History of MI5* (Penguin, 2010)

Andrew, Christopher, and Oleg Gordievsky, *Instructions from the Centre: Top Secret Files on KGB Foreign Operations, 1975–85* (Hodder & Stoughton, 1991)

Bower, Tom, *The Perfect English Spy: Sir Dick White and the Secret War, 1935–90* (William Heinemann Ltd, 1995)

Boyle, Andrew, *Climate of Treason: Five Who Spied For Russia* (Hutchinson, 1979)

Callaghan, James, *Time & Chance* (HarperCollins, 1987)

Campbell, John, *Roy Jenkins: A Well-Rounded Life* (Jonathan Cape, 2014)

Carter, Miranda, *Anthony Blunt: His Lives* (Macmillan, 2001)

Cavendish, Anthony, *Inside Intelligence* (HarperCollins, 1990)

Chapman Pincher, Harry, *Dangerous to Know: A Life* (Biteback Publishing, 2014)

—— *Their Trade is Treachery* (Sidgwick & Jackson, 1981)

—— *Traitors: The Labyrinths of Treason* (Sidgwick & Jackson, 1987)

Corera, Gordon, *The Art of Betrayal: Life and Death in the British Secret Service* (Weidenfeld & Nicolson, 2011)

Costello, John, *Mask of Treachery* (HarperCollins, 1988)

Dalyell, Tam, *The Importance of Being Awkward* (Birlinn Ltd, 2011)

Deacon, Richard, *'C': A Biography of Sir Maurice Oldfield* (The Book Service Ltd, 1985)

Dictionary of National Biography (OUP, 2004)

Dorril, Stephen, *MI6: Fifty Years of Special Operations* (Fourth Estate, 2001)

—— and Robin Ramsay, *Smear! Wilson and the Secret State* (Fourth Estate, 1991)

Foot, Paul, *Who Framed Colin Wallace?* (Macmillan, 1989)

Harvey, R. A., *The Story of the School of Grace, Lady Manners* (J. W. Northend Ltd, 1982)

Hennessy, Peter, *The Secret State: Preparing for the Worst 1945–2010* (Penguin, 2010)

Hermiston, Roger, *The Greatest Traitor: The Secret Lives of Agent George Blake* (Aurum Press, 2013)

Hinsley, F. H., E. E. Thomas, C. F. G. Ransom and R. C. Knight, *British Intelligence in the Second World War* (Stationery Office Books, 1979)

Horne, Alistair, *But What Do You Actually Do? – A Literary Vagabondage* (Weidenfeld & Nicolson, 2011)

Jeffery, Keith, *MI6: The History of the Secret Intelligence Service 1909–1949* (Bloomsbury, 2011)

Judd, Alan, *The Quest for C: Mansfield Cumming and the Founding of the Secret Service* (HarperCollins, 2000)

Kauffer, Rémi, *Histoire Mondiale des Services Secrets* (Librairie Académique Perrin, 2015)

Knightley, Phillip, *Philby: KGB Masterspy* (André Deutsch Ltd, 2003)

Bibliography

Leigh, David, *The Wilson Plot: How the Spycatchers and Their American Allies Tried to Overthrow the British Government* (Pantheon Books, 1988)

Lownie, Andrew, *Stalin's Englishman: The Lives of Guy Burgess* (Hodder & Stoughton, 2015)

Macintyre, Ben, *A Spy Among Friends: Kim Philby and the Great Betrayal* (Bloomsbury, 2014)

Martin, David C., *Wilderness of Mirrors* (HarperCollins, 1980)

Murphy, David, Sergei A. Kondrashev and George Bailey, *Battleground Berlin: CIA vs. KGB in the Cold War* (Yale University Press, 1997)

Pearce, Martin, and Mike Dabell, *Unreliable Memories* (Blurb, 2009)

Philby, Kim, *My Silent War* (MacGibbon & Kee, 1968)

Pilger, John, *A Secret Country: The Hidden Australia* (Alfred A. Knopf, 1991)

Rimington, Stella, *Open Secret: The Autobiography of the Former Director-General of MI5* (Hutchinson, 2001)

Roberts, Andrew, *The Storm of War: A New History of the Second World War* (Penguin, 2010)

Routledge, Paul, *Public Servant, Secret Agent: The Elusive Life and Violent Death of Airey Neave* (Fourth Estate, 2003)

Saunders, Frances Stonor, *Who Paid the Piper? – The CIA and the Cultural Cold War* (Granta Books, 1999)

Stafford, David, *Spies Beneath Berlin* (John Murray, 2002)

Stewart, Brian, and Samantha Newbery, *Why Spy? – The Art of Intelligence* (C. Hurst & Co. Publishers Ltd, 2015)

Straight, Michael, *After Long Silence* (W. W. Norton & Co., 1983)

Summers, Anthony, and Stephen Dorril, *Honeytrap: The Secret Worlds of Stephen Ward* (Weidenfeld & Nicolson, 1987)

Taylor, A. J. P., *A Personal History* (Coronet Books, 1984)

Thatcher, Margaret, *The Downing Street Years* (HarperCollins, 1993)

Thomas, Evan, *The Very Best Men: The Daring Early Years of the CIA* (Simon & Schuster, 2007)

Verrier, Anthony, *Through the Looking Glass: British Foreign Policy in an Age of Illusions* (W. W. Norton & Co., 1983)

West, Nigel, *At Her Majesty's Secret Service: The Chiefs of Britain's Intelligence Agency, MI6* (Greenhill Books, 2006)

Wright, Peter, *Spycatcher: The Candid Autobiography of a Senior Intelligence Officer* (Viking, 1987)

Articles

Cockburn, Andrew, 'Secretary of Nothing', *Harper's Magazine*, December 2013

Knightley, Phillip, 'A Spymaster Recalls the Twists of the Game', *Independent*, 26 July 1997

McKittrick, David, 'Oldfield's Job Sets the Tongues Wagging', *Irish Times*, 6 October 1979

MacManus, James, 'Spymaster's Fall from Grace', *Sunday Telegraph*, April 1987

Massie, William, and Chris Logan, 'MI6 Used Bishop as Secret Agent', *Sunday Express*, 10 January 1988

Milmo, Cahal, and Andrew Rosthorn, 'Revealed: The Spymaster and Nazi Peacemaker Rudolf Hess', *Independent on Sunday*, 14 September 2013

Morris, Sophie, Joanna Busk, David Hancock, Fiona Stapley and Jackie Bates, 'The 50 Best Country Pubs', *Independent*, 18 May 2012

Obituary of Betty Kemp (*Daily Telegraph*, 16 June 2007; *Guardian*, 12 July 2007)

Obituary of Kenneth Skelton (*Independent*, 4 August 2003; also *Daily Telegraph*, 1 August 2003, *Guardian*, 4 August 2003)

Obituary of Michael Straight (*Daily Telegraph*, 17 January 2004)

Pilger, John, *Other People's Wars* (documentary)

Bibliography

Ryder, Chris, 'Pub Incident that Exposed a Spymaster', *Sunday Times*, 26 April 1987

Tiley, Marc, 'Britain, Vietnam and the Special Relationship', *History Today*, 12 December 2013

Index

Abwehr, 66, 67, 68, 76, 77
Acheson, Dean, 247
Agiraki, Anna, 69
Ahmed (chauffeur), 134, 195, 196, 330
Ala, Hossein, 194
Alamein, El, battles, 68, 70–1, 74
Albania, 119–20, 148
All Souls College, Oxford, 11, 104, 365, 375–6, 409, 419
Amery, Catherine (Macmillan), 175
Amery, Julian, 21, 174–5, 409
Amin, Idi, 349, 350, 354
Andrew, Christopher, 88, 227
Angleton, Cicely, 151, 216
Angleton, James Jesus:
    appearance, 113; background, 113; CAZAB, 331; character, 113–14; influence on MI6, 275, 279, 280–3, 288, 291–4, 297, 303, 342, 365; OSS career, 113–14; relationship with Golitsyn, 227, 232, 256, 261–2, 265, 268–70, 271–2, 275; relationship with MO, 216–19, 241, 249, 261–2, 271–2, 279, 281–2, 291–2, 303; relationship with Philby, 114,
    129, 151, 155–6, 218; report on Burgess, 155–6; retirement, 326, 347; view of Penkovsky, 241, 248, 292
Anglo-Iranian Oil Company (AIOC), 171–3, 192–3
Archer, Jane, 122–3
Argentina, 175, 176
Armstrong, Robert: investigation of MO, 405–6, 430; MO's admission of homosexuality, 405–6, 414, 426–7; on Kincora, 421–4; on MO's Falklands achievements, 361; on Northern Ireland, 393; on Wilson's MI5 interview, 338
Army, British: demobilization, 101–2; Intelligence Corps, 60–3; Jewish Brigade, 87; Littlejohns case, 312; murder of Irish nationalists, 394; Northern Ireland, 16, 23, 307, 310, 381–2; Northern Ireland Security Coordinator's role, 385–93, 397–8; Soviet penetration, 314
Ascherson, Neal, 177–8, 179
Ashby, Peter, 267

Athenaeum Club, 165, 276, 296, 420
Atkins, Humphrey: MO's
    appointment, 20–2; MO's
    death, 413; MO's report, 384;
    MO's resignation, 401;
    Northern Ireland issues, 16,
    17, 388, 390
Attlee, Clement: cabinet, 54;
    Doctrine, 131, 231; election
    defeat (1951), 159; Iran
    policies, 171; Malaya policies,
    139; Palestine policy, 86, 101;
    US intelligence relations, 119
Australia, 185, 292, 330–3
Australian Secret Intelligence
    Service (ASIS), 131, 161–2,
    194, 331

Bagley, Pete, 268–70
Barnes, Janet, 216
Barnes, Tracy, 211, 216
Bayliss, Sir Richard, 410
Bay of Pigs, 235, 237, 244, 264
Bedell Smith, Walter, 155–6
Begin, Menachem, 90
Beirut: MO's undercover work,
    66; MO's visits, 173; Philby
    in, 124, 188, 257–60; Philby's
    flight, 260–1; SIME
    headquarters, 74; wartime
    spying, 69–70
Berlin: Canadian mission, 255;
    crossing points, 154–5, 282,
    357; MO's studies, 48, 68;
    strategic importance, 243–1,
    246; tunnel operation, 212–14,
    224, 225–6; Wall, 242
Berry, Halle, 28
Bevin, Ernest, 87–8, 92, 119
Bibbee, Bill, 57
Bissell, Richard, 235
Blair, Tony, 199, 243
Blake, George: anti-hero status,
    257; background and career,

224–5; Berlin tunnel
    operation, 213, 224, 225–6;
    betrayal of British agents,
    225, 226, 240; British
    imprisonment, 226, 237, 250;
    escape from prison, 297;
    unmasked, 225–6, 237, 259;
    work for KGB, 224, 225–6,
    308, 364
Blaker, Sir Peter, 402, 403, 415
Bletchley Park, 60, 168, 266, 302
Blunt, Anthony, 14, 71–2, 266–8,
    274, 430
Bond, James, 4, 167, 256, 319, 352,
    369
Bonzos (double agent), 69
Bossard, Frank, 292–3
Boyne, Harry, 206, 207
Brandt, Willy, 326
Brezhnev, Leonid, 295, 306, 335
Briggs, Sir Rawdon, 160
Briggs Plan, 160, 161
British Guiana (Guyana), 255
Brooman-White, Richard, 187–8
Broome, Robert (great-
    grandfather of MO), 26
Brown, George, 289–91
Bruce-Lockhart, John, 169
Bulganin, Nikolai, 189
Bulik, Joe, 237
Burgess, Guy: anti-hero status,
    257; background and
    character, 150, 217, 258, 265;
    caricature of Libby Harvey,
    151, 155, 216; CIA report on,
    155–6; escape to Moscow,
    152–4, 167, 185–6, 188;
    Golitsyn's evidence, 227, 232,
    256; life in Soviet Union,
    185–6; recalled to London,
    152; recruitment efforts, 265;
    relationship with Philby,
    150–2, 155, 167, 169, 188;
    spying activities, 7, 174, 211,

Index

217, 430; Washington position, 150–2; White Paper on, 186
Burke, Lardner, 231–2
Burnham, Forbes, 256
Bush, George H. W., 330
Buss, Gerald: background, 202–3; career, 202–3, 204, 208, 294–6; 'Friend' of MI6, 204, 305, 335; memories of MO, 203–4, 325, 395–6, 412, 427; relationship with MO, 203–5, 356, 395–6
Buss family, 202, 395–6
Butler, Rab, 274

'C' (head of MI6), 5, 316
Cabell, Charles, 235
Cairncross, John, 267
Callaghan, James: avowal of SIS, 9; currency devaluation, 307; Falklands policy, 359–60; fall of government, 15; Greece policy, 347–9; Prime Minister, 346–8; relationship with MO, 335–6, 340–1, 356
Cambridge spy ring, 109–10, 223, 224, 256, 266
Canada, Department of External Affairs, 255
Canaris, Wilhelm, 67–8, 76–8, 83
Cardona, José Miró, 223
Carew Hunt, Robert, 157, 165
Carrington, Lord, 14, 20, 401
Castro, Fidel, 233–5, 244–5, 251–3
Castro, Raúl, 252
Catling, Dick (later Sir Richard), 100
Cavendish, Anthony (formerly Tony Castle): defence of MO, 416, 417, 424; hunt for Burgess and Maclean, 153–4; journalism, 202; Middle East intelligence work, 96, 98–100, 102; memories of MO, 95,

362–3, 406–7, 414, 427; name, 95, 371; relationship with MO, 21, 95–6, 206, 216–17, 278, 366, 395, 412; relationship with Philby, 123–4; view of smear source, 429; view of Wilson resignation, 342–3
Cavendish, Elspeth, 395
Cawley, Clara, 32–3
CAZAB, 292, 331
Chan, Irene, 276
Chan, Michael, 206, 210, 275–6, 410, 417–18
Chebab, Emir Farid, 210–11
Chilcot, John, 400
China, 156–7, 158, 335
Chisholm, Janet, 240, 245, 250
Chisholm, Ruari, 240, 250
Churchill, Winston: election victory (1951), 159–60, 171; instruction to SOE, 60; intelligence reports and briefings, 71–2, 168; Iron Curtain speech, 119; Malaya policy, 160; Middle East policy, 87; on Alamein, 70–1; retirement, 185; view of Baldwin's policies, 109
Churchill, Winston (grandson of above), 338
CIA (Central Intelligence Agency): anti-Mosaddegh operation, 172; Australian policy, 331–2; Blake case, 224–7; Blake's escape, 297; Cuba policies, 233–4, 235, 246–9; Fluency committee, 279–81, 283; Four Square Agreement, 181, 200; Golitsyn influence, 227, 232, 268–9, 281; headquarters, 222; Krotkov's information, 283; lie detector tests, 221–4, 408; MI5 relations, 124–5; MI6

467

CIA (*cont.*)
    relations, 119–20, 124–5,
        144–8, 156, 168–70, 212–14,
        249, 260–1; MO relations,
        144–5, 181, 211–12, 215–19,
        361; mole, 269; Nosenko's
        information, 268–72, 282;
        Penkovsky's information,
        235–42, 244–7, 249–50, 305;
        Philby's escape, 260; Philby's
        position, 124–5, 147–8, 156;
        South East Asia, 114–15; style,
        128, 151; Suez Crisis, 185, 193
CIFE (Combined Intelligence Far
    East), 130–1, 195
Clarke, Dudley, 65–6, 70
Climber operations, 117–19
Cline, Ray, 200, 217, 223, 247, 248
Clockwork Orange operation,
    322, 337, 341
Colby, William (Bill), 326, 330,
    331–2
Colchester, Halsey, 120, 302, 409,
    413
Colchester, Rozanne, 302, 404, 409
Cold War: Cuban Missile Crisis,
    242, 252; development, 148;
    Germany, 167; Gordievsky's
    defection, 334; MO's
    retirement, 11; Penkovsky's
    defection, 238, 240;
    polygraph, 221; start of, 97
Colhoun, Vernon, 123
Cooke, Albie, 37
Cooke, Alistair, 165
Cooper, Frank, 322–3
Cordeaux, John 'Bill', 106
Cornwell, David (John le Carré):
    George Smiley character, 1, 8,
    373–4, 375; meeting with
    MO and Guinness, 371–4;
    memories of MI5, 264;
    memories of MO, 244, 299;
    MI6 interview, 179; on

homosexuality, 431
Cowgill, Felix, 124
Crabb, Lionel (Buster), 189–90
Cram, Cleveland, 213, 218–19,
    283, 411
Creasey, Timothy, 381–2, 387
Crompton, James (Jimmy), 42,
    46, 50
Crosland, Anthony, 289, 346, 354
Crossman, Richard, 285
Cuba: MO's activities, 252; US
    relations, 233–5, 243
Cuban Missile Crisis: end, 252,
    253, 262, 354; MO's
    involvement, 7, 217, 246–9;
    origins, 242–4; public
    responses, 242; Soviet missile
    bases, 244–6, 250–1; US
    response to missile bases,
    245–6, 249–52, 264, 265
Cumming, Sir Mansfield Smith,
    5, 11–12, 24
Curwen, Sir Christopher, 426

da Silva, John, 288
Dalley, John, 141–2
Dalyell, Tam, 285, 416, 425
Darbyshire, Norman, 172
de Gaulle, Charles, 247, 302
de Mowbray, Stephen, 272, 279,
    304, 306, 326, 342
de Silva, Desmond, 343–4, 394–5
Deacon, Richard, 246, 248
Dean, Elsa, 57
Deep Chat, 327
Delmer, Sefton (Tom), 206–7, 286
Demetrios (double agent), 69
Dempster, Fergie, 181–2
Dennys, Rodney, 120–1
Deutsch, Arnold, 109–10
Dewhurst, Claude, 95–6, 100
'Dick' (agent), 252
Dicken family, 28
Dixon, Robin, 395

Dobb, Maurice, 107
Donald, Sir Alan, 17
Donoughue, Bernard, 336, 337–8, 339, 341
Dorril, Stephen, 263, 343
Dougherty, Hermenia, 378
Dougherty, Pat, 317
Douglas-Home, Alec (*earlier* 14th Earl of Home): Blunt's immunity, 266; election defeat, 284; Foreign Secretary, 311, 314; government, 274; Prime Minister, 265; Operation Foot, 314–15; relationship with MO, 265, 315, 333, 340–1
Duff, Sir Antony, 17, 400
Dulles, Allen: Berlin tunnel plan, 213; career, 107, 213; Castro overthrow plans, 233, 235; office desk, 386–7; relationship with MO, 181; relationship with Rennie, 301; resignation, 235
Dwyer, Peter, 120
Dyer, Ken: bodyguard, 21, 22, 278, 318, 378, 428; career, 248–9; memories of MO, 248–9, 303; MO's investiture, 340

Easton, Jack (Sir James): career, 124–5, 169, 191; home life, 203, 205; present at Philby's interrogation, 168–9; relationship with MO, 163; relationship with Robber Barons, 182; view of Philby, 169
Eden, Anthony: career, 161, 185; Crabb affair, 189–91; Foreign Secretary, 187–207; MI6 relations, 189–91; Philby parliamentary statement, 187–8; Prime Minister, 185; relationship with MO, 340–1;

Suez Crisis, 192–3
Egypt, 61, 62, 82, *see also* Suez
Eisenhower, Dwight D., 171, 233
ELLI (codename for mole), 280
Elliott, Nicholas: Blake case, 225; career, 287; Crabb affair, 189–91; immunity offer to Philby, 259–60, 263; MI6 selection panel, 179; relationship with MO, 180, 191; relationship with Philby, 169, 184, 259–60; Vermehren case, 75–6, 122
Ellis, Charles Howard 'Dick', 106, 116, 162, 293–4
Enigma, 74
Entebbe hostage crisis, 349–50
Eppler, Johannes, 81
European Economic Community (EEC), 302, 333, 334–5, 347
Evans, L. G. (Tubby), 30, 31
Ewer, Denis 'Jakes', 54
Ewer, 'Trilby', 54

Faber, Olive, 33, 358–9
Falkland Islands (1976–7), 359–61
FBI: HOMER investigation, 149; Philby case, 187, 260; Philby's view of, 127–8, 152; view of MO's lodgers, 276
Figures, Sir Colin, 391
Finucane, Patrick, 394
Fitt, Gerry, 421
Fleming, Ian, 4, 190, 200, 319–20
Floud, Bernard, 54, 267, 268
Fluency committee: Gaitskell death allegations, 306; investigations, 280–1, 283; MO's view of, 292; sackings, 291; set up, 280; suspects, 292–3, 342
Foot, Michael, 346
Foote, Alexander, 80–1
Footman, David, 247

Foreign Office: Arabists, 88, 92–3; Cambridge spy ring, 126, 150, 153–4; International Research Department, 299; MI6 leadership, 297–8, 301, 311; MI6 officers, 4; MO's career, 50, 51, 59, 104–5, 317, 356; Namier's career, 47–8, 50, 104, 165; Radó case, 81–3; Vassall case, 227; Volkov case, 94
Four Square Agreement, 181, 200
Franco, General, 67, 110–11, 112
Franks, Sir Arthur (Dickie), 10, 21, 236–7, 365, 416, 428
Fuchs, Klaus, 127, 149
Fuller, Kate, 166, 359, 424
Fuller, Patricia, 358
Fulton, James, 131, 425
Furnival Jones, Martin, 291–2, 314

Gaddafi, Colonel, 391
Gaitskell, Hugh, 261, 289, 306
Gent, Sir Edward, 139–43
Glentoran, Baron, 395
Glushchenko, B. G., 314
Goldsmith, Sir James, 428
Goleniewski, Michael, 224, 268
Golitsyn, Anatoliy: analysis of his theories, 261–2; claims debunked, 283; defection, 227, 259, 269; identification of spy ELLI, 280; list of suspected moles, 261; London visit, 292; MO's view of, 269, 281, 291–2, 303; relationship with Angleton, 227, 232, 256, 261, 262, 265, 268–9, 271, 275; search for moles, 263, 265, 269; theories, 227–8, 232, 256, 275, 306; view of Nosenko, 271; view of Penkovsky, 261; White's view of, 274–5; Wilson Soviet agent claim, 336; work on MI5 files, 263, 306

Goodhart, Philip, 175
Goodhart, Valerie, 175
Gordievsky, Oleg, 264, 324, 347
Gordon Walker, Patrick, 284
Gouzenko, Igor, 97, 116, 280
Granatstein, Jack, 97
Gray, Irvine, 64, 73
Greene, Graham, 112, 181, 186, 369–71
Greenhill, Denis, 276, 298–9, 304, 315
Gromyko, Andrei, 245–6, 314
GRU (Soviet Military Intelligence Agency), 79, 235, 237, 239, 262, 314
Guevara, Che, 252
Guinness, Alec, 371–4, 375
Gurney, Sir Henry, 143, 159, 160

Hair, Gilbert, 146
Hair, John, 145–6
Halpern, Sam, 146, 181, 200
Hamilton, Archie, 426
Hankey, Lord, 185
Hanley, Michael, 293, 310, 342
Harris, Tomas, 258
Hart, Sir Anthony, 422
Hart, Jenifer, 267
Hart, John Leland, 411
Harvey, Clara, 216
Harvey, Libby, 151, 155, 216
Harvey, Reginald, 31, 35, 43, 214
Harvey, William King (Bill), 151, 156, 213, 216, 218, 226
Havers, Michael, 423–4
Hayter, William, 120, 128
Heath, Edward (Ted): EEC policy, 302; elections, 309, 335; Northern Ireland policies, 310, 421; Operation Foot, 314; relationship with MO, 309–10, 315, 333, 340–1; smears, 337, 428
Helms, Richard (Dick), 215, 220, 221, 291, 326

Henry Worthington File, 342
Hermon, John, 382
Hess, Rudolf, 367–8
Hillenkoetter, Roscoe H., 128
Historical Institutional Abuse
    (HIA) Inquiry, 407, 422
Hitler, Adolf: abolition of Abwehr,
    76; Delmer's interview with,
    206; German attitudes to, 48,
    67, 79; Hess case, 367; invasion
    of Czechoslovakia, 51; invasion
    of Poland, 193; plots against,
    75–8, 286; refugees from, 48, 86
Hockaday, Sir Arthur, 20, 400–1
Hoffman, Barry, 253
Hollis, Roger: death, 347;
    investigated, 263–4, 268, 280–1,
    293, 326, 342, 411; Philby
    evidence, 258; retirement,
    287; suspension of Martin,
    267; Vassall case, 256–7
Hoover, J. Edgar, 127, 187, 260
Hope Commission, 331, 332
Hopkin, Bryan and Renee, 105
Horne, Sir Alistair: career, 96–8,
    102, 166; memories of MO, 75,
    92, 95–8, 102, 123, 371, 433;
    memories of Roberts, 75, 115;
    MO's death, 412; relationship
    with MO, 95, 97–8, 166–7;
    SIME Green Card, 98–9; view
    of MO's character, 369, 371,
    408; view of Pincher, 425
Hulme Hall, 42, 45, 49, 52
Hungarian uprising, 201–2
Hunt, Sir John, 9, 21
Hussein, King of Jordan, 286

Ingham, Bernard, 393
INLA (Irish National Liberation
    Army), 15, 376–7, 391
Intelligence Corps, 46, 59–61, 96,
    160; Field Security Section,
    59, 61, 74

IRA: Army role against, 381; back
    channels, 323; Lazin
    connection, 392; Libyan arms
    supplies, 391; Littlejohns
    affair, 312; MI6 agents, 311;
    Mountbatten assassination,
    14–15; PLO links, 391;
    possible KGB links, 310;
    Provisional, 310; targeting
    MO, 324–5, 357, 377; view of
    MO, 421
Iraq: debates (2003), 285; 'dodgy
    dossier', 10, 243, 364;
    Khomeini's exile, 362
Irgun (IZL), 87, 89, 92, 98, 100
Isham, Sir Gyles, 102
Ivanov, Yevgeny, 262

Jacob, Ernest, 44, 47, 104
Jagan, Cheddi, 255–6
Jantzen, Jane, 145–6
Jantzen, Robert J. (Red), 145–6,
    200
Jebb, Gladwyn, 120
Jeffery, Keith, 116
Jeffes, Maurice, 106
Jellicoe, Earl, 120, 166
Jenkins, Roy, 41, 307, 346
Jewish Agency, 91, 100–1
John, Otto, 286–7
Johnson, Ben, 225
Johnson, Lyndon B., 220, 284
Johnson Smith, Geoffrey, 312
Joyce, Robert, 120

Kagan, Joe, 338–9, 342
Keeler, Christine, 262
Kellar, Alec, 102
Kemp, Betty: appearance, 43;
    career, 43, 85, 104; education,
    43; Joe's funeral, 216;
    marriage proposal to MO,
    276–7; MO's call-up, 57–8;
    Over Haddon visits, 278;

Kemp, Betty (*cont.*)
relationship with Crompton, 46; relationship with MO, 21, 43, 84, 164, 366, 404, 409; *Sunday Telegraph* interview, 425; view of MO, 432

Kennedy, John F.: Bay of Pigs, 233–4, 235; Cold War poker game with Khrushchev, 240, 241–2; Cuba policy, 8, 233–5; Cuban Missile Crisis, 242, 245–51, 265, 270; death, 264, 270; election, 233; relationship with MO, 7–8, 219–20, 246–7, 248–9

Kennedy, Robert, 252

Kenyatta, Jomo, 230–1, 350

Kerr, Sir John, 332

KGB: agents, 55, 71–2, 224, 257, 338–40, 367, 424; agents of influence, 261, 282, 336, 339; border guards, 295–6; British sources, 334; Cambridge spy ring, 110; defectors, 227, 259, 268–71; double agents, 334; honeytraps, 227; IRA links, 310; MI6 agent captured by, 303; officers, 114, 313, 333; Operation Foot, 313–15, 338; Philby's autobiography, 8, 299; Philby's flight, 260, 369, 370; poisoning department, 261; training section, 221

Khomeini, Ayatollah, 173, 362–3

Khrushchev, Nikita: British state visit, 189–90; Cold War poker game, 240, 241–2, 246, 335; Cuban Missile Crisis, 243–4, 250–2, 261–2; Cuban missile sites, 244–6, 251; nuclear power, 238, 243

Killick, Sir John, 17, 19–20

Kincora Boys' Home, Belfast, 337, 421–4, 429

Kisevalter, George, 237, 268, 270

KISS (agent), 89–90

Klugmann, James, 53–4

Knightley, Phillip, 355–6, 366–7, 369–70

Kollek, Teddy: background and career, 91, 286; Philby's wedding, 108, 218; relationship with Angleton, 114; relationship with MO, 91–2, 95, 100, 286, 329; view of terrorism, 91–2, 101

Kopatzky, Aleksander, 227

Krotkov, Yuri, 271, 282

Lady Manners School: alumni, 29, 136, 234, 365; careers fair, 356; headmaster, 34–6; MO at, 32–6; MO's achievements, 38–9; MO's nephew at, 242; MO's role as governor, 409–10; MO's scholarship, 30–1; MO's sisters at, 31, 36, 55; MO's Speech Day address, 158, 214; sport, 31, 33–4, 52; status, 107, 123; teachers, 30–1, 358–9; uniform, 40

Lai Teck, 141–2

Laidlaw, Marion, 197–8, 204–5, 404, 413

Lamphere, Robert, 151

Lancaster, Donald 'Butch', 177–8

Lancaster, Osbert, 127, 178

Lathkill View Hotel: bomb alert, 378; licensee, 26, 28, 31, 317; location, 26–7, 28; MO at, 43, 84, 103, 106, 164, 278, 317, 318, 378; MO's leaving party, 57; Sadie's wedding reception, 84

Laub, Levi, 252

Lawson, Richard, 382

Lazin, Viktor, 392

le Carré, John, *see* Cornwell, David

Lecky, Terence, 225

Lee Kuan Yew, 198–9, 219, 329–30
Leigh, Martin, 318
Liddell, Guy, 101, 122, 149, 169, 266
Lim, David, 196
Lim Yew Hock, 199
Lindsay, Frank, 120
Liossis, George, 69
Lipton, Marcus, 187
Littlejohn, Keith and Kenneth, 312–13, 327
Livingstone, Ken, 425
Long, Leo, 267
Lonsdale, Gordon (Konon Molody), 224, 250
Low, N. I., 134–5, 195
Lunn, Peter, 258–60, 299
Lupton family, 26, 29
Lyalin, Oleg, 313–14

'M' (James Bond's boss), 319–20
Maadi Interrogation Camp, 78, 81
MacDonald, Alec, 280, 292
Macdonald, Ian Pendlebury, 34–6
MacDonald, Malcolm, 130, 139–43, 201
Mackenzie, Bruce, 229–30, 349–51
Maclean, Donald: anti-hero status, 257; background and career, 126–7, 217, 265; escape to Moscow, 152–5, 188; Golitsyn's evidence, 227, 232, 256; HOMER codename, 110, 149, 152; life in Soviet Union, 185–6; relationship with Philby, 126–7, 152–3, 155, 167, 188; spying activities, 7, 126, 174, 211; Venona team's hunt for, 126, 149, 152–3; Washington position, 126–7; White Paper on, 185–6
Maclean, Melinda, 152, 153
Macmillan, Harold: Cuban Missile Crisis, 250, 265; EEC membership rejection, 302; Philby case, 258; Philby parliamentary statement, 188; Philby review, 186; Profumo affair, 263; relationship with MO, 340–1; son-in-law, 174–5; successor, 264–5; Vassall case, 256–7; 'Wind of Change' speech, 229; 'you've never had it so good', 307
Maitland, Sir Donald, 17
Malayan Communist Party, 137, 139, 140, 141
Malayan Emergency, 130, 137, 143, 159–61, 199, 208
Malayan National Liberation Army (MNLA), 137–42
Malayan Security Service (MSS), 141
Maly, Theodore, 110
Manchester University: Betty Kemp's arrival, 43; Hulme Hall, 42, 45, 49, 52; MO's arrival, 40; MO's Fellowship, 49–50; MO's graduation, 49; MO's Masters studies, 42, 49, 51, 110; MO's papers, 3; MO's place at, 39; MO's politics, 44–5; MO's postwar return, 84–5, 104; MO's room, 42; MO's social life, 42–3, 45–6; MO's student activities, 48–9, 51–2; MO's teachers, 43–4, 46–7
Manhattan Project, 125
Mao Zedong, 54, 261–2
Marshall, David, 198
Martin, Arthur: Blunt interview, 266, 267; Fluency committee, 280, 306; Golitsyn's theories, 261–2; Krotkov defection, 283; mole hunting, 263–4, 268, 280, 291; Philby case, 258; Straight interview, 265; surveillance of Mitchell,

Martin, Arthur (*cont.*)
263–4; suspension and
transfer, 267; suspicions of
Hollis, 263–4
Mason, Roy, 376–7
Maudling, Reginald, 314
McCarger, James, 120
McCone, John, 226, 248
McGuinness, Martin, 324
McNamara, Robert, 247
McNee, David, 405, 423
Mellor, Jim, 56
Melville, William, 24
Menzies, Sir Stewart:
background, 168; Chief of
MI6, 93–4, 106, 168; Philby's
career, 122, 149, 156, 168–9;
retirement, 162, 163; Secret
Service Committee, 106;
successor, 168, 170; Volkov
case, 93–4, 122, 165
MI5: Beirut station, 74; Blunt
interviews, 266–8; CIA
relations, 124–5; CIFE, 130–1,
195; Chiefs, *see* Duff,
Furnival Jones, Hanley,
Hollis, Petrie, Rimington,
Sillitoe, Smith (Sir Howard),
White; files, 263, 306;
Fluency committee, 280, 291;
history, 88, 227, 345; Jewish
Agency relations, 100;
Maclean's escape, 153–4; MI6
relations, 74, 130, 137–8, 191,
340, 429; MO interrogations,
406, 407, 414; MO smears,
423, 429; mole hunting, 261–6,
267–8, 274, 293, 326, 342;
Northern Ireland, 16, 310,
322, 386, 429; Operation
Foot, 313–14; Philby
investigations, 167, 168–9,
170, 186–7, 263; Profumo
affair, 262; *Spycatcher* affair,

416, 418; territory, 4, 61, 130–1,
231, 232; 'Watchers', 153;
Wilson investigation, 336,
338, 341–2
MI6: agents, 9; 'agents of influence',
4–5; anti-Mosaddegh operation,
172–3; Australian operations,
330–2; briefing Leader of
Opposition, 9, 20, 356; budget,
305–6; Chief ('C'), 5–6, 8–9, 24,
433–4, *see also* Cumming,
Curwen, Figures, Franks,
Menzies, Oldfield, Rennie,
Sawers, Sinclair, White; CIA
relations, 119–20, 124–5, 144–7,
156, 168–9, 212–14, 249, 260;
CIFE, 130–1, 195; Crabb affair,
189–90; Cuba intelligence, 234;
Cuban Missile Crisis, 249–51;
Deep Chat, 327; European
intelligence gathering, 347–9;
files, 115–16, 368, 423, 442;
Fluency committee, 280–1;
German Station, 182;
headquarters (Broadway
Buildings), 105, 106, 121, 125,
129, 156, 162, 165, 167, 170, 175,
183, 193, 200, 225, 273, 320;
headquarters (Century House),
273–4, 301, 321; history, 115–16,
442; The Horrors, 170, 180, 183,
211, 301, 311, 322; interviewing
panel, 176–9; MI5 relations, 74,
130, 137–8, 191, 340, 428–9;
MO's papers, 3; mole hunt,
271–2, 279–80, 283–4, 303–5,
314–15, 322, 326; Northern
Ireland, 310, 315, 322–5, 386,
421, 428–9; officers, 4–5;
Operation Foot, 314–15;
Operation Valuable, 119–21;
organization, 106; Penkovsky's
information, 235–41, 244–8,
249–50, 305; Philby interview,

Index

186–7; Philby's escape, 260; purge of senior officers, 304; R5 Station, 104, 112, 115–16, 124; recruitment policies, 107–8, 176–9; reforms, 326–7; reorganization, 106; Robber Barons, 167–71, 179–80, 184, 185, 189, 191, 211, 275, 287; Secret Service Committee, 106; Section V, 112; Section IX, 124; Soviet Bloc operations, 305–6; stations, 4–5; Suez Crisis, 184–6, 192–3; territory, 4–5, 130–1, 231; vetting, 216–17, 228, 352–3, 402, 406, 408, 430; WWII, 61, 76

Miller, Eric, 344
Mitchell, Graham, 263, 326
Modin, Yuri, 152–3, 186, 189
Montgomery, Bernard, 70–1, 74, 107
Moran, Lord, 17
Morgan, Ellis, 288
Morrison, Herbert, 71
Mosaddegh, Mohammad, 171–4, 192–3
Mossad, 210, 349, 351
Mountbatten, Lord, 14, 139, 239, 337, 376
Moyne, Lord, 87
Muggeridge, Kitty, 46
Muggeridge, Malcolm, 46

Namier, Lewis, 44, 47–9, 50, 104, 165
Nasser, Gamal Abdel, 185, 192–3
Neave, Airey, 15, 20
Newman, Sir Kenneth, 100, 380–2, 386, 387
Nitse, Paul, 247–8
Nixon, Richard, 233, 325–6
Noakes, Michael, 344–5
Northern Ireland: back channels, 323; informers, 388–9, 392; MI6 involvement, 310–13, 324–5, 388–9; peace process, 8, 324; Planning Staff, 385–7; Security Coordinator role, 16–23, 382–90, 393, 399–400; the Troubles, 7, 11, 14–15, 376
Nosenko, Yuri, 268–71, 282
Novicov, Lieutenant Colonel, 80
Nunn May, Alan, 54–5
Nunn May, Ralph, 54–5

Oatley, Michael, 322–4
Oehlers, George, 133
Oldfield, Annie (Ada Annie Dicken, mother of MO): children, 29, 36–7, 50, 83–5; death, 412–13; family background, 28; finances, 30–1, 36–7; husband's death, 216; London visit, 103; marriage, 28; old age, 12, 317, 377, 380, 396
Oldfield, Anthony Joe (nephew of MO), 164
Oldfield, Brian (brother of MO), 29, 50, 83, 317
Oldfield, Catherine (sister of MO), 83
Oldfield, Derrick (brother of MO), 29, 83
Oldfield, Fred (grandfather of MO), 26–8, 37
Oldfield, Freda (sister of MO), 29, 36, 83
Oldfield, Herbert (uncle of MO), 28
Oldfield, Jane (niece of MO), 357
Oldfield, Joe (brother of MO): Bakewell Market, 12; birth, 29; daughter's Berlin visit, 357; farming, 13, 50, 83; memories of MO, 1–2, 412; MO's last visit, 378; sister's wedding, 84; village hall committee, 164
Oldfield, John (brother of MO), 29, 83

Oldfield, Joseph (Joe, father of
   MO): childhood, 27–8, 29;
   children, 29, 36–7, 50, 83–4;
   death, 215, 216; family
   background, 26, 27; farming,
   31, 36, 50, 52–3, 83, 203;
   finances, 29–31, 36–8, 52–3;
   grave, 378; harmonium, 32;
   Joseph Oldfield Cup, 279;
   landlord of the Lathkill, 28,
   31; London visit, 103; marriage,
   28; photograph, 210; village
   hall committee, 164
Oldfield, Margaret (Lupton,
   grandmother of MO), 26–7
Oldfield, Margaret (sister of MO),
   see Pasley
Oldfield, Sir Maurice:
   CAREER (in chronological
      order): 175, 183–4, 194, 195,
      208–9, 273–4, 279, 297–8,
      313, 315, 363–5, 375–6;
      introduction to world of
      intelligence, 49; Foreign
      Office attachment, 50, 51, 59,
      105, 86; war service, 57, 59;
      Intelligence Corps training,
      59; Suez Field Security
      Section, 61; Passport Control
      at Kantara, 62–3; SIME
      position, 62–7, 74; work with
      'A' Force, 68–70; work as
      secret agent, 72; head of 'A'
      Section, 78–9; head of 'B'
      Division, 89; temporary
      Chief of SIME, 91–2;
      demobilization and MBE,
      102–3; joining MI6, 104;
      deputy chief of R5 Section,
      104, 116; Singapore posting,
      129, 130; Deputy Head of
      Station (Far East), 131, 135,
      143–5, 156–9; Assistant
      Secretary (Foreign Office),
      162, 163, 176, 183–4; on MI6's
      interviewing panel, 176–9;
      First Secretary and Head of
      Station (Singapore), 194, 195;
      recruitment of 'Friends' of
      MI6, 204, 206–9; return to
      London, 209, 210; Counsellor
      at the British Embassy in
      Washington DC, 209, 211–12,
      214–22, 254–6, 260–1, 264–5;
      vetting lies, 221–3, 402, 406,
      430; Cuban Missile Crisis,
      234–5, 242, 243, 246–9; return
      to London, 272, 273–4; Deputy
      Chief of MI6, 274, 277–8,
      299–300, 301–4; Director of
      Counterintelligence, 274, 277–8,
      279, 303; Chief of MI6, 7, 313,
      315, 316–17, 319–23, 325–9,
      361; succession issue, 353–4;
      retirement, 8, 10–12, 363–6,
      428; Security Coordinator for
      Northern Ireland, 21–3, 375–6,
      382–93; resignation from
      Northern Ireland post, 399–401,
      406–8
   PERSON: aliases, 29; allegations
      against, 402–7, 416–18, 426–7,
      428–31; appearance, 12, 40, 42,
      74–5, 95–6, 179, 205, 316–17,
      319, 336, 410; birth, 25;
      bodyguards, 21, 22, 174, 248–9,
      318, 340, 378, 396, 419–20, 428;
      character, 2, 40–1, 51–2, 65,
      254–5, 303, 371; childhood, 25,
      28–9; club, 165–6, 276, 296,
      420; death, 2, 3, 403, 411–12;
      driving, 32, 50–1, 73, 84;
      education, 30–6, 38–9, 43–9,
      92–3, 110; family background,
      1–2, 6, 25–30, 92–3, 105–6,
      163–4, 278–9; finances, 39,
      49–50, 52–3; funeral, 413;
      health, 2, 159, 215, 396–7,

399, 400, 401, 406, 409–12;
Highwayman pub story, 405,
415, 418–21, 424, 427;
homosexuality, 21, 41, 164,
276–7, 298, 351–3, 396, 406–
8, 412, 419–20, 422; honours,
8, 102–3, 114, 200–1, 316–17,
340, 363–4; horsemanship,
32; languages, 48, 143;
London flats, 14, 165, 210,
214, 268, 275–6, 292, 296,
316, 325, 410, 417, 428;
marriage question, 204–5,
275–7, 352; music, 32, 51, 57,
73, 164, 196; nicknames, 115,
328; papers, 3, 404;
passports, 3, 144, 173, 234;
political views, 44–5;
religion, 21, 64, 132–3, 166,
196, 254–5, 277, 303, 318, 353,
431, 434; rumours about, 2,
298, 351–2, 396, 405–6, 413,
414–16, 418–20, 428–31;
smoking, 159, 210, 341, 406,
409; speech, 2, 179; sports,
33–4, 52, 205–6; threats
against, 21, 324–5, 357;
writings, 11–12

Oldfield, Renee (sister of MO):
birth, 29; dealing with press,
317; education, 31; living with
mother, 13, 317; memories of
MO, 350, 378; MO's investiture,
340; panic button, 307;
wartime service, 56, 84

Oldfield, Sadie (sister of MO), *see*
Pearce

Oldfield, Sarah (great-
grandmother of MO), 26

Oldfield, Walter (uncle of MO), 28

Onslow, Lady Pamela, 312

Operation Bertram, 70

Operation Boot, 172–3, 182

Operation Foot, 314, 338

Operation Gold (Stopwatch),
212–14

Operation Silver, 212, 225

Operation Valuable, 119–21, 128,
148, 154, 167, 202

Ormsby-Gore, David, 219, 234

Orr-Ewing, Anne, 293

Ortiz, Vicki, 252

OSS (Office of Strategic Services),
82, 112, 113, 114, 119

Oster, Hans, 68, 79

Oswald, Lee Harvey, 170

Owen, David, 9, 354, 360, 427–8, 433

Page, Chantry Hamilton, 94

Palestine, 86–9

Palme, Olof, 326

Pantcheff, Theodore 'Bunny', 293

Parker, Robert, 418

Pasley, Margaret (Oldfield, sister
of MO), 29, 72, 84

Pasley, Richard (nephew of MO),
72, 164

Paterson, Geoffrey, 154

Payne, Denis, 322–3

Pearce, Carolyn (wife of John,
mother of author), 358, 408–9

Pearce, John (nephew of MO,
father of author): Bakewell
Market, 12; car, 278, 319,
357–8; childhood, 129, 164;
farming, 13; memories of
uncle Maurice, 129, 164, 378;
Private Eye cartoon, 321;
sports, 230, 296, 321, 357–8,
366; uncle Maurice's work,
242

Pearce, Sadie (Oldfield, sister of
MO, grandmother of author):
birth, 29; brother Maurice's
investiture, 340;
correspondence with Skelton,
230, 231; education, 36, 56;
father's death, 216; memories

Pearce, Sadie (*cont.*)
  of brother Maurice, 36, 363;
  mother's old age, 380, 396;
  relationship with brother
  Maurice, 1, 2, 48, 341, 346;
  threat in prayer book, 21, 357;
  war service, 55–6; wedding,
  83–4
Pearce, Thomas, 31
Pearce, Warren (brother-in-law of
  MO): Bakewell Home Guard,
  56; Bakewell Market, 12; car,
  278, 319; land, 43;
  relationship with MO, 13,
  296, 378; wedding, 83
Penkovsky, Oleg (HERO):
  Angleton's view of, 241, 261,
  292; arrest in Moscow, 250;
  background and career, 235;
  British visit, 237–9; Chisholm
  contacts in Russia, 240, 245,
  250; codename, 242–3;
  Cuban Missile Crisis, 243–9;
  death, 250, 334; defection,
  235–7; double agent, 230;
  funding, 239, 245; Golitsyn's
  view of, 261; information
  from, 232, 238–40, 240–1,
  243–5, 262, 334; MO's view
  of, 241, 246–7, 271, 305;
  Profumo affair, 262; return
  to Russia, 239–40; tests for,
  241–4; Wynne contact, 236–7,
  244–5, 250
Perón, Juan and Eva, 176
Petrie, Sir David, 71, 88
Petrov, Vladimir, 185–6, 194
Petty, Alan (Judd), 12
Philby, Aileen (Furse), 111–12,
  150–1, 257
Philby, Dora, 107, 122
Philby, Eleanor, 257, 260
Philby, Kim (H. A. R.):
  appearance, 108, 117, 147;
autobiography (*My Silent
  War*), 126, 299–300, 316;
  background, 54, 107–8, 123,
  217, 265; Blake comparison,
  224–5; career, 106–7, 111–15,
  123, 168, 188, 257–8, 273,
  286; CIA view of, 154–6, 168,
  169, 174, 211, 215; cleared of
  Third Man accusation, 188;
  Climber operations, 117–18,
  120; club, 165; drinking, 149,
  186, 257, 259; escape to
  Moscow, 260; FBI relations,
  127–8, 187; finances, 169, 186;
  Golitsyn's work, 227, 191, 261,
  263, 280; handler, 186, 189;
  immunity offer, 258–60, 266;
  interrogation by MI5, 168–9,
  191; interviewed by MI6, 186–7;
  joining MI6, 107, 111, 112, 188;
  journalism, 110, 123, 168, 257;
  life in Beirut, 257–8; life in
  Moscow, 369–70; Maclean tip-
  off, 152–4, 155–6, 167, 186;
  marriages, 108–9, 111–12, 257;
  MI6 response to his treachery,
  162, 167–70, 184; MI6 review,
  186–7; MO's suspicions, 122–6;
  named as Third Man, 187–8;
  Operation Valuable, 120, 128,
  148, 154–5, 167; pay-off from
  MI6, 169; press conference,
  188–9; recall from Washington,
  156, 167, 209; recruitment of
  spy ring, 109–10; relationship
  with Angleton, 113, 114, 128–9,
  149–52, 156, 218; relationship
  with Burgess, 150–2, 155–6,
  167, 169, 188; relationship with
  Greene, 369–71; relationship
  with Maclean, 126, 152, 155,
  167, 188; spying activities, 7,
  154–5, 364; stammer, 108, 169;
  STANLEY codename, 110, 149,

150, 152; supporters at MI6,
167–70; unmasked, 227, 232,
258–60; Venona investigation,
149, 152; Vermehren case, 122;
view of MO, 425; Washington
position, 124–9, 147–56, 209;
White's suspicions, 256
Philby, Litzi (Friedmann), 108–10,
111
Philby, St John, 107, 111
Philby, Tommy, 123
Phillipps, Diane, 279
Phillpotts, Christopher:
appearance, 288; candidate
for MI6 Chief, 298; career,
288, 299, 304; Director of
Counterintelligence, 304,
365; 'Gestapo methods', 293–
4; influence on Rennie, 304;
mole hunt, 279, 291, 293, 342,
365; relationship with MO,
291; retirement, 299, 326;
return to London, 288, 291;
Washington position, 272,
279, 288
Pile, William, 17–18
Pilger, John, 332
Pincher, Chapman: accusations,
54; allegations about MO,
356, 405, 417, 423–5;
autobiography, 321; journalism,
321, 340, 355; relationship
with MO, 321, 350–1, 411, 417
Pine Gap satellite tracking base,
331, 332
Pool, Phoebe, 267, 268
Porro, Ricardo, 252–3
Portland Spy Ring, 224
Powers, Gary, 236
Prague Spring uprising, 306, 334
Private Eye, 14, 320–1, 339–40,
341–2, 352, 365
Profumo, John, 262, 263
Purseglove, John, 136–7, 234, 252

Pym, Francis, 16, 17, 20, 401

Queen Elizabeth II, 344–5
Quinn, Frank, 223
Quinn, William, 114

Radó, Dr Alexander, 79–83, 98,
121
Ramphal, Shridath 'Sonny', 234,
252, 256
Reed, Ronald, 42, 46, 52, 433
Rees, Goronwy, 266
Rees, Merlyn, 337
Rennie, Charles, 315
Rennie, John Ogilvy (Jack):
background and career, 298–
9; character, 301, 303–4, 322;
Chief of MI6, 298–9, 301;
Foreign Office relations, 310–
11; knighthood, 340; mole
hunting, 303–4, 306; name,
320; Northern Ireland, 310;
Operation Foot, 313–14;
retirement, 315, 316, 322;
risky operations, 310–11
Repiton-Préneuf, Paul, 64
Rhodesia, 13–14, 231, 232
Richards, Sir Francis 'Brooks',
400–1
Rimington, Stella, 268
Roa, Raúl, 235
Roberts, Andrew, 74
Roberts, Douglas: appearance,
95; background and career,
65, 74; demobilization, 102;
fear of flying, 91, 94; head of
R5 Section, 104, 115; head of
SIME, 78, 89; illness, 397;
relationship with Menzies,
93, 165; relationship with
MO, 65, 74–5, 91, 102, 104,
115; successor, 102; Suez
Interrogation Centre, 100;
Volkov mission, 94–5, 121, 165

Roberts, Elizabeth, 208, 397
Robinson, John, 45
Rommel, Erwin, 70, 74, 77, 78
Roosevelt, Kermit, 174
Rote Kapelle spy ring, 79, 82
Rothschild, Victor, 127, 257–8, 342, 406–7, 409
Routledge, Paul, 15
Rowley, Allan, 322
Royal Ulster Constabulary (RUC): Chief Constable, 100, 380–1, 382; coordination with other agencies during Troubles, 16, 310; Highwayman pub, 420–1; joint staff proposal, 23, 385; murder of Irish nationalists, 394; Planning Staff, 385–6, 387; relationship with Army, 381, 385–90, 392–3, 398; role, 385–6; Special Branch, 394; Stevens inquiries, 394
Ryder, Chris, 415, 418

Saddam Hussein, 5, 362
SAVAK, 329, 362
Sawers, Sir John, 364
Schlesinger, Arthur, 265
Schlesinger, James, 326
Scott, Sir Robert, 201
Scott-Hopkins, James, 356
SD (Sicherheitsdienst), 66
Shah of Iran (Mohammad Reza Pahlavi): Anglo-American activities, 172–3; death, 363; exile, 363; forced from office, 363; illness, 363; MO's promise not to spy in Iran, 329, 361; MO's visits, 194, 285, 303, 329; Mosaddegh appointment, 171; Mosaddegh sacking, 172–3; relationship with MO, 11, 174, 199, 303, 329; relationship with

Saddam Hussein, 362;
SAVAK, 329, 362
Shamir, Yitzhak, 90
Shergold, Harold (Shergy): Blake interrogation, 225, 237; funding for Wynne and Penkovsky, 239; Penkovsky interview, 237, 240–1; Soviet Bloc chief, 288, 294, 305; Suez Interrogation Centre, 100; view of Angleton, 292
Sherrat, Joe, 56
Shipp, Cecil, 407, 414, 430
Sillitoe, Percy, 88
SIME (Security Intelligence Middle East), 62–3, 65, 67, 69–70, 78–9, 89; 'A' Force, 65, 68–70; 'A' Section, 78–9
Sinclair, Sir John (Sinbad): appearance and character, 170, 181–2, 322; Chief of MI6, 163, 168, 170, 183; Iran operation, 172; relationship with Robber Barons, 170, 181–2, 184; replacement, 184, 189, 322; retirement, 180, 191; successor, 191
Singapore: ASIS officers, 162; churches, 132, 196; Four Square Agreement, 181; Head of Station, 131; headquarters, 131; MO's arrival, 130; MO's first posting, 130–7, 158–9, 320; MO's hospitality, 136; MO's house, 134–5, 195; MO's neighbours, 134–6, 195–6; MO's posting as First Secretary and Head of Station, 194, 195–8; MO's relationships with political leaders, 198, 208–9; MO's research and reports, 156; MO's return from, 163; MO's travels from, 144, 201; MO's visits as Chief of MI6,

Index

329–30, 351; recruitment of 'Friends', 136–7, 207–8; sponsorship of children's education, 196–7; tennis, 205–6

SIS (Secret Intelligence Service), 4–5, 8–9, 24

Skelton, Kenneth, 84, 230–2

Smiley, George: Guinness's meeting with MO, 372–4, 375; Guinness's performance, 8, 372, 375; image, 169; model for, 373–4, 375; resemblance to MO, 1, 8, 200

Smith, Alan, 425

Smith, Sir Howard, 21, 407

Smith, Ian, 232

Smith, Joseph, 145

Smith, Vic, 50–1, 73

SOE (Special Operations Executive), 60, 61, 106, 139, 400

Solomon, Flora, 257–8

South Staffordshire Regiment, 57, 59

Special Branch: bomb discovery, 325; Burgess's flight, 153; Dyer's career, 248; Highwayman pub story, 404–5, 407, 417, 419–21; protection of MO, 319, 325, 377, 379–81, 395–6

Spry, Charles, 194

SS, 66

Starnes, John, 252, 255

Stauffenberg, Claus von, 76–8

Steele, Frank, 310, 322–3, 324

Stern, 315, 316

Stern, Avraham, 87, 89

Stern Gang (Lehi), 87–9, 92, 98

Sternberg, Rudy, 339

Stevens, Sir John, 394

Stevenson, Adlai, 235

Stewart, Brian, 10, 143, 160, 278, 353, 382–3

Stewart, Michael, 284, 298

Stobie, William, 394

Stokes, Michael, 237, 239

Stowe, Sir Kenneth, 387, 425

Strachey, John, 54

Straight, Michael, 265–7

Suez: Canal, 61–2, 184–5, 192, 193–4; Crisis, 193–4, 201, 275, 284, 327; Interrogation Centre, 100; Zone, 61–2, 89, 102

Sullivan, Bill, 265

Taylor, A. J. P., 44, 46, 48, 104

Taylor, Jim, 56

Taylor, Margaret, 46

Taylor, Peter, 324

Templer, Gerald, 60, 160–1, 383

Thatcher Foundation Archive, 407

Thatcher, Margaret: intelligence briefings as Leader of Opposition, 356; invitation to retired MO, 13–16, 20–2, 379; MO's resignation, 399–401; Neave murder, 15; Northern Ireland policy, 16, 381; parliamentary statement on MO, 402–4, 405, 414–16, 427, 431; relationship with MO, 341, 356; secrecy of Secret Service, 9; security briefing, 393, 399–400; Security Coordinator post, 16–22, 389, 399–401; visit to MO in hospital, 412, 414, 415

Their Trade is Treachery, 411

Thomas, Dylan, 46

Thurlby, Jack, 56

Timberlake, Roy, 54

Tinker Tailor Soldier Spy, 371, 374, 375

Tong Dow, 197, 330

Townsend, Peter, 166

Trend, Sir Burke, 287

Trento, Joseph, 332

Trepper, Leopold, 79, 80, 82, 98

Trethowan, Monty, 62–3, 65, 72, 74

Triads, 157
Truman, Harry S., 88, 119, 171
Tudor Hart, Edith, 108
Turner, Stansfield, 361
Tweedy, Bronson, 211, 291
Tyrer, William, 411

U Thant, 251
Ulster Defence Association
    (UDA), 394
Unison Committee for Action,
    337
Urquhart, Edmund, 318, 403, 410,
    413, 424, 425

Vassall, John, 227–8, 232, 256–7,
    268, 270, 430
Venona Project, 125, 149, 152, 154
Vermehren, Elisabeth, 75–6, 83,
    121–2
Vermehren, Erich, 75–6, 83,
    121–2
Vietnam, 144, 158, 177, 181, 199,
    201
Vietnam War, 11, 208, 285, 331
Vivian, Valentine, 111
Volkov, Konstantin, 93–5, 121,
    155, 165, 167, 280

Wadsworth, A. P., 164
Wadsworth, Janet, 164, 404
Wallace, Colin, 337, 421–4, 426,
    429
Waller, Ian, 206, 207
Ward, Stephen, 263
Warner, Gerry, 294, 305, 327–8,
    365, 369, 426–7
Washington: MO's position, 209,
    211–12, 214–28, 232, 252,
    254, 260, 265, 272; Philby's
    position, 124–9, 147–56, 167
Watkins, John, 282
Waugh, Auberon, 320–1, 339–40,
    341–2

Wavell, Sir Archibald, 65
Way, Keith, 131
Wheeler, Geoffrey, 247
White, Sir Dick: accusations
    against, 304; background,
    192; Blake case, 225, 226;
    Blunt case, 266, 274–5; career
    after retirement, 304; Chief
    of MI5, 186; Chief of MI6,
    191, 273, 287, 301, 322, 364;
    comparison with MO, 276;
    Deputy Chief issue, 274;
    family life, 275; knighthood,
    340; listening to MI6
    interview, 186–7; meeting
    with Angleton and Golitsyn,
    291–2; mole hunting, 279–81,
    282–3, 291–2, 304, 322; MO's
    Washington brief, 218, 260–1;
    Penkovsky case, 239–41, 250,
    292; Philby broken, 259–60;
    Philby escape, 260; Philby
    interrogation, 186, 191;
    Philby suspicions, 256, 258;
    relationship with Angleton,
    280, 282–3, 291–2;
    relationship with MO, 211,
    276, 278, 291, 293–4, 297–8;
    relationship with Robber
    Barons, 191, 275; retirement,
    297–8; sackings, 291;
    successor question, 287, 288,
    297–8; Suez Crisis, 193;
    Vietnam War question, 284–5
White, Kate, 275
Whitehead, Phillip, 287, 365
Whitelaw, William, 20, 322, 405
Whitlam, Gough, 330–3
Whitmore, Sir Clive, 13, 20,
    400–1
Wigg, George, 284
Wildgoose, Anne and Mary
    (great-great-aunts of MO), 26
Wilks, Leslie, 35

Index

Williams, Marcia, 337–8, 339, 341
Wilson, Harold: Angleton's view of, 326; connections investigated, 306–7, 336–40, 342–5; conspiracy theories about, 306–7, 326, 342, 344–5; dementia speculations, 343; EEC membership rejection, 302; election defeat (1970), 309; election victory (1964), 284; election victory (1966), 289; election victory (1974), 335; Golitsyn's theories, 261, 306, 336; honours list, 337–8, 339, 344; leadership election (1963), 289; MI5 activities, 306–7, 342, 344–5, 418, 423; MI6 budget, 305; Northern Ireland policy, 386; office burgled, 343–4; possibility of coup against, 336–7; *Private Eye* coverage, 321, 339–40; relationship with MO, 285, 340–1, 342–3, 345, 347; resignation, 343, 346; smear campaign against, 337; Vietnam War, 8, 284–5
Wiseman, David, 42
Wisner, Frank, 120, 181
Wolf, Markus, 370
Woodhouse, Monty, 172
Woods, Robin, 132
Woolsey, Edmund, 312

Wright, Sir Oliver, 17
Wright, Peter: background, 268; Blunt interviews, 268; Fluency committee, 280; Hollis suspicions, 280, 287, 411; meetings with Angleton and Golitsyn, 292; mole-hunter-in-chief, 268, 291; relationship with Angleton, 283, 291; relationship with MO, 293, 423; *Spycatcher*, 411, 418, 423; Wilson investigation, 306, 336, 342, 343
Wrigley, Michael, 102, 166, 192, 354
Wynne, Greville, 236–7, 239, 245, 250

Young, George Kennedy: anti-Mosaddegh operation, 172; career plans, 170, 180, 191, 308; character, 191; Deputy Chief of MI6, 170, 191, 275, 308; MI6 selection panel, 179; political views, 170, 308, 337; relationship with MO, 180; relationship with Philby, 169; Robber Baron, 169, 308; Suez Crisis, 192–3, 275; support for MO, 199–200, 202, 424; view of MO smears, 424, 429; view of Sinclair, 182

Martin Pearce is Sir Maurice Oldfield's nephew. He grew up getting postcards from around the world from his mysterious uncle, who turned out to be the real-life 'M'.

This is his first book.